D0948694

ALL ■ IN ■ ONE

Java 2

Certification

EXAM GUIDE

THIRD EDITION

William Stanek

Osborne / McGraw-Hill
New York • Chicago • San Francisco • Lisbon
London • Madrid • Mexico City • Milan • New Delhi
San Juan • Seoul • Singapore • Sydney • Toronto

Osborne/**McGraw-Hill**
2600 Tenth Street
Berkeley, California 94710
U.S.A.

To arrange bulk purchase discounts for sales promotions, premiums, or fund-raisers, please contact Osborne/**McGraw-Hill** at the above address. For information on translations or book distributors outside the U.S.A., please see the International Contact Information page immediately following the index of this book.

Java 2 Certification All-in-One Exam Guide, Third Edition

1234567890 DOC DOC 01987654321

Book p/n 0-07-219170-8 and CD p/n 0-07-219171-6
parts of

ISBN 0-07-219169-4

Publisher
Brandon A. Nordin

Vice President & Associate Publisher
Scott Rogers

Acquisitions Editor
Michael Sprague

Project Manager
Jenn Tust

Acquisitions Coordinator
Paulina Pobocha

Technical Editor
Steve Kapp

Compositor and Indexer
MacAllister Publishing Services, LLC

Cover Design
Greg Scott

ACKNOWLEDGMENTS

Author's Acknowledgements

One of my major concerns in writing the previous edition of *All-in-One Java 2 Certification Exam Guide* was to ensure the book had as few errors as possible. We spent over a year working on the book and hired top-notch technical editors and reviewers to scour the book from end to end. We did a great job.

As you might imagine, writing *Java 2 Certification All-in-One Exam Guide, 3rd Edition* was also a huge undertaking. Instead of starting over from scratch, I decided to revise and expand what I knew was a good book. The result is the book you hold in your hand. Inside, you'll find hundreds of new pages. Dozens of new examples, exercises and questions. We've also included a new test simulator that closely approximates the testing environment at Sylvan Prometric. The test engine contains several full-length tests that you can take to prepare for the exam.

But no man is an island and this book couldn't have been written without help from some very special people.

First of all, I would like to offer a huge thank you to Michael Sprague and Paulina Pobocha. Michael is the acquisition editor for the book and the one who convinced me that this time things would go well—and he was absolutely correct. Paulina was the project coordinator for the book and she did a terrific job, ensuring timely flow of materials between all members of the team and helping to manage the timeline so that the book could be completed on time.

I would also like to thank the editorial staff at McGraw Hill. It was challenging to get this project moving forward. We went through a lot of twists and turns but I think the result is a first-class book. Thank you to everyone on the editorial staff and to Andy Stone at MacAllister Publishing Services! Andy worked very hard on the copy editing and final proof stages.

A special thanks goes to the technical editor and reviewer, Steve Kapp. Steve scoured the code and found every single typo and inconsistency possible. His insight and comments on structure/additions helped make this an excellent resource reference as well as an exam guide. Thank you, Steve!

I would also like to thank Studio B Literary Agency and my agents David Rogelberg and Neil Salkind. Thanks also to Sherry and Craig who managed to straighten out last minute contractual issues.

Hopefully, I haven't forgotten anyone but if I have, it was an oversight. *Honest. ;-)*

Publisher's Acknowledgement

The publisher would like to recognize that the first edition of this title was written by Barry Boone and portions of this work were written by him.

ABOUT THE AUTHORS

William Stanek has over 15 years of business and technology experience. He is a leading network technology expert and an award-winning author. Over the years, his practical advice has helped millions of programmers, developers, and network engineers all over the world. He is also a regular contributor to leading publications like *PC Magazine*. He has written, co-authored, or contributed to over 30 computer books, which are sold all over the world and have been translated in many languages.

Back in the early days of Java, William wrote *Peter Norton's Guide to Java Programming* and he has been writing, teaching, and lecturing about Java ever since. He frequently runs seminars and has written and conducted training courses for Digital Think, Digital Education, and Microsoft. He has written technical white papers on XML, XSL, Java, and much more.

William has been involved in the commercial Internet community since 1991. His core business and technology experience comes from over 11 years of military service. He has experience in developing server technology, encryption, Internet development, and a strong understanding of e-commerce technology and its deployment. In 1994, he founded Virtual Press, an Internet consulting, design, and publishing firm. During 1998 and 1999, he worked as a senior member of the technical staff at Intel Corporation's IDS New Business Unit at iCat. His latest venture is Stanek & Associates, a management consulting firm he owns and operates.

He has an MS in Information Systems with distinction and a BS Computer Science degree magna cum laude. He is proud to have served in the Persian Gulf War as a combat crew member on an electronic warfare aircraft. He flew on numerous combat missions into Iraq and was awarded nine medals for his wartime service, including one of the United States' highest flying honors, the Air Force Distinguished Flying Cross.

William currently resides in the Pacific Northwest with his wife and four children.

Barry Boone is a Sun Certified Java Programmer and Sun Certified Java Developer. He'll share his experiences from taking these tests in these pages.

Barry lives in Seattle, but he travels all around the country teaching. He loves teaching. The thrill of working with students when they "get it" and understand a concept is always an exciting moment. Books are a natural extension of his love of learning and teaching, and he hopes this fun comes across while you're studying.

He is the author of two previous books on Java, *Java Essentials for C and C++ Programmers* and *Learn Java on the Macintosh*, with Dave Mark. He's had some great conversations with readers since these books were first published. He has taught classes in Java and object-oriented programming throughout the United States. In doing so, he's discovered what confuses students learning Java and what they need to know to get through the tougher concepts.

He's consulted to and worked for Fortune 500 companies on object-oriented design and development for the past 11 years, writing many real-world applications that play a role in this book.

ABOUT THE REVIEWER

Steve Kapp is the Chief Technologist for EMRT Consultants. He has 13 years of software and systems development experience, focused mainly on embedded imaging systems. Steve has worked on projects of all sizes, ranging from microcode to database and scripting languages. He specializes in bringing complex products and systems to market.

Steve has also spoken at various industry forums, such as JavaOne and the Embedded Systems Conference, and written extensively about technology-related issues. He holds a BS in Electrical Engineering and Applied Physics from Case Western Reserve University. Steve invites contact and may be reached at skapp@emrt.com.

BRIEF CONTENTS

CONTENTS

Chapter 16   Essential java.lang and java.util **301**

INTRODUCTION

What This Book Is All About

To distinguish yourself from the growing crowd of Java programmers and developers, you should become Sun certified. To prepare for the certifications exams, you should read this book.

What Does It Mean to Become Sun Certified in Java?

Sun offers certification in the Java language at three levels:

- At the programmer level, which tests for basic understanding of the language and your ability to code given a set of specifications.

- At the developer level, which tests for advanced Java knowledge in putting together real-world applications using Java.

- At the architect level, which tests skills for building and deploying enterprise applications and for the ability to resolve application design issues.

When you are Sun certified as a Java programmer and Java developer, your employers, peers, and friends know that you can walk the walk and talk the talk. It's not just you saying so; it's Sun, the inventor of the Java language.

As you know, the Java programming market is red-hot. Companies are paying huge sums to programmers who can demonstrate expertise in Java. Consulting and contracting firms specializing in personnel placement cannot get knowledgeable Java programmers fast enough.

As the Java market heats up even more, programmers will need a way to distinguish themselves as Java experts in an increasingly crowded field. Certification is your means of separating yourself from those less knowledgeable.

Why Use the Java 2 Certification All-in-One Exam Guide to Prepare for the Exams?

The exams are not free, and they are not easy. We know of a number of Java instructors who failed the test on their first try, because they did not study!

It's best to have a clear idea of what you need to know before you plunk down your money and walk into the exam. After all, you don't want to fail, and you don't want to waste your time and money when you can pass the first time with a little preparation. The *Java 2 Certification All-in-One Exam Guide* helps programmers with a basic understanding of Java take and pass the Java certification exams with flying colors.

The *Java 2 Certification All-in-One Exam Guide* is written as a study guide. This book explains the specific concepts and coding assignments found in the Certification exams. It carefully separates what is and is not on the test. This book also contains complete practice tests and programming assignments similar to the ones on the exams — all with detailed answers — so that when you walk into the test, you'll know you'll pass. This book aims to make you a Java expert.

In addition to helping programmers pass these exams, this book can help Java programmers become experts in their field. We cover important Java features that are not on the test at the end of each chapter. That way, even when the test does not explicitly require you to know a particular topic, you'll still learn about the topic in detail. After all, as a certified programmer, you'll be expected to be a Java expert.

The CD that comes with this book contains all the source code presented in this book, the sample questions, and many other resources to help programmers study for these tests.

Where Else Can You Go to Prepare for the Test?

A number of Internet and Web-based resources add information to what appears in this book. McGraw-Hill maintains a wonderful Web site for this book. It's at **http://www. computing.mcgraw-hill.com/**. Sun posts information regarding the certification exams at **http://suned.sun.com/US/certification/java/index.html**. You can find the most up-to-date numbers to call to sign up for the exam and all the test locations throughout the U.S. and the world at this Web site.

Sun also offers instructor-led courses you can attend through Sun Educational Services. You can find these courses by following the Internet link in the previous paragraph.

And finally, William's company, Stanek & Associates, offers products and services to help you learn Java. Drop by William's Web page at **http://www.tvpress.com/java/** to learn more.

What Should You Know Before You Start Studying?

We assume you already know something about programming in Java. This book does not teach Java programming from scratch; many great books are available on that topic. Just peruse the bookshelves at your local bookstore, or visit one of the excellent Web-based bookstores, such as Amazon.com or cbooks.com, and search for "Java programming."

We expect that you know how to do things like write a simple "Hello, world" program and how to define a class with instance variables and instance methods. You don't need to be an expert to begin studying for the exams, but you should have done some Java programming before. If you're not sure you know enough to begin studying for the exams, try this simple exercise.

Exercise 0.1

For example, you should be able to invoke your program from the command line by typing

```
java Hello William
```

and, in the standard output, the program should display "Hello, William." (We know that some development environments, such as Metrowerks CodeWarrior, ask you to enter command-line parameters in a separate window. Follow the procedures for your particular development environment when working through the instructions in this book.)

You might not realize it at first glance, but if you can write this program, you know how to do many basic things in Java, including

- Define a class.
- Write a static method.
- Work with an array.
- Invoke a method.
- Access a class variable.
- Work with Java's String class.
- Write a String to the standard output.

Even though this list appears fairly long, the program itself can be written in four or five lines of code. The answer to this exercise appears at the end of this introduction.

The majority of test questions for both exams are quite a bit more complicated and trickier than this exercise, but the point is that you should already know something about Java before you begin to study for the exam. If you feel comfortable writing this simple program, you're ready to use this book to start preparing to become a Sun Certified Java Programmer and a Sun Certified Java Developer—and win the accolades and respect that go with these titles.

How Is This Book Organized?

This book is structured like a self-study course. Each chapter contains sections describing:

- Objectives for that chapter

- The concepts for that chapter

- Examples of how to use Java to implement these concepts

- Exercises you can work through to ensure you have learned the objectives

- Review questions

- The complete answers to the exercises and review questions to make sure you've learned what you need to learn

The *Java 2 Certification All-in-One Exam Guide* is divided into three sections.

- The first section helps make sure you can figure out how an existing program works and that you can program in Java given a set of specifications. These skills are at the heart of the Programmer exam. At the end of this section, you'll find three practice exams. These practice exams are modeled on the actual exams and are of the the same degree of difficulty that you'll find in the real test.

- The second section ensures you can use Java to solve problems, design a solution, and write your own code. These abilities are the crux of the Developer exam. At the end of this section, you'll find a practice programming assignment and practice essay exam. The practice assignment and exam are modeled on the actual exams and are of the same degree of difficulty that you'll find in the real tests.

- The third section contains the appendices. The appendices details what's on the CD-ROM and provide some additional information on the JDK.

The *Java 2 Certification All-in-One Exam Guide* covers in depth those topics that are on the test. However, if we only covered the material on the test questions, this would not be a complete Java review. In addition to becoming an expert, sometimes you just want to know about the other stuff. So, we try to provide additional information where possible, ensuring that you know that this information isn't on the test. This will help round out your knowledge of Java and might even provide you with some insight into topics that are on the test.

To help you reconcile the divergent paths of studying as quickly as possible and studying as thoroughly as possible, we've used a variety of call-outs to make sure you can easily distinguish between what you need to know to pass the exam, what is good background information, and what you'll be expected to know by your peers as you enter the world as a certified programmer and developer.

What Do You Do Once You're Ready to Take the Test?

Once you've studied and feel comfortable that you know what you need to know, you can sign up for the test. To become a Sun Certified Java Programmer, you need to take and pass exam 310-025 for Java 2. This test is administered through Sylvan Prometric™. You can schedule an exam by calling Sun Educational Services or an Authorized Prometric Test Center. Part III of this book provides phone numbers to call to schedule your exam.

To become a Sun Certified Java Developer, you need to first be a Sun Certified Java Programmer. Then you must successfully complete a programming assignment and pass exam 310-027. These exams are also administered through Sylvan Prometric.

No matter where you are, don't worry—test centers are located throughout the U.S. and around the world, so you'll find a place you can go to get certified.

Onward!

You're ready to prepare for the test. Good luck, and have fun as you become a certified expert in the Java programming language.

Answers to the Exercises

Exercise 0.1

Here's a version that fulfills the requirements of the exercise:

```
public class Hello {
  public static void main(String[] args) {
    System.out.println("Hello, " + args[0]);
  }
}
```

This version is fine, but we can improve it by checking whether the user has supplied a command-line argument so we don't get an ArrayIndexOutOfBoundsException if a name was not supplied:

```
public class Hello {
  public static void main(String[] args) {
    if (args.length > 0) //safety feature
      System.out.println("Hello, " + args[0]);
    else
      System.out.println("Hello, someone");
  }
}
```

Whether you wrote the exact program we've written is not important. What is important is that you should feel familiar with defining a class, writing a main()method, accessing an element in an array, and writing to the standard output. If you can do these things, you probably know enough Java to tackle this book. If you know much more than this, that's fine, too. Either way, we'll help you focus on what the test will cover so that you'll pass on your very first try.

PART I

Studying for the Programmer's Exam

Programmer Exam Roadmap

In this chapter, we'll introduce the topics covered in the Sun Certified Programmer for the Java 2 Platform exam (Exam number 310-025). As you study the chapters in Part I, you can refer to the exam roadmap to check on specific exam objectives. The chapter also provides tips for taking the Programmer exam.

What Is the Programmer Exam Like?

The exam contains 59 questions. The exam is 120 minutes long, which means that on average you'll have two minutes to answer each question. The questions consist mostly of analyzing programming snippets, identifying true and false statements about the way the language works, and supplying short class definitions and method calls.

For the programming snippets, you'll be asked a variety of questions. Do they produce the expected results? What do they write to the standard output? Do they even compile in the first place?

Three types of programming questions are asked:

- **Multiple choice**   You select as many valid answers as are listed.
- **Single choice**   There is only one right answer from a list.
- **Short answer**   You'll be asked to enter a single line of code—or sometimes just a single word, such as a specific class name or keyword.

The Programmer test focuses on all the basics of Java, including classes, objects, methods, exceptions, threads, user interfaces, applets, and some of Java's core classes, such as String and Math. To pass the exam, you'll need to get a score of 61 percent, which means you'll need to get at least 36 questions right out of 59.

What's on the Exam

Previous versions of the Programmer exam had a wide list of objectives. For the Java 2 exam, this list of objectives has been narrowed to 33 objectives. Fewer objectives doesn't mean the exam is easier; it isn't. In fact, in many ways, the latest exam is more difficult. The Sun Certified Programmer for the Java 2 Platform exam focuses on the core programming language and core API packages.

The specific exam objectives are organized by topic. The topics and objectives supplied by Sun follow.

Declarations and Access Control

- Write code that declares, constructs, and initializes arrays of any base type using any of the permitted forms both for declaration and for initialization.

- Declare classes, inner classes, methods, instance variables, static variables, and automatic (method local) variables, making appropriate use of all permitted modifiers (such as public, final, static, abstract, and so forth). State the significance of each of these modifiers both singly and in combination, and state the effect of package relationships on declared items qualified by these modifiers.

- For a given class, determine if a default constructor will be created and, if so, state the prototype of that constructor.

- State the legal return types for any method given the declarations of all related methods in this or parent classes.

Flow Control and Exception Handling

- Write code using if and switch statements and identify legal argument types for these statements.

- Write code using all forms of loops, including the labeled and unlabeled use of break and continue, and state the values taken by loop control variables during and after loop execution.

- Write code that makes proper use of exceptions and exception-handling clauses, (try, catch, finally) and declares methods and overriding methods that throw exceptions.

Garbage Collection

- State the behavior that is guaranteed by the garbage collection system and write code that explicitly makes objects eligible for collection.

Language Fundamentals

- Identify correctly-constructed source files, package declarations, import statements, and class declarations (of all forms, including inner classes). Also, identify interface declarations and implementations (for java.lang.Runnable or other interfaces described in the test), method declarations (including the main method that is used to start the execution of a class), variable declarations, and identifiers.
- State the correspondence between index values in the argument array passed to a main method and command-line arguments.
- Identify all Java programming language keywords and correctly-constructed identifiers.
- State the effect of using a variable or array element of any kind when no explicit assignment has been made to it.
- State the range of all primitive data types and declare literal values for String and all primitive types using all permitted formats, bases, and representations.

Operators and Assignments

- Determine the result of applying any operator, including assignment operators and instanceof, to operands of any type, class, scope, or accessibility, or any combination of these.
- Determine the result of applying the boolean equals(Object) method to objects of any combination of the classes java.lang.String, java.lang.Boolean, and java.lang.Object.
- In an expression involving the operators &, |, &&, ||, and variables of known values, state which operands are evaluated and the value of the expression.
- Determine the effect upon objects and primitive values of passing variables into methods and performing assignments or other modifying operations in that method.

Overloading, Overriding Runtime Type, and Object Orientation

- State the benefits of encapsulation in object-oriented design and write code that implements tightly-encapsulated classes and the relationships "is a" and "has a."

- Write code to invoke overridden or overloaded methods and parental or over-loaded constructors. Also describe the effect of invoking these methods.

- Write code to construct instances of any concrete class, including normal top-level classes, inner classes, static inner classes, and anonymous inner classes.

Threads

- Write code to define, instantiate, and start new threads using both java.lang.Thread and java.lang.Runnable.

- Recognize conditions that might prevent a thread from executing.

- Write code using synchronized, wait, notify, and notifyAll to protect against con-current access problems and to communicate between threads. Define the interac-tion between threads and between threads and object locks when executing synchronized wait notify or notifyAll.

The java.awt Package—Layout

- Write code using component, container, and layout manager classes of the java.awt package to present a graphic user interface (GUI) with a specified appearance and resize behavior. Also distinguish the responsibilities of layout managers from those of containers.

- Write code to implement listener classes and methods, and in listener methods, extract information from the event to determine the affected component, mouse position, nature, and time of the event. State the event class name for any specified event listener interface in the java.awt.event package.

The java.lang Package

- Write code using the following methods of the java.lang.Math class: abs, ceil, floor, max, min, random, round, sin, cos, tan, and sqrt.

- Describe the significance of the immutability of String objects.

The java.util Package

- Make an appropriate selection of collection classes/interfaces to suit specified behavior requirements.

The java.io Package

- Write code that uses objects of the file class to navigate a file system.

- Write code that uses objects of the classes InputStreamReader and Output-StreamWriter to translate between Unicode and either platform default or ISO 8859-1 character encoding. Also distinguish between conditions under which platform default encoding conversion should be used and conditions under which a specific conversion should be used.

- Select valid constructor arguments for FilterInputStream and FilterOutputStream subclasses from a list of classes in the java.io.package.

- Write appropriate code to read, write, and update files using FileInputStream, FileOutputStream, and RandomAccessFile objects.

- Describe the permanent effects on the file system of constructing and using FileInputStream, FileOutputStream, and RandomAccessFile objects.

How Does the Text Map to the Programmer Exam Objectives?

Chapters 1 through 20 cover all the objectives on the Programmer exam. Like the exam itself, the chapters do not go through the exam objectives sequentially. Instead, the chapters examine specific subjects, such as control flow, exceptions, and layout managers. The chapters also cover subjects that don't have specific objectives. For example, the exam doesn't have specific objectives that cover the Image class, yet a chapter in this book covers creating, loading and displaying images. The reason for this is that a working knowledge of the Image class is needed to be an effective Java programmer.

How the Test Is Administered

The Programmer exam is a given as a computer-based test. The exam questions appear on the computer screen one at a time. You can answer the question at that time or skip the question and come back to it later. You can also move forward and backward through the exam questions at any time.

The Programmer test is administered by a company called Sylvan Prometric. They have test centers all over the United States and the world. When you show up, you sign in, identify yourself by showing two forms of ID (one with a picture, and both with signatures), and then you take the test at your scheduled time.

You can't bring any paper into or out of the testing room. They don't want you taking a crib sheet in with you or writing out test questions during the test. (Of course, once you leave the testing area, you can try to recall as many questions as possible. However, be aware that the tests are copyrighted, so you can't turn around and publish the questions, make copies of them, and so on.)

You also can't bring in any pagers or cellular phones. After all, in this day and age, it would be a simple matter to have your local Java guru talk you through the test.

Even though you can't take any paper in with you, the people at Sylvan Prometric do give you either some scratch paper, or a small marker board and a marker to help you work out answers.

How to Sign up for and Take the Exams

You must call Sun and buy a voucher (or buy or get a voucher from your company, who has in turn purchased a voucher through Sun). The idea behind the voucher system is that your company may offer vouchers for free or at a discount to the regular price of the test if they are encouraging you to become certified.

The main number for Sun Educational Services in the United States is 1-800-422-8020. Listen to the options from the phone menu and make sure you tell them what test you want to sign up for. Outside the United States, check out the Web site at **http://suned.sun.com/** for additional phone numbers

Once you have a voucher, you need to register for the test. You can do this by calling Sylvan Prometric. Their number is 1-800-795-EXAM. (I know; I hate dialing by letters, too. Their number in numbers is 1-800-795-3926.) Or you can register online at **www.2test.com**.

Whether you register on the phone or online, you'll have to give Sylvan your social security number for identification, and they'll ask you some questions, such as which company you're with, your phone number, and your address. Then they'll schedule you for a test.

When they schedule you, they'll find a time that's convenient for you to visit one of their testing centers. You need to be there on time, because you can't stay past your stop time—the computer will shut you off! What they do is distribute the test electronically to the test center you'll be at.

If they can fit you in the next day (and that's what you want), they'll do their best to accommodate you. The only possible problem might be that a space is not available at the test center closest to you.

Just in case your friendly neighborhood Java expert doesn't show up in your place as a ringer, you need to bring two forms of ID, one of which must be a photo ID. If you want to postpone for some reason—if you're panicking or you just can't make it—you can do so up until the day before the test.

You'll find out immediately whether or not you've passed the exam, because the software that administers the test prints out your results. Remember, you need to get at least 36 questions (61 percent) right to pass. You can always restudy and take it again if you do fail, and, since it's a difficult test, lots of people go this route.

Test-Taking Tips for the Programmer Exam

Before taking the test, you should know what to expect. The sections that follow contain test-taking tips. You'll find these tips to be helpful as you set out to become a certified Java programmer.

What the Test Program Looks Like for the Programmer Exam

When you first sit down at the computer, you'll be asked to type in your test-taking ID, which is most likely your social security number (Sylvan Prometric will tell you). The test software will then ask whether or not you're familiar with the application. If you'd like, you can take a short tutorial. The test does not begin until you look at the first question, so looking over the tutorial doesn't take away from your testing time. If you're ready, then go ahead and start the exam.

The font is large and easy to read. Buttons on the bottom of the screen will take you to the next or a previous question.

The program that administers the test is very friendly. A clock in the top right of the screen counts down, showing you the remaining time. You can double-click this clock to see what time you started, the maximum time allowed for the exam you're taking, and the current time.

You can go through most of the test just by clicking. Two types of multiple choice questions are used: exclusive and non-exclusive. The non-exclusive questions allow you to pick as many answers as are valid. The exclusive answer questions have round radio buttons. The multiple answer questions have square check boxes. In addition to the way the check boxes look for the different question types, a small message at the bottom of the question indicates whether you should select just one right answer or all valid answers.

The questions that require you to type in a response have a single-line text field, so this is a good indication to you that all of your typed responses should be short—no full-class definitions, no algorithms. All you'll need to do is invoke a method or specify a class name. You should click in the text field to begin typing.

At the end of the test, after you've answered the last question, you'll see a list of all the questions and your responses. You can double-click on a question/answer in this list to jump to it and review it.

You'll also see a little check box in the top left that says "mark." If you click this, when you go to review your questions at the end, you'll see a little yellow square with the letter "m" beside your question in the question/answer list. This little yellow square can remind you that you had a question about something and wanted to go back to review your answer.

If you have any incomplete answers, you'll see this in the review screen at the end as well. Incomplete answers have a red square with an "I" to indicate their incomplete status.

A help button is available that provides a good overview of what you're seeing on the screen. If a serious problem occurs, you can always call someone into the room to help.

Be Careful!

Sometimes a question is too long to fit in one screen. This is usually the case when the question contains a code snippet or a full program for you to analyze. If you want to scroll down, you might inadvertently click in the answer area instead of over the scroll bar. If that happens, check your answers! If you click over the same row as an answer, even if it's all the way over to the right, the test application recognizes that click and will mark the answer in that row.

Take Your Time and Answer the Easy Ones First

You have close to two minutes per question. Believe me, unless you fall asleep, you won't run out of time; you'll have plenty of time to read over each question and think about it.

Not all questions take the same amount of time. Some questions you'll answer right off the bat. Some are so easy you'll read them over a second time, thinking you missed some trick. Most take about a minute to answer.

If you get impatient with a long question involving a big class definition, feel free to skip it and go back to it later. You can answer all the easy ones first, and then return to the more difficult or long questions later. All questions are worth the same number of points, so you might as well. Sometimes this strategy works particularly well, because a later question might inadvertently contain the answer to something you were pondering earlier.

You might remember from your days in high school or graduate school that one of the tricks in taking the SATs or GREs is to eliminate the wrong answers first in order to increase your odds. That's a great technique for this test as well. You'll find some answers that are obviously wrong (trust me, you will). When you do, you'll be that much closer to picking the right one.

It's also better to answer a question than to not answer it at all. You're only marked for right answers—there's no penalty for a wrong answer, so you should always at least guess rather than leaving something blank.

Beware of Tricks

Sometimes the test questions try to trick you. For example, a particular question might present answers where you should pick all the valid ones. For example, you might see a question like this:

> Which identifiers are valid in Java?
> a. max_num
> b. max-num
> c. 3DogNight
> d. star*power
> e. (train)

Since this question allows more than one correct answer, you might think that there must be more than one correct answer. But that's not so. In fact, only one of these is a valid Java identifier: a. max_num. The rest are not valid at all.

Another trick is to present some irrelevant information in a question. For example, check out the following:

Given the following preliminary specification for a class that will be shared by different packages, write the beginning of a class definition that indicates the new class' access control keywords (if any) and what the new class inherits from.

"A Satellite is a SpaceCraft. It maintains information for its orbital information, which is an array of six double values."

This might lead you to think your answer should look something like this:

```
public class Satellite extends SpaceCraft {
   double[] orbitalInfo = new double[6];
}
```

However, the question asked only to indicate the access control for the class and which class it inherits from. What's more, you can only enter one line anyway for short answer questions. So, the answer it's really looking for is simply

```
public class Satellite extends SpaceCraft
```

The test is assembled semi-randomly from components in a question database. (The assembly of questions is not completely random, because the program that assembles the questions makes sure that any particular area doesn't have too many of the same type of question.) Sometimes there will be multiple answers for a question that allows multiple answers, but sometimes there won't be. And sometimes more information will appear in a question than you need to answer that question. Don't be fooled. Think about the question and give the best answer you can, not what you think the question requires for an answer.

Understand Why the Question Is on the Test

One great way to feel good about an answer to a question is to understand why it is on the test. For example, imagine the following question.

Given the following code,

```java
class ClassA {
  public static void main(String[] args) {
    ClassA a = new ClassA();
    ClassB b = new ClassB();
    ClassA a2 = b;

    System.out.println("test() for a is: " + a.test());
    System.out.println("test() for a2 is: " + a2.test());
  }

  String test() {
    return "ClassA";
  }
}

class ClassB extends ClassA {
  String test() {
      return "ClassB";
  }
}
```

if you invoke main() for ClassA, what messages appear in the standard output?

a)

```
test() for a is: ClassA
test() for a2 is: ClassA
```

b)

```
test() for a is: ClassA
test() for a2 is: ClassB
```

c)

```
test() for a is: ClassB
test() for a2 is: ClassA
```

d)

```
test() for a is: ClassB
test() for a2 is: ClassB
```

You probably have this narrowed down to either a or b. The answer is b. The reason is that the method that is invoked depends on the actual object type referenced by the variable, not on the declared type of variable.

Once you realize this, it's obvious why this question would appear on the test. It's making sure you understand this concept.

Know Your Test Center

It's helpful to show up early to get the feel for what the test center is like. And it can eliminate problems—I showed up about 20 minutes early and was told that my name wasn't on the list of test takers for that day. The people at the test center had to call Sylvan Prometric's "hot line" and ask them to download the test right then, which took some time. By the time this was accomplished, it was time to take the test.

Not all test centers are created equal. Some have 14-inch monitors and some have 17-inch monitors; some have Pentiums and some don't. If you're lucky enough to have a choice of test centers, call ahead and ask what their screen size is and what kind of computers they use. I'd say your first priority is a big screen, followed by a fast processor as a close second. Some questions (in fact, most questions) take up more screen real estate than a 14-inch monitor can supply. Long code snippets are particularly annoying to look at when you have to keep on scrolling up and down. It's not tragic if you have a 14-inch screen; I had one and it wasn't debilitating. However, that said, the bigger the screen, the better.

And the faster the computer, the better. Remember, your test is being administered by a computer. The last thing you want to do is wait around for the question to pop up on your screen.

What Happens When You're Done?

When you tell the computer you're done, it will grade your exam right there on the spot. It then displays the percentage of questions you got right and whether you passed or not. If you pass, the computer will print a certificate, which the people at your Sylvan test center will then emboss, stamp, and hand to you for your safe-keeping.

At that point, it's official. You're a Sun Certified Java Programmer!

Sun's Take on Certification

In talking with a number of people at Sun Educational Services, including those responsible for creating the certification program, we have come to a good understanding of how they view the certification process. Following is a summary of their thoughts, many of which I'll touch on throughout this book.

Java certification is a way for individuals to differentiate and promote their skills and for employers and clients to know that a programmer is credible.

Sun needed to implement a certification program because Java is so new. It's simply not possible for a programmer to claim he has several years of experience with Java. So it's a challenge to employees to demonstrate they know what they say they know. Becoming certified in Java is a recognized way of validating your skills.

If you'd like to get up to speed as quickly as possible, Sun Educational Services offers courses that cover many of the topics that are part of Java certification. Other courses (both live and on the Web) cover these topics as well, as do books, seminars, and lectures. There is also no substitute for real-world experience. Regardless of how you learned Java in the first place, remember to study for the test. You can't know too much going into the exams!

As you prepare, you should also give some thought as to what your goals are for becoming certified. Are you studying just to pass the exams, or are you truly trying to become an expert?

You are certified according to a particular Java release. Therefore, you are Java certified in JDK 1.1, or Java 2, depending on when you took the certification exam. If you would like to be certified in a new version of the language, you must take the certification exams again (which means paying the testing fees once more).

When you become certified, Sun sends you some material in the mail. This includes a logo that you can place on your business cards to tell the world you're Sun certified, a certificate, and a lapel pin (so others can see you're certified without even glancing at your business cards).

How Sun Manages the Certification Process

Sun Educational Services sends the questions to Sylvan Prometric with all the right answers. The Programmer exam takes into account that a question may have more than one right answer. For example, the difference between a comma and a semicolon could be that one's right and one's wrong. But the question, "What if I put spaces around my parameters in a parameter list?" has a different answer. They're both right, and the test will mark both answers as correct.

Sun is constantly monitoring the feedback they receive from test takers to make sure they did not miss anything.

Sun does not publish numbers of how many people take the test and how many people pass. Sun does not want this to be the kind of test where you can just walk in, sign your name, and pass. This is not simply certification on paper. Passing really means you know your stuff.

Where Certification Is Heading

Sun certification is becoming the standard in the industry. Other companies are looking to Sun, as the inventors of the Java language, to verify their skills. For example, IBM's own certification program will include Sun's Java certification exams.

Java certification is part of the 100-percent pure Java initiative. JavaSoft administers the application and system side of this initiative; Java certification represents the people side. Java certification answers the question: "do you have the capability to develop 100-percent pure Java programs?"

Java certification is also becoming important in corporate education. For example, when an employee is trained in Java, how does a company know if the training hit the mark? Java certification is a standardized way to make sure that employees learn what they need to know.

CHAPTER 2

Java Programming Fundamentals

Objectives for This Chapter

- Identify the characteristics of objects.
- Explain encapsulation and message passing.
- Describe classes and class structures.
- Describe packages and their hierarchy.
- Explain inheritance.
- Identify and describe access controls.
- Describe Java's architecture and design.
- Detail Java's key features.
- Describe feature changes in various Java versions.

As you set out to become a certified Java programmer, you'll need to study many different things. Every Java programmer must have a solid understanding of object-oriented programming concepts. This understanding is the key to your success as a Java programmer. Object-oriented programming concepts are just the beginning, however. A skilled Java programmer should also be able discuss the feature differences between various Java versions. You should know which features are added and which features are deprecated, meaning they've fallen out of favor and shouldn't be used in new programs.

Java Programming Concepts

Java is an object-oriented programming language and you should be able to explain and describe its core concepts, including

- Objects
- Classes
- Packages
- Encapsulation
- Inheritance
- Access controls

Objects

The fundamental unit in Java programming is the object. Java, like other languages that follow object-oriented concepts, describes the interaction among objects. All objects have a state and a behavior.

The state of an object pertains to data elements and their associated values. Everything the object knows about these elements and values describes the state of the object. Data elements associated with objects are called *instance variables*.

The behavior of an object depends on the actions the object can perform on the instance variables defined within the object. In procedural programming, such a construct would be called a *function*. In Java, this construct is called a *method*. A method belongs to the class it is a member of, and you use a method when you need to perform a specific action more than once.

Thus, the state of an object depends on the things the object knows, and the behavior of the object depends on the actions the object can perform. If you create a software object that models your computer, the object would have variables describing the computer's current state, such as it is powered on, two applications are running, and six peripherals with input are coming from the keyboard. The object would also have methods that describe the permissible actions, such as starting or shutting down the computer, running an application, receiving input from the keyboard, and displaying output to the monitor.

Classes

A class is a representation of a complex data type in the Java programming language. You can think of a class as the blueprint from which an object is made. When you create an object from a class, you are said to have created an instance of the class. The object describing the functions of your computer, for example, could be an instance of a class of objects called Computer. When you use the statement

```
Computer comp = new Computer();
```

you are using the new operator to create a new instance of the Computer class. A single class can be used to instantiate multiple objects. This means that you can have many active objects or instances of a class.

Keep in mind that each object within a class retains its own states and behaviors. By encapsulating objects within a class structure, you can group sets of objects by type. The Java Application Programming Interface (API) describes many classes. Each class in the API specifies a set of objects that perform related functions and share common characteristics. Classes you create can serve a similar purpose.

Packages

Java uses the term *package* to describe a collection of related classes. Just as classes encapsulate objects, packages encapsulate classes in Java. This additional layer of encapsulation makes it easy to control access to methods.

Inheritance

Inheritance is a powerful aspect of Java that allows you to easily reuse code. You use inheritance to create a new class that inherits the functionality of an existing class. A class that inherits features of an existing class is called a *subclass*. The class from which objects are inheriting features is called a *superclass*.

Continuing the previous example using computer-related objects and classes, the Computer class could have subclasses for Laptop, Desktop, and Workstation. These new subclasses would not be limited by the instance variables or methods of the superclass (Computer) and could include instance variables and methods not defined in the superclass. The new subclasses could also override inherited methods.

Encapsulation

Objects encapsulate instance variables and related methods into a single identifiable unit. Therefore, objects are easy to update, maintain, and reuse. An object can invoke one or more methods to accomplish a task. You initiate a method by passing a message to an object. A message must contain the name of the object you are sending the message to, the names of the methods to perform, and the values needed by those methods.

The object receiving the message uses this information to invoke the appropriate methods with the specified values.

The benefit of encapsulation of instance variables and methods is that you can send messages to any object without having to know how the object works. All you have to know is what values a method will accept. Therefore, the software object describing your computer could be extremely complex, but all you or the end user has to know in order to use the Computer object is how to trigger the necessary actions. The press of a key on the keyboard or the click of a mouse button sends a message to the computer, telling it which method to perform and the new input values for the method.

Access Controls

By default, the methods and variables you declare in Java are accessible by any class and objects in the same package. The advantage of this is that objects in a particular package (generally a set of related classes) can access each other without limitation. To further control access, you'll need to use an access control keyword. Through encapsulation, you can control which parts of a program can access the members of a class. By controlling access, you prevent misuse of objects and their features.

Java defines several types of access controls, which are designated using the keywords: **public, protected,** and **private.** These modifiers are used as follows:

- **public**   The public modifier enables a class or interface to be accessed outside of its package. The modifier also enables a variable, method, or constructor to be accessed anywhere its class may be accessed. Thus, public members can be accessed without limitation.

- **protected**   The protected modifier enables a variable, method, or constructor to be accessed by classes or interfaces of the same package or by subclasses of the class in which it is declared. The advantage of this is that only members in the same package or a subclass of a class can access the items without limitation.

- **private**   The private modifier prevents a variable, method, or constructor from being accessed outside of the class in which it is declared. The advantage of this is that only members of a specific class can access the items without limitation.

If no modifier is used, the default access controls are used. This means the class, interface, variable, method, or constructor can be accessed by any class or interface of the same package.

The keywords **public** and **protected** do not affect access between classes and members in the same package. The keyword **private,** however, does restrict access to the class that defines the **private** member. Table 2-1 shows what happens when a class within

Table 2-1 Access for a Class Within the Same Package as a Public and Default Class

	Public class	**Default class**
Public member	Yes	Yes
Protected member	Yes	Yes
Private member	No	No
Default member	Yes	Yes

the same package as a **public** and default class tries to access members of the **public** and default classes. These members are defined with different access control keywords.

In the table, the entry "yes" indicates a class can access the member in the class type named for that column; the entry "no" indicates a class cannot access the member. (In the table, a default class is a class defined without any access control keywords; a default member is a member defined without any access control keywords.)

> **EXAM TIP:**   Classes in the same package can access each others' variables and methods, except for private members. Classes outside of the package can only see classes that are defined as public and can only access methods and variables defined using the public or protected keyword. What's more, only subclasses of classes with protected members can access those protected members outside a package.

Table 2-2 depicts a method in a class outside the same package as a public and default class trying to access members with different access control keywords.

Table 2-2 Access for a Class Outside a Package Defining a Public and Default Class

	Public class	**Default class**
Public member	Yes	No
Protected member	Yes*	No
Private member	No	No
Default member	No	No

TIP: Notice that access is much more restrictive than when the accessing class is in the same package as the public and default class. Packages allow you to fine-tune how and when others can make use of your classes.

Java's Characteristics

Java has many powerful characteristics. These characteristics are the source of Java's power and the reason for Java's widespread popularity. The more you work with Java, the more you'll understand how many of these characteristics are interrelated. Java is designed to be

- Simple
- Architecture-neutral
- Distributed
- Dynamic
- Interpreted and compiled
- Network-ready and compatible
- Multithreaded
- Object-oriented
- Portable
- Robust
- Secure

The sections that follow examine the key characteristics.

Design for Distributed Networks

A key ingredient for a successful programming language designed for an environment as complex as the Internet is the capability to run on heterogeneous and distributed platforms. Java can do this because it is architecture-neutral, meaning that Java executables can run on any platform that has the Java runtime environment.

Another key ingredient for a successful programming language designed for complex network environments is performance. Java has many features that make it a high-performance language. High-performance features include Java's compiler and runtime system. Java's interpreter can execute bytecode at speeds approaching that of code compiled to a purely machine-readable format.

Design for Multithreading

Unlike many other programming languages, Java has built-in multithreading capabilities. *Multithreading* is the capability to run more than one process thread at a time. Multithreading allows Java's interpreter to run processes such as garbage collection and memory management in the background. Processes that run in the background take advantage of idle time for your computer's central processing unit (CPU). In the real world, many things occur simultaneously. The doorbell rings, the phone rings, and your child runs into the kitchen screaming. You cannot answer the phone, the door, and give Johnny a hug all at the same time. So what you do is grab Johnny with one arm, grab the phone with the other, and tell the person at the door to wait a moment.

To accomplish all three tasks in successive order, you prioritized. Your child was priority one. The phone call you have been waiting for all afternoon was priority two. The mail carrier delivering a package was priority three. Programs that are multithreaded are capable of prioritizing as well. When the computer is waiting for input from the user, background processes can be busily cleaning up memory. Or when the computer pauses for an instant after crunching a number, a background process can squeeze in a few clock cycles to prepare a section of memory for use. Being able to run background processes while a foreground process waits for input from a user or pauses momentarily is essential for optimal performance.

Design for Ease of Use and Reuse

Although Java's object-oriented design is the key feature that makes code reuse possible, Java's designers know that complex network environments tend to change rapidly. Therefore, to ensure that Java developers could easily reuse code even if the environment changed, Java is designed to be dynamic and robust. Java accomplishes this by delaying the binding of objects and through the dynamic linking of classes at runtime, which avoids errors if the environment has changed since the program was compiled. Another way Java avoids errors is that it checks data structures at compile time and runtime.

Robustness and reliability go hand in hand. For Java to be robust, it must be reliable as well. As stated before, pointers and memory management are the source of many problems in C/C++ programs. Therefore, Java ensures robustness and reliability by not using pointers; by using dynamic boundary checking, which ensures that memory boundaries cannot be violated; and by providing for automatic memory management, which guards against memory leaks and memory violations.

Design for Security

Security features in distributed networked environments are essential, especially in an automated world where computer viruses abound. Many Java characteristics ensure that it is extremely secure. For example, malicious programmers cannot access system heaps, stacks, or protected sections of memory because Java does not use pointers to memory and only allocates memory at runtime. This prevents malicious programmers from reaching restricted sections of the system.

Java also ensures system security at runtime by making the Java interpreter pull double duty as a bytecode verifier. Before the Java interpreter executes a program, it performs a check to make sure the program is valid Java code. Java proves the validity of code using a theorem prover that guards against access violations, forged pointers, illegal data conversions, incorrect values and parameters, malicious alteration or misuse of classes, overflow and underflow of the stack, and suspicious or unwarranted activity.

Working with Java Applets and Applications

In Java, you can create

- Applets

- Applications

Java applets are programs that are designed for use on the World Wide Web. Java applets require an external viewer program, such as a Web browser or an applet viewer. Although applets are typically thought of as small programs, the smallness of an applet is entirely relative. The key thing to keep in mind is that applets are designed for use with external viewers.

Java applications are programs that are designed for standalone use and do not require an external viewer program. This means that you can execute a Java application directly using the Java interpreter. Keep in mind that some Java programs can run both as applets requiring an external viewer and as standalone applications.

The program file containing the actual instructions in the Java programming language is called the *source* or *source code*. You will name source code files for Java with the .java extension. These files should be plain text files. When you compile the source using the Java compiler, javac, you compile the source to bytecode that can be executed.

The executable code is generally stored according to the class structure. After you compile your Java source code, you will have one file for each class you declared in the source. Each of these files will be named with the .class extension.

The Java Specification and the API

The first official version of Java was released in January 1996. Shortly after the version 1.0 release, work began on Java 1.1. The features added by Java 1.1 were significant and had great impact on Java programmers. Java 1.1 added many new elements and redefined the way events were handled by applets. It also changed many of the features in the 1.0 API. Key changes included deprecating many of the original features in Java 1.0.

Feature changes have continued through the most recent Java releases. Let's take a quick look through the recent changes, starting with Java 1.1.

Java 1.1

Java 1.1 introduced many important features to the Java programming language. Most of the changes occurred in the core packages of the Java API. For example, some methods of the Date class were deprecated and moved into the Calendar and DateFormat classes. Some of the methods were also updated to enhance existing features.

Java 1.1 also added

- Inner classes, which allow one class to be defined within another class

- Built-in support for Unicode character streams

- Improved event handling

- Enhanced security, introducing digital signatures, access control lists, key generation, and message digests

- Reflection, which helps determine fields, constructors, and methods of a Java object at run-time

- Serialization, which allows you to save and restore the state of objects

- Remote Method Invocation (RMI), which allows a Java object to revoke methods of another Java object that is located on a different computer

- Java Beans, which are software components written in Java

- Java Database Connectivity (JDBC), which allows Java programs to connect to databases

- Java Native Interface (JNI), which provides interfaces into code libraries written in other programming languages

Java 2: JDK 1.2

With the release of the Java Developer Kit version 1.2, the Java programming language was renamed as Java 2 and Sun introduced the Java 2 platform. JDK 1.2, like its predecessor, introduced many new features and deprecated others. Key features added to the language included the following:

- Collections, which are groups of objects that help you solve common programming issues. For example, collections exist for hash tables, linked lists, and dynamic arrays.

- Java 2D, which provides advanced features for working with text, images, and shapes.

- Drag and Drop, which allows you to create programs that can transfer data between applications using standard editing techniques.

- Accessibility, which provides enhancements for persons with disabilities.

- Java Swing, which provides a standard set of interface components that can be platform-independent or platform-specific.

- Object Request Broker (ORB) and Interface Definition Language (IDL) support through a standard ORB and an idltojava compiler.

- The Just In Time (JIT) compiler is now included. This improves performance.

- Security enhancements and support for digital certificates. Policy files can be used to define permissions for applications. Digital certificates provide a method for establishing the identity of a user.

- Additional tool enhancements and implementation of the Java plug-in to enable direct connection to the Java Runtime Environment.

- Support for the input of Japanese, Chinese, and Korean characters from the keyboard.

- Playback of additional audio file formats, which means you can play back AU, AIFF, MIDI, RMF, and WAV audio files.

Java 2: JDK 1.3

Version 1.3 of the Java 2 platform extends and enhances the functionality of the Java programming language. Again, new features have been added to the language. These include the addition of

- The Java Naming and Directory Interface (JNDI), which was previously an extension to the language and is used to provide directory services.

- RMI over IIOP, which allows applications connecting to remote objects to use the Internet InterORB Protocol (IIOP). This allows you to program Common Object Request Broker Architecture (CORBA) servers and applications via RMI.

- CORBA 2.3.1-compliant ORB, which allows for distributed computing using IIOP.

- MOTIF 2.1 support, which is the graphical environment used on the Solaris 7 and Solaris 8 operating systems. Previously, JDK 1.2 and earlier supported MOTIF 1.2, which is the version used on Solaris 2.6.

JDK 1.3 also brings many enhancements, including the following:

- Jar file enhancements allow for the automatic installation of extensions and indexing. With the automatic installation of extensions, the correct versions of the extensions are installed without requiring repeated downloads each time an applet is loaded. With Jar indexing, functionality can be broken down into multiple Jar files, each of which can be distributed separately.

- RMI serialization improvements allow strings longer than 64 KB to be serialized and they improve performance as well as exception handling.

- The Java IDL compiler has been updated and is now 100-percent pure Java without a preprocessor. The new version is idlj, and it has more features than idltojava.

- Drag and Drop adds new methods in the class java.awt.datatransfer.DataFlavor.

- Java Sound has a new API for capturing, processing, and playing back audio and MIDI data, plus additional enhancements.

- Java 2D has been updated for multiple monitor support, Portable Network Graphics (PNG) support, dynamic font loading, and more.

- Java Swing and the Abstract Windows Toolkit (AWT) contain many changes and enhancements to improve performance. Use the new java.awt.Robot class to automate the testing of AWT components.

- Java networking now supports TCP half-close sockets and HTTP keep-alive for maintaining connections. It also includes HTTL 1.1. client-side support.

Review Questions

1. What are the fundamental units in Java programming?
   a. Objects
   b. Classes
   c. Packages
   d. Interfaces

2. If the Laptop class is based on the Computer class, which is the subclass and which is the superclass?
   a. Neither class is a super or subclass.
   b. Laptop is a subclass of the Computer superclass.
   c. Computer is a subclass of the Laptop superclass.
   d. Both are subclasses of each other.

3. By default—that is, without keywords—all classes can access all members, except for those defined:
   a. Using the final keyword
   b. Using the abstract keyword
   c. In another package
   d. In the same package

4. Which keyword can you give a class so that only classes within the package this class is defined in can access the class?
   a. Don't give the class a keyword at all.
   b. private
   c. final
   d. protected

5. You compile a Java source code file that defines five classes and 18 methods. How many bytecode files are generated when you compile the source code file and what are the file extensions?
   a. 23 bytecode files with the .class and .meth extensions
   b. One bytecode file with the .class extension
   c. Five bytecode files with the .java extension
   d. Five bytecode files with the .class extension

Answers to Review Questions

1. a. Objects are the fundamental unit of Java programming.
2. b. A class that defines another class is a superclass. A class that inherits features of an existing class is a subclass.
3. c. All classes can access all members, by default, except for those defined in another package. To access classes and members in another package, those classes must be declared using the public keyword, and the members must also be declared public (or protected, if the accessing class is a subclass of the class defining the protected member).

4. **a.** The default access control for a class—that is, defining a class without a keyword—restricts other classes in other packages from accessing the class. The protected keyword doesn't work here because subclasses of classes with protected members can access those protected members outside a package.

5. **d.** Source code files are named with the .java extension. After compiling source code, you will have one file for each class you declared in the source. Each of these files will be named with the .class extension.

CHAPTER 3

Java Keywords

Objectives for This Chapter

- Identify all Java keywords.
- State what each Java keyword is used for.

Keywords are reserved words. You cannot use a reserved word as the name of a class, variable, or method. You've no doubt seen all the keywords in Java in your travels through the language—or have you? This chapter makes sure you're familiar with Java's keywords by listing them all by category (under headings such as exceptions, access control, and so on) and by providing examples of how to use each of them.

An Alphabetical List of All the Keywords

The Java language specifies 50 keywords. These keywords cannot be used as identifiers for variables, methods, classes, or labels. Two keywords are reserved but are currently unused in Java 2. These keywords are const and goto.

The complete list of Java keywords follows:

abstract	const	final	instanceof	private	synchronized	volatile
boolean	continue	finally	int	protected	this	while
break	default	float	interface	public	throw	
byte	do	for	long	return	throws	
case	double	goto	native	short	transient	
catch	else	if	new	static	true	
char	extends	implements	null	super	try	
class	false	import	package	switch	void	

For the rest of this chapter, we've divided the keywords into their logical categories and provided explanations for each one. Feel free to skim over these sections if this is mostly a review for you. You can reference this chapter later if you want to quickly look up a keyword or find an example of how to apply it.

Organizing Classes

package   Specifies that classes in a particular source file should belong to the named package. You use the package keyword at the top of a source file, followed by the name of the package:

```
package shapes;
```

import   Requests the named class or classes be imported into the current application.

Any number of import keywords can follow the package keyword. Each import statement specifies the name of a package to import:

```
import shapes.*;
```

Defining Classes

class   Defines a class as a collection of related data and behavior that can also inherit data and behavior from a superclass.

You can define a class by writing the word class followed by the class name. The class definition follows within a set of curly braces:

```
class Circle
```

extends   Indicates which class to subclass. Write the keyword extends after the class name if you would like to extend a class other than class Object:

```
class Circle extends Shape
```

interface   Defines class constants and abstract methods that can be implemented by classes. Interfaces can extend other interfaces.

Specify an interface by writing the keyword interface followed by the interface name. The interface definition follows within a set of curly braces:

```
interface Editable
```

implements   Indicates the interface that a new class will supply methods for.

The implements keyword appears after the name of the superclass you are extending, or after the name of the class you are defining if you are simply extending class Object:

```
class Circle implements Editable
class Circle extends Shape implements Editable
```

Keywords for Classes and Members

public   Means the class, method, or variable can be accessed from classes outside of the package in which they're defined.

Place the public keyword in front of the class or member:

```
public Circle
public double radius;
public double area()
```

private   Means only the class defining the method or variable can access it (classes cannot be private).

Place the private keyword in front of the member:

```
private double radius;
private double area()
```

protected   Means that when a class inside a package defines a member as protected, the only classes outside of the package that can access the protected member are subclasses (classes cannot be protected).

Place the protected keyword in front of the member:

```
protected double radius;
protected double area()
```

abstract   Specifies the class cannot be instantiated directly. You must declare a class as abstract if

- Any of its methods are abstract
- It inherits from a class that defines abstract methods and does not implement them
- It extends an interface but does not implement its methods

Optionally, you can also decide you do not want other programmers instantiating your class and can declare your class to be abstract, even if your class does not contain any abstract methods.

The *abstract* keyword is placed in front of the class definition if the class is abstract, and in front of a method definition if the method is abstract:

```
abstract class Shape
abstract void draw()
```

 TIP: By convention, access control keywords are placed first.

static   Indicates a member belongs with the class. You can place the static keyword in front of the member:

```
static double radius;
public static double area()
```

synchronized   Indicates only one thread can access the synchronized methods for a particular object or class at a time.

You can define a synchronized method by placing this keyword in front of the method:

```
synchronized void initCircle()
```

You can also define a synchronized block of code by writing the keyword synchronized, followed by an object or class that will be used to obtain the monitor or lock (there's much more information on threads and synchronization in Chapter 13):

```
synchronized (this) { }
```

volatile   Tells the compiler a variable may change asynchronously due to threads.

Declaring a variable to be volatile makes the compiler forego optimizations that might turn the variable into a constant and eliminate the possibility of it changing asynchronously:

```
volatile int numCircles;
```

final   Means this variable or method cannot be changed by subclasses.

A final member can be optimized by the compiler and turned into a constant if it is a variable and inline code if it is a method. A final method keeps programmers from changing the method's contract, its agreed-upon behavior:

```
public static final int RADIUS = 20;
final double area()
```

native   Indicates a method is implemented using native, platform-dependent code (such as C code).

The native keyword indicates the method is not written in Java but in some platform-dependent language:

```
native double area()
```

Simple Data Types

We'll discuss Java's data types in Chapter 5. Here's a quick list of all the primitive data types:

long   64-bit, signed intege r value

int   32-bit, signed integer value

short   16-bit, signed integer value

byte   8-bit, signed integer value

double   64-bit, floating-point value

float   32-bit, floating-point value

char   16-bit, Unicode character

boolean   True or false value

Values and Variables

false   Boolean value

true   Boolean value

this   Refers to the current instance in an instance method

The keyword this is really a "magic" object reference that refers to the object responding to a method. With this, you can pass the current object to another method or refer to an instance variable when a local variable might hide the instance variable:

```
addToList(this);
this.length = length;
```

super   Refers to the immediate superclass in an instance method.

The keyword super is really a "magic" object reference that refers to an object responding to a method and the object's type is the superclass of the responding object. With super, you can pass a method call up the class hierarchy:

```
super.draw();
```

null   Indicates no value is assigned and represents the value held by an object reference before that reference is initialized.

void   Indicates a method does not return a value. You can use void instead as the return type of a method to indicate that the method does not return a value:

```
void draw()
void writeToScreen(String s)
```

Exception Handling

There's more explanation concerning these keywords in Chapter 8, which covers exception handling.

throw   Signals that an exception has occurred. You must write a Throwable object following this keyword.

Typically, a new instance of an Exception class is created on the spot. Exception implements the Throwable interface:

```
throw new IOException();
```

try   Marks the stack so that if an exception is thrown, it will unwind to this point.

The previous explanation for try is a cryptic way of saying that you try to execute a block of code, and following the try block, you catch any exceptions that methods you invoked might have thrown. You can also execute a finally block following the try block:

```
try { }
// followed by exception handling and/or a finally block
```

catch Handles an exception.

A catch block follows a try block. Catch blocks are handlers for specific exception types. After the catch keyword, write the type of exception that your **catch** block will handle. This exception type is written in parentheses, similar to a method parameter:

```
//a try block precedes a catch block
catch (IOException x) { }
```

finally Says "execute this block of code regardless of control flow statements."

A finally block can follow a try block or a try/catch block:

```
// following a try or try/catch block
finally { }
```

throws Indicates the types of exceptions a method is allowed to throw.

Methods that might throw a checked exception must indicate the exception type with a throws clause in the method declaration. Checked exceptions inherit from the Exception class.

Methods can optionally indicate that they throw *unchecked* exceptions. Unchecked exceptions inherit from RuntimeException or Error:

```
void pauseGame(int seconds) throws InterruptedException { }
double area(String area) throws NumberFormatException { }
```

Instance Creation and Testing

new Creates new instances.

Following a new keyword, specify the class name you'd like to create an instance of, and supply the appropriate parameters for the constructor you want to invoke. The new keyword returns an object reference to the new object:

```
Circle c = new Circle();
Circle c = new Circle(40, Color.blue);
```

instanceof Tests whether an instance derives from a particular class or interface.

This keyword is really an operator that tests an object reference to see what it derives from. The instanceof operator will respond true if the object reference refers to an object that is an instance of the class being tested, if it is an instance of a subclass of that class, or if it is an instance of a class that implements the interface specified with this operator:

```
if (objRef instanceof Cloneable)
if (objRef instanceof Shape)
```

Control Flow

Java's control flow statements are similar to the control flow statements in other languages, such as C.

switch   Tests a variable.

case   Executes a particular block of code according to the value tested in the switch.

default   Means the default block of code executes if no matching case statement is found.

break   Jumps out of the block of code in which it is defined.

The switch-case construct is a convenient way to pick from a variety of possible values for an expression and take different actions for each of them, rather than writing lots of nested if-else statements:

```
String nobelWinner = null;
switch (year) {
  case (1938):
    nobelWinner = new String("Enrico Firmi");
    break;
case (1921):
    nobelWinner = new String("Albert Einstein");
    break;
case (1903):
    nobelWinner = new String("Marie Curie");
    break;
default:
    nobelWinner = new String("unknown");
    break;
}
```

for   Signifies iteration.

A for statement contains three parts: initialization of the loop index, a test for halting the loop, and modification of the loop index. These are separated by semicolons.

You can place more than one expression in any of these three parts by separating them with a comma.

continue   Continues with the next iteration of a loop.

The continue statement can be a convenient way to skip over code and go on to the next loop iteration:

```
for (int index = 0; index < limit; index++) {
  if ((result = calculate(index)) == 0)
    continue; // loop back to the for loop
  //more code in this loop. . .
}
```

You can also use labels with a continue or break statement. Then, instead of continuing with the next loop iteration in the block where the continue is used, or instead of breaking out of the block the break is defined in, you can continue or break to the block defined by the label. Examples of this will be shown in Chapter 7.

return   Returns from a method, optionally passing back a value.

if   Tests for a condition and performs some action if true.

else   Performs some action if an if test is false.

```
String nobelWinner = null;
if (year == 1938)
  nobelWinner = new String("Enrico Firmi");
else if (year == 1921)
    nobelWinner = new String("Albert Einstein");
else if (year == 1903)
    nobelWinner = new String("Marie Curie");
else
    nobelWinner = new String("unknown");
}
```

do   Performs some statement or set of statements.

while   Performs some action while a condition is true.

To perform a block of code conditionally, you can use while without do, as in

```
while (condition == true) {
  doThis();
}
```

To perform a block of code at least once, and thereafter conditionally, you can use while in conjunction with do:

```
do {
doThis();
} while (condition == true);
```

Exercises

Exercise 3-1

Sort the following list into reserved and non-reserved words:

- for
- do_while
- Integer
- int
- implements
- equals
- Object
- java
- switch
- break
- test
- code
- goto

Exercise 3-2

List all the keywords that can be used to define control flow statements.

Exercise 3-3

List the keywords reserved by Java but not used in Java 2.

Answers to the Exercises

Exercise 3-1

Don't mistake class names for reserved words!

Reserved Words

- for
- int
- implements
- switch
- break
- goto

Nonreserved Words

- do_while
- Integer
- equals
- Object
- java
- test
- code

Exercise 3-2

The keywords used with control flow statements are do, while, if, else, for, break, continue, case, switch, default, and return.

Exercise 3-3

The two unused keywords are const and goto.

Review Questions

1. Which word is not a Java keyword?
   a. integer
   b. double
   c. float
   d. default

2. Which keyword is not used to control access to a class member?
   a. public
   b. protected
   c. private
   d. default

3. Identify the keywords from this list:

   ```
   abstract     class       object      reference
   double       character   Boolean     this
   ```

   boolean is the primitive data type; Boolean is the wrapper object class. Here it is purposefully listed as Boolean, which is not a keyword.
   a. abstract, class, object, double, this
   b. class, object, this
   c. abstract, class, double, this
   d. abstract, class, object, double, character, this
   e. abstract, class, object, double, this, Boolean

Answers to Review Questions

1. a. The integer data types are int, long, byte, and short, but there is no integer type. (Integer, with a capital I, is a class name.)

2. d. The default keyword is used with switch-case statements.

3. c. The others (object, reference, character, and Boolean) are not keywords. Note that boolean is a keyword, which refers to the primitive data type. Boolean is a wrapper object class for booleans.

CHAPTER 4

Java Building Blocks

Objectives for This Chapter

- Understand what identifiers are and what they mean to Java.
- Know the difference between various types of literals.
- Identify operators and separators.
- Understand and use comments in code.

In the previous chapter, we examined keywords, which are one of the basic building blocks of the Java programming language. Other building blocks include identifiers, operators, separators, and comments. These building blocks are very important to Java and they are referred to as tokens. Every Java programmer should know how to work with these basic building blocks.

At compile time, the Java compiler examines the source code and pulls out specific information. First, the Java compiler takes out escape sequences from the raw byte codes. It determines if the escape sequences are line terminators or input characters. Next, the Java compiler takes out whitespace that is not internal to a string, including the ASCII space character, carriage return, line feed, and horizontal tab. Then the compiler gets down to the business of pulling out tokens, which includes keywords, identifiers, operators, separators, and comments.

Identifiers

Identifiers are used for class names, method names, and variables. Identifiers can be named anything as long as they begin with an alphabet character, a dollar sign, or an underscore. Identifiers cannot begin with numeric characters.

NOTE: We do not recommend that you use the dollar sign or begin an identifier name with an underscore. The Java libraries use these symbols and you'll have a much easier time debugging programs if you don't use these symbols.

Java identifiers are case-sensitive. This means you can use uppercase, lowercase, or mixed-case words as identifiers. For example, you could use truck, Truck, or TRUCK as identifiers and they would all be seen as different.

CAUTION: Sometimes Java gives you just enough rope to get into interesting knots. For example, char is a reserved word in Java. However, Char, CHAR, or variations thereof are not reserved, meaning you could use these values as identifiers if you really wanted to. However, this would make debugging difficult and it would also make it difficult to maintain the program.

Literals

In Java, data is represented by *literals*. Similar to literals in other programming languages, Java literals are based on character and number representations. The types of literals are boolean, character, string, integer, and floating-point.

Every variable consists of a literal and a data type. The difference between the two is that literals are entered explicitly into the code. Data types are information about the literals, such as how much memory is reserved for that variable, as well as the possible value ranges for the variable.

Boolean Literals

Boolean literals are logical values that represent whether an item is true or false. A boolean literal can have one of two values. It is either *true* or *false*. Unlike other programming languages, no numeric value such as 0 or 1 can be assigned. Therefore, the value of a boolean literal is literally true or false. Booleans are used extensively in program control flow logic.

Character Literals

Java uses the Unicode character set. Characters in Java are represented in this character set and are 16-bit values that can be converted into integers and manipulated with integer operators, such as the addition or subtraction operator.

When you assign a character literal as part of a value, you enclose the character literal in single quotes, such as

```
'a'
```

or

```
'\u0061'
```

Programmers often use a single character as a value. In Java, this is represented by character literals. The value of a character literal is enclosed by single quotes. An example is 'b', which represents the character b. Any visible ASCII character can be directly entered inside the single quotes. This means you can use the letters a through z or A through Z; numerals 0 through 9; or other characters, such as !, @, #, $, %, ^, &, or *.

Some characters are reserved in the language or cannot be directly entered and must be escaped before you can use them. For example, you must escape the single-quote character ('), the double-quote character ("), and the backslash character (\). You escape characters by prefixing them with the backslash character—even the backslash character itself. This means you would use \' for the single quote character, \" for the double quote character, and \\ for the backslash character. Table 4-1 shows the character escape sequences.

NOTE: Compile-time errors occur if the character after \ is anything but b, t, n, f, r, ", ', \, 0, 1, 2, 4, 5, 6, or 7.

Table 4-1   Character Escape Sequences

Escape Sequence	Description
\nnn	Octal character
\unnnn	Hexadecimal character
\'	Single quote
\"	Double quote
\\	Backslash
\b	Backspace
\f	Form feed
\n	New line (line feed)
\r	Carriage return
\t	Tab

Java also supports a technique for directly entering character values using octal and hexadecimal. For octal notation, use the backslash followed by the three-digit octal value for the character, such as \141 for the letter a. For hexadecimal notation, use the backslash followed by the letter u and then the four-digit hexadecimal value for the character, such as \u0061 for the letter a in the ISO-Latin-1 character set.

Exercise 4-1

Given the following characters and associated values in the ISO-Latin-1 character set,

0061 = a
0062 = b
0063 = c
0064 = d
0065 = e

create separate character literal representations of these characters in hexadecimal notation. Be sure to enclose the character literals in single quotes.

String Literals

String literals are a sequence of characters enclosed in double quotes, such as

```
"This is a string literal"
```

or

```
"Hello World"
```

The Java compiler does not strip out whitespace from within string literals. String literals can be concatenated. For example, if one string contained

```
"This is the beginning"
```

and another string contained

```
" of a wonderful relationship"
```

then they could be concatenated together using the plus sign. The representation would be

```
"This is the beginning" + " of a wonderful relationship"
```

It is not necessary to have spaces on either side of the plus sign.

You could also use ((for a null character string. An important note concerning string literals is that they cannot span more than one line. This means Java strings must begin and end on the same line. Unlike other programming languages that have line continuation characters, no such value exists in Java.

As with the character literal, the backslash indicates the beginning of an escape sequence and is used with characters that cannot be typed or otherwise could not be used, such as the single-quote character ('), the double-quote character ("), and the backslash character (\). This means you could use \', \" and \\ within string literals.

 NOTE: Unlike C/C++ and some other programming languages, Java does not implement strings as arrays of characters. Instead, strings are actually implemented as objects. You'll learn more about Java's string handling in Chapter 16.

Exercise 4-2

Create string literals for the following sentences, making sure to use the appropriate escape codes:

Wilma asked, "Aren't you getting ready for the Java exam?"

Fred answered, "Yabba yabba right!"

Integer Literals

Integers are whole numbers, such as 1, 2, 3, and 500. Any whole number value can be an integer literal. Integer values can be represented in decimal (base 10), octal (base 8), or hexadecimal (base 16). Integer literals create an int value, which in Java is a 32-bit value.

Decimal values can be positive, zero, or negative. Decimal literals cannot start with 0, as in 0123. After the first number, a decimal literal can consist of the numbers 0 through 9. Numbers beginning with 0 are reserved for octal and hexadecimal literals. Therefore, when using decimals, do not right-justify with leading zeros. The upper limit of a positive decimal integer is $2^{31}-1$, or 2,147,483,647. The lower limit is $-2,147,483,648$ or -2^{31}.

Octal literals start with 0 and can be followed by any number 0 through 7. They can be positive, zero, or negative. The maximum value of an octal literal is 017777777777, which is equivalent to $2^{31}-1$.

Hexadecimal integer literals start with 0x or 0X followed by one or more hexadecimal digits (0–9, A–F). The letters A through F represent the numbers 10 through 15 and can be uppercase or lowercase. As with other integer literals, hexadecimal integers can be positive, zero, or negative. The upper limit of a positive hexadecimal literal is 0x7fffffff, which is, once again, equivalent to $2^{31}-1$.

NOTE: Java is a strongly typed language, but it does allow for an integer literal to be assigned to one of Java's integer types, such as byte or long, without causing a type mismatch error. When an integer literal is assigned to a byte or short variable, no error is generated if the literal value is within the acceptable range for the assigned variable type. Integer literals can always be assigned to long variables. However, you must explicitly tell the compiler that the literal value is of type long. You do this by appending an upper- or lowercase l to the literal such as 0x155l or 8764l.

Floating-Point Literals

Floating-point literals represent numbers with decimal values. Java standards specify that floating-point numbers must follow the industry standard specification as written in IEEE-754. This means that floating-point values can be expressed using either standard or scientific notation. Standard notation consists of a whole number followed by a decimal point, such as 3.14, 8.567, or 2.0. Scientific notation uses a standard notation plus a suffix that specifies a power of 10 by which the number is to be multiplied. The exponent is indicated by an e or E followed by a decimal number, which can be positive or negative such as 7.654E15, 2.345E−04, or 7e+50.

Floating-point literals in Java can have two different precisions. Single-precision floating-point numbers consist of a 32-bit space and are designated by an uppercase or lowercase *f*. Double-precision numbers are allotted a 64-bit space and are designated by uppercase or lowercase *d*. Double-precision floating-point numbers are the default. Therefore, 3.1429 is a double-precision floating-point number, and 3.1429f is a single-precision floating-point number. The largest magnitude single-precision floating-point literal is 3.40282347e+38f, and the smallest is 1.40239846e−45f. The largest double-precision floating-point number is 1.79769313486231570e+308, and the smallest floating-point number is 4.94065645841246544e−324.

Separators

Java uses a group of special characters as separators. The compiler uses these separators to divide the code into segments. The separators used are described in Table 4-2.

Operators

Operators are symbols used for arithmetic and logical operations. Arithmetic symbols define operations that apply to numbers, such as

```
18 + 32
```

Table 4-3 lists all the Java operators. Most operators can only be for arithmetic calculations. The exceptions are the logical operators (&, |, ^, !, &&, ||, ?:) and the + operator. Logical operators can be used with Boolean (true/false) expressions and the + operator can be used to concatenate strings. You'll find a complete discussion of these operators and their usage in Chapter 7.

Table 4-2 Java Separators

Symbol	Description
{}	Braces are used to define blocks of code for classes, methods, and local scopes. They are also used to contain the values of automatically initialized arrays.
[]	Brackets are used to declare array types. Also used when dereferencing array values.
,	A comma separates consecutive identifiers in variable declarations. It is also used to chain statements together inside for statements.
()	Parentheses are used to contain lists of parameters in method definitions and invocation. They are also used for defining precedence in expressions, containing expressions in control statements, and enclosing cast types.
.	A period is used to separate packaged names from subpackages and classes. Also used to separate a variable or method from a refernce variable.
;	A semi-colon terminates Java statements.

Table 4-3 Java Operators Listed Alphabetically by Operation

Operation	Operand
Addition assignment	+=
Addition	+
AND assignment	&=
Assign value	=
Bitwise AND	&
Bitwise complement	~
Bitwise OR	|
Bitwise XOR	^
Conditional (ternary)	?:
Decrement by 1	--
Divide assignment	/=
Division	/
Equal	==
Greater than	>
Greater than or equal	>=
Increment by 1	++
Left shift	<<
Left shift assignment	<<=
Less than	<
Less than or equal	<=
Logical AND	&
Logical OR	|
Logical XOR	^
Modulus	%
Modulus assignment	%=
Multiplication	*
Multiply assignment	*=
Not	!

Operation	Operand
NOT assignment	^=
Not equal	!=
OR assignment	|=
Right shift	>>
Right shift assignment	>>=
Short-circuit AND	&&
Short-circuit OR	||
Subtract assignment	-=
Subtraction	-
Zero fill right shift	>>>
Zero fill right shift assignment	>>>=

Exercise 4-3

Sort the following list into Java operators and non-Java operators:

- *
- +
- +=
- -=
- --
- !=
- !!
- ++
- #
- %

Exercise 4-4

List all the operators that can be used with non-arithmetic operations.

Comments

Comments are used to add non-code elements to the text for the purposes of documentation or simply to explain what a particular block or line of code is doing. Comments should be used throughout code to explain key elements and they also can be used to block out certain code sections for testing purposes.

Java has three types of comments, two of which are used for standard comments and the remaining one is used for creating documentation automatically from source code. Table 4-4 provides a summary of Java comments as well as the end designator if any.

The standard comments are used as follows:

```
// Enter your comment text on one line
/* Enter your comment text on multiple lines
Making sure to end with */
```

Documentation comments can be inserted into code manually or be machine-generated.

 NOTE: Comments can be used anywhere in code without affecting the code's execution or logic. Be sure to terminate the comment, or the compiler will get confused. If you forget to terminate a comment, you will see strange results when you try to compile or run the program. Basically, what happens is that the compiler interprets everything up to the next end comment indicator as part of the comment, which can cut out entire sections of your program.

Table 4-4   Comment Indicators

Start	Text	End Comment
/*	text	*/
/**	text	*/
//	text	Everything to the end of the line is ignored by the compiler.

Answers to the Exercises

Exercise 4-1

The character literals are

'\u0061' for the letter a

'\u0062' for the letter b

'\u0063' for the letter c

'\u0064' for the letter d

'\u0065' for the letter e

Exercise 4-2

The string literals for the sentences "Wilma asked, 'Aren't you getting ready for the Java exam?', " and "Fred answered, 'Yabba yabba right!'," are

```
"Wilma asked, \"Aren\'t you getting ready for the Java exam?\""
"Fred answered, \"Yabba yabba right!\""
```

Exercise 4-3

The following are Java operators:

- *
- +
- +=
- -=
- --
- !=
- ++
- %

The following are not Java operators:

- !!
- #

Exercise 4-4

Operators that can be used with non-arithmetic operations include logical operators (&, |, ^, !, &&, ||, ?:) and the + operator.

Review Questions

1. How would you present the value 3 as a character literal using octal, decimal, and hexadecimal notation? (Hint: 3 is the 51st character in the ISO-Latin-1 character set.)

   a.

   ```
   Octal
   '\033'
   Decimal
   '33'
   Hexadecimal
   '\u0033
   ```

   b.

   ```
   Octal
   '\063'
   Decimal
   '51'
   Hexadecimal
   '\u0033
   ```

   c.

   ```
   Octal
   '\063'
   Decimal
   '3'
   Hexadecimal
   '\u0033
   ```

   d.

   ```
   Octal
   '\63'
   Decimal
   '51'
   Hexadecimal
   '\0033'
   ```

2. If you wanted to concatenate the string literals "Bang," "Zoom," "Straight," "To," "The," and "Moon," which of the following are acceptable ways to do this?

   a. "Bang," Zoom, "Straight," "To," "The," "Moon"
   b. "Bang," "Zoom," "Straight," "To," "The," "Moon"
   c. Bang Zoom Straight To The Moon
   d. "Bang"+"Zoom"+"Straight"+"To"+"The"+"Moon"

3. Which of the following are valid Boolean literals?

    a. 0

    b. 1

    c. true

    d. false

4. The output of the following code

```
/* Print to screen
System.out.println("Welcome to my world!");
```

    is

```
Welcome to my world!
```

    a. True

    b. False

Answers to Review Questions

1. **c.** Octal '\063', Decimal '3', Hexadecimal '\u0033'. For octal, 063 is the equivalent of the decimal value 51 (the ASCII character value for 3). For decimal, the value is simply 3 because any visible ASCII character can be directly entered inside the quotes including the numerals 0 through 9. For hexadecimal, 0x0033 is the equivalent of decimal 51 (the ASCII character value for 3).

2. **d.** Strings are concatenated together using the plus sign and it is not necessary to have spaces on either side of the plus sign.

3. **c.** and **d.** only. In Java, you can only use the values true and false to represent Booleans. You cannot use 0 or 1.

4. **b.** False. The code wouldn't display anything. The programmer forgot to terminate the comment. To resolve this, the code would need to be rewritten as follows:

```
/* Print to screen */
System.out.println("Welcome to my world!");
```

Memory and Garbage Collection

Objectives for This Chapter

- Identify when an object referred to by a local variable becomes eligible to be garbage collected (in the absence of compiler optimization).
- Describe how finalization works and the behavior Java guarantees regarding finalization.
- Distinguish between modifying variables containing primitive data types and object references, and modifying the objects themselves.
- Identify the results of Java's pass-by-value approach when passing parameters to methods.

Java manages your program's memory. This eliminates all manner of bugs that creep into programs built with languages where you must access and manage memory directly. Java's role in managing memory eliminates bugs involved with the following:

- Freeing memory too soon (resulting in a dangling pointer)
- Not freeing memory soon enough or at all (resulting in a memory leak)
- Accessing memory beyond the bounds of the allocated memory (resulting in using uninitialized values)

When you want to define a new data type, you define a new class. You can allocate an instance of a class by using the new keyword, which returns an object reference. This object reference is essentially a pointer to the object in memory—except in Java you cannot manipulate this object reference like a number. You cannot perform pointer arithmetic.

Objects are allocated from a garbage-collected heap. You cannot directly alter the memory in this heap. You can only get at the objects in this heap by using object references. Since Java manages the heap, and since you cannot manipulate object references, you must trust the Java Virtual Machine (JVM) to do what's right: free memory when it should, allocate the correct amount of memory when needed, and so on. But don't worry; the JVM is very good at its job—much better than any of us error-prone humans.

Garbage Collection

For the exam, you'll need to be able to identify when an object referred to by a local variable becomes eligible to be garbage collected (in the absence of compiler optimization). Since Java manages the garbage-collected heap, which is where all your objects live, you've got to trust Java to manage the memory for you. This includes believing that the JVM really will free memory that you no longer need when it runs low.

When Does an Object Become Eligible for Garbage Collection?

An object becomes a candidate for garbage collection when your program can no longer reference it. Here is an example. Let's say you allocate an object and only assign it to a method variable. When that method returns, you have no way to ever refer to that method variable again. Therefore, the object is lost forever. That means that when the method returns, the object is a candidate for garbage collection.

As another example, you might create an object, assign this object to an object reference, and then set this object reference to null. As soon as you lose the reference to the object, that object becomes a candidate for garbage collection.

Just because your program might lose a reference to an object does not mean that the JVM will reclaim that object's memory right away, or even at all. The JVM will only perform garbage collection if it needs more memory to continue executing. For almost all simple programs, including the ones you've seen so far, the JVM doesn't even come close to running out of memory.

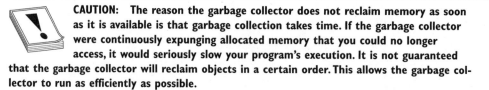

CAUTION: The reason the garbage collector does not reclaim memory as soon as it is available is that garbage collection takes time. If the garbage collector were continuously expunging allocated memory that you could no longer access, it would seriously slow your program's execution. It is not guaranteed that the garbage collector will reclaim objects in a certain order. This allows the garbage collector to run as efficiently as possible.

Even though a new keyword exists, notice that you do not explicitly indicate how much memory to set aside. The JVM determines this for itself. The JVM determines the memory your object requires based on

- The amount of memory needed to maintain instance variables for the object

- A standard overhead required by all objects

What's more, even though Java supplies the keyword *new*, no corresponding delete is available, nor any other way to directly free memory. The way you indicate you are through with an object is to set its object reference to null or to some other object. Or, as mentioned, when a method returns, its method variables will no longer be valid, so the garbage collector also knows any objects referenced by method variables are candidates for garbage collection.

Invoking the Garbage Collector

Even though you cannot free objects explicitly, you *can* directly invoke the garbage collector. This will make the garbage collector run, which will reclaim candidates for garbage collection.

They way you run the garbage collector is to perform two steps:

1. Get an object that represents the current runtime.

2. Invoke that object's gc() method.

Here is a snippet that does this:

```
Runtime rt = Runtime.getRuntime();
rt.gc();
```

Exercise 5-2 asks you to work through an example of this.

Finalization

For the exam, you'll need to know when finalization takes place. In most situations, you'll never know when garbage collection has occurred. Java runs the garbage-collecting process as a low-priority background thread. The garbage collector will run whenever memory gets low.

However, you can get into the act of garbage collection. If you want to perform some task when your object is about to go away, you can override a method called finalize().

Java will invoke the finalize() method exactly once for every object in your program. finalize() is declared as protected, does not return a value, and throws a Throwable object.

Java invokes the finalize() method just before an object is about to be garbage collected. You might take advantage of this notification to clean up any resources that have been allocated outside this object. A classic example is a file that an object has opened that might still be open. The object can check to see if the file has been closed in finalize() and, if not, it will close the file.

 CAUTION: Although you can use try and catch blocks in finalize(), uncaught exceptions are ignored. The official documentation says that finalize() will be run for all objects when the program exits. However, on some platforms and in earlier versions of Java, this is not always the case. Sometimes finalize() simply does not run unless the JVM runs out of memory or, if it does not, you explicitly invoke the garbage collector.

You can also invoke your own object's finalize() method. Typically, you would not invoke finalize() yourself, but would allow the JVM to do this for you. If you do invoke finalize(), remember that finalize() is declared as throwing a Throwable, and that it is declared as protected, so only objects with the proper access can invoke this method.

It's easy to forget that finalize() could be implemented in a superclass. Always be certain to invoke your superclass's finalize() method so that you don't break code you inherit from. Since Java only invokes finalize() once per object, you should not resurrect an object in finalize(). If you did and the object was finalized again, its finalize() method would not get called. Instead, you should create a clone of the object if you really need to bring the object back to life.

 TIP: Always invoke your superclass's finalize() method if you override finalize().

Exercise 5-1

Write a class called Test with objects that writes the message, "We're in finalize," to the standard output when their finalize() methods are run.

Exercise 5-2

Given the following code for a class called GC, create a new Test object in GC's test() method and then make that object a candidate for garbage collection. Do this before the call to fullGC() in test().

When this code is working, running GC with the Test class you wrote should cause the message "We're in finalize" to appear in the standard output automatically, without you explicitly invoking finalize().

```
class GC {
    public static void main(String[] args) {
        GC gc = new GC();
        gc.test();
    }
    void test() {
        fullGC();
    }
    void fullGC() {
        Runtime rt = Runtime.getRuntime();
        long isFree = rt.freeMemory();
        long wasFree;
        do {
            wasFree = isFree;
            rt.gc();
            isFree = rt.freeMemory();
        } while (isFree > wasFree);

        rt.runFinalization();
    }
}
```

Accessing Members

You should be able to distinguish between modifying variables containing primitive data types and object references, and modifying the objects themselves. Given an object reference, which variable you access and which method you invoke depend on different things. The type of the *object reference* determines which variable you access. The type of the *underlying object* determines which method you invoke.

As an example, consider the following code:

```
class Acc {
  public static void main(String[] args) {
      First s = new Second();
      System.out.println(s.var);
      System.out.println(s.method());
  }
}

class First {
    int var = 1;
    int method() {
        return var;
    }
}
```

```
class Second extends First {
   int var = 2;
   int method() {
      return var;
   }
}
```

What do you expect this program to display in the standard output? Notice that the variable s in main() is defined as an object reference for the First type, but we've actually allocated a new object of type Second, a subclass of First.

When we use s to access a variable, the type of s—in this case, First—is used to grab the variable. So, we access var from First, which is 1. So, in the first println() statement, 1 appears in the standard output.

When we use s to invoke a method, the type of the object referenced by s—in this case, Second—is used to invoke the method. So, we invoke method() in Second, which accesses its local variable named var. This makes the second println() statement display 2 in the standard output.

What would happen if we changed the class definition of Second so that it no longer overrode method()? In that case, even though s.method() will look first in the Second class to access method(), the call will get passed up the class hierarchy. The method() that's defined in First will execute, which will access its local var variable, which is 1, so the second println() statement would display 1.

Exercise 5-3

When you invoke a method given an object reference, is there a way to force the JVM to invoke the overridden method that's defined in that object's superclass instead of invoking the method in the class type of the object itself? For example, given classes First and Second defined in the previous section, is it possible to invoke method() defined in First, rather than method() defined in Second, given an object reference of type Second?

Passing Parameters to a Method

For the exam, you'll need to be able to identify the results of Java's pass-by-value approach when passing parameters to methods. When Java passes method parameters *by value*, Java makes a copy of the parameter and passes this copy to the method.

For a primitive data type—such as an int, float, boolean, or char—the result of passing by value should be clear: anything that happens to that value inside the method does not affect the original value in the calling code.

Here's an example:

```
public class C {
    public static void main(String[] args) {
        double pi = 3.1415;

        System.out.println("before: pi is " + pi);
        zero(pi);
        System.out.println("after: pi is " + pi);
    }

    static void zero(double arg) {
        System.out.println("top of zero: arg is " + arg);
        arg = 0.0;
        System.out.println("bottom of zero: arg is " + arg);
    }
}
```

First, we set a value for a variable named pi, and then we pass this value to a method that sets this value to 0. The value of pi gets to the method named zero() just fine, and zero() does its job of setting the value it receives to 0. However, zero() has received a copy. The original value of pi in main() is not affected.

The output from this program is

```
before: pi is 3.1415
top of zero: arg is 3.1415
bottom of zero: arg is 0
after: pi is 3.1415
```

Although the same call by value rule is in place when the argument is an object reference rather than a primitive data type, unraveling what's really going on involves some careful thinking.

Let's redo the previous program, this time making the variable pi an object reference that refers to an instance of a class we'll create called Pi. This class will have one instance variable and will look like this:

```
class Pi {
    double value = 3.1415;
    public String toString() {
        Double d = new Double(value);
        return d.toString();
    }
}
```

TIP: By overriding the method toString(), we provide a way to place the object reference directly in a println() statement to display its value. You can use this trick in your own programs to help make your code easier to read and your objects easier to work with.

Let's rework the original program to use an instance of the Pi class instead of passing the value of pi directly as a double:

```
public class D {
    public static void main(String[] args) {
        Pi pi = new Pi();

        System.out.println("before: pi is " + pi);
        zero(pi);
        System.out.println("after: pi is " + pi);
    }

    static void zero(Pi arg) {
        System.out.println("top of zero: arg is " + arg);
        arg.value = 0.0;
        System.out.println("middle of zero: arg is " + arg);
        arg = null;
        System.out.println("bottom of zero: arg is " + arg);
    }
}
```

What do you expect the outcome of this program to be? To answer this question correctly, you need to have a picture in mind of what's going on in memory.

In main(), after creating the instance of Pi and assigning it to an object reference called pi, we have something like Figure 5-1.

We will refer to a chunk of memory somewhere in the program by using the name pi. This chunk of memory (which is four bytes long, to be exact) points to an object that's somewhere else in memory. Notice that an object reference like pi is a pointer, even though Java offers no means of manipulating pi as if it were a pointer, as you can in C or C++. The object referenced by pi has an instance variable set to 3.1415, so that's how we've depicted it in the figure.

As soon as we invoke the method named zero(), Java needs to keep track of another object reference—the method parameter (that is, the variable) we've named arg. The variable arg is completely separate from the variable pi, because parameters are passed by value, and so Java makes a copy of the variable. However, as with the double values

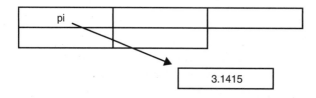

Figure 5-1   An object reference accessing an object in the garbage-collected heap

in the previous example, the contents of each variable are the same. Hence, arg also points to the same object as pi (see Figure 5-2).

Now, if we use the variable arg to change the object, we change the object directly. The code, for example, sets arg.value to 0 (see Figure 5-3).

The final section of code in the method zero( ) sets the value of arg to null. This does nothing to the object itself or to any other object references—setting arg to null only changes the object reference named arg (see Figure 5-4).

The variable arg loses its reference to the object, but the object itself is still intact. Also intact are any other references to the object. If arg were the only object reference to the underlying Pi object, then the object would become a candidate for garbage collection.

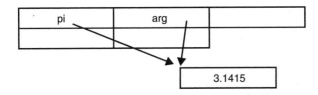

Figure 5-2   Two object references pointing to the same object in the garbage-collected heap

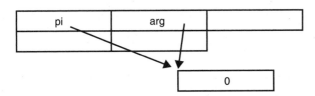

Figure 5-3   Changing the same object by using the second object reference

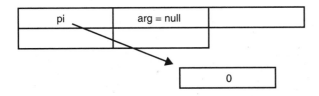

Figure 5-4   Setting one of the object references to null, but the object is untouched

However, arg is just a parameter, and there is another reference to the underlying object —the reference in the calling code.

The output of this code, then, looks like this:

```
before: pi is 3.1415
top of zero: arg is 3.1415
middle of zero: arg is 0
bottom of zero: arg is null
after: pi is 0
```

Exercise 5-4

Find a way to change the following code so that you can pass the values a, b, and c in test() to calc(). Then have calc() update these values and return them to test(). As the values are currently defined, there is no way to pass them to calc() and then return them to test(). The reason for this is that the values are defined as primitive data types. Perhaps you can pass another data type to calc() so that this will work?

```java
class DataPassing {
    public static void main(String[] args) {
        DataPassing a = new  DataPassing();
        a.test();
    }
    void test() {
        int a = 10;
        int b = 13;
        int c = 24;

        System.out.println("before: a = " + a);
        System.out.println("before: b = " + b);
        System.out.println("before: c = " + c);

        calc(a, b, c);

        System.out.println("after: a = " + a);
        System.out.println("after: b = " + b);
        System.out.println("after: c = " + c);
    }
    void calc(int a, int b, int c) {
        a *= 2;
        b *= 3;
        c *= 4;
    }
}
```

Forcing Garbage Collection

Exercise 5-2 contained some code that used a Runtime object to force garbage collection. This is not something that is on the test, but it's useful to know how to do this.

Runtime defines four methods that you can use to help keep track of and interact with the garbage collector:

- **gc()** By the time this method returns, the JVM has performed garbage collection.

- **runFinalization()** By the time this method returns, the JVM has run the finalize() method for all objects awaiting garbage collection that have not had their finalize() methods run yet.

- **totalMemory()** This method returns an int containing the total amount of memory available in the JVM for allocating objects.

- **freeMemory()** This method returns an int containing the total amount of free memory in bytes. Free memory is the amount of memory available for allocating objects. This amount will always be less than the value returned by totalMemory().

Answers to the Exercises

Exercise 5-1

You can write a Test class that overrides finalize() like this:

```
class Test {
    protected void finalize() throws Throwable {
        super.finalize();
        System.out.println("We're in finalize");
    }
}
```

Remember, as the text says, finalize() is declared as protected and throws a Throwable.

Exercise 5-2

Your test method in GC should now look like this:

```
void test() {
    Test t = new Test();
    t = null;
    fullGC();
}
```

Exercise 5-3

No, you can reference super from a method, but you cannot invoke a method defined in a superclass given only an object reference.

Exercise 5-4

One way to solve this problem is to create a new class that has three int values for a, b, and c, pass an instance of this class to calc(), and have calc() operate on the instance variables of this object.

Another way is to create an array of int values and to pass the array to calc(). Remember, an array is an object, so you can pass the array to a method and if the method modifies the elements of the array, these changes will appear in the calling method's array as well. Here is an example of this:

```java
class DataPassing2 {
    public static void main(String[] args) {
        DataPassing2 b = new DataPassing2();
        b.test();
    }
    void test() {
        int[] arr = {10, 13, 24};

        for (int i = 0; i < arr.length; i++)
            System.out.println("before: a" + i + " = " + arr[i]);

        calc(arr);

        for (int i = 0; i < arr.length; i++)
            System.out.println("after: a" + i + " = " + arr[i]);

    }
    void calc(int[] arr) {
        arr[0] *= 2;
        arr[1] *= 3;
        arr[2] *= 4;
    }
}
```

Review Questions

1. What would the result be in the standard output if you executed the class named Acc2, listed here?

```java
class Acc2 {
    public static void main(String[] args) {
        First s = new Second();
        Second s2 = (Second)s;
        System.out.println(s2.var);
        System.out.println(s2.method());
    }
}
```

```
class First {
    int var = 1;
    int method() {
        return var;
    }
}

class Second extends First {
    int var = 2;
    int method() {
        return var;
    }
}
```

   a. 2
       2
   b. 2
       1
   c. 1
       2
   d. 1
       1

2. How many objects are candidates for garbage collection by the end of the following code snippet?

```
String s = "kanga";
s = "kanga" + "roo";
int[] arr = {1, 4, 9, 25};
arr[3] = 16;
arr = new int[4];
s = null;
```

   a. 1
   b. 2
   c. 3
   d. 4

3. Which answer defines a legal finalize() method?

   a.

```
protected void finalize() {
    super.finalize();
    System.out.println("finalize");
}
```

b.

```
private void finalize() throws Throwable {
  super.finalize();
  System.out.println("finalize");
}
```

c.

```
protected void finalize() throws Throwable {
  super.finalize();
  System.out.println("finalize");
}
```

d.

```
void finalize() {
  super.finalize();
  System.out.println("finalize");
}
```

4. What happens if you attempt to compile and run this code?

```
class Clean {

    public static void main(String[] args) {

        Dirty d = new Dirty();

        d.finalize();

        d = null;
        Runtime r = Runtime.getRuntime();
        r.gc();
        r.runFinalization();
    }
}

class Dirty {
    protected void finalize() throws Throwable {
        System.out.println("Dirty finalization");
    }
}
```

    a. The code will not compile because of a problem invoking finalize().
    b. The code will compile but will display nothing.
    c. The code will compile and will display "Dirty finalization" once.
    d. The code will compile and will display "Dirty finalization" twice.

Answers to Review Questions

1. **a.** Since we cast the object reference s from a type First to a type Second, we then access Second's var and method.

2. **c.** Let's take this line by line:

   ```
   String s = "kanga";
   s = "kanga" + "roo";
   ```

   At this point, we have created two objects. The first String object contained the characters "kanga." The second contained the characters "kangaroo." Since we can no longer reference the first String object—we have reused the s object reference —this is the first object now available for garbage collection.

   ```
   int[] arr = {1, 4, 9, 25};
   arr[3] = 16;
   ```

   At this point, we have created a new int array and accessed one of its elements:

   ```
   arr = new int[4];
   ```

   Now we create a new int array and assign it to the object reference arr. Therefore, we lose track of the first array that contained 1, 4, 9, and 25. This is the second object that is now available for garbage collection.

   ```
   s = null;
   ```

   Setting s to null makes us lose the reference to the String containing "kangaroo." This object is now available for garbage collection as well.

3. **c.** The finalize() method is protected and throws an object of type Throwable.

4. **a.** The problem with invoking finalize() is that it is declared as throwing an object of class Throwable. That means the direct call to finalize() must be placed within a try-catch block. There's a full explanation of exception handling in Chapter 14.

Data Types and Values

- State what strongly typed means.
- Define the range of values for all primitive data types.
- Describe numeric promotion of integers and floating-point values.
- Construct literal char values using both quoted formats and Unicode escape sequences.
- Identify the default values of instance and static variables.
- Define one dimensional and multi-dimensional arrays.
- Determine the default values for elements in an array.
- Use curly braces {} as part of an array declaration to initialize an array.

As with most programming languages, Java supports several types of data. This chapter examines how to use those data types, what their default values are, and how to declare them. We also look at declaring, constructing, and initializing arrays.

Data Types

Java is a strongly typed language. This means that every variable and expression has a type, and that every type is strictly defined. It also means that all assignments are checked for type compatibility whether they are explicitly defined or assigned via parameter passing in method calls.

Unlike some other programming languages, Java doesn't perform automatic conversion or coercion of conflicting data types either. The Java compiler checks all expressions and parameters to ensure that the types are compatible. Any type mismatches or errors reported must be corrected before the compiler will complete its operation.

Variables and Data Types

In Java, variables store data. The type of data that can be stored in a variable is defined by the data type it is assigned. The data type also sets the size limits of the data.

An example specifying a variable and data type is

```
int myInt;
```

Here, you create the definition of the myInt identifier as the type int. The myInt variable at this point has the value of 0, which is the default value of type int.

Another example of defining variables and data types follows

```
int valueA, valueB, valueC;
```

This example defines three variables: valueA, valueB, and valueC. Each of them is of type int and has the default value of zero.

Primitive Data Types

Java defines eight primitive data types. Primitive data types represent single values, meaning they can have only one value at a time. They do not reference other data or indicate sequence in a group of data. They are primitive in that they are the simplest forms of data in Java and do not represent objects. The reason for this is efficiency. Primitive data types are highly efficient and make the Java programming language much more robust than it would be if primitive data types were represented as objects.

The primitive data types are

```
Data Type        Size in Bits
byte             signed 8-bit integer
short            signed 16-bit integer
int              signed 32-bit integer
long             signed 64-bit integer
float            signed 32-bit floating-point
double           signed 64-bit floating-point
char             16-bit Unicode character
boolean          either true or false (special values built-in Java)
```

The primitive data types have a strictly defined range. The explicit range is necessary because of Java's portability requirement. Explicit ranges ensure that the size of a data type on one platform is the same on other platforms. This allows you to create programs that are guaranteed to run on other platforms without having to port the code from one platform to another.

For the exam, you'll need to be able to state the range for all primitive data types. The ranges are as follows:

```
Data Type      Range
byte           -2^7 to 2^7 [nd] 1 (-128 to 127)
short          -2^15 to 2^15 - 1 (-32,768 to 32,767)
int            -2^31 to 2^31 - 1 (-2,147,483,648 to 2,147,483,647)
long           -2^63 to 2^63 - 1
float          Float.MIN_VALUE to Float.MAX_VALUE, Float.NaN,
               Float.NEGATIVE_INFINITY, Float.POSITIVE_INFINITY
double         Double.MIN_VALUE to Double.MAX_VALUE, Double.NaN,
               Double.NEGATIVE_INFINITY, Double.POSITIVE_INFINITY
char           0 to 2^16 - 1  (0 to 65,535)
boolean        either true or false (special values built into Java)
```

If you do not supply a default value for member variables, they use a standard default value. These default values are

```
Type           Default Value
boolean        false
byte           0
char           \u0000
short          0
int            0
long           01
float          0.0f
double         0.0d
```

Not defining a default value for a local variable results in a compile-time error.

Integer Data Types

Java defines four integer types: byte, short, int, and long. Each can handle a different range of numbers, as summarized previously, and are all signed, positive, and negative values. Although Java doesn't implement unsigned integers, the language does allow for unsigned operations on values using the unsigned right shift operator. This operator is primarily used to manipulate the high-order bits for 32-bit and 64-bit values.

The bit size of an integer type should not be thought of as the amount of storage it uses. Instead, the size defines the valid range for variables and expressions of that type. Different runtime environments can implement storage usage in different ways. For example, in some implementations, bytes and shorts are stored as 32-bit values rather than 8- and 16-bit values. The reason for this is to improve performance (most computers used 32-bits as the standard word size).

As you work with integers, you'll find that bytes, ints, and longs each have their uses, although shorts are rarely used. Bytes are useful when you work with raw binary data that may not be compatible with Java's other built-in types. Ints are useful when you want to create a number for counting, controlling loops, indexing arrays, or performing integer math. Longs are useful when you are working with large values that cannot be represented as ints.

Following are examples of integer declarations:

```
byte ByteVal;      //8 bits
short ShortVal;    //16 bits
int IntVal;        //32 bits
long LongVal;      //64 bits
```

You can perform operations on mixed integer types. Whenever two integers of varying length are operated on, the computation proceeds by widening the smaller bit size to equal the larger bit size. This means anytime you perform an operation involving bytes, shorts, ints, or literal numbers, the values are widened to ints by numeric promotion before the operation is performed. Similarly bytes, shorts, ints, and literal numbers are widened to longs by numeric promotion before an operation involving a long is performed. The result is always expressed as an int or long as appropriate.

Integer operations rarely result in ArithmeticException. The only case in which an exception occurs is when there is an attempt to divide by zero. To prevent this, you should always test the right-hand operand to see if it is zero before attempting a divide operation.

Other interesting things happen in Java when the value of an integer underflows or overflows its defined range. ArithmeticException will not occur. Instead, the value wraps around to the other end of the numeric range for that type. Here is an example:

```
class WrapNumber {
public static void main (String args[]) {
   byte BaseNumber = 120;
   byte TheNumber;
   int  IncValue;
   TheNumber = BaseNumber;
   for (IncValue=0; IncValue < 10; IncValue++) {
    System.out.println("BaseNumber(" + BaseNumber + ") + IncValue
(" +
    IncValue + ") = " + TheNumber);
    TheNumber++;
    }
   }
 }
```

The output is

```
BaseNumber(120) + IncValue (0) = 120
BaseNumber(120) + IncValue (1) = 121
BaseNumber(120) + IncValue (2) = 122
BaseNumber(120) + IncValue (3) = 123
```

```
BaseNumber(120) + IncValue (4) = 124
BaseNumber(120) + IncValue (5) = 125
BaseNumber(120) + IncValue (6) = 126
BaseNumber(120) + IncValue (7) = 127
BaseNumber(120) + IncValue (8) = -128
BaseNumber(120) + IncValue (9) = -127
```

In this example, the byte value overflows and begins incrementing at the lowest value possible (-128). Similarly, a short would overflow to –32,768 and an int would overflow to –2,147,483,648.

Character Values

In Java, the data type used to store characters is char. A variable defined as a char can contain any Unicode character. The range of a char is 0 to 65,536. There are no negative character values.

The standard ASCII character set is in the range from 0 to 127. The extended ISO-Latin-1 character set is in the range from 0 to 255. Other character sets, including Arabic, Cyrillic, Greek, and Hebrew, are defined above these values.

The char data type can be assigned to variables in several ways. You can use a specific value, which is an index into the Unicode character set, such as

```
myChar = 90; //code for Z
```

myChar is assigned the value 90, which is the ASCII (and Unicode) value that corresponds to the letter Z.

You can use the escape sequence '\udddd' to represent any Unicode character, where d is a hexadecimal digit. The ASCII characters are all found in the range '\u0000' to '\u00ff,' which as stated previously, are the values 0 to 127. Here is an example of assigning a value using an escape code:

```
myChar = '\u0090'; //code for Z
```

Another way to assign a character value is to use a string literal, such as

```
myChar = 'Z'; //assigns letter Z
```

Although chars are not integers, you can operate on them as if they were integers. This means you can add two characters together and you can increment the value of a character. Consider the following example:

```
class IncChar {
public static void main (String args[]) {
   char MyChar;
   int IncValue;
```

```
MyChar = 'A';

for (IncValue=0; IncValue < 26; IncValue++) {
  System.out.println("MyChar is: " + MyChar);
  MyChar++;
  }

  }
}
```

The output generated by this program is

```
MyChar is: A
MyChar is: B
MyChar is: C
MyChar is: D
MyChar is: E
MyChar is: F
 . . .
MyChar is: Z
```

 CAUTION: The default value for any class variable or instance variable declared as a char is '\u0000.' Don't confuse '\u0000' with a space character, which is '\u0020.'

Floating-Point Arithmetic

Floating-point or real numbers are used when evaluating expressions that require fractional precision. Java implements the IEEE-754 set of floating point types, which are float and double. Type float designates that the variable is a single-precision, 32-bit, floating-point number. Type double is a double-precision, 64-bit, floating-point number.

Examples declaring floating-point variables are

```
float Velocity;
double DistanceTraveled;
```

Unlike integer data types, floating-point data types never throw an exception if some ill-defined state arises when performing arithmetic. For example, if you divide by 0 using floating-point types, Java assigns the value to infinity (of the appropriate sign matching the numerator). The class "wrapper" types double and float even define class constants called POSITIVE_INFINITY and NEGATIVE_INFINITY that you can use to acquire these values. If the result is not a number at all, the result is NaN. NaN constants of both float and double type are predefined as Float.NaN and Double.NaN.

Following is a table that shows various outcomes with 0, finite values, and infinity.

x	y	x/y	x%y
finite	0.0	infinity	NaN
finite	infinity	0.0	x
0.0	0.0	infinity	NaN
infinity	finite	infinity	NaN
infinity	infinity	NaN	NaN

The sign of infinity depends on the signs involved in the arithmetic expression. Any arithmetic expression involving NaN yields NaN.

With both float and double you can perform operations using mixed integer and floating-point types. Anytime you perform an operation involving integers and floats, the values are widened to floats by numeric promotion before the operation is performed. Similarly integers and floats are widened to doubles by numeric promotion before an operation involving a double is performed. The result is always expressed as a float or double as appropriate.

Booleans

Booleans are logical values that can only have a value of true or false. You use boolean values with relational and conditional expressions, such as b>c or if (b == true). Booleans are used to determine the control flow used with if, while, do, and for statements.

Other programming languages have boolean values of 0 for false and 1 for true. Although Java doesn't use 0 or 1, you can get Java to mimic this behavior if necessary. As in the C programming language, x!=0 will convert the integer x to a boolean in which 0 equals false and anything else equals true. On the other hand, y?1:0 will convert the boolean variable y to 0 for false and 1 for true.

Casting

You cannot implicitly coerce a data type with greater accuracy into a data type with less accuracy. In fact, trying to do so results in compile-time error.

This means, for example, that you cannot write code that looks like this:

```
int i = 5;
byte b = i;
```

because an int holds larger numbers than a byte. An int is more accurate. The Java compiler will complain that these are incompatible types for the = operator, and that you need an explicit cast to convert the int into a byte.

The way to do this is to write

```
int i = 5;
byte b = (byte)i;
```

The same is true with floating-point values. You cannot assign a double to a float, because a double is more accurate than a float. So, you must explicitly cast it.

Similarly, you cannot assign any kind of floating-point number to an integer type without an explicit cast.

Exercises

Exercise 6.1

What is the smallest integer data type you could use to hold the following?

the number of letters in the alphabet

the net worth of Bill Gates in U.S. dollars

the number of pages in this book

the number of people in the United States

Exercise 6.2

Write a program that displays the default values for each integer type.

Exercise 6.3

What is wrong with the following program? How would you fix this code?

```
class Test {
    public static void main(String[] args) {
        int index;
        boolean found;
        for (index = 0; index < 10 && !found; index++) {
            if (index > Math.PI) {
                System.out.println(index + " is greater than Pi");
                found = true;
            }
        }
    }
}
```

Arrays

For the exam, you'll need to be able to declare, construct, and initialize arrays. Arrays are groups of variables that are referred to by a common name and can have one or more dimensions. Think of going grocery shopping. The grocery list acts as the array. Each item on the list is an element, the smallest part of an array. It is referenced by its place in the array, such as the first, second, or third item on the list. If you are going grocery shopping at two different stores, you could create a two-dimensional array where the first element indicates the store you are shopping at and the second element indicates the item you want to buy at that store.

Declaring and Initializing Arrays

You can declare arrays in several ways. You can declare an array without initializing it. In other words, the array variable itself is created, but no space is allocated in memory for array objects until the array is initialized or values are assigned to the elements of the array. Or you can declare the array and initialize it to a specific size. Here you initialize an array to a specific size, and memory is allocated to hold the array's elements.

Elements can be of any primitive type, as in float, char, or int. Elements can also be a class or interface type. Arrays can consist of other arrays as well. All the elements of an array must be of the same type, however.

Arrays of data types can be declared by writing square brackets after the data type, as in

```
int[] myIntArray;
```

or

```
MyClass[] myClassArray;
```

These two array declarations create variables whose types are an array of ints and an array of objects, respectively.

Arrays are objects. Use new to create the array and allocate the array to the appropriate size. For example,

```
MyClass[] myClassArray = new MyClass[5];
```

allocates an array large enough to hold five elements. In this case, we have allocated an array of object references. The first element in an array is element 0. The last element is element length $-$ 1.

You'll also need to determine the default values for elements in an array. Java sets each element in an array to its default value when the array is created. For myClassArray, defined previously as an array of objects, each element is set to null when the array is first allocated. For an array of int values, each element would be set to 0.

One-Dimensional Arrays

One-dimensional arrays are like the grocery list in the previous example. There is only one way to reference the items: by using a subscript to indicate which element number to access. The number used to reference the specific element of an array is called the component. This concept is represented in Java as

```
char MyArray[] = new char[3];
```

In this example, MyArray is the name of the array. The [3] declares that there are three elements in the array. All elements are of type char. The elements are referenced by MyArray[0], MyArray[1], and MyArray[2]. In Java, the subscripts always start at zero and go to the length of the array minus 1. The new command initializes the array to null characters. Memory space is allocated to the array here so that values can be assigned to the array. Reference to elements in the array is by subscript or component. Therefore, MyArray[0] = 'a' assigns the value of a to the first component in the array.

Something interesting about arrays in Java: because they are objects allocated at runtime, you can use a variable to set their length—something you cannot do in C/C++, for example, where you must lay out the memory for an array at compile time. For example, you can write

```
String[] attendees = new String[numAttendees];
```

Initializing an Array
When it is Allocated

You don't have to use new explicitly to allocate and initialize an array. Instead, you can use curly braces to set its size and default values in one fell swoop. For example, you can create and initialize an array like this:

```
String[] movies = { "The Red Shoes", "Jeremiah Johnson",
"Ninotchka" }
```

The example allocates the movies array to three elements and initializes each element with a new String instance. This works just as well with object references in place of string literals. For example, you can write

```
String s1 = "The Red Shoes";
String s2 =  "Jeremiah Johnson";
String s3 = "Ninotchka";
String[] movies = {s1, s2, s3};
```

This type of array initialization also works for primitive data types. For example, you can write

```
int[] arr = {1, 2, 3};
```

to declare and allocate an array of three integers whose elements are 1, 2, and 3. By the way, the array declaration

```
String movies[];
```

works just like

```
String[] movies;
```

TIP: Although the first version uses the same syntax as C/C++, the second version is preferred, because **String[ ]**, not **String**, is the data type of the variable **movies**.

You can find the length of an array—how many elements it was allocated to—by using the special array variable length, as in

```
int numMovies = movies.length;
```

CAUTION: The curly braces used to initialize an array can only be used when the array is declared. That is, the curly braces can only be used as an initializer.

To illustrate the previous caution, you cannot write something like this:

```
int[] arr = new int[5];
arr = {1, 2, 3, 4, 5}; //will not compile!
```

To correct the problem, you would need to rewrite the code as follows:

```
int[] arr = {1, 2, 3, 4, 5}; //this compiles!
```

Exercise 6.4

Write a program that calculates the first ten squares (1, 4, 9, 16, and so on) and places each entry in an array of integers. Then, create a new array and use curly braces to initialize the new array to the values in the old array. At the end of the program, write out all the entries in the second array to verify that the program worked. Be sure your array has ten elements and that your values range from 1 to 100.

Arrays of Arrays

In theory, all Java arrays are one-dimensional. You create multi-dimensional arrays by defining arrays of arrays.

You can define an array of arrays by using multiple sets of square brackets. For example, a two-dimensional array could be declared like this:

```
int[][] chessBoard = new int[8][8];
```

You can also use curly braces when declaring and initializing an array of arrays, as in

```
double[][] identityMatrix = {
  { 1.0, 0.0, 0.0 },
  { 0.0, 1.0, 0.0 },
  { 0.0, 0.0, 1.0 }
};
```

So that this doesn't trip you up, take note: you can place a comma in the last line of a multi-array initialization, or not. There's no comma in the third line in the previous array initialization. There is a comma in the third line of the initialization in the following snippet:

```
double[][] identityMatrix = {
  { 1.0, 0.0, 0.0 },
  { 0.0, 1.0, 0.0 },
  { 0.0, 0.0, 1.0 },
};
```

Either version will compile successfully.

Just as you might expect, you can find the length of each array within the array. For a two-dimensional array, you might think of the first entry as the row number and the second as a column. To find the number of columns for row 0 in a two-dimensional matrix called catalog, you can write

```
catalog[0].length;
```

You can also allocate the length of each column one at a time. You can start by allocating the number of rows in an array. Let's say our catalog array is an array of string arrays:

```
String[][] catalog = new String[100][];
```

Notice that the number of columns is left undefined at first. This allows us to work with one column at a time, and each column in our array of arrays can be of variable length

```
catalog[0] = new String[5];
catalog[1] = new String[10];
```

and so on. Then, we can refer to each element in the array by specifying its row and column. For example, the first element is

```
catalog[0][0]
```

and we can set this to a String object, as follows:

```
catalog[0][0] = new String("shirt");
```

We can refer to other rows and columns as we'd like to.

Where Arrays Fit into the Class Hierarchy

If arrays are objects, what is their class type? Where do these classes fit into the class hierarchy?

Arrays follow a parallel hierarchy of the class types they hold. For example, if you have a class hierarchy involving Vehicle, Car, and SportsCar that looked like what's in Figure 6-1, then the hierarchy of arrays looks like what's in Figure 6-2.

In other words, Vehicle[] is a sibling of Vehicle, Car[] is a sibling of Car, and Sports-Car[] is a sibling of SportsCar. As the figure shows, Vehicle[] inherits directly from Object[], just as Vehicle inherits from Object. Of course, all arrays are objects, so Object[] in turn inherits from Object.

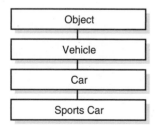

Figure 6-1   A hierarchy involving three classes

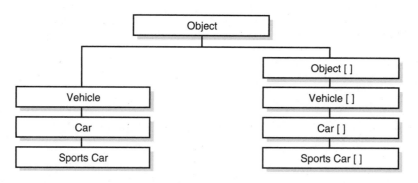

Figure 6-2   The parallel hierarchy of arrays

Answers to the Exercises

Exercise 6.1

A byte holds values up to 127. It could hold the number of letters in the alphabet (26).

An int is not large enough to hold the net worth of Bill Gates (what is it now, around 50 billion dollars?). A long holds values up to 9,223,372,036,854,775,807. (However, if Microsoft stock splits a few more times . . .)

A short can hold values up to 32,767. This is large enough to hold the number of pages in this book. A byte would be too small.

An int can hold up to around 2 billion, which is enough to keep track of the number of people in the United States for some time to come. A short would be too small.

Exercise 6.2

Here is one possible solution to this exercise:

```
class Def {
   byte b;
   short s;
   int i;
   long l;
   public static void main(String[] args) {
      Def d = new Def();
      d.defaults();
   }

   void defaults() {
      System.out.println("default values:");
      System.out.println(b);
```

```
        System.out.println(s);
        System.out.println(i);
        System.out.println(l);
    }
}
```

Exercise 6.3

The method variable named found is not initialized before being used. This results in a compile-time error. You must set this variable to false for this program to compile and work as intended.

```
class Test {
    public static void main(String[] args) {
        int index;
        boolean found = false;
        for (index = 0; index < 10 && !found; index++) {
            if (index > Math.PI) {
                System.out.println(index + " is greater than Pi");
                found = true;
            }
        }
    }
}
```

The variable index is initialized in the for loop before it is referenced.

Exercise 6.4

One possible solution is

```
class Squares {
    public static void main(String[] args) {
        int[] first = new int[10];
        for (int i = 1; i <= 10; i++)
            first[i-1] = i * i;
        int[] second = {first[0], first[1], first[2], first[3],
            first[4], first[5], first[6], first[7], first[8],
            first[9]};
        for (int i = 1; i <= 10; i++)
            System.out.println("entry " + i + " is " + second[i-1]);
    }
}
```

Review Questions

1. The range of values for the integer data types is
   a. $-2\verb|^|15$ to $2\verb|^|15 - 1$
   b. $-2\verb|^|$(number of bits $- 1$) to $2\verb|^|$(number of bits $- 1$)
   c. $-2\verb|^|31$ to $2\verb|^|31 - 1$
   d. $-2\verb|^|$(number of bits) to $2\verb|^|$(number of bits) $- 1$

2. What are two ways to set a char variable named c to a blank space?
   a. c = " " and c = ' '
   b. c = " " and c = '\u0000'
   c. c = ' ' and c = '\u0020'
   d. c = " " and c = '\u0020'

3. What is the result of trying to compile and run this program?

```
class Q3 {
    int instVar1 = 1;
    int instVar2;
    public static void main(String[] args) {
        int localVar = 3;
        Q3 q3 = new Q3();
        System.out.println(q3.instVar1 + q3.instVar2 + localVar);
    }
}
```

   a. 4
   b. 0
   c. The code does not compile because localVar is not initialized correctly.
   d. The code does not compile because instVar2 is not initialized at all.

4. How can you initialize an array of three boolean values to all true?
   a. boolean[] b = new boolean[3];
   b. boolean[] b = {true, true, true};
   c. boolean[3] b = {true, true, true};
   d. boolean[] b = new boolean[3]; b = {true, true, true};

Answers to Review Questions

1. **d.** The range of values for an integer data type depends on the number of bits. For an int, which holds 32 bits, the range goes from -2^{31} to $2^{31} - 1$. The number of bits is 8 for a byte, 16 for a short, 32 for an int, and 64 for a long.

2. **c.** A char value can be set using single quotes or the format '\udddd'. The value '\u0020' is a blank space.

3. **a.** This code compiles and runs successfully. An instance variable, such as inst-Var2, is set to 0 if it is not explicitly initialized.

4. **b.** This example shows how to use curly braces in an initializer to set the values for an array. (Because the default value for a boolean is false, answer A will not work).

Operators

Objectives for This Chapter

- Determine the result of applying any operator, including assignment operators and instanceof, to operands of any type, class, scope, or accessibility, or any combination of these.

- In an expression involving the operators &, |, &&, ||, and variables of known values, state which operands are evaluated and the value of the expression.

- Use the instanceof operator correctly.

- State the difference between the == operator and equals().

- Determine the result of applying the == comparison operator and the equals() method to instances of class String, Boolean, and Object.

- Determine the effect upon objects and primitive values of passing variables into methods and performing assignments or other modifying operations in that method.

Java has lots of operators: most of them are quite simple. There are the standard arithmetic operators +, −, *, /, and %. However, there are also some others that you might feel less familiar with. Guess what? Those are the ones on the test! We'll cover them thoroughly in this chapter.

The test covers the bitwise operators. If you're like most programmers, you probably don't use these operators on a day-to-day basis.

The bitwise operators include

- right shift (>>)
- left shift (<<)
- right shift, don't keep the sign bit (>>>)

There are other bitwise operators we'll cover in this chapter.

The test also makes sure you know how operators used with objects and object references work. These include the +, ==, and instanceof operators. You should know the difference between == and equals(), and which classes respond differently to equals() than the class Object.

Operators and Expressions

The expression a = 4 uses the equals operator (=) to assign the value 4 to variable a. Expressions are Java's way of performing a computation. Operators are used in expressions to do the work of the program and to operate on variables. Expressions in Java are similar to, although a subset of, C and C++.

Variables used in expressions must be declared before they are used. An error will occur if you try to operate on an undeclared variable.

It is necessary to understand what Java expects of its operators and the correct syntax of its expressions to get anything accomplished in this language. Every expression results in a value. The operators tell the Java compiler how to manipulate the variables and other data to give the appropriate result.

Arithmetic Operators

In standard arithmetic expressions, Java supports both unary and binary operators. An operator that manipulates a single value is called a *unary operator. Binary operators* act on two values.

The unary operators are useful to modify variables in place. That is, a variable can be operated on in some instances without an intermediate variable and then reassigned to the original variable. The increment and decrement operators are examples of unary operators. For example, after g++ is executed, the value of the variable g is incremented by one. Likewise, g−− will actually decrement g by one. Using increment and decrement in this manner is the same as writing

```
g = g + 1;
```

or

```
g = g - 1;
```

It is useful to note that unary operators don't always change the original value of a variable. For example, after !g is executed, the value of g will remain unchanged.

Unary negation multiplies the variable by −1, which in effect reverses the sign of an integer from positive to negative or negative to positive. The sign reversal is only in effect during the operation. The variable itself is not affected (unless you reassign the value to the original variable).

The following example demonstrates unary negation:

```
class UnaryNegation {
 public static void main (String args[]) {
    int num, currCount;
    num = -5;
    currCount = -num + 1;            //equals 6
    System.out.println("num equals " + num);
    System.out.println("currCount equals " + currCount);
 }
}
```

The output is

```
num equals -5
currCount equals 6
```

To see how binary operators are used, let's look at the simple expression:

```
c = b + 8;
```

In this example, b + 8 is the binary operation. Only variable c is changed as it is assigned the value of whatever is the result of b plus 8. Variable b is unchanged. Whereas this seems to be common sense, more complex expressions aren't so clear. It is possible to combine unary operations such as increment with binary operations to create a complex expression, changing more than one variable in the expression. Break these out in separate expressions if possible. This will help later in debugging and maintenance.

Complex expressions require the use of separators to avoid unpredictable results. Separators such as parentheses notify the compiler of the order in which operations should be completed. In other words, separators set precedence. For example, the result of 5 * 3 + 4 is 19, but 5 * (3 + 4) is 35. In this situation, the separator overcomes the natural precedence of Java. We'll talk more about precedence later in the chapter.

Table 7-1 summarizes arithmetic operators. Study the examples and be sure you understand how the results are achieved.

NOTE: Note that although the string concatenation operator (+) isn't really an arithmetic operator, it doesn't fit into any of the other tables. Therefore, I've added it here rather than have a separate table with one element.

Table 7-1 Arithmetic Operators

Operator	Operation	Example	Result
+	Positive	+4	4
−	Negation	a=2;−a	−2
+	Addition	2 + 2	4
−	Subtraction	2−1	1
*	Multiplication	2 * 3	6
/	Division	3 / 3	1
%	Modulus	5 % 5	0
++ (Prefix)	Increment	a=2; b=++a;	a=3; b=3;
++ (Postfix)	Increment	a=2; b=a++;	a=3; b=2;
−− (Prefix)	Decrement	a=2; b=−−a;	a=1; b=1;
−− (Postfix)	Decrement	a=2; b=a−−;	a=1; b=2;
+ (String)	Concatenation	"y" + "ou"	"you"

The most difficult arithmetic operator to understand is modulus. Modulus returns the remainder from a division operation. If you divide 5 into 12, the remainder is 2 and thus a modulus operation returns 2. Consider the following example:

```
class ModulusArithmetic {
public static void main (String args[]) {
  int a;
  a = 12 % 5;
  System.out.println(" a is equal to " + a);
 }
}
```

The output is

```
a is equal to 2
```

Prefix and postfix notations are difficult concepts to understand. When using a prefix notation, you

1. Perform the operation on the original value.

2. Assign the result to the original value.

3. Evaluate the expression.

To get a better understanding of prefix notation, consider the following example:

```
a = 3;
b = ++a;
```

Here, the increment occurs before a is assigned to b. This results in both a and b being equal to 4 and is the same as writing:

```
a = 3;
a = a + 1;
b = a;
```

When you use a postfix notation,

1. Evaluate the expression.

2. Increment the original value.

To get a better understanding of postfix notation, consider the following example:

```
a = 3;
b = a++;
```

Here, the increment occurs after a is assigned to b. This results in b being equal to 3 (the original value of a) and a being incremented to 4. Another way to write this expression is

```
a = 3;
b = a;
a = a + 1;
```

CAUTION: Although prefix and postfix notation are useful, be careful when using them within expressions. If improperly used in an expression, these operators can cause bugs that are difficult to track down and correct.

Assignment Operators

An assignment operator stores a specific value in the memory area allocated to a variable. For example, in the expression a += 5; 5 is added to the original value of variable a, and the old value is replaced. Here are more examples:

```
a = 8;     // assigns to a the value 8
a -=5;     // assigns to a the result of a - 5
a *=4;     // assigns to a the result of a * 4
a /=3;     // assigns to a the result of a / 3
```

As with modulus arithmetic, modulus assignment is difficult to understand. With modulus assignment, you divide the variable by the modulus value and then store the remainder in the variable. Consider the following example:

```
class ModulusAssignment {
 public static void main (String args[]) {
   int a;
   a = 12;
   a %=5;
   System.out.println(" a is equal to " + a);
 }
}
```

The output is

```
a is equal to 2
```

which is the same value as when you used

```
a = 12 % 5;
```

Table 7-2 summarizes the assignment operators and their usage. For these examples, the value of a is 4 and the value of b is 2 initially.

Comparison Operators

Comparison operators are used to compare one operand to the other. They determine equality and ordering and always return a boolean value, which is either true or false.

Table 7-3 provides an overview of the comparison operators. We'll discuss the instanceof operator in greater detail later.

Table 7-2 Assignment Operators

Operator	Operation	Example	Result
=	Assign value	a = 4	a=4; b=2
+=	Add to current variable	a += b	a=6; b=2
-=	Subtract from current	a -= b	a=2; b=2
*=	Multiply current	a *= b	a=8; b=2
/=	Divide current	a /+ b	a=2; b=2
%=	Modulus current	a %= b	a=0; b=2

Table 7-3   Comparison Operators

Operator	Operation	Example	Result
==	Equal	3 == 2	false
!=	Not equal	3 != 2	true
<	Less than	3 < 2	false
>	Greater than	3 > 2	true
<=	Less than or equal	3 <= 2	false
>=	Greater than or equal	3 >= 2	true
instanceof	Check for class instance	"hello" instanceof String	true

Comparison operators are typically used in expressions that control the flow, such as if conditional statements as well as for, do, and while loops. You can use the equality operator (==) and the inequality operator (!=) with any Java data type to determine whether elements are equal to or not equal to each other. Only numeric types can be compared with the ordering operators (<, >, <=, >=). This means you can use the ordering operators to determine whether one float is larger than the other.

As you work with the comparison operators, keep in mind that Java doesn't define true and false as numeric values. True and false are nonnumeric values, which do not relate to zero or non-zero. This means, unlike C and C++, you cannot use the following statements:

```
//perform operations that set a flag then check
//the value of the flag to determine what to do next
int flag;
if (flag) x++;
if (!flag) x--;
```

And must explicitly use a comparison operator, such as:

```
if (flag== 0) x++;
if (flag != 0) x--;
```

Logical Operators

Java's logical operators are shown in Table 7-4. Generally, these operations result in true or false. The exception is the conditional operation which returns a value based on whether the first operand evaluates to true or false. If the first operation results in true,

Table 7-4   Logical Operators

Operator	Operation	Example	Result
&	logical AND	true & false	false
|	logical OR	true || false	true
^	logical XOR	true ^ false	true
!	Not	! false	true
&&	short-circuit AND	false && true	false
||	short-circuit OR	false || true	true
?:	conditional (ternary)	false ? 5 : 8	8

the value of the second operand is returned. If the first operation results in false, the value of the third operand is returned.

NOTE: Note that the conditional operator (?:) really isn't a logical operator but it doesn't fit into any of the other tables, so I've added it here so I can discuss it in terms of logical operations.

The easiest way to consider logical AND, OR, and XOR is to use truth tables. Table 7-5 shows the result of logical AND operations given the forms shown.

Table 7-5   Truth Table for Logical AND, OR, and XOR Operations

a	b	a & b	a | b	a ^ b
false	false	false	false	false
false	true	false	true	true
true	false	false	true	true
true	true	true	true	false

Two types of logical operators give programmers the most problems: conditional and short-circuit. Conditional or ternary operators have the basic syntax of

```
operand1 ? operand2 : operand3
```

With ternary operators, operand1 must be a boolean type. When the operation is performed, the value of operand1 is evaluated. If the value is true, the operation returns the value or operand2. Otherwise, the operation returns the value of operand3. Consider the following example:

```
class Ter {
  public static void main(String args[]) {
    for(int i=0;i<10;++i)
      System.out.print((i%2==0)?("" + i) : " ");
  }
}
```

If you run the previous example, you'll get the following result:

```
0  2  4  6  8
```

Short-circuit operators can also give you problems if you aren't paying attention. The && and || operators are called short-circuit operators because they don't always evaluate the second operand before returning a result.

When the first operand is false and you use the && operator, false is returned without checking the second operand. Otherwise, the second operand is evaluated and its result of true or false is returned.

When the first operand is true and you use the || operator, true is returned without checking second operand. Otherwise, the second operand is evaluated and its result of true or false is returned.

Bitwise Operators

Java's bitwise operators are summarized in Table 7-6. These operators are the most challenging operators to understand and key operators are covered in the sections that follow.

Table 7-6 Java Bitwise Operators

Operator	Operation	Binary Example	Binary Result
&	Bitwise AND	10011011 & 11010101	10010001
|	Bitwise OR	00001010 | 00001000	00001010
^	Bitwise XOR	00001010 ^ 00001000	00000010
<<	Left shift	00000010 << 1	00000100
>>	Right shift	10101011 >> 2	11101010
>>>	Zero-fill right shift	10101011 >>> 2	00101010
<<=	Left-shift assignment	00000001 <<= 5	00100000
>>=	Right-shift assignment	10100000 >>= 5	11111101
>>>=	Zero-fill right-shift assignment	10100000 >>>= 5	00000101
		Decimal Example	Decimal Result
~	Bitwise complement	~3	-4

The >> Operator

The >> operator shifts the bits in a number the specified number of places to the right. For example, if you run the following program,

```java
class Bit {
  public static void main(String[] args) {
    int i = 0x00000010;
    int ans;

    System.out.println("before: " + i);
    ans = i >> 1;
    System.out.println("after: " + ans);
  }
}
```

the result will be

before: 16

after: 8

because the hex number 0x00000010 is 16 in base 10. The 32 bits representing this number are

$$0000\ 0000\ 0000\ 0000\ 0000\ 0000\ 0001\ 0000$$

Shifting the bits once to the right yields the bit pattern

0000 0000 0000 0000 0000 0000 0000 1000

which is the hex number 0x00000008, or 8 in base 10.

Another example where the most significant bit is 1 might better illustrate how a right shift is performed. Consider the following example:

```
class Bit2 {
  public static void main(String[] args) {
    int i = 0x10000010;
    int ans;

    System.out.println("before: " + i);
    ans = i >> 1;
    System.out.println("after: " + ans);
  }
}
```

Here, the hex number we're working with 0x10000010. The result is now

before: 268435472

after: 134217736

because the hex number 0x10000010 is 268,435,472 in base 10. The 32 bits representing this number are

1000 0000 0000 0000 0000 0000 0001 0000

Shifting the bits once to the right yields the bit pattern

0100 0000 0000 0000 0000 0000 0000 1000

which is the hex number 0x08000008, or 134,217,736 in base 10.

Negative numbers might yield results you did not expect, because the sign bit is moved to the right even though the number stays negative. Here's the most simple example. Running the program,

```
class Neg {
  public static void main(String[] args) {
    int i = 0x80000000;
    int ans;

    System.out.println("before: " + i);
    ans = i >> 1;
    System.out.println("after: " + ans);
  }
}
```

yields the following result:

before: −2147483648

after: −1073741824

The variable i is assigned the hex value 0x80000000, which, as a bit pattern, is

1000 0000 0000 0000 0000 0000 0000 0000

Now, in Java's 2's complement notation, this is a negative number—the most negative an int can be. Java. You can see this in the result for i in the "before" printout: −2147483648, which matches the value in java.lang.Integer.MIN_VALUE. Then, moving this bit one to the right, but keeping the sign, yields the bit pattern:

1100 0000 0000 0000 0000 0000 0000 0000

which is the same as the base 10 number in the "after" printout.

The >>> Operator

To get around this strange "the sign bit both stays and moves to the right" syndrome, you can use the >>> operator instead. For example,

```
class Neg1 {
  public static void main(String[] args) {
    int i = 0x80000000;
    int ans;

    System.out.println("before: " + i);
    ans = i >>> 1;
    System.out.println("after: " + ans);
  }
}
```

yields the result

before: −2147483648

after: 1073741824

In other words, the bit pattern went from

1000 0000 0000 0000 0000 0000 0000 0000

to

0100 0000 0000 0000 0000 0000 0000 0000

TIP: The $>>>$ and $>>$ operators yield the same results when the number is positive.

The $<<$ Operator

There is one more similar operator, the $<<$ operator, which moves all the bits to the left the indicated number of places. The result of applying this operator is straightforward, but you might wonder what happens when the bit pattern moves from

0100 0000 0000 0000 0000 0000 0000 0000

one step to the left, as in the program

```
class Back {
  public static void main(String[] args) {
    int i = 0x40000000;
    int ans;

    System.out.println("before: " + i);
    ans = i << 1;
    System.out.println("after: " + ans);
  }
}
```

Does the number change sign? Yes, indeed. The printout reads

before: 1073741824

after: −2147483648

What about moving the bit pattern

1000 0000 0000 0000 0000 0000 0000 0001

one to the left using the $<<$ operator? Does the number stay negative or become positive? It becomes positive. The bit that indicates the sign gets shifted out completely. The result is

before: −2147483647

after: 2

The &, |, and ^ Operators

With binary operations, the operators &, | and ^ mean "bitwise and." "bitwise or," and "bitwise xor" respectively. These operators work on integers and yield integer results, not boolean results. The & operator turns bits on if both bits are on, and off if either or both bits are off. The | operator turns bits on if either or both bits are on, and off if both bits are off. The ^ operator turns bits on only when one of the bits is on and off when both bits are on or both bits are off.

It's easier to look at a simple example than it is to comprehend these operators by reading about them. If you perform the operation,

```
3 & 2
```

the result is 2. You can see this clearly if you look at the following bit patterns (we'll only look at the last 4 bits to make this easier to read):

```
0011 &
0010
- - - -
0010
```

If you perform the operation

```
3 | 2
```

the result is 3. Here are the bits:

```
0011 |
0010
- - - -
0011
```

However, if you perform the operation

```
3 ^ 2
```

the result is 1. Here are the bits:

```
0011 ^
0010
- - - -
0001
```

As with logical AND, OR, and XOR, a truth table can help you understand bitwise AND, OR, and XOR. With this in mind, take a moment to study Table 7-7.

Table 7-7   Truth Table for Logical AND, OR, and XOR Operations

a	b	a & b	a | b	a ^ b
0	0	0	0	0
0	I	0	I	I
I	0	0	I	I
I	I	I	I	0

Exercises

Exercise 7.1

Write a class that stores two short integers in a single int variable. Write methods called putVar1(), putVar2(), getVar1(), and getVar2() to save and retrieve this value into the upper or lower half of an int.

You'll probably have to use the >> and << operators to make this work, as well as & and | to mask the bits when you set the int's value.

Testing for an Object's Class Type

For the exam, you'll need to know how to use the instanceof operator correctly. The operator instanceof tests to see whether a particular object is an instance of a class or a subclass of that class. It can also test whether an object's class or subclass implements an interface.

Here are some examples. Let's say you have the following code:

```
class Fruit { }
class Apple extends Fruit {
  public static void main(String[] args) {
    Apple a = new Apple();
    if (a instanceof Apple)
      System.out.println("A is for Apple");
    if (a instanceof Fruit)
      System.out.println("A is a Fruit");
    if (a instanceof Object)
      System.out.println("A is an Object");
  }
}
```

Running this code writes "A is for Apple," "A is a Fruit," and "A is an Object" to the standard output, because the instanceof operator returns true for each test.

Here's another example that deals with interfaces:

```
interface Fruit { }
interface Apple extends Fruit { }
class GrannySmith implements Apple {
  public static void main(String[] args) {
    GrannySmith gs = new GrannySmith();
    if (gs instanceof Apple)
      System.out.println("gs inherits from Apple");
    if (gs instanceof Fruit)
      System.out.println("gs inherits from Fruit");
  }
}
```

The strings "gs inherits from Apple" and "gs inherits from Fruit" appear in the standard output when you run this program.

CAUTION: Some compilers, such as Sun's JDK, will not allow code to compile if they can determine with the available classes that a particular object cannot possibly inherit from a class specified in instanceof.

Exercise 7.2

Use the Apple and Fruit classes shown in the previous section (you can replace main() with your own code). Write a program that shows that an Apple array inherits from a Fruit array, that a Fruit array inherits from an Object array, and that an Object array inherits from Object.

equals( ) and ==

For the exam, you'll need to know the difference between the == operator and equals() and be able to determine the result of applying the == comparison operator and the equals() method to instances of class String, Boolean, and Object.

The equals() method is used to test the value of an object. For example, do two object references refer to objects whose fields contain similar values? The == operator is used to test the object references themselves. For example, are two object references the same?

Identical object references can be in different variables. By default, equals() returns true only if the objects reside in the same memory location—that is, if the object references are equal. So, by default, equals() and == do the same things. This will be the case for all classes that do not override equals().

The classes String, BitSet, Boolean, Date, Calendar, File, and Primitive Wrappers all override equals(). Each class uses the data in its fields to determine whether the object represents the same thing:

- String objects are equal if they represent the same character strings.

- Boolean objects are equal if they have the same value.

- Wrapper objects—including Integer, Long, Float, Double, Character, and Boolean —are equal if they represent the same primitive data type.

- BitSet objects are equal if they represent the same sequence of bits.

- Date and Calendar objects are equal if they represent the same date and time.

- File objects are equal if they represent the same path—not if they refer to the same underlying file. (The danger here is that the path name might be a relative path name. In that case, they might easily represent two different files in the system.)

EXAM TIP: The exam objectives specifically state that you must know how to determine the result of applying the boolean equals() method to objects of any combination of the classes java.lang.String, java.lang.Boolean, and java.lang.Object. You don't have to know about the other classes that override equals(). There are more than listed here. Still, it is helpful to understand how key classes are affected in comparisons.

TIP: You can override equals() for your own classes, just as the classes in the list above do, to perform whatever test for equality you feel is important.

Exercise 7.3

Show that String objects and Date objects return true for equals() if they are created with the same data (the Date class is defined in java.util). What happens if you use the no-args constructor for Date and separate the creation of the Date objects by a few lines of code? Why aren't these Date objects equivalent, even though you supplied the same data—namely, no data at all—to the Date's constructor?

Exercise 7.4

Write your own equals() method for the following two classes.

```
class Employee {
   private String id;
   public Employee (String id) {
     this.id = id;
   }
}

class Movie {
   String name;
   boolean thumbsUp;
   int year;
}
```

Operator Precedence and Evaluation Order

Java evaluates expressions from left to right. When multiple operators are used, the order of evaluation is determined by the precedence order shown in Table 7-8. From the table, you can see that operators that are on the same line are evaluated using the normal left to right order. For example, if both a + and a - operations occur in the same expression, Java will resolve the expression from left to right. However, if * and + are used, the multiplication takes place first because it has a higher precedence.

The separators [] and () change precedence. Everything within these separators will be computed before Java looks outside them. Java will evaluate the expression in separators using its regular rules of precedence, as in the following expression:

```
varA = (2 * 2 + 3) + (6 + 4 / 2);
```

The value of varA is 15. Multiplication is a higher precedence than addition, so 2 * 2 is the first operation, which is then added to 3. In the next set of parentheses, division is a higher precedence than addition, so 4 / 2 is the first operation, the result of which is then added to 6. The values from each set of parentheses, 7 and 8, are then added together and assigned to variable varA.

To get a better understanding of operator precedence, here's another example:

```
class CheckExp {
   public static void main (String args [])
   {
       int IntA, IntB = 2;
       IntA = (IntB+=2) * (IntB+3);
```

Table 7-8   Operator Precedence, from High to Low

[ ] ( )
++ (Postfix) −− (Postfix)
++ (Prefix) −− (Prefix), + (Positive), − (Negative), !, ~
(Type)
* / %
+ (Addition) − (Subtraction)
<< >> >>>
< > <= >= instanceof
== !=
&
^
|
&&
||
?:
= += −= *= /= %= &= ^= |= >>= <<= >>>=

```
        System.out.println("IntB = " + IntB);
        System.out.println("IntA = " + IntA);
    }
}
```

This is the output of the previous code:

```
IntB = 4
IntA = 28
```

In the previous example, variables IntA and IntB are declared to be type int and initialized to 2. Then the value of variable IntB is incremented by 2, resulting in 4. The new value of IntB is increased by 3, resulting in 7. The result of the two values in parentheses, 4 and 7, are now multiplied. This value, 28, is then assigned to IntA.

Using Arrays in Expressions

You can use arrays and elements of arrays in the same way as any other variable. It is not necessary to use any intermediate variable. For example,

```
MyArray[0] = 4;
MyArray[1] = MyArray[0] * 500;
```

assigns the value of the first element in the array multiplied by 500 to the second element in the array. This example increments the value of the third element of MyArray by one:

```
MyArray[2]++;
```

As you can see, arrays act as any other variable in an expression. The array structure is in place to group like items together for easy access.

Using chars in Expressions

Expressions are not just for numeric data types. Character variables are also assigned by means of an expression. The following example gets a character from the keyboard:

```
class GetChar {
    public static void main (String args[])
    throws java.io.IOException
    {
        char KeyboardChar;
        System.out.println("Type a key: ");
        KeyboardChar = (char) System.in.read();
        System.out.println("The key you pressed is " + KeyboardChar);
    }
}
```

Answers to the Exercises

Exercise 7.1

Here is a class called Half that stores two short values in one int variable:

```
class Half {
    int value;

    void putVar1(short s) {
```

```
        value &= 0xFFFF0000;
        value |= s;
    }

    void putVar2(short s) {
        value &= 0x0000FFFF;
        value |= (s << 16);
    }

    short getVar1() {
        return (short)(value);
    }

    short getVar2() {
        return (short)(value >> 16);
    }
}
```

You can run a class such as Tester, listed as follows, to verify this class named Half is doing what it's supposed to:

```
class Tester {
    public static void main(String[] args) {
        Half h = new Half();
        h.putVar1((short) 100);
        h.putVar2((short) -91);

        System.out.println(h.getVar1());
        System.out.println(h.getVar2());
    }
}
```

Exercise 7.2

```
class Fruit { }
class Apple extends Fruit {
    public static void main(String[] args) {
        Apple[] a = new Apple[1];
        Fruit[] f = new Fruit[1];
        Object[] o = new Object[1];
        if (a instanceof Fruit[])
            System.out.println("a inherits from Fruit[]");
        if (f instanceof Object[])
            System.out.println("f inherits from Object[]");
        if (o instanceof Object)
            System.out.println("o inherits from Object");
    }
}
```

Exercise 7.3

```
import java.util.Date;
import java.util.GregorianCalendar;

class Eq {
    public static void main(String[] args) {
        String s1 = new String("a");
        String s2 = new String("a");

        Date d1 = new Date();

        Date d2 = new GregorianCalendar(97, 2, 14).getTime();
        Date d3 = new GregorianCalendar(97, 2, 14).getTime();

        Date d4 = new Date();

        System.out.println(s1.equals(s2));
        System.out.println(d2.equals(d3));
        System.out.println(d1.equals(d4));
    }
}
```

This program displays "true, true, false." The reason the two Date objects d1 and d4 are not equal is because the no-args Date constructor initializes the Date objects to the current date and time to the nearest millisecond. So, their internal data is different.

Exercise 7.4

```
class Employee {
    private String id;
    Employee (String id) {
        this.id = id;
    }
    public boolean equals(Object obj) {
        if (obj instanceof Employee) {
            Employee e = (Employee)obj;
            if (e.id == id)
                return true;
        }
        return false;
    }
}

class Movie {
    String name;
    boolean thumbsUp;
    int year;
    public boolean equals(Object obj) {
        if (obj instanceof Movie) {
            Movie m = (Movie)obj;
```

```
        if (name.equals(m.name) && year == m.year)
            return true;
    }
    return false;
}
}
```

Notice that we cast the object to the type being tested. Also, note the equals() test for Movie: the String object is tested using equals(), and the thumbsUp variable is not considered, since the movies might still be the same even if two different people rated them differently.

Review Questions

1. What is the result of the following expression?

```
5 & 2
```

    a. 0
    b. 2
    c. 5
    d. 7

2. What is the result of the following expression?

```
10 | 2
```

    a. 0
    b. 2
    c. 10
    d. 14

3. What happens when you attempt to compile and run the following code?

```
class Tree { }
class Pine {
    public static void main(String[] args) {
        Pine[] p = new Pine[1];
        if (p instanceof Tree[])
            System.out.println("p inherits from Tree[]");
    }
}
```

```
      }
```

   a. The compiler complains that Tree[ ] cannot inherit from Pine[ ].

   b. The compiler complains that Pine[ ] cannot inherit from Tree[ ].

   c. The program compiles and runs but does not display anything in the standard output.

   d. The program compiles and runs and displays "p inherits from Tree[ ]" in the standard output.

4. What is the result of invoking main() for classes A, B, and C?

```java
class A {
   public static void main(String[] args) {
      Integer myInt = new Integer(5);
      Integer otherInt;
      otherInt = myInt;
      if (otherInt == myInt)
         System.out.println("equal");
      else
         System.out.println("not equal");
   }
}

class B {
   public static void main(String[] args) {
      Integer myInt = new Integer(5);
      Integer anotherInt = new Integer(5);
      if (anotherInt == myInt)
         System.out.println("equal");
      else
         System.out.println("not equal");
   }
}

class C {
   public static void main(String[] args) {
      MyClass mc1 = new MyClass(1);
      if (mc1.operatorEquals(mc1))
         System.out.println("equal");
      else
         System.out.println("not equal");
   }
}

class MyClass extends Object {
   int value;
   MyClass(int value) {
      this.value = value;
   }
```

```
boolean operatorEquals(MyClass test) {
    return (this == test);
}
}
```

  a. A: equal; B: equal: C: equal

  b. A: equal; B: not equal; C: equal

  c. A: not equal; B: not equal; C: equal

  d. A: not equal; B: not equal; C: not equal

5. What is the result of 0x800028FF >> 3?

  a. 0x900005FF

  b. 0x1000051F

  c. 0x1000011F

  d. 0xF000051F

6. What is the result of trying to compile and run the following program?

```
class Phone implements Cloneable {
    public static void main(String[] args) {
        Phone p = new Phone();
        if (p instanceof Object)
            System.out.println("Object");
        if (p instanceof Cloneable)
            System.out.println("Cloneable");
    }
}
```

  a. The program does not compile.

  b. The program compiles and runs and writes "Object" to the standard output.

  c. program compiles and runs and writes "Cloneable" to the standard output.

  d. The program compiles and runs and writes both "Object" and "Cloneable" to the standard output.

Answers to Review Questions

1. a. It's clear if you look at the bits:

```
101 fi
&
010
- - -
000
```

2. c. The bits are:

```
1010
0010
- - - -
1010
```

3. b. When the compiler can figure out that an object cannot inherit from another object, it will not even compile the program. That's what Sun's JDK does in this case.

4. b. The only one that is not equal is class B, which checks for equivalence of object references. Since this check uses two different objects, the object references are different.

5. d. Translate the hexadecimal into a bit pattern to see this. 0x800028FF is:

```
1000 0000 0000 0000 0010 1000 1111 1111
```

Shifting each bit 3 positions to the right, and using sign extension, yields:

```
1111 0000 0000 0000 0000 0101 0001 1111
```

or

```
0xF000051F
```

6. d. The object referenced by p will return true to the instanceof test with Object and Cloneable.

Control Flow

Objectives for This Chapter

- Write if and if ... else statements.
- Write while and do-while loops.
- Write for statements and nested loops using a loop counter.
- Use the break and continue keywords with and without labels.
- Use switch constructs and understand default value usage.
- Write nested if-else and switch constructs.
- Identify the legal argument expression type for if and switch.
- Use the operators && and || and determine their effects on control flow statements.

Control flow instructs the program how to make a decision and how further processing should proceed on the basis of that decision. The building blocks of control flow are the { and } block delimiter characters and the if, while, do, for, and switch keywords. Each of these can be used to control how your program executes by determining if a condition exists and then executing various sections of code based on the result.

The basic control flow elements of looping and branching are similar to those in other programming languages. In fact, Java uses all of the same keywords as C/C++, with some minor modifications.

Most of this chapter examines the basics of Java's control flow keywords. This chapter also covers the details (the differences between Java and C/C++) that might confuse you on the test. The test covers if and switch statements as well as all forms of loops. You'll need to know how to use labels to break out of nested loops, break statements, and continue statements as well.

Using if and if . . . else Statements

Conditional expressions generally execute one of several sections of code on the basis of a conditional test. This code can be as simple as a single statement, but more complex sections of code can be made up of many statements. The simplest conditional expression is the if statement.

if Statements

An if statement makes up a conditional expression of the form

```
if (expression) statement;
```

or

```
if (expression)
{
   statement(s);
}
```

When the expression in the parentheses evaluates to true, the statement is executed. When the expression evaluates to false, the statement is skipped and execution continues at the statement following the if statement. The following example shows how this works:

```
int MyNumber;
MyNumber = System.in.read();
if ( (MyNumber % 2) == 0 ) System.out.println("Even");
```

Here a key is read from the keyboard and then tested to determine if its numeric value can be divided evenly by 2. If the value can be evenly divided, the System.out.println statement is executed and Even is displayed. You could also use a block style to define the if statement, such as

```
int MyNumber;
MyNumber = System.in.read();
if ( (MyNumber % 2) == 0 ) {
   System.out.println("Even");
}
```

if . . . else Statements

Another way to enhance if statements is with if . . . else constructs. Here, the statement following the if expression is executed only when true and the statement following the else expression is executed only when the if expression evaluates to false. You can use if . . . else as shown in the following example:

```
int MyNumber;
MyNumber = System.in.read();
if ( (MyNumber % 2) == 0 ) {
   System.out.println("Even");
} else {
   System.out.println("Odd");
}
```

Nested if Statements

if statements can be nested inside other if statements. For example, you can write

```
if (expression)
   statement
else if (expression)
   statement
else if . . .
```

CAUTION: There's a gotcha as far as nested if statements are concerned that can undermine the best laid plans: be sure that indentations of nested if-else statements don't cause you to mistake which else goes with which if.

As an example of this warning, check out the following snippet:

```
if (result >= 0) if (result > 0) System.out.println("positive");
else System.out.println("negative"); //wait a minute . . .
```

Here's the same code written with different indentation so you can see what's really going on:

```
if (result >= 0)
  if (result > 0)
    System.out.println("positive");
  else
    System.out.println("negative"); //wait a minute . . .
```

So, we'll get the message "negative" even if result is equal to 0. This is anything but good.

To help avoid these situations, you can use curly braces to delimit your blocks of code. Using curly braces with conditionals is a good coding style to adopt. So, you can write

```
if (result >= 0) {
  if (result > 0) {
    System.out.println("positive");
  }
} else {
  System.out.println("negative");
}
```

Legal Values for if Statements

The expression for an if statement must evaluate to a Boolean. This is simple enough to remember, unless you're coming from an entrenched background in C. Then, you've got to write 10 times, so that you don't forget, "I will only use a Boolean in my if tests."

C programmers are familiar with using 0 and null to mean false. But in Java, you cannot coerce one to the other. Keep this in mind for the || and && operators, as well. These operators combine Boolean arguments to achieve another Boolean.

NOTE: These same rules apply to while statements.

Exercise 8.1

```
class Exp {
    public static void main(String[] args) {

        int i = 10;

        int j = 12;

        if ((i < j) || (i = 3)) {
            System.out.println("hello");
        }
        System.out.println(i);
    }
}
```

Fix this code so that it works as intended.

Looping Expressions

Looping Expressions are used to repeatedly execute a section of code until a certain condition is met. Some looping expressions check the condition before executing the code. Other looping expressions check the condition after executing the code.

while Statements

while loops are used to repeatedly execute blocks of code as long as a Boolean condition remains true. while loops use the form

```
while ( expression ) statement;
```

or

```
while ( expression )
{
    statement(s);
}
```

When a while loop is encountered, the expression is evaluated first. If it evaluates to true, the statement or block following the while statement, known as the body of the while loop, is executed. When the end of the body is reached, the expression is evaluated again. If the expression is false, execution will continue with the next statement following the while loop. If the expression is still true, the body of the while loop will be executed again. The body will continue to be executed until the expression evaluates to false.

Here is an example:

```
while (theChar != 'x')
{
    theChar = (char)System.in.read();
    StoreChar(theChar);
}
```

This expression tests whether theChar is equal to the character x. If it is not, the body of the while loop is executed, causing a character to be read from the keyboard and then stored. This will continue until the character x is read in.

The expression used with a while loop must evaluate to a Boolean value. Because the initial while expression is evaluated first, it is possible for the statements making up a while loop not to execute if the initial expression evaluates to false. It is also possible for a while loop to execute forever if the expression never evaluates to false. This is known as an infinite loop.

A common cause of an infinite loop is that the programmer forgot to put a statement that changes part of the expression in the body of the loop. If the expression never changes, it will always evaluate the same and an infinite loop occurs.

do-while Statements

The do-while loop enables your code to repeatedly execute a block of code until a Boolean expression evaluates to false. It is almost identical to the while loop, except the expression is evaluated at the bottom of the loop rather than the top. This means that the contents of the loop will always be executed at least once. do-while loops have the form

```
do statement; while ( expression );
```

```
or
do
{
   statement(s);
} while ( expression );
```

The keyword do begins the do-while construct. A statement or a block follows this. Next is keyword while, followed by the parentheses containing an expression that must evaluate to a Boolean.

When a do-while loop is encountered, the statement or block following the do keyword is executed. When the do-while loop body completes, the expression is evaluated. If it is false, execution will continue with the next statement following the do-while loop. If it is true, the body of the do-while loop will be executed again. The body will continue to be executed until the expression evaluates to false.

Here is an example:

```
do
{
   theChar = (char)System.in.read();
   StoreChar(theChar);
} while (theChar != 'x')
```

In this example, the body of the do-while loop is executed, which reads in a character and then stores it. The expression is then evaluated to determine if theChar is equal to the character x. If it is, execution will continue with the first statement after the do-while loop. If it is not, the do-while loop body will be executed again. This continues until the character x is read in.

Compare this looping expression with the while loop shown previously. It does not need to initialize theChar because the variable will be read in at the beginning of the loop. This is the most common reason for choosing a do-while loop instead of a while loop.

Like the while loop, it is possible to create an infinite loop by forgetting to add a statement that changes part of the expression in the body of the loop.

Legal Values for while and do-while Statements

The expression for while and do-while statements must evaluate to a Boolean. As with if statements, this is simple enough to remember, unless you have a background in C programming. C programmers are familiar with using 0 and null to mean false. But in Java, you cannot coerce one to the other. Keep this in mind for the || and && operators, as well. These operators combine Boolean arguments to achieve another Boolean.

Iteration with for loops

for loops enable code to execute repeatedly until a Boolean expression evaluates to false. for loops are similar to a while loop but is more specialized. As in a while loop, an expression is evaluated at the top of the loop. However, it provides a more explicit means for initializing the loop variable and modifying it at the end of the loop.

for Statements

for loops use the form

```
for (initialization; expression; modification) statement;
```

or

```
for (initialization; expression; modification)
{
    statement(s);
}
```

The construct begins with the for keyword. The parentheses contain three elements: an initialization, an expression, and a modification. The initialization can be a statement of any kind but typically its purpose is to initialize part of the expression. Initialization is followed by a semicolon (;), then by the expression. Like while and do-while loops, the expression must evaluate to a Boolean. This is followed by another semicolon and then modification. Modification can be any statement, but again is typically used to modify a control variable used as part of the expression. The construct is completed with a statement or a block of code.

When a for loop is encountered, initialization occurs first, then the expression. If the expression evaluates to true, the body of the for statement is executed. When the end of the body is reached, modification occurs. The expression is then evaluated again. If it is false, execution continues with the next statement following the for loop. If it is true, the body of the for loop is executed again. The body continues to be executed until the expression evaluates to false.

Here is an example:

```
for (index = 0; index < limit; index++) {. . .}
```

TIP: In this case, index is assumed to be an integer. However, it could also be a floating-point number, in which case the ++ operator would increment by 1.0, as you would expect.

Each of the three parts of the for loop—initialization, termination, and modification —can be made of multiple expressions, separated by commas. For example, you can write

```
for (row = 0, col = 0; row < numRows; row++, col++) {. . .}
```

This loop could be used to look at the main diagonal in a square matrix, for example.

Controlling for Loops with Expressions

A for loop without any expressions loops forever. The loop

```
for ( ; ; ) {. . .}
```

is an infinite loop. As with while and do-while loops, it is possible to create an infinite loop by forgetting to put a statement that changes part of the expression in the body of the loop.

You can also define a loop variable within the initialization expression of a for loop. Java programmers do this all the time, because it is so convenient.

Here's an example:

```
for (int index = 0; index < limit; index++) {. . .}
```

 CAUTION: A loop index created on-the-fly, as in the previous code snippet, goes out of scope at the end of the loop.

An example of the previous warning is the following, which is not legal:

```
for (int index = 0; index < limit; index++) {
   // do stuff here.
}
System.out.println("The final value for index is " + index);
//the code won't compile!
```

Nested for Loops

for loops can be nested. To loop through an array of arrays, you could write

```
for (int row = 0; row < numRows; row++)
   for (int col = 0; col < numCols; col++)
      System.out.println(arr[row][col]);
```

Switch and Case Statements

A switch statement can be used to test a variable or expression and jump to a corresponding case statement containing a constant equal to that expression.

switch case

A switch case construct takes the following form:

```
switch (expression)
{
   case value:
       statement(s);
       break;
   case value:
       statement(s);
       break;
             .
             .
             .
   default:
       statement(s);
       break;
}
```

The case statement works by evaluating the expression and then scanning down the case statements until an exact match is found. At this point the corresponding group of statements between the case and break will be executed. When the break is encountered, execution will resume at the first statement following the switch construct.

A default statement is optional. If none of the constants in the case statements match the value of the variable in the switch statement, execution jumps to the default statement. If there is no default statement and none of the case statements match the switch expression, the switch block is, in effect, skipped altogether.

EXAM TIP: The expression in a switch statement must be of type int or char. The values in each case statement must be constants.

A case block will fall through to the case block that follows it, unless the last statement in a case block is a throw, return, or break. Often, you will write code that follows the same approach as the following snippet:

```
switch (season) {
  case 0:
    System.out.println("Spring");
```

```
      break;
  case 1:
    System.out.println("Summer");
    break;
  case 2:
    System.out.println("Fall");
    break;
  case 3:
    System.out.println("Winter");
    break;
  default:
    throw new IllegalSeasonException();
}
```

The break statements at the end of each case jumps control out of the switch to keep execution from flowing to the next, unrelated case statement. A case statement does not have to have a break associated with it. If break is not present, program execution falls through to the next case statement. It keeps executing that group of statements until a break is encountered, so be sure to place appropriate breaks if this is not the intended action.

TIP: If you want execution to flow from one case statement to the next, it is often a good idea to place a comment at the end of the case statement. That way it is clear to others looking at the code that the lack of a break statement is intentional.

Nested switch case

As with for loops and if statements, you can also nest switch statements inside each other by placing a second switch statement within one of the case statements.

For example, you can follow this pattern:

```
switch (season) {
  case 0:
    System.out.println("Spring");
    switch month {
      case 3:
        System.out.println("March");
        break;
      case 4:
        System.out.println("April");
        break;
      case 5:
        System.out.println("May");
        break;
    }
```

```
      break;
   case 1:
      System.out.println("Summer");
                 .
                 .
                 .
   }
```

Using Jump Statements

Java supports several jump statements, including break, continue and return. These statements transfer control to another part of a program. The statements discussed in this section are break and continue. For a discussion of return and return types, see Chapter 9.

break

The break statement can be used to break out of the middle of loops and other control constructs. When a break statement is encountered, execution of the inner loop immediately stops and resumes at the first statement following the current loop.

You could use break with a for loop as follows:

```
int i;
for (i=0; i < ArraySize; i++) {
   if (Array[i] < 0) {
      System.out.println("Value improperly initialized,
breaking.");
      System.out.println("index = " + i);
      break;
   }
   ProcessArray(Array[i]);
}
```

This code uses the for loop to check each array value looking for improper entries. By including the break statement, execution of the loop stops at the first negative entry. In this example, a negative entry might be considered so severe that no other processing should be done. Also notice that no else statement is needed because if an error occurs, execution will jump to the end of the loop, skipping the entry processing code.

continue

The continue statement can be used to short-circuit part of a loop. When a continue statement is encountered, execution of the current loop immediately resumes at the top of the loop, skipping all other code between it and the end of the loop.

Here is an example using the continue statement:

```
int i;
for (i=0; i < ArraySize; i++)
{
  if (Array[i] < 0)
    {
      System.out.println("Value improperly initialized,
continuing.");
        System.out.println("index = " + i);
        continue;
    }
    ProcessArray(Array[i]);
}
```

This code uses the for loop to check each array value looking for improper entries. By including the continue statement, execution of the loop stops and then continues at the top of the loop with the next value in the array. In this example, a negative entry might be considered illegal and should not be processed. However, it is not so severe that it stops processing other entries. Again notice that an else statement is not needed. Here, if an error occurs, execution will continue at the top of the loop, skipping the entry processing code.

Labeled Loops

If break and continue only take you to the end or beginning of the current loop, what do you do if you have nested loops and need to get out of more than just the current loop? Don't worry, Java provides an extended version of break and continue for this purpose. By adding a label to a loop and referencing it in a break statement, you can make execution resume at the end of a labeled block.

Here's an example using labeled loops with break:

```
outer:
for (i=0; i < ArraySize; i++)
{
  inner:
    for (j=0; j < ArraySize; j++)
    {
        if (Array[i][j] < 0)
        {
        System.out.println("Value improperly initialized,
breaking.");
        System.out.println("index = " + i + "," + j);
        break outer;
        }
        ProcessArray(Array[i][j]);
    }
}
```

In this example, the array is extended to two dimensions; two for loops are used to step through all elements of the array. If an improperly initialized entry is encountered, execution will break out of the inner loop and resume at the end of the outer loop. This means when the inner loop breaks to the outer loop, both loops are terminated.

> **NOTE: The ability to jump out of the middle of a loop is handled in C++ and some C implementations with a goto statement. Because goto statements can be used to branch anywhere in the code, you can often get undesirable results. The labeled loop concept in Java allows you to break out of code blocks while limiting the scope and is a good compromise.**

To learn more about breaking to labels, consider the following example: We want to look over all the positions in a game board. If we see a mole, we want to bang it. After a swing of our mole bat, it's the next player's turn—we don't want to allow the user more than one swing of the mole bat per turn.

In the example below, the break statement doesn't quite do what we want:

```
for (int row = 0; row < 8; row++) {

    for (int col = 0; col < 8; col++) {

        if (moleAt(row, col)) {
            bangIt(row,col);
            break;
        }

    }

}
```

Unfortunately, the break statement only breaks out of the inner loop. The outer loop —the one going through the rows—keeps going, allowing the user to bang at more moles.

One way out of this predicament is to supply a label for the outer loop. We can then tie the break statement to the outer loop by using this label. Here's how we could update the code:

```
outer: for (int row = 0; row < 8; row++) {

    for (int col = 0; col < 8; col++) {
        if (moleAt(row, col)) {
            bangIt(row,col);
```

```
        break outer;
    }

  }

}
```

Here, execution breaks out of the inner loop and resumes at the end of the outer loop. This causes both loops to be terminated.

Any line of code can be labeled. However, when you set a label, you should define the label for an enclosing block of code. The following is an example of poor label placement:

```
//Poor label placement causes problems
class BadBreakLabelPlacement {
    public static void main(String args[]) {
    firstArray:
    for (i=0; i < ArraySize; i++) {
       if (firstArray[i] < 0)
       {
       System.out.println("Value improperly initialized,
breaking.");
       System.out.println("index = " + i);
       break secondArray;
       }
       ProcessArray(firstArray[i]);
    }
    secondArray:
    for (j=0; j < ArraySize; j++) {
       if (secondArray[j] < 0)
       {
       System.out.println("Value improperly initialized,
breaking.");
       System.out.println("index = " + j);
       break firstArray;
       }
       ProcessArray(secondArray[j]);
    }
  }
}
```

Labels can also be used with continue statements. Here, the label describes which enclosing loop to continue. With an inner and outer loop, the continue label could be used to terminate the inner loop and continue with the next iteration of the outer loop. For example,

```
outer: for (int row = 0; row < 8; row++) {

    for (int col = 0; col < 8; col++) {
       if (moleAt(row, col)) {
          bangIt(row,col);
```

```
        continue outer;
    }

  }

}
```

This program changes the behavior of the mole program, possibly allowing for multiple players to bang moles at the same time.

Exercise 8.2

Rewrite the following code snippet so that it uses both a label and a continue statement to jump out of the inner loop instead of the inCheck array element:

```
boolean[] inCheck = new boolean[8];


for (int row = 0; row < 8; row++) {
    for (int col = 0; col < 8 && inCheck[row] == false; col++) {
        if (isKingInCheck(row, col))
            inCheck[row] = true;
    }
}
```

Using && and ||

The operators && and || enable you to combine Boolean values for if and while conditions. The && operator means "logical-AND," and the || operator means "logical-OR."

The expressions are evaluated in order from left to right. As soon as the condition of the if or while clause is resolved, no more expressions for that condition are evaluated.

For example, in the if test

```
if (5 > 3 || 2 < 1). . .
```

The second expression, 2 < 1, is never evaluated. Since 5 > 3 is known to be true before 2 < 1 is evaluated, the JVM already knows the entire if condition is true.

If, however, the test was

```
if (5 > 3 && 2 < 1) . . .
```

then if the first expression was true (which it is in this example), the second expression would be evaluated as well, because the entire if clause would only be true if both expressions were true. However, if the first expression was false, then the entire condition would be false; in that case, the second expression would not have to be evaluated.

Exercise 8.3

What is the result of this program?

```
class Exp {
  public static void main(String[] args) {

      int i = 10;
      int j = 12;

      if ((i < j) || (i == 3)) {
         System.out.println("hello");
      }

      System.out.println(i);

   }
}
```

Run this code if it helps to see what's going on.

Answers to the Exercises

Exercise 8.1

The expression

```
i = 3
```

in the if test is the problem. Even though this expression will never be evaluated (since i is less than j), i = 3 does not yield a Boolean. In fact, its result is an integer—the value of i—which is set to 3. Since an integer is not a legal argument for the || operator, this code will not compile.

Exercise 8.2

```
boolean[] inCheck = new boolean[8];
   rows: for (int row = 0; row < 8; row++) {
           for (int col = 0; col < 8; col++) {
              if (isKingInCheck(row, col)) {
                inCheck[row] = true;
                continue rows;
              }
           }
        }
```

Exercise 8.3

This program writes "hello" and "10." Since the first expression in the if test,

```
(i < j)
```

is true, the second part of this test,

```
(i == 3)
```

is not evaluated.

Review Questions

1. The legal expression for an if statement is:
   a. an integer
   b. a boolean
   c. a or b
   d. neither

2. Given the following code snippet:

```
char c = 'a';
switch ( c ) {
   case 'a' :
      System.out.println("a");
      break;
    default:
      System.out.println("default");
}
```

What will happen if you attempt to compile and run the code that includes this snippet?
   a. The code will not compile because the switch statement does not have a legal expression.
   b. The code will compile and run but nothing will be written to the standard output.
   c. The code will compile and run and the letter "a" will be written to the standard output.
   d. The code will compile and run and the word "default" will be written to the standard output.

3. Given the following code snippet:

```
int myInt = 3;
if (myInt < 5)
  if (myInt < 3)
    System.out.println("< 3");
else
  if (myInt > 2)
    System.out.println("> 2");
else
  System.out.println("Other");
```

What will appear in the standard output?

  a. "< 3"

  b. "> 2"

  c. "Other"

  d. nothing

4. What type of code line can have a label?

  a. Any line of code

  b. Only lines of code associated with a loop (just before, at the loop, or just after)

  c. Only the line of code at the start of a loop

  d. Only the line of code defining the most outer loop

Answers to Review Questions

1. b. An if statement only works with a boolean.

2. c. This is perfectly valid code and the letter "a" appears in the standard output.

3. b. To see this, a better way to indent this code is

```
int myInt = 3;
if ( myInt < 5 ) {
   if (myInt < 3) {
      System.out.println("< 4");
   }
   else {
      if (myInt > 2) {
         System.out.println("> 2");
      }
```

```
        else {
            System.out.println("other");
        }
    }
}
```

4. **a.** Any line of code can be labeled.

Methods

Objectives for This Chapter

- Define methods and their valid returned types.
- Distinguish between overloaded and overridden methods.
- Identify legal return types for overloaded and overridden methods.
- Write code for an overridden method that uses the special reference super.
- State what occurs when you invoke an overridden method in a base class and a derived class.

Methods encode behavior. You can define static methods, which belong to the class, and instance methods, which belong to objects created from the class. Generally, static methods access static data; instance methods access instance data.

Methods must be uniquely identified by name and signature—if there is more than one method with the same name, that method is said to be overloaded. Subclasses can override methods by defining their own method with the same name and signature as a method in any of its ancestors.

The Programmer exam is big on overloading and overriding methods. Although the concept is fairly straightforward if you're familiar with object-oriented concepts, the details can be tricky. There are rules you should know about when overloading and overriding methods you inherit. These rules will help you move quickly through questions on the test, and we'll cover them in this chapter.

Defining Methods

We have been using methods throughout this book, but now a better definition of methods is in order. As you've seen, methods are similar to functions in C and C++. They provide a way to group a block of code together and then refer to it by name.

Methods make use of arguments and return types. Arguments are parameters that are passed to a method when it is called so that the method can be made to do different tasks. The return type is a value that can be returned to the code that called the method. The return type can be any valid Java type or void. If the method throws any checked exceptions, these exception types must be listed in a throws clause after the method's signature. (You can also list any unchecked exceptions in the throws clause, if you wish.)

Method Definitions

To define a method, simply declare the method within the class it belongs to, stating the method's keywords, return type, name, parameters, and any exceptions it might throw. Access control keywords include public, protected, and private. Other keywords (mostly relating to a method's place in the class hierarchy) include abstract, final, static, strictfp, native, and synchronized.

Following is a simple method definition:

```
void test() { }
```

This method does not use any keywords, does not return a value, does not take any parameters, and does not throw any checked exceptions.

Following is an example of defining a method for a class called Movie:

```
class Movie {
  static int id;
  String name;
  int runningTime;
  boolean thumbsUp;
  boolean letsSeeIt() {
    return thumbsUp && (runningTime < 130);
  }
}
```

The letsSeeIt() method says that we'll see movies that have been given a thumbs-up by the reviewer and that have a running time of less than two hours and ten minutes.

More complicated method definitions can include keywords and access controls, such as

```
public abstract Object test(String[] args, boolean b)
  throws IOException, MyOwnException;
```

This method is public, meaning it can be accessed by any other method that can access the class defining it. The method is also abstract (and so does not provide a method body). The method returns an instance of class Object, takes two parameters, and throws two exceptions: IOException and MyOwnException. (This definition packs quite a wallop.)

Return Types

Methods can return any valid Java type or void. This could be a char, a boolean, an array, an object, and so on. The return type immediately precedes the method name, such as

```
boolean isRed (Color color) {
   if (color == red)
      return (true);
   else
      return (false);
}
```

The method body tests whether the color passed is red. If it is, the method uses the return keyword to return true to the calling method. Otherwise, it will use return to return false to the calling method.

Void is a special return type in Java that indicates that there is no return type of any kind. This is used for methods that have no need to return anything to the calling program, or that modify only method arguments and global variables.

An example of a method that does not need to return anything is one that only prints output to the screen. Because there is no further processing to be done, there is no need to return anything and no need to use keyword return anywhere in the method.

Method Modifiers

Method modifiers control the way a method is accessed and declare its type. The four levels of access are defined:

Level	Access Allowed
Public	All other classes
Private	No other classes
Protected	Subclasses or same package
<Default>	Same package only

Several method types are defined, including static, abstract, final, strictfp, synchronized, and native. The strictfp keyword is discussed in Chapter 6 under "Floating-point Arithmetic."

Public

Public methods are very open for access. Any class that can access the method's class can access a public method. If a class in package 1 wants to access the method of a class defined in package 2, the class in package 2 must be declared public so that the first class can get to it. Then, the first class can access any methods that are declared as public. Following is an example declaring a public method:

```
public void DisplayResults (String str) {
   ....
}
```

Private

You can restrict all access to a particular method from all classes except the class in which it is defined by using the keyword private on the method. This can be used to completely hide a method from all other classes. If no other classes can access the method, it can be changed as needed without causing problems. Following is an example declaring a private method:

```
private boolean CheckResults (String str) {
   ....
}
```

Protected

A protected method can only be accessed by classes within the same package, or by subclasses in the same or different packages from the method's class. This allows access for objects that are part of the same application, but not other applications. Following is an example:

```
protected boolean CheckResults (String str) {
   ....
}
```

Default

If no modifier is used, the default access controls are used. This means a class or interface in the same package can access the method. Following is an example:

```
void DisplayResults (String str) {
   ....
}
```

Static

A static method belongs with the class and does not operate on any instance of a class. Static methods can only access static fields. Further, because a static method is not associated with a particular object, you cannot use this or refer to an instance member by name as you would from a nonstatic method. If a method needs to access a nonstatic instance field of an object, it cannot be a static method (or the method must first obtain an instance variable).

The main method of a Java program is declared as static, as in

```
public static void main(String[] args) {
    ...
}
```

Because main is static, you don't need to create an instance of the class in order to call it. When you call the Java interpreter with the name of the class in which the main method is defined, the interpreter starts the main method without creating an instance of the class. Because of this, access to elements both within and outside the class are restricted and the main method can only access static instance fields in the class in which it is defined. To get around this limitation, most Java programs use the method to create an object of its own class, such as

```
public class MyApp {
    public static void main(String[] args) {
        MyApp app = new MyApp();
            //Now you can work with methods
    }
}
```

Now when you type **java MyApp** at the command line, the program starts and the main method executes. Main then creates an object of type MyApp and can then invoke instance methods of that object.

Abstract

An abstract method defines the method's signature, return value, and the exceptions it might throw, but it does not define the code that implements the method. In this way, abstract methods are used to create template methods, which are very similar to function prototypes in C and C++.

```
abstract void CheckValid (Object obj) {
}
```

If you define a method as abstract, you must also define the class as abstract. Subclasses are then required to implement the abstract method and supply a body.

Final

A final member cannot be changed after it is defined. That means that a final method cannot be overridden by subclasses. The two benefits of a final method are with security (enforcement of the API) and optimization (placing code inline). A final member provides these benefits on a member-by-member basis, rather than for an entire class as a whole.

Synchronized

A synchronized method can only be invoked by one thread at a time. A synchronized method can belong to an object or a class. If a thread enters a synchronized instance method, no other thread can invoke any other synchronized instance method for that object. If a thread enters a synchronized static method, no other thread can invoke any other synchronized static method for that class.

There's much more information on synchronized methods in Chapter 15.

Native

Declaring a method to be native means that it is implemented in a language "native" to the platform you're running on. In other words, it is written in a language, such as C, and compiled for a particular platform.

Following is an example:

```
public native void method();
```

A native method does not have a body, not even an empty set of braces. Although a native method *can* throw exceptions; it *cannot* be abstract.

Exercise 9.1

What is wrong with this class definition? Fix it so it works when you invoke main():

```
class Avg {
  public static void main(String[] args) {
    double a = 5.1;
    double b = 20.32;
    double c = 32.921;
    System.out.println(findAvg(a, b, c));
  }

  double findAvg(double a, double b, double c) {
    return (a + b + c) / 3.0;
  }
}
```

Overloading a Method

You can overload a method by defining more than one method with the same name in the same class. If you defined more than one method with the same name in the same class, Java must be able to determine which method to invoke based on the number and types of parameters defined for that method.

The return value does not contribute towards distinguishing one method from another; it does not affect which method Java invokes. The exceptions a method might throw also do not matter. All that matters is that the method is sufficiently different in its parameters that the JVM can determine which method to invoke.

Following is a simple example of overloading a method named test():

```
class Ex1 {
  public static void main(String[] args) {
      Ex1 e = new Ex1();
      e.test();
      e.test(1.0, 1);
  }
  void test() {
  }
  void test(double i, int j) {
  }
}
```

The JVM can easily determine which version of test() to invoke from main(). One version takes no parameters. The other takes a double and an int.

What if, instead of invoking the second version by writing

```
e.test(1.0, 1);
```

we wrote

```
e.test(1, 1);
```

In other words, we have two int values. In this case, there's still no confusion. The JVM can also determine which version to invoke. It's a simple matter to coerce an int to a double. This code will compile and run successfully.

Following is an example that doesn't work. In this case, the methods are not different enough for the JVM to determine which one to invoke:

```
//THIS WILL NOT COMPILE!
class Ex2 {
   public static void main(String[] args) {
      Ex2 e = new Ex2();
      e.test(1, 1); //CONFUSION!
```

```
    }
    void test(int i, long j) {
    }
    void test(long i, int j) {
    }
}
```

This code won't even compile. The compiler will complain that the overloaded test() methods are too similar to each other to invoke using

```
e.test(1, 1);
```

However, there is nothing inherently wrong with the two test() methods. They are, in fact, different. If we changed the line where we invoke test() to clear up which one to call, then this code compiles and runs fine. We can do that, for example, by writing

```
e.test(1L, 1);
```

Exercise 9.2

Write a class that defines two static methods. One should find the average for an int array, the other should find the average for a double array.

Overriding a Method

Subclasses can override methods defined in their superclasses. To pass the method invocation up the class hierarchy (that is, to pass the method call to your superclass so that its version of the method is also invoked), you can use the special object reference super.

This special object reference is an object whose type matches the superclass. Using super, an object can access the variables and methods defined by the superclass.

Following is a simple example of using super:

```
class Super {
    public static void main(String[] args) {
        Sub s = new Sub();
        s.test();
    }
    void test() {
        System.out.println("Superclass");
    }
}
class Sub extends Super {
    void test() {
        super.test();
        System.out.println("Subclass");
```

```
    }
}
```

This program writes "Superclass" followed by "Subclass" to the standard output. Following are some rules involving overriding methods.

Access Control to Subclasses

You cannot make a method in a subclass more private than it is defined in the super-class, though you can make it more public. For example, given the following method

```
class Super {
  protected void test() {
  }
}
```

you cannot make the subclass look like this:

```
class Sub extends Super {
  private void test() {
    super.test();
  }
}
```

Inheriting Synchronized and Abstract

A subclass may make an inherited method synchronized, or it may leave off the synchronized keyword so that its version is not synchronized. If a method in a subclass is not synchronized but the method in the superclass is, the thread obtains the monitor for the object when it enters the superclass's method. (There's more about threads in Chapter 12.)

You could also declare an inherited method to be abstract, but then there would be no way to get to the behavior in the hierarchy above the abstract declaration. It is important to note that an abstract method cannot be declared synchronized.

NOTE: Why does an abstract method stop inheritance? Because you cannot invoke your superclass's behavior if your superclass defines the method to be abstract, because an abstract method does not define any behavior for the method. Hence, you cannot pass a method call up the class hierarchy beyond the abstract method declaration.

Also, as covered in previously in the chapter, you cannot override a final method.

Return Types

Return types must match the overridden method in the superclass exactly.

Parameter Types

The parameters of the overridden method must match those in the superclass exactly. Java does not coerce parameters, as it can do with overloaded methods.

Exceptions

A method in a subclass cannot add exception types to the exceptions defined in the superclass. However, it can leave off exceptions.

In the previous chapter, we covered exceptions in relation to overriding a method. Following is the key concept from that chapter that stated the rule.

 EXAM TIP: When you override a method, you must list those exceptions that the override code might throw. You can only list those exceptions, or subclasses of those exceptions, that are defined in the method definition you are inheriting from. (A method can also throw any unchecked exception, even if it is not declared in its throws clause.)

Exercise 9.3

Create a subclass of Calculator, called FancyCalculator, that is able to provide all of Calculator's functions, plus sin, cos, and tan. Following is the class definition for Calculator:

```
class Calculator {

    private String[] functions = {"+", "-", "*", "/", "="};

    String getFunctions() {
        String s = functions[0];
        for (int i = 1; i < functions.length; i++)
            s += ", " + functions[i];
        return s;
    }
}
```

You can use the following code to test the Calculator class and your new class:

```
class Tester {
    public static void main(String[] args) {
        Calculator c = new Calculator();
        System.out.println(c.getFunctions());
        FancyCalculator f = new FancyCalculator();
        System.out.println(f.getFunctions());
    }
}
```

The point of this exercise is to override a method and invoke the superclass' version of this method successfully.

Object References to Base and Derived Classes

For the exam, you'll need to be able to state what occurs when you invoke an overridden method in a base class and a derived class. A variable declared as an object reference for a certain class type can in fact hold an object reference for that class or an object reference for any subclass of that class. For example, suppose you have two classes. One is named Base, and it derives directly from class Object. The other is named Derived, and it extends class Base.

You can create new classes and assign them to variables like this:

```
Base b = new Base();
Derived d = new Derived();
```

As you can see, the class type defines the type of object reference. But you can also define a new object and assign its reference to a variable like this:

```
Base b_d = new Derived();
```

Even though b_d is defined as a type of class Base, this type includes subclasses of Base, such as class Derived. This has interesting effects when accessing data. For example, imagine we've defined the Base and Derived classes like:

```
class Base {
    int i = 1;
}

class Derived extends Base {
    int i = 2;
}
```

It's perfectly legal to have two different instance variables with the same name if they are defined in different two classes where one inherits from the other. Which variable we access depends on the type of the object reference that the variable was declared to hold. For example, if we accessed and displayed the values for i like this:

```
System.out.println(b.i);
System.out.println(d.i);
System.out.println(b_d.i);
```

then what gets displayed depends on the object reference's declared type. The variable b is declared as a Base class. So, b.i accesses i in the Base class and displays "1." The variable d is declared as a Derived class. So, d.i accesses i in the Derived class, and displays "2."

The variable b_d is trickier. We have created an instance of the Derived class and assigned it to this variable. However, as our rule says, the variable that gets accessed depends on the declared type of the object reference, which in this case is Base. So, b_d.i accesses i in the Base class, and displays "1."

In contrast to which variable gets accessed, the method that gets invoked depends on the underlying object. Imagine if our Base and Derived classes looked like this:

```
class Base {
    int i = 1;
    String test() {
        return "Base";
    }
}

class Derived extends Base {
    int i = 2;
    String test() {
        return "Derived";
    }
}
```

As you can see, the Derived class overrides the method test() defined in the Base class. Now, we create new instances as before:

```
Base b = new Base();
Derived d = new Derived();
Base b_d = new Derived();
```

This time, what happens when we invoke the test() method for each object reference and print the results, as in

```
System.out.println(b.test());
System.out.println(d.test());
System.out.println(b_d.test());
```

The method that gets invoked depends on the actual type of the object itself, not on the declared type. So, b.test() invokes test() in the Base class, which displays "Base." d.test() invokes test() in the Derived class, which displays "Derived." And, following our rule, b_d.test() invokes test() in the Derived class, because that is the actual object assigned to the variable b_d.

Answers to the Exercises

Exercise 9.1

What's wrong here is that the static method attempts to invoke the non-static method named findAvg(). Because there is no instance of Avg to use to invoke findAvg(), this is a compile-time error. To fix this, we could either make findAvg() static or create an instance of Avg and use that when invoking findAvg().

Exercise 9.2

```
class Avg2 {

    static double avg(double[] arr) {
        double sum = 0.0;
        if (arr.length > 0) {
            for (int i = 0; i < arr.length; i++)
                sum += arr[i];
            sum /= arr.length;
        }
        return sum;
    }

    static int avg(int[] arr) {
        int sum = 0;
        if (arr.length > 0) {
            for (int i = 0; i < arr.length; i++)
                sum += arr[i];
            sum /= arr.length;
        }
        return sum;
    }

    public static void main(String[] args) {
        // Test the methods.
        int[] intArray = {1, 2, 3, 4, 5};
        double[] doubleArray = {10, 20, 30, 40, 50};
        System.out.println(avg(intArray));
        System.out.println(avg(doubleArray));
    }

}
```

Exercise 9.3

Following is the new FancyCalculator class:

```
class FancyCalculator extends Calculator {
    private String[] functions = {"sin", "cos", "tan"};

    String getFunctions() {
        String s;
        s = super.getFunctions();
        for (int i = 0; i < functions.length; i++)
            s += ", " + functions[i];
        return s;
    }
}
```

Review Questions

1. What is the result of trying to compile and run this program?

```
class Example1 {
    public static void main(String[] args) {
        Example1 e = new Example1();
        e.test(5);
    }

    int test(int i) {
        System.out.println("int");
        return 1;
    }

    void test(long i) {
        System.out.println("long");
    }

}
```

    a. The program does not compile because the compiler cannot distinguish between the two test() methods provided.

    b. The program compiles and runs but nothing appears in the standard output.

    c. The program compiles and runs and "int" appears in the standard output.

    d. The program compiles and runs and "long" appears in the standard output.

2. What is the result of trying to compile and run this program?

```
class Example2 {
    public static void main(String[] args) {
        Example1 e = new Example1();
        e.test(5, 5.0, 5L);
    }

    void test(double a, double b, double c) {
        System.out.println("double, double, double");
    }

    void test(int a, float b, long c) {
        System.out.println("int, float, long");
    }

}
```

    a. This code will not compile.

    b. The code will compile and run and display "double, double, double."

    c. The code will compile and run and display "int, float, long."

3. What is the result of attempting to compile and run this program?

```
class Over {
    public static void main(String[] args) {
        Under u = new Under();
        u.test();
    }

    int test() {
        System.out.println("Over");
        return 1;
    }
}

class Under extends Over {
    short test() {
        super.test();
        System.out.println("Under");
        return 1;
    }
}
```

    a. This code does not compile.

    b. This code compiles and runs and displays "Over" followed by "Under."

    c. This code compiles and runs and displays "Under" followed by "Over."

Answers to Review Questions

1. c. The program compiles fine. When it runs, the word "int" appears in the standard output. Remember, the return type is not part of the signature of a method. An overloaded method can have different return types and the code will still be legal. Also, the Java Virtual Machine can determine which version to invoke because literals, such as 5, are int values.

2. b. The second parameter is 5.0. Floating-point numbers in Java are double by default. So, even though the first and second parameters are int and long and match the second definition of test(), the second parameter would have to be coerced to a float. Java invokes the first version of test(), where no values have to be explicitly coerced.

3. a. The compiler complains because the method in the subclass Under returns a different type than the method in the superclass. Unlike an overloaded method, the return type for an overridden method must match the superclass's return type for that method.

Constructors

Objectives for This Chapter

- State what constructors are and how they are used.
- Describe the default constructor.
- Identify situations when the default constructor is created for you.
- Identify situations when the default constructor is not created for you.
- Overload and override constructors.
- Use this( ) and super( ) to invoke constructors in the current or parent class.

Constructors are used to initialize objects upon creation. In some ways, constructors are similar to methods. However, instead of directly calling a constructor, Java executes a constructor for you just after Java allocates the memory for your object, and after Java has set the object's instance variables to their initialization values. As with methods (which were discussed in depth in Chapter 9), you can override and overload constructors. Java will invoke the constructor that corresponds to the parameters supplied with the new statement.

Constructor Essentials

Having to initialize all of the variables each time you created a class instance would be time-consuming and tedious. What you want to happen instead is for objects to initialize themselves when they are created. Java allows objects to be initialized using constructors.

Constructors initialize objects immediately upon creation and have the same name as the classes in which they reside. Syntactically, constructors are similar to methods. You declare constructors using constructor methods, which are used to initialize objects of a given class. Within a constructor method declaration, you give instance variables their initial state.

The following example defines a constructor method for the Record class:

```
public Record (String n, String a, String c, String, s, String z)
{
    name = n;
    address = a;
    city = c;
    state = s;
    zipcode = z;
}
```

Constructor methods do not have a return type and do not use void. This is because the implicit return type of the constructor is the class itself. It is the job of the constructor to set the initial state of the object's variables so that it is usable by the caller.

Although constructors don't have to take parameters, you can use parameters whenever necessary. In the previous example, the following code snippet defines five parameters for the constructor:

```
String n, String a, String c, String, s, String z
```

These parameters are then used in the constructor to set the value of the instance variables. The name, address, city, state, and zipcode variables are set with the following code:

```
name = n;
address = a;
city = c;
state = s;
zipcode = z;
```

The new keyword is always used together with a constructor to create an object of the related class. When you use the new keyword, the constructor is called immediately after the object is created and just before the new operation completes. In the following example, a new instance of the Record class is created:

```
theRecord = new Record("William R. Stanek","123 Main St.",
                       "Seattle","WA","97232");
```

The instance fields of the object are then initialized as follows:

```
name = "William R. Stanek";
address = "123 Main St.";
city = "Seattle";
state = "WA";
zipcode = "97232";
```

When you work with constructors, keep in mind that you cannot create an instance of a class without initializing the instance variables, either implicitly or explicitly. If you do not set instance variables to a specific value, they are implicitly initialized to the default value for the variable type; zero for numbers, null for objects, and false for booleans.

You cannot apply a constructor to an existing object to reset the instance fields. Instead, you should create mutator methods that perform those actions for you. For example, you could create a clear method for the Record class to set all the variables to an empty string (" ").

To sum all this up, the following rules apply when you work with constructors:

- Constructors always have the same name as their respective class.

- Constructors may use zero or more parameters.

- Constructors are always called with the new keyword.

- Constructors have no return value.

The Default Constructor

For a given class, you'll need to be able to describe the default constructor. You'll also need to be able to identify situations when the default constructor is created for you and when it is not created for you. Basically, if you do not define a constructor explicitly, Java defines one for you. This *default* constructor takes no arguments and invokes its superclass no-args constructor.

Here's a simple example for a class named Queue. This class is a subclass of Vector. (A queue stores values using a first-in, first-out strategy.)

```
import java.util.Vector;
class Queue extends Vector {
    void enqueue(Object obj) {
        addElement(obj);
    }
```

```
    Object dequeue() {
        Object obj = firstElement();
        boolean success = removeElement(obj);
        return obj;
    }
}
```

Given this class definition, you can create Queue objects by writing code like this:

```
Queue q = new Queue();
```

Here, you invoke the default constructor for the class. As discussed earlier, the new keyword is always used together with a constructor to create an object of the class. You can add() objects to and get() objects from this Queue object by invoking Queue's methods.

The default constructor automatically initializes all instance variables to zero, null, or false. As you work with constructors, keep in mind that if you create a constructor, the default constructor is no longer used.

Defining, Overloading, and Overriding a Constructor

Now that you've reviewed constructor essentials, lets take a close look at defining, over-loading, and overriding constructors. The Queue class created in the previous example works fine except for one thing: It does not support other constructors defined by Vec-tor. These constructors are defined in the documentation within java.util (where Vector is defined) as:

```
public Vector(int initialCapacity);
public Vector(int initialCapacity, int capacityIncrement);
public Vector(Collection c);
```

As with methods, the Java Virtual Machine determines which constructor to execute by the arguments you supply when creating a new object. These additional constructors overload the default Vector constructor. If you do not override one of these overloaded constructors in the Queue class and try to create a Queue object like this:

```
Queue q = new Queue(100);
```

and you think that this would invoke the correct Vector constructor to set the initial capacity of this Queue/Vector, think again. The only constructor Java provides for you is the no-args constructor. So the above line wouldn't work with the code we've written so far—Java would say there is no constructor for Queue that takes an int as a parameter. To make this work, you've got to write the appropriate constructor in the Queue class.

You can define a constructor for a class by writing any access control keywords, the class name, a set of arguments in parentheses, any exceptions the constructor might throw, and then the body of the constructor—just as you would for a method, except that you do not define a return value. As stated previously, constructors *never* return a value—if you specify a return value, Java will interpret your intended constructor as a method.

The constructor we need for Queue could take an int and invoke the corresponding constructor defined in Vector by using super():

```
Queue(int capacity) {
   super(capacity);
}
```

Now, the line of code:

```
Queue q = new Queue(100);
```

runs without a hitch. We could also write a constructor for Queue to handle the second Vector constructor—the one that takes two int parameters, an initial capacity, and an increment.

This Queue class now works fine, except we can no longer create a Queue object the way we did before by writing:

```
Queue q = new Queue();
```

What gives? We've fixed one problem and created another. The problem is that Java only supplies the default, no-args constructor if you do not define any other constructor. Since we have now supplied a constructor that takes an int, Java does not define a no-args constructor for us. The way around this problem is to supply a no-args constructor ourselves. Here is a complete definition for our new Queue class:

```
import java.util.Vector;
  class Queue extends Vector {

   Queue() {
      super();
   }

   Queue(int capacity) {
      super(capacity);
   }
```

```
Queue(int capacity, int increment) {
    super(capacity, increment);
}

void enqueue(Object obj) {
    addElement(obj);
}

Object dequeue() {
    Object obj = firstElement();
    boolean success = removeElement(obj);
    return obj;
}
}
```

Invoking Another Constructor

You can invoke one of the overloaded constructors by supplying the appropriate parameters in super(). Placing a call to super() in any line other than the first one results in a compiler error. If you do not invoke a superclass' constructor yourself, Java will attempt to invoke the no-args constructor in your superclass. If the superclass does not have a no-args constructor, the Java compiler will detect this situation if it can and issue a compiler error. Otherwise, if the compiler doesn't detect this situation (because of classes loaded dynamically at runtime), Java will throw runtime exception when it encounters trouble.

You can use this() and super() to invoke constructors in the current or parent class. If you do invoke another constructor directly, make that direct call as the first line of your constructor. For example, let's say you want to define a constructor for Queue that takes an array of objects to place into the Queue, and you want to set the initial capacity of that Queue to the length of the array. You can write such a constructor like this:

```
Queue(Object[] objs) {
    this(objs.length);
    for (int index = 0; index < objs.length; index++)
        addElement(objs[index]);
}
```

This constructor invokes a constructor in the same class that takes an int value (the constructor that takes the int value defines the initial capacity). The constructor then performs some additional processing to add the objects in the array to the Queue.

Instance Variables in Constructors

As you've seen in previous examples, overloading constructors can be a very useful technique when you want to construct an object in several different ways. One thing we haven't looked at is how overloaded constructors can be used to set different initial states for instance variables. It is always a good idea, regardless of how you construct an object, to ensure that all instance variables are set to meaningful values. Additionally, it is poor practice to rely on Java to set all the instance variables to default values as occurs when the default constructor is called.

When you set instance variables, there are times when you'll want all constructors of a class to set the instance variable to the same value and times when you'll want all constructors of a class to set the instance variable to a unique value. Both cases are handled in different ways.

In the first case where you want to use the same value, you should assign the value in the class definition. Going back to the Record class used earlier in the chapter, you may find that you want to set a credit rating of 1 for all new customers until their credit reports are reviewed and updated by the organization's credit department. This could be done as shown in the following example:

```
class Record {
    public Record (String n, String a, String c, String, s,
String z) {
        name = n;
        address = a;
        city = c;
        state = s;
        zipcode = z;
    }
    . . .
    private String name, address, city, state, zipcode;
    private int creditRating = 1;
}
```

In the second case where you want the value to be unique, you should set the instance variable inside the constructor. With the Record class, you may want to generate a unique account number for each new record. You could do this as shown in the following example:

```
class Record {
    public Record (String n, String a, String c,
    String, s, String z) {
        name = n;
        address = a;
        city = c;
```

```
        state = s;
        zipcode = z;
        accountNumber = Account.getNewNumber();
    }
    . . .
    private String name, address, city, state, zipcode;
    private int creditRating = 1;
    private int accountNumber;
}
```

Whenever you work with constructors, be very aware of the local variable and instance variable names that you use. Java doesn't allow you to declare two local variables with the same name inside the same or enclosing scopes. However, you can declare local variables that have the same names as the instance variables of a class. When local variables have the same name as instance variables, the local variables hide the instance variables, which as you might imagine can cause confusion for other programmers who read your code and may also be the source of bugs within the code.

While it may be easier to simply use different names for local variables and instance variables, there is another solution. You can use this to refer directly to the object and avoid any namespace conflicts that may occur between the local variables and the instance variables. Consider the previously defined constructor for the Record class:

```
public Record (String n, String a, String c, String, s, String z) {
    name = n;
    address = a;
    city = c;
    state = s;
    zipcode = z;
}
```

In this example, the parameters are set as n, a, c, s, and z instead of name, address, city, state, and zipcode. If the parameters had been set as name, address, city, state, and zipcode, the parameter names would have hidden the instance variables. To avoid this problem and be able to use the same parameter names, you could use this when specifying the instance variables. An example follows:

```
public Record (String name, String address, String city, String
state, String zipcode) {
    this.name = name;
    this.address = address;
    this.city = city;
    this.state = state;
    this.zipcode = zipcode;
}
```

The key thing to remember is that it is poor programming practice to use the same local and instance variable names. Whether you use different names or this to counter, this problem is a matter of preference. Your technique should be consistent, however, whenever possible. You'll learn more about this in upcoming chapters as well.

Exercise 10.1

Create a subclass of class Frame called MyFrame. Define MyFrame so that you can create a new MyFrame object with a title. The Frame class defines a constructor that takes a title as a String as in:

```
Frame (String s);
```

(The Frame class is a real Java class defined in java.awt.)

Exercise 10.2

Here is a class named Bridge:

```
class Bridge {
    int length;
    Bridge(int length) {
        this.length = length;
    }
}
```

Modify this class definition to construct a new Bridge instance without explicitly supplying the Bridge's length, like this:

```
Bridge b = new Bridge();
```

Exercise 10.3

Given this class definition:

```
class Railroad {
    String name;
    Railroad() {
        System.out.println("I've been working on the railroad");
    }
    Railroad(String name) {
        this.name = name;
    }
}
```

How could you adjust the second constructor (the one that takes the String) most efficiently so that it also displays the message "I've been working on the railroad" when it is invoked?

Answers to the Exercises

Exercise 10.1

To create a class called MyFrame that defines a title, you've got to override the Frame's constructor that takes a String and pass that String object up to the Frame's constructor, like this:

```
import java.awt.Frame;
class MyFrame extends Frame {
    MyFrame(String s) {
        super(s);
    }
}
```

Exercise 10.2

The no-args constructor is only supplied for you if you have not defined another constructor. In this case, since there is already another constructor, you've got to write the no-args constructor explicitly:

```
class Bridge {
    int length;
    Bridge(int length) {
        this.length = length;
    }
    Bridge() {
    }
}
```

You do not have to supply any code for this no-args constructor. The Java Virtual Machine will invoke your superclass' no-args constructor for you, and since length is already set to 0 as its default value, you do not need to initialize length in the constructor itself.

Exercise 10.3

You can invoke the no-args constructor in the Railroad class using this(), as in:

```
class Railroad {
   String name;
   Railroad() {
     System.out.println("I've been working on the railroad");
   }
   Railroad(String name) {
      this();
      this.name = name;
   }
}
```

Review Questions

1. What is the result of attempting to compile and run the following code?

```
class Ex {
   public static void main(String[] args) {
      Fx f = new Fx();
   }
   Ex(int i) {
   }
}

class Fx extends Ex {
}
```

    a. The code does not compile because the Ex class does not define a no-args constructor.

    b. The code does not compile because the Fx class does not define a no-args constructor.

    c. The code does not compile because there is no code in the Ex(int i) constructor.

    d. The code compiles and runs successfully.

2. What is the result of attempting to compile and run the following code?

```
class Ex {
   public static void main(String[] args) {
      Fx f = new Fx(5);
   }
   Ex() {
      System.out.println("Ex, no-args");
   }
   Ex(int i) {
      System.out.println("Ex, int");
   }
}
```

```
class Fx extends Ex {
   Fx() {
      super();
      System.out.println("Fx, no-args");
   }
   Fx(int i) {
      super(i);
      this();
      System.out.println("Fx, int");
   }
}
```

    a. The messages "Ex, int," "Fx, no-args," and "Fx, int" appear in the standard output.

    b. The messages "Ex, no-args," "Ex, int," "Fx, no-args," and "Fx, int" appear in the standard output.

    c. The code does not compile because the Fx(int i) constructor is not defined legally.

    d. The code does not compile because the Fx() constructor is not defined legally.

3. What is the result of attempting to compile and run the following code?

```
class Ex {
   public static void main(String[] args) {
      Fx f = new Fx(5);
   }
   Ex() {
      System.out.println("Ex, no-args");
   }
   Ex(int i) {
      System.out.println("Ex, int");
   }
}

class Fx extends Ex {
   Fx() {
      super();
      System.out.println("Fx, no-args");
   }
   Fx(int i) {
      this();
      System.out.println("Fx, int");
   }
}
```

    a. The messages "Ex, int," "Fx, no-args," and "Fx, int" appear in the standard output.

    b. The messages "Ex, no-args," "Fx, no-args," and "Fx, int" appear in the standard output.

  c. The code does not compile because the Fx(int i) constructor is not defined legally.

  d. The code does not compile because the Fx() constructor is not defined legally.

Answers to Review Questions

1. **a.** The default constructor in Fx will attempt to invoke a no-args constructor in Ex. Since Ex already defines a constructor, Java does not supply a no-args constructor by default. The compiler will catch this problem and complain.

2. **c.** The Fx(int i) constructor is defined like this:

```
Fx(int i) {
    super(i);
    this();
    System.out.println("Fx, int");
}
```

  However, a direct call to a constructor must appear as the first thing in a constructor. While super(i) is first, this() is second, and this() is also a direct call to a constructor. This is illegal.

3. **b.** First, Java invokes the constructor Fx(int i). This calls Fx(), which invokes the no-args superclass constructor Ex(). This writes "Ex, no-args" to the standard output. Then the Fx() no-args constructor continues, which writes "Fx, no-args" to the standard output. Then the Fx(int i) constructor continues, which writes Fx, int to the standard output.

Objects and Classes

Objectives for This Chapter

- Define classes, including member variables and member methods.
- Use the class controls public, abstract, strictfp and final appropriately.
- Declare variables and methods using the private, protected, public, static, final, native, volatile, strictfp, or abstract controls.
- Identify when variables can be accessed based on access control keywords.
- Create object-oriented hierarchies using 'is a' and 'has a' relationships.
- Define inner classes and describe how they are used.
- Use anonymous classes and static inner classes.

In this chapter, we'll examine objects and classes in greater detail than we have in previous chapters. Everything you write in Java is inside a class. While the Java API defines thousands of classes, you still have to create your own classes to describe the objects that you want to create. A class instance is a specific implementation of an object. Objects use declarations, expressions, and other structures to do the real work of the language. The idea is to use these pieces of code in appropriate ways so you don't have to keep rewriting them for each use. Reusability is what makes object-oriented programming and Java so powerful.

As you've seen in previous chapters, classes can be built on other classes. In fact, all classes are built on a base class called Object. When you extend the base class or any class for that matter, the new class initially has all the properties and methods of its parents. That is, classes receive their characteristics through inheritance. You can choose whether to modify methods of the parent class or define new methods for the child class.

Objects

Objects are containers for information. Objects can be instantiated in your programs to contain and manage information. The information an object contains is its data. The data in an object is usually called its instance variables or fields. Objects manage data using methods.

Objects are encapsulated so that they hide the implementation of their data from users. All objects have behavior, state, and identity.

An object's *behavior* is defined by the messages it accepts and the actions it can perform. An object's *state* is determined by the current values of its fields. The state of an object can be changed over time as messages are sent to the object. An object's *identity* serves to uniquely identify the object to the runtime environment. Each object that is instantiated has a unique identity, even objects that are instances of the same class.

Creating and Destroying Objects

Data space for objects is not preallocated in Java. Instead, it is created as needed. Space is used for as long as something is accessing the data and then memory is automatically deallocated. This is similar to using the malloc and free system calls in C. The biggest difference between Java and C is that there is no need to release memory explicitly after the program finishes with it. In Java, an automatic garbage collection system finds any memory that is not in use and automatically frees it.

Java and C++ have differences, also. In C++, constructor and destructor functions run whenever an object is created or destroyed. Java has an equivalent to the constructor function, named constructor, but there is no exact equivalent to a C++ destructor. All objects in Java are removed using automatic garbage collection. There is no way to invoke destructors manually. There is a method named finalize that can be used like a C++ destructor to do final cleanup on an object before garbage collection occurs. However, finalizers have several limitations.

Creating an Instance

Java allocates memory space similar to malloc in C using the keyword new. new creates an object of virtually any type, the exceptions being primitive data types. An example of this follows:

```
StringBuffer sb;
sb = new StringBuffer(8);
```

This allocates enough space in memory for an 8-character string and names it sb. sb is now considered an object of type StringBuffer and has all the methods associated with class StringBuffer.

Method invocation in Java differs from that in C. In a procedural language like C, the variable sb is normally passed as an argument to the appropriate function call. In Java, the object associated with sb already has all the methods it inherited from the String class.

Destroying an Instance

When an object is no longer referenced by any other objects, Java reclaims the memory space using garbage collection. Java calls a destructor method before garbage collection takes place. This method is called *finalize*. The *finalize* method always has a return type of void and overrides the default destructor in java.object.Object.

Java calls finalize automatically and do not pass any arguments at that time. Because of this, the basic structure of a finalize method is

```
void finalize() {
  //insert body of finalize method here
}
```

 NOTE: A program can call finalize directly just as it would any other method. However, calling finalize will not initiate any type of garbage collection. It is treated as any other method if called directly. When Java does garbage collection, finalize is still called even if it has already been called directly by the program.

A key difference between finalize and a C++ destructor is that the system-only calls finalize when it is ready to reclaim the memory associated with the object. This is not immediately after an object is no longer referenced. Cleanup is scheduled by the system on an as-needed basis. There can be a significant delay between when the application finishes and when finalize is called. This is true even if the system is busy, but there is no immediate need for more memory. For these reasons, it may be better to invoke the garbage collector directly at program termination rather than wait for garbage collection to invoke it automatically. You invoke the garbage collector directly using the Runtime.gc() method as discussed in Chapter 5.

Classes

Classes describe the objects you want to create. Classes are made up of instance variables (fields) and member methods. Each real member of a class is referred to as an *instance*. Classes follow a specific hierarchy that allow for both superclasses and subclasses. A *superclass* is the top-level class of every application. In Java, the root superclass is automatically the Object class. This means that if a class does not implicitly declare its superclass, or next higher class level, then it is a subclass of Object. *Subclasses* extend the superclass and create a new variation of the class. They inherit the characteristics of the preceding class.

Declaring a Class

In Java, all classes are ultimately derived from the system class named Object. This makes Object the root of the class hierarchy and means that all methods and variables in the Object class are available to all other classes. It is this class structure that makes code reuse in Java possible.

Class declarations without controls follow this general format:

```
class Name {
    //methods and variables associated with the class
}
```

Classes can be named anything as long as they begin with an alphabetic character, a dollar sign, or an underscore. By convention however, a class name should begin with a capital letter. This makes the class easily distinguishable from methods, variables, and so on. The Java class libraries follow this convention and it is highly recommend.

Java supports single inheritance of classes. Therefore, each class except Object has only one superclass. This means that any class you create can extend or inherit the functions of only a single class. Although this may seem like a limitation if you have programmed in a language that allows for multiple inheritance of classes, Java does support multiple inheritance of class methods, which is accomplished through the class interface. You define a class interface with an interface declaration.

Most class definitions have some or all of these components:

```
[keywords] class MyClass [extends Superclass]
  [implements Interface] {
  //class variables
  //static initializers
  //instance initializers
  //instance variables
  //constructors
  //class methods
  //instance methods
```

These components are discussed later in the chapter.

Application Class Structures

You can create two types of programs in Java: applications and applets. *Applications* are standalone and can be run directly from the command line. Every Java application must define one method named main, which is similar to main in C and C++. When a Java application is invoked, the Java interpreter looks for the method named main and begins execution there. If main is not declared, the interpreter will complain.

Main methods must always be declared public. It would be impossible for a program outside Java to even start the Java application if main were not declared public.

The main method itself must be declared in a fixed format:

```
public static void main (String args[]) {
  //body of main
}
```

The public declaration enables main to be accessed from external programs. static indicates that this method cannot be modified by subclasses. void means that this method does not return a value of any kind. main is the required name of the method. (String args[]) indicates that main will have command line arguments consisting of an array of type String. This array contains the command line arguments specified when this application was started.

Here's a simple application that uses a main method:

```
public class Yesterday {
   public static void main (String args[]) {
      System.out.println("Yesterday was a good day.");
      System.out.println("Today is a great day.");
      System.out.println("Tomorrow will be even better.");
   }
}
```

To compile the example, type the following:

```
javac Yesterday.java
```

When the compiler finishes, invoke the Java interpreter as follows:

```
java Yesterday
```

The output from the application should be as follows:

```
Yesterday was a good day.
Today is a great day.
Tomorrow will be even better.
```

Applet Class Structures

Applets rely on an external program to interface with the user. They cannot be run by themselves. To run an applet, you can use Web browsers and the JDK's appletviewer.

Applets are an extension of an existing Java class, java.applet.Applet. This means an applet is really an example of a subclass.

To declare an applet, you use the following syntax:

```
class AppletName extends Applet {
   //applet body
}
```

This notifies the compiler that an applet is a subclass of another class, in this case a subclass of java.applet.Applet.

Applets begin execution differently than applications. Applications begin program execution by calling method main. Applets instead use methods init and start. The browser or viewer running the applet invokes the init method followed by the start method every time an applet is started. As the methods are defined in the Applet class, these do not have to be explicitly declared in an applet. For example, the following applet will run just fine without declaring init or start methods:

```
import java.awt.*;
import java.applet.*;

public class Yesterday extends Applet {
   public void paint (Graphics g){
      g.drawString("Yesterday was a good day.", 10, 10);
      g.drawString("Today is a great day.", 10, 30);
      g.drawString("Tomorrow will be even better.", 10, 50);
   }
}
```

This is an example of an applet beginning execution without an explicit declaration of methods init and start, instead relying on default init and start methods. Notice also that there is no call to invoke paint, yet the screen was painted anyway. This happens because the default start method automatically calls the repaint method, which invokes the update method and ultimately the paint method. paint must be explicitly declared for anything to be written to the screen.

init, start, and paint aren't the only methods defined in the Applet class. Other key methods include stop and destroy. Lets take a closer look at these methods now to get a better understanding of how applets work.

init

The init method is called when an applet is loaded into a viewer. The call only occurs once. You can use the init method to get parameters from the HTML page in which the applet was invoked and to initialize variables. (Arguments and parameters are discussed in Chapter 13.)

The init method must always have a return type of void, be declared public, and cannot have arguments. An example of an init method is

```
public void init () {
    counter = 0;
}
```

This example initializes a counter, setting its value to zero.

An init method is not required. Declaring an init method in an application overrides an existing init method in class java.applet.Applet, which is why the name, return type, and other information are fixed.

start

The start method is called after the init method the first time an applet is loaded into a viewer or if an applet has been suspended and must be restarted. If the compiler can't find a start method explicitly declared in the applet, it will default to the start method in java.applet.Applet.

Like the init method, the start method must always have a return type of void, be declared public, and cannot have arguments. An example of a start method follows:

```
public void start() {
    run = true;
    while (run == true) {
        counter++;
        repaint();
        try {Thread.sleep(1000);}
        catch(InterruptedException e) {}
    }
}
```

This start method sets variable called run to true and then enters a while loop that will run as long as run is equal to true. The loop increments the counter that was initially set to zero in the init method. The repaint call causes the screen to be repainted after every increment. The try and catch lines cause the program to sleep for 1,000 ms after every counter increment. (try and catch are exceptions covered in Chapter 14, "Exception Handling.")

A start method is not required. Like init, it actually overrides the default start method provided by java.applet.Applet.

stop

The stop method is called whenever an applet must be stopped or suspended. Without the stop method, the applet continues to run, consuming resources even when the user has left the page on which the applet is located. There may be times when continued execution is desirable, but in general it is not.

The stop method must always have a return type of void, be declared public, and cannot have arguments. An example of the stop method follows:

```
public void stop() {
    run = false;
}
```

This stop method sets the run variable to false. This causes the loop in the start method from the previous example to exit the loop and fall through the end of the method. The result is that the application stops running. Note that only the run variable is changed.

As with the init and start methods, a stop method is not required. It overrides the default stop method provided by java.applet.Applet.

paint

The paint method is used to paint or repaint the screen. It is automatically called by repaint or can be called explicitly by an applet. Applets call paint when the browser requires a repaint, such as when an obscured applet is brought to the front of the screen again.

The paint method has a fixed format. It always must have a return type of void and be declared public. However, unlike init, start, and stop, it does have an argument of type Graphics. This is a predefined type in Java that contains many of the methods for writing graphics to the screen. Here is an example of a paint method:

```
public void paint(Graphics g) {
    g.drawstring("counter = " + counter, 10, 10);
}
```

This method writes the value of counter to the screen each time it is invoked.

The compiler does not require a paint method. It overrides the default method provided by java.applet.Applet. However, if you do not override paint, you will not be able to write anything to the screen.

destroy()

The destroy method is always called when an applet has completed or is being shut down. Any final cleanup takes place here. The destroy method must have a return type of void, be declared public, and have no arguments. An example of a destroy method follows:

```
public void destroy() {
    counter = 0;
}
```

This destroy method only sets the variable counter to zero.

A destroy method is not required. It is overrides the existing destroy method in class java.applet.Applet.

Class Variables

Chapter 6 discusses variables as they relate to data types and values. This section shows how variables are used in classes.

Variables are used in classes to hold data to be used later. Good programming form places variables immediately following the class declaration statement, such as:

```
class ShowVariables {
    int IntA, IntB;  //declare some integer variables
    int IntC = 25;  //declare and initialize a variable
    char MyChar;    //declare a character type variable;
    float FloatArray[];  //declare single dimensional
                         //array of floating-point values
    boolean b;       //declare boolean variable
    . . .
}
```

The variable declaration statements in this example just set up the variables to be used in the class. No methods or expressions are defined at this point.

Every class can have variables associated with it. Variables fall into two categories: those that are particular to an instance, called *instance variables*, and those that are global to all instances of a particular class, known as *class variables*. The use of the variable determines its type.

Here is an example of a class that inherits from class Object and defines three instance variables.

```
class Show {
    String ShowName;
    int RunTime;
    boolean Rating;
}
```

The first instance variable is an object reference to an instance of class String. The next two are primitive data types. These instance variables allow Show objects to store their own unique values.

A static variable belongs to the class, not to the objects.

```
class Show {
    static int id;
    String ShowName;
```

```
    int RunTime;
    boolean Rating;
}
```

The id variable can be accessed from any class that can access Show, starting from when the Show class is first loaded by the Java interpreter. Because it is declared as static, the id variable exists exactly once, no matter how many objects are created—even if no objects are created. In addition to static, we'll get into the other keywords for member variables (public, protected, private, and final) later in this chapter.

Instance Variables

Instance variables exist only for a particular instance of an object. This means that different instances of a given class each have a variable of the same name, but Java stores different values for that variable in different places in memory. Each of these instance variables is manipulated individually. If an instance goes away, so does the variable. You can access instance variables from other instances, but the variable itself exists only in a particular instance.

Instance variables have been shown in the examples so far in this chapter. They are declared after a class declaration but before method declarations. Every instance of that class has a copy of this variable and can modify it as needed without affecting any other instance copies of the variable. Here is an example of an instance variable declaration:

```
class Book {
    String[] name;
    String[] ISBN;
    int pageCount;
}
```

Here every instance of class Book has a name, ISBN, and pageCount variable used to store information about a particular item. If you had two books and wanted to put them on your Web page, you could specify the name, ISBN, and page count of each book in individual instances without worrying about overwriting the information.

Static Variables

You can modify variable (and method) declarations with the *static* modifier. *Static variables* exist in only one location and are globally accessible by all instances of a class. A variable cannot be changed by a subclass if it has been declared static and *final*. Further, static variables have the same information in all instances of the class.

This is a valuable tool in situations in which a variable is shared by several instances of a class and/or subclasses. All instances will have the same value for the variable. All classes accessing that variable point to the same place in memory. This variable will remain there until the last instance accessing the variable is flushed from memory.

A static variable is declared in the same way as an instance variable but has the keyword static in front of it. In the following code, the variable bookType is declared static and is thus the same for all instances of class Book:

```
class Book {
    static String bookType[] = "hardcover";
}
```

In this way, all the instances can check this variable for the value of bookType. An external class can query this variable for the same information. Its value needs to be specified only once and stored in one location because the information is the same for all instances of class Book.

Predefined Instances

Java comes with three predefined object values: null, this, and super. They are used as shortcuts for many common operations in Java.

null

What happens when the class being created is a superclass? An object can be created that is simply a placeholder for subclasses to fill with values. In this situation, the object can be declared null, meaning that no value is assigned to a variable, such as:

```
class Book{
    static String name = null;
    public static void main (String args[]) {
        Book book = new Book();
        if (book.name == null) {
            GetName("Enter name> ");
        }
    }
}
```

In this example, the String object name is initialized to null. It is then tested in main to determine whether it is a null object. If so, the user is prompted to enter the book's name. Note that null cannot be used with primitive data types. It can only be used with objects.

this

To refer to the current object, you can use the keyword this. this allows the current instance of an object to be referenced explicitly. This is valuable when the current instance of an object is to be passed to another class that will also use the object, such as:

```
void GetName (String prompt){
    StringBuffer name;
    char ch = '\0';
    name = new StringBuffer();
    System.out.print(prompt);
    System.out.flush();
    Wwhile (ch != '\n') {
        try {ch = (char)System.in.read(); }
        catch (IOException e) {};
        name.append(ch);
    }
    this.name = name.toString();
}
```

The compiler understands implicitly that the current instance of a class variable is this. Do not explicitly reference the current instance unless necessary.

super

super is a reference to the superclass. It is often used as a shortcut or explicit way to reference a member in the superclass of the current class. In the following code, a subclass named ComputerBook uses the super keyword to reference the method GetName in its superclass, Book:

```
class ComputerBook extends Book {
    void getBookInfo {
        super.GetName();
    }
}
```

ComputerBook would look for a method called GetName in the current class if super were not used, generating a compile error.

Object-Oriented Relationships Using 'is a' and 'has a'

'is a' and 'has a' relationships are an example of the kind of thing you've got to understand for the exam and to be an effective Java programmer. How would you define a class hierarchy with these classes?

- An Employee class that maintains an employee number
- A Full-time employee class that
  - maintains an employee number
  - maintains the number of hours worked that week
  - calculates its own pay using its own salary() method
- A Retired employee class that
  - maintains an employee number
  - maintains the number of years worked
  - calculates pay using its own salary() method

Then, using these classes and the resulting class hierarchy, create an object for a full-time employee named Ralph Cramden.

Think about for this for a moment, then read on.

Perhaps you're thinking of something like this for the class hierarchy.

At first blush, the example hierarchy seems to work. We have Employee at the top level, defining an instance variable and an abstract method that both Full-time and Retired employees inherit. We would create a new instance of the Full-time employee class for Ralph. Figure 11-1 certainly fits the classes into a class hierarchy. So what's the problem? Here's an example of where the design in Figure 11-1 falls apart.

Ralph Cramden is hired as a bus driver when he's 25. At that time, the program creates a new Full-time instance for him. Over the years the application accumulates references to this object throughout the system, because Ralph's on various lists for medical benefits, employee phone numbers, and so on. The application runs fine for years. But after 20 years he decides to retire to spend more time with his wife. Now we want to represent Ralph as an instance of the Retired class. Does this mean we create a new object for him, that we try to find all the references to the old object and replace it

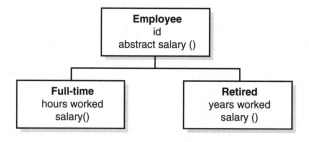

Figure 11-1   A hierarchy that works in theory

with the new object? And what happens if he takes time off in the middle of his career? What happens if he works in a temporary position in which his salary is calculated differently from other employees? Do we constantly create new objects to represent our employee named Ralph Cramden?

We only want to create one object for Ralph. Clearly, then, something's wrong with the design. What's wrong is that we did not fully grasp the difference between 'is a' and 'has a' for our particular domain.

 EXAM TIP: The phrase 'is a' defines a direct relationship between a superclass and a subclass: a subclass is a type of a superclass. The phrase 'has a' describes a relationship between a part of an object and another object, usually of a different type: an object has a part that is another object.

Sure, a Full-time employee or a Retired employee 'is an' Employee. However, we would be much better off saying that the Employee class 'has a' part that 'is a' Status, and that an employee's Status is either Full-time or Retired. Now our hierarchy looks like Figure 11-2.

With this arrangement, we can keep the same Employee object forever and simply change its status when we need to. We can add to our status hierarchy as the needs of the application change. If Ralph took a leave of absence at the birth of his son, we can define a class to represent that new type of status and use a new instance of this class as Ralph's current status. If Ralph worked part-time for a while as he pursued a bowling career, an instance of a class called Part-time could be swapped in as his new status.

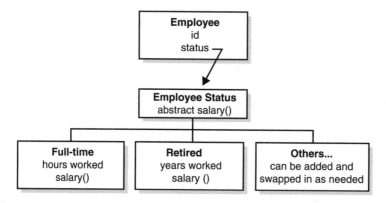

Figure 11-2 A hierarchy that works in practice

Our hierarchy works smoothly because we have used 'has a' and 'is a' correctly for our domain: an Employee 'has a' status; Part-time, Full-time, or Retired 'is a' Status.

 TIP: This example shows why creating class hierarchies falls somewhere between engineering and craft. You use your skills to make trade-offs until you find something that works in practice. The primary skills you use are your ability to discern between 'is a' and 'has a' relationships for the domain you're working in, and your ability to imagine scenarios that typify your design.

Our next step is to start implementing the classes and class hierarchies you design.

Exercise 11.1

Create classes for 2DShape, Circle, Square, and Point. Points have an (x, y) location. Circles have an (x, y) location, as well as a radius. Squares have an (x, y) location, as well as a length. Which are the superclasses, and which are the subclasses? Are any classes related by a 'has a' relationship?

Exercise 11.2

Define a class hierarchy to represent a shipment of coffee beans. The beans have some different characteristics and behavior in an inventory system depending on whether they are *unexamined*, or whether they have been examined and found to be *stale* or *fresh*. A shipment of beans is first entered into the inventory system before it is examined. What classes might you need? How are these classes related in 'is a' and 'has a' relationships? Which kind of class should you create an instance of when the shipment first arrives, before it is examined? What should you do after the shipment is examined?

Class Keywords

Classes can be modified from their default state using any of three keywords: public, abstract, strictfp, and final. As you've seen, the public keyword relates to access control; you'll see in a moment how the abstract and final keywords relate to your design.

public

If you import a package, you can only access those package classes that are declared to be public. All of the classes you see in the Java APIs are declared public. Since each of these classes is defined in a different package from your application, declaring them public is the only way you can get at them.

abstract

An abstract method consists of a method declaration without a body. That is, you define the keywords, return type, name, parameters, and the exceptions the method throws, but no instructions between a set of curly braces. Here's an example:

```
public abstract double area(double radius)
    throws IllegalGeometryException;
```

Since there is no code supplied for the area() method, the class itself cannot be instantiated. If it could be, then there is nothing stopping some other code from instantiating the class and invoking its area() method—but there are no instructions yet for area(). This flies in the face of Java's philosophy of doing its best to keep the programmer from making mistakes involving how the pieces fit together.

If you have defined any methods as abstract, then you must define your class to be abstract, as well. You can declare a class to be abstract, even if no methods are declared as abstract. Subclasses are automatically concrete. Two examples of this are Java's own Container and Component classes, defined in java.awt. Again, declaring the class as abstract forces programmers to instantiate subclasses of these classes. So, instead of allowing a programmer to instantiate Component, a programmer must instantiate Button, Choice, Checkbox, or some other subclass. However, an object reference of type Component can refer to any of these.

NOTE: Why declare a method to be abstract? Can there possibly be a good reason for not providing any behavior at all and insisting that the class itself be abstract?

Yes, the reason has to do with design. Declaring a class to be abstract organizes your class hierarchy a certain way and forces a programmer using this class hierarchy to do things according to your understanding of the domain. For example, the java.lang package defines a class called Number. This class is abstract. This class defines the abstract methods intValue(), longValue(), floatValue(), and doubleValue(). The role of the Number class is to organize and unite a variety of "wrapper" classes into the same branch in the class hierarchy, and to specify what their interface will be. Concrete subclasses of Number are Integer, Long, Double, and Float. These subclasses implement the behavior for the abstract methods they inherit and make this behavior mean something specific to their class type.

The reason these methods are declared to be abstract, (rather than, for example, defining a method that returns a default value such as 0), is because the Number class is never intended to be instantiated. According to the design, it makes no sense to instantiate Number. The purpose of the subclasses is to put an object-oriented wrapper around a primitive data type that corresponds to the class name—int, long, double, or float. However, there is no generic number type. So making a Number object has no meaning.

Making Number abstract forces programmers to instantiate the classes that were intended to be instantiated. You can do the same thing in your design, so that programmers use your classes as you intended.

One of the benefits of this type of design—that is, of uniting the wrapper types under the same branch in the class hierarchy, even if you cannot instantiate the superclass—is that you can define an object reference to be the superclass type. Then, this object reference can refer to any subclass of that type.

For example, you can write something like:

```
Number n;
String s = getInput();
if (isInteger(s))
    n = new Integer(s);
else if (isFloatingPoint(s))
    n = new Double(s);
```

The variable n can be used to invoke methods that are defined in Number, including Number's abstract methods that are implemented in the subclasses. Since Number defines intValue(), longValue(), floatValue(), and doubleValue(), we can invoke any of these methods using the variable n.

strictfp

You can use the strictfp keyword with for methods and classes to ensure that floating-point calculations are handled strictly. You can apply strictfp on a method-by-method basis or to an entire class. With methods, floating-point values used in the method follow the strict floating-point rules automatically. With classes, all methods in the class follow the strict floating-point rules.

If you do not use the strictfp keyword, the default floating-point calculation rules are used. These rules relax the computational model by not requiring the truncation of certain intermediate values that occur during a computation, which allows use of an extended exponent range to represent intermediate results where exclusive use of the float or double value set might otherwise result in underflow or overflow. The result is that the correct answer might be returned instead of an underflow or overflow.

final

A final class makes all of its methods final as well, since a final class cannot be extended. As an example of a final class, the classes Integer, Long, Float, and Double are declared as final, so all of their methods are final, as well. None of these wrapper classes can be subclassed. If you would like to make your own type of wrapper, you must extend the class Number. Another commonly used class that's declared as final is String.

EXAM TIP: If you want to stop programmers from ever making a subclass of a particular class, you can declare that class to be final.

NOTE: The final keyword optimizes your code and makes your design more secure. First, let's look at optimization. When a variable is declared to be final, Java knows its value is a constant. A final variable must be initialized when it is declared, because it can never be changed later. Since this value is a constant, the compiler could feel free to optimize by replacing references to that variable with its constant value, eliminating the need to look up its value when it is referenced. As an example, the variables PI and E in the Math class in java.lang are defined as final.

When a method is declared to be final, Java knows that the method can never be overridden. A final method must be fully defined when it is declared—you cannot have an abstract final method, for example. Since Java knows the method can never be overridden by subclasses, the Java compiler can replace the call to the method with inline code if it wants. This eliminates all sorts of class look-ups to find the method in the class hierarchy and makes the method invocation much faster.

How about security? Declaring a method to be final is one way to guarantee that its contract—its published API—will never be violated. For example, the method getClass() in class Object is declared as final. No subclass can override this method so that it violates its contract and returns some other class type to hide its identity.

Exercise 11.3

Given the following class definition:

```
abstract class Shape {
  abstract double perimeter();
}
```

Create a subclass of Shape named TwoDShape, and a subclass of 2DShape named Square. Like Shape, TwoDShape should also be an abstract class, but Square should be concrete and should know how to calculate its perimeter. Define whatever instance variables you need for Square.

Exercise 11.4

Modify the classes you created above so that programmers cannot make subclasses of your Square class.

Variable Keywords

You should be able to declare variables using controls. First, we'll present keywords that are used with variables. Then, we'll summarize the access control keywords for variables.

static

As we mentioned earlier, a static variable belongs with the class. A static variable always exists exactly once for a class, no matter how many instances are created.

final

A final variable cannot be changed after it is defined. That means that a final variable is a constant. As we mentioned when describing what it means to declare an entire class to be final, the two benefits of a final variable are with security (enforcement of the API) and optimization (placing code inline). A final variable provides these benefits on a variable-by-variable basis, rather than for the class as a whole.

transient

A transient variable is not stored as part of an object's persistent state. It indicates that a variable may not be serialized and is used to protect sensitive data from being written to a stream. For example, if you wanted to protect sensitive data regarding a customer's account number, you could designate it as transient. In this way, the account number wouldn't be written to a stream outside the Java Virtual Machine.

Transient variables may not be declared as final or static.

volatile

The volatile modifier indicates that a variable can be modified asynchronously in a multiprocessor environment. While this modifier isn't covered in the exam, it is a good idea to use this modifier whenever a variable may be accessed by two or more threads without synchronization.

Exercise 11.5

What is wrong with this class definition? Fix it so that is works when you invoke main().

```
class Avg {
    public static void main(String[] args) {
        double a = 5.1;
        double b = 20.32;
        double c = 32.921;
        System.out.println(findAvg(a, b, c));
    }

    double findAvg(double a, double b, double c) {
        return (a + b + c) / 3.0;
    }
}
```

Access Control Keywords

For the exam, you'll need to be able to identify when variables and methods can be accessed based on access control keywords. You've already seen a couple of tables regarding access control for class members. Here's a quick summary of these keywords. We'll follow this summary with a number of exercises involving access control.

If there are no access control keywords on a class, then only those classes defined in the same package can attempt to access members of that class. If there are no access control keywords on a member, then only those classes in the same package can access that member.

public

A public member can be accessed by any class that can access the member's class. If a class in package number 1 wants to access the member of a class defined in package number 2, the class in package number 2 must be declared public so that the first class can get to it. Then, the first class can access any members that are declared as public.

private

You can restrict all access to a particular member from all classes except the class in which it is defined by using the keyword private on the member.

protected

A protected member can only be accessed by classes within the same package, or by subclasses in the same or different packages from the member's class.

The following exercises deal with keywords that you can place on classes and class members.

Exercise 11.6

Imagine this hierarchy:

```
Tree (defines a protected instance variable named age)
Deciduous extends Tree
Evergreen extends Tree
Pine extends Evergreen
Forest
```

This hierarchy is shown in Figure 11-3. Now, create the following objects:

```
Deciduous d = new Deciduous();
Evergreen e = new Evergreen();
Pine p1 = new Pine();
Pine p2 = new Pine();
Forest f = new Forest();
```

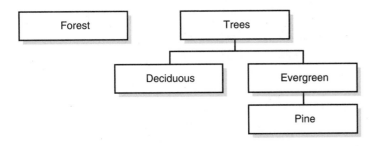

Figure 11-3   A hierarchy of tree classes

Which objects can access the protected field in class Tree if all of these classes are defined as part of the same package? Which objects cannot access this protected field?

Exercise 11.7

What if each of the classes in Exercise 11.6—Forest, Tree, Evergreen, Deciduous, and Pine—were defined in different packages? Which objects could then access the Tree's protected field?

Exercise 11.8

Tie together the Violin and Guitar classes presented below with a superclass, and make the Violin class unable to be subclassed. Use Java's abstract and final keywords where appropriate.

```
class Violin {
   int numStrings;
   void play() {
      System.out.println("mmm")
   }
}

class Guitar {
   int numStrings;
   void play() {
      System.out.println("twang")
   }
}
```

Exercise 11.9

Change the following class definition for Employee. Restrict access to the Employee id to be read-only. (You can use a combination of a keyword on this variable and a new method to achieve this.) In addition, outside of this package, id should be able to be accessed by only the Employee class and Employee subclasses.

Maintain an id counter internally in the class. Start the id counter at 1 for the first employee, and for each new employee add 1 to the counter. Any class should be able to create a new employee—even classes in other packages. Use the keywords private, protected, public, and static, as necessary.

```
class Employee {
   int id;
   Employee(int id) {
      this.id = id;
   }
}
```

Exercise 11.10

Here are a few questions and thought experiments about combinations of keywords. If you're not sure of the answers, write some code and try to compile it.

1. Can an abstract method be final?
2. Can an abstract method be static?
3. Can you define a public protected field?

Casting Classes

You can cast one object type to another type. If you cast down the hierarchy, you must cast the class type. If you cast up the hierarchy, you can assign an object to a superclass reference without casting. For example, imagine these three simple classes:

```
class Parent {
    public static void main(String[] args) {
        Derived1 d1 = new Derived1();
        Derived2 d2 = new Derived2();
        Parent p = new Parent();
        // we'll add code here. . .
    }
}

class Derived1 extends Parent{}

class Derived2 extends Parent{}
```

Let's replace the comment "we'll add code here" with some actual code. If we want to set d1 to p, that's no problem. All we need to do is write:

```
p = d1;
```

That's because we've cast up the hierarchy. All Derived1 objects are also of type Parent, so this assignment is perfectly legal.

TIP: Interestingly, this does not change the object type as far as invoking a method. The actual object type referenced by p is still of type Derived1. So, if Derived1 overrides a method in Parent, invoking that method using p (now pointing to a Derived1 object) will still invoke the version of that method in Derived1.

If, instead of

```
p = d1;
```

we wrote

```
d1 = p;
```

the code would not compile. This kind of cast is somewhat similar to trying to assign a float value to an int. You are attempting to assign a value with more detail to a type that knows less detail.

If we were dealing with float and int, we could cast the float to an int to make the compiler and runtime know that everything was okay and that we're aware of what we're doing. The same is true with classes—we can cast Parent to Derived1 and the code will compile.

```
d1 = (Derived1)p;
```

However, just because the compiler allows for the possibility that this is a legal cast, that does not mean that it actually is. Whether or not this is legal depends on what the object's type is at runtime. According to the code we've written, the object reference p refers to an instance of class Parent. Parent does not inherit from Derived1, so, at run-time, this code would throw a ClassCastException.

If, instead, we had created a new object and assigned it to p like this:

```
Parent p = new Derived1();
```

then this code:

```
d1= (Derived1)p;
```

would both compile and run successfully.

You can only cast up and down the hierarchy—for example, you cannot cast between two classes that are siblings. To illustrate this warning, you could not write:

```
d1 = d2;
```

or even

```
d1= (Derived1)d2;
```

because d1 and d2 are not in the same branch of the class hierarchy. The compiler would complain that this is an invalid cast.

Inner Classes

An inner class is a class defined within another class. For the exam, you'll need to know how to declare and use inner classes. We haven't covered inner classes in previous chapters, so we'll cover this now as the last item you'll need to know for the programmer exam.

In Java 1.1 and later, you can define classes inside other classes. If you define an inner class at the same level as the enclosing class' instance variables, the inner class can access those instance variables—no matter what their access control (even private)—just as a method can access the variables of the class it is defined in. If you define an inner class within a method, the inner class can access the enclosing class' instance variables and also the local variables and parameter for that method.

If you do reference local variables or parameters from an inner class, those variables or parameters must be declared as final to help guarantee data integrity. (A new feature in Java 1.1 is that parameters and local variables can now be declared final.)

Creating Inner Classes

Creating inner classes allows you to better organize your classes in tune with your program. For example, if a class is really only used by one other class, that class can be placed within the class that refers to it. In a sense, the first class owns the helper class.

Here's an example (you already saw this program in Chapter 11). This applet displays a new number every second. It displayed prime numbers in red and nonprimes in blue:

```java
import java.awt.*;
import java.applet.Applet;

public class Ex1 extends Applet {
    Color       color = Color.red;
    int         candidate = 3;
    PrimeThread prime;

    public void init() {
        prime = new PrimeThread(this);
        prime.start();
    }

    public void paint(Graphics g) {
        g.setColor(color);
        g.drawString(new Integer(candidate).toString(), 30, 40);
    }
}
```

```
class PrimeThread extends Thread {
    Ex1 target;

    PrimeThread (Ex1 target) {
        this.target = target;
    }

    public void run() {
        int candidate;
        for (candidate = 3; ; candidate++) {
            if (isPrime(candidate))
                target.color = Color.red;
            else
                target.color = Color.blue;

            target.candidate = candidate;
            target.repaint();

            try {
                sleep(1000);
            } catch (InterruptedException ie) {
            }
        }
    }

    public boolean isPrime(int number) {
        boolean isPrime = true;

        for (int i = 2; i < number - 1 && isPrime; i++) {
            if ((number % i) == 0)
                isPrime = false;
        }
        return isPrime;
    }
}
```

Let's take this applet and turn PrimeThread into an inner class. When we do this, we'll no longer have to keep tabs on the applet itself in the target variable. Now, PrimeThread, as an inner class, can directly reference its enclosing class' variables and methods:

```
import java.awt.*;
import java.applet.Applet;

public class Ex2 extends Applet {
    Color       color = Color.red;
    int         candidate = 3;

    public void init() {
        new PrimeThread().start();
    }
```

```
public void paint(Graphics g) {
    g.setColor(color);
    g.drawString(new Integer(candidate).toString(), 30, 40);
}

class PrimeThread extends Thread {

    public void run() {
        for ( ; ; candidate++) {
            if (isPrime(candidate))
                color = Color.red;
            else
                color = Color.blue;

            repaint();

            try {
                sleep(1000);
            } catch (InterruptedException ie) {
            }
        }
    }

    public boolean isPrime(int number) {
        boolean isPrime = true;

        for (int i = 2; i < number - 1 && isPrime; i++) {
            if ((number % i) == 0)
                isPrime = false;
        }
        return isPrime;
    }
}
}
```

We can go even further and move this class definition into the applet's init() method so that the new class is declared right before we create an instance of it, just as we might declare a variable right before its use:

```
import java.awt.*;
import java.applet.Applet;

public class Ex3 extends Applet {
    Color        color = Color.red;
    int          candidate = 3;

    public void init() {

        class PrimeThread extends Thread {

            public void run() {
```

```
            for ( ; ; candidate++) {
                if (isPrime(candidate))
                    color = Color.red;
                else
                    color = Color.blue;

                repaint();

                try {
                    sleep(1000);
                } catch (InterruptedException ie) {
                }
            }
        }

        public boolean isPrime(int number) {
            boolean isPrime = true;

            for (int i = 2; i < number - 1 && isPrime; i++) {
                if ( (number % i) == 0)
                    isPrime = false;
            }
            return isPrime;
        }
    }

    new PrimeThread().start();
}

public void paint(Graphics g) {
    g.setColor(color);
    g.drawString(new Integer(candidate).toString(), 30, 40);
}
}
```

Where you define your class is in part a matter of style. You should define your classes where they make the most sense in your design. If you'd like to refer to the current instance of the enclosing class, you can write:

```
EnclosingClassName.this
```

If you need to refer to the inner class using a fully qualified name, you can write:

```
EnclosingClassName.InnerClassName
```

Anonymous Classes

You can also define an *anonymous* class—a class without a name. What does this mean? If we were to rewrite the prime number applet to define PrimeNumber as an anonymous thread, we could rewrite the init() applet like this:

```
public void init() {
   Thread t = new Thread() {
       //The old PrimeThread definition goes here . . .
   };
   t.start();
}
```

As you can see, the new expression states that it is creating an instance of class Thread. Actually, it's creating a subclass of Thread that we have not named, although we have supplied a definition for this subclass.

Note also the ending semicolon for anonymous class. The anonymous class is defined like a statement, so it needs a semicolon at the end.

Anonymous classes cannot have constructors. Java invokes their superclass constructor implicitly.

Anonymous classes are great if you have a very simple class that's pretty much self-documenting because of the straightforward code and familiar context. This might not necessarily be the case with the PrimeThread class we were working with. In that case, an inner class with a name might be a better choice. In Java, anonymous classes are often used to perform simple event handling for user interfaces.

Static Inner Classes

If your inner class is not defined as static, you can only create new instances of this class from a nonstatic method. Static inner classes don't receive an implicit OuterClass.this pointer and this is why they can be instantiated from a static method in an enclosing class. Here's an example of a static inner class:

```
public class Outer {
   private StaticInner a = new StaticInner();
   private NonStaticInner b = new NonStaticInner();

   static class StaticInner {
      public String getName() {
         return "StaticInner";
      }
      public String getOuterName() {
         // this line will not compile since class is static
         //return Outer.this.getName();
         return "I can't do that";
      }
   }
   class NonStaticInner {
      public String getName() {
         return "NonStaticInner";
      }
      public String getOuterName() {
```

```
            return Outer.this.getName();
        }
    }

    public String getName() {
        return "Outer";
    }

    public static void main(String args[])  {
        Outer o = new Outer();
        System.out.println(o.getName());
        System.out.println(o.a.getName());
        System.out.println(o.b.getName());
        System.out.println(o.a.getOuterName());
        System.out.println(o.b.getOuterName());
    }
}
```

Exercise 11.11

In this exercise, you'll update an applet use inner classes. The applet code is:

```
import java.awt.*;
import java.awt.event.*;
import java.applet.Applet;

public class ClickApplet extends Applet {
    public void init() {
        Button b = new Button("Click me!");
        b.addMouseListener(new OurClickHandler());
        add(b);
    }
}

class OurClickHandler implements MouseListener {
    public void mouseClicked(MouseEvent e) {
        System.out.println("button clicked");
    }

    // Left-over interface methods.
    public void mousePressed(MouseEvent e) { }
    public void mouseReleased(MouseEvent e) { }
    public void mouseEntered(MouseEvent e) { }
    public void mouseExited(MouseEvent e) { }
}
```

Turn OurClickHandler into an inner class.

Then make it an inner class defined within the init() method.

Then make it an anonymous class.

One question you may have is, how do you implement an interface as an anony-mous class? You cannot use implements with an anonymous class. Try your solution, and if you have questions check out the answer.

Answers to the Exercises

Exercise I I.I

This is a classic example of knowing when to use 'is a' and 'has a.' The confusion comes with the fact that points, circles, and squares all have a position on the screen. Here is one way to do the hierarchy, where it looks as though you have pushed as much information up the hierarchy as possible.

Figure 11-4 shows one way to do the hierarchy, where it looks as though you have pushed as much information up the hierarchy as possible.

The problem here is not that 2D shapes such as circles and squares don't have a screen position—they do. The problem is that 2D shapes are not special kinds of points as depicted in Figure 11-4. In other words, points are not well represented as circles with a zero radius. This does not feel right or represent the situation as you think of it in the real world. Instead, it might make more sense to have the 2DShape class refer to a Point instance as depicted in Figure 11-5. In other words, a 2DShape 'has a' point—a position on the screen—but a 2DShape 'is not a' point.

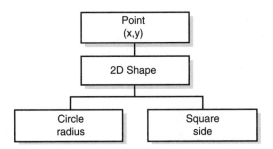

Figure II-4   An awkward class hierarchy—do you agree?

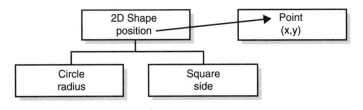

Figure II-5   A better class hierarchy

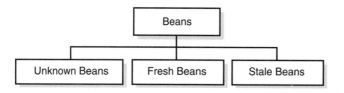

Figure 11-6 A beans class hierarchy—will this work well with our inventory systems?

Exercise 11.2

There are many possible answers to this question. One possible class hierarchy for coffee beans is shown in Figure 11-6.

Before this discussion, you might have been tempted to say the shipment can be represented by an instance of class Beans. But when it is determined to be stale or fresh, what class would you use then? The instructions to this exercise state that the beans have some different characteristics and behavior depending on whether they're unexamined, fresh, or stale. You could simply keep a flag in the class itself that indicates state, but then you'd have to write an if-else or switch-case statement in the class to perform the correct behavior depending on whether the beans have been examined or not, and if they have been, what the outcome was. Using control flow to determine something that can be done using subclasses is a strong indication that you're not taking full advantage of object-oriented programming and that it's time for some reworking of your class hierarchy.

The hierarchy presented above will work fine, but in conjunction with another class. One way to make this work, for example, is to define a class named Shipment. The Shipment class can delegate its responses to the method calls that depend on its state to a Beans object reference. At first, the shipment is assigned an object of type UnknownBeans. Once the Shipment is tasted, its Beans object reference can be assigned a new object, of type FreshBeans or StaleBeans, as appropriate.

Now, the relationship is that Shipment 'has a' taste, and that taste is either unknown, fresh, or stale.

Exercise 11.3

```
File Shape.java
abstract class Shape {
   abstract double perimeter();
}
File Square.java
abstract class TwoDShape extends Shape {
}
```

```
class Square extends TwoDShape {
   double side;
   double perimeter() {
      return 4 * side;
   }
}
```

Exercise 11.4

All you have to do to stop programmers from making subclasses of a class is declare it using the final keyword. For the Square class, you could write:

```
final class Square extends TwoDShape {
   double side;
   double perimeter() {
      return 4 * side;
   }
}
```

Exercise 11.5

What's wrong here is that the static method attempts to invoke the nonstatic method named findAvg(). Since there is no instance of Avg to use to invoke findAvg(), this is a compile-time error. To fix this, we could either make findAvg() static or create an instance of Avg and use that when invoking findAvg().

Exercise 11.6

The protected keyword is commonly defined as restricting access of a member to the same class or to a subclass of that class. However, protected is not as straightforward as that. Actually, within a package, any class can access any other class's protected field. So, all objects in this example—d, e, p1, p2, and f—can access any protected fields in Tree.

Exercise 11.7

Outside of the package a class is defined in, only subclasses can access a superclass's protected field. So: d, e, p1, and p2 could access the protected field; f could not.

If you have an object reference, say to object e, can the object p1 access e's protected field defined in Tree? The answer is yes. However, could e access p1's protected field defined in Tree? Here, the answer is no. The reason is that the object accessing the protected field must be of at least the type of the object reference. p1, a Pine, is of type e, an Evergreen, so it can access e's protected field. However, the reverse is not true. An Evergreen is not (always) a Pine, so e cannot access p1's protected field.

Similarly, p1 could not access d's protected field, since Pine does not inherit from Deciduous.

Exercise 11.8

```
abstract class StringedInstrument {
   int numStrings;
   abstract void play();
}

final class Violin extends StringedInstrument {
   void play() {
      System.out.println("mmm");
   }
}
class Guitar extends StringedInstrument {
   void play() {
      System.out.println("twang");
   }
}
```

Exercise 11.9

Here is one possible answer to this exercise:

```
public class Employee {
   private static int next_id = 1;
   private int id;
   public Employee() {
      id = next_id++;
   }
   protected int getId() {
      return id;
   }
}
```

Exercise 11.10

1. Can an abstract method be final? No. An abstract method must be overridden by a subclass, but final methods cannot be overridden.

2. Can an abstract method be static? No. You cannot override a static method (think about it—there is no this or super, because there is no current object responding to a static method, so there's no way to invoke the superclass's behavior). Because you cannot override a static method, a static method cannot be abstract.

3. Can you define a public protected field? No. Only one access control keyword can be used at a time. (There is an oversight in earlier versions of Java where protected private was allowed, but it no longer is.)

By the way, you cannot define an abstract method to be native, either.

Exercise 11.11

Here's the original program, now with an inner class:

```
import java.awt.*;
import java.awt.event.*;
import java.applet.Applet;

public class ClickApplet1 extends Applet {
    public void init() {
        Button b = new Button("Click me!");
        b.addMouseListener(new OurClickHandler());
        add(b);
    }

    class OurClickHandler implements MouseListener {
        public void mouseClicked(MouseEvent e) {
            System.out.println("button clicked");
        }

        // Left-over interface methods.
        public void mousePressed(MouseEvent e) { }
        public void mouseReleased(MouseEvent e) { }
        public void mouseEntered(MouseEvent e) { }
        public void mouseExited(MouseEvent e) { }
    }
}
```

And here's how we can place the class within the init() method itself, bringing it very close to where the instance is used:

```
import java.awt.*;
import java.awt.event.*;
import java.applet.Applet;

public class ClickApplet2 extends Applet {
    public void init() {
        Button b = new Button("Click me!");
        class OurClickHandler implements MouseListener {
            public void mouseClicked(MouseEvent e) {
                System.out.println("button clicked");
            }

            // Left-over interface methods.
            public void mousePressed(MouseEvent e) { }
            public void mouseReleased(MouseEvent e) { }
            public void mouseEntered(MouseEvent e) { }
            public void mouseExited(MouseEvent e) { }
        }

        b.addMouseListener(new OurClickHandler());
        add(b);
    }
}
```

As for the anonymous interface implementation, you just write it as if it were an instance of an interface—of course, this is not possible. What's really happening is that Java extends class Object and implements the interface. Here's a solution:

```
import java.awt.*;
import java.awt.event.*;
import java.applet.Applet;

public class ClickApplet3 extends Applet {
    public void init() {
        Button b = new Button("Click me!");
        b.addMouseListener(myClickHandler());
        add(b);
    }

    private MouseListener myClickHandler() {

        return new MouseListener() {

            public void mouseClicked(MouseEvent e) {
                System.out.println("button clicked");
            }

            // Left-over interface methods.
            public void mousePressed(MouseEvent e) { }
            public void mouseReleased(MouseEvent e) { }
            public void mouseEntered(MouseEvent e) { }
            public void mouseExited(MouseEvent e) { }
        };
    }
}
```

Similarly, it's easy to rewrite the first program in Chapter 15 (Scribble.java) so that the adapter classes are inner classes or even anonymous classes.

You could also extend MouseAdapter here; the returned anonymous class would start out:

```
return new MouseAdapter() { . . . }
```

Review Questions

1. What happens if you try to compile code that looks like this:

```
class MyString extends String {
}
```

a. The code compiles successfully.
b. The code does not compile because you have not defined a main() method.

    c. The code does not compile because String is abstract.

    d. The code does not compile because String is final.

2. If you have this class definition:

```
abstract class Shape{
   abstract void draw();
}
```

    what happens if you try to compile the following class definition?

```
class Square extends Shape{
}
```

    a. Everything compiles succesfully.

    b. Shape compiles, but Square does not compile.

    c. Square compiles, but Shape does not compile.

    d. Neither Shape nor Square compiles.

3. What happens if you try to compile the Shape and Square class from Question 2 if the Shape class is declared like this:

```
abstract class Shape {
}
```

    a. Everything compiles fine.

    b. Shape compiles, but Square does not compile.

    c. Square compiles, but Shape does not compile.

    d. Neither Shape nor Square compiles.

4. The following class definitions:

```
class Bridge {
   Road road;
}

class Road {
   String name;
}
```

    represent:

    a. An 'is a' relationship

    b. A 'has a' relationship

    c. Both

    d. Neither

5. What keyword can you give a class so that classes outside of the package this class is defined in cannot access the class?

a. Don't give the class a keyword at all

b. private

c. final

d. protected

6. To restrict access to a static member to the class itself:

a. Use the final keyword

b. Use the private keyword

c. Do not use a keyword at all for the member

d. A static member cannot be restricted in this way

7. Which of the following statements is false?

a. An instance method can be both protected and abstract.

b. A static variable can also be final.

c. A static method can also be protected.

d. A static method can also be abstract.

8. By default—that is, without keywords—all classes can access all members except for those defined:

a. Using the final keyword

b. Using the abstract keyword

c. In another package

d. In the same package

9. Static classes receive an implicit OuterClass.this pointer.

a. True

b. False

10. How can you rewrite the following two classes so that the second becomes an inner class of the first? (The resulting program should still work like the original.)

```
class First {
    public static void main(String[] args) {
        new Second().sayGoodnightGracy();
    }
}
class Second extends First {
    void sayGoodnightGracy() {
        System.out.println("Goodnight, Gracy");
    }
}
```

a.

```
class First {
    public static void main(String[] args) {
        System.out.println("Goodnight, Gracy");
    }
}
```

b.

```
class First {
    public static void main(String[] args) {
        new First() {
            void sayGoodnightGracy() {
                System.out.println("Goodnight, Gracy");
            }
        };
    }
}
```

c.

```
class First {
    public static void main(String[] args) {
        new Second().sayGoodnightGracy();
    }
    class Second extends First {
        void sayGoodnightGracy() {
            System.out.println("Goodnight, Gracy");
        }
    }
}
```

d.

```
class First {
    public static void main(String[] args) {
        new First().test();
    }
    void test() {
        new Second().sayGoodnightGracy();
    }

    class Second extends First {
        void sayGoodnightGracy() {
            System.out.println("Goodnight, Gracy");
        }
    }
}
```

11. Java invokes the superclass constructor for anonymous classes implicitly.
    a. True
    b. False

Answers to Review Questions

1. **d.** String is defined using the keyword final. Therefore, it cannot be subclassed, and the compiler will tell you that extending String is not allowed.

2. **b.** Square will not compile because it should either be declared as abstract, or it should implement the draw() method.

3. **a.** A subclass of an abstract class that does not declare any abstract methods is not abstract by default.

4. **b.** A Bridge 'has a' Road, represented by the instance variable road inside Bridge. Neither class extends another class (except for class Object, so in that sense, it does represent an 'is a' relationship).

5. **a.** The default access control for a class—that is, defining a class without a keyword—restricts other classes in other packages from accessing the class.

6. **b.** You can restrict access to a member by using the private keyword, regardless of whether that member is static or nonstatic.

7. **d.** A static method cannot be overridden: therefore, it cannot be abstract.

8. **c.** All classes can access all members, by default, except for those defined in another package. To access classes and members in another package, those classes must be declared using the public keyword, and the members must also be declared public (or protected, if the accessing class is a subclass of the class defining the protected member).

9. **b.** False. Static inner classes don't receive an implicit OuterClass.this pointer.

10. **d.** Only this program defines an inner class that keeps the output of the original code. Answer c does not work because you cannot define an inner class within a static method if the inner class is not also declared as static.

11. **a.** True. Anonymous classes cannot have constructors. Java invokes their superclass constructor implicitly.

CHAPTER 12

Packages, Inheritance, and Interfaces

Objectives for This Chapter

- Specify the difference between the default (unnamed) package and named packages.
- Declare new packages and place them in the appropriate directory locations.
- Define the usage of the CLASSPATH environment variable.
- Identify the proper order for package and import statements in class files.
- Understand access control for packages.
- Reuse class names and share classes between applications using packages.
- Understand the importance of inheritance.
- Declare and use interfaces.
- Clone Objects by implementing the Cloneable interface.
- Define and use static initializers.

Packages, inheritance, and interfaces are subjects that a Java programmer must understand very well to be successful on the exam and on the job. While previous chapters have looked at these subjects briefly, we haven't taken a close look at these subjects until now.

Packages

Packages are containers for classes and interfaces that are used to organize the name-space into discrete hierarchies. In previous chapters, we primarily worked with classes in the JDK, which for the most part are grouped in the core package called java. You can also create your own packages to group classes. The key is that each name for a class must be unique within a package.

Declaring a Package

Unless you state otherwise, Java uses the current path and generally assumes that your compiled code is in the current directory when you run a Java program. To tell Java where to look for class files that are not defined in the JDK, you use package statements. Package statements follow the form:

```
package PackageName
```

If you plan to create applications in Java and want the classes and objects you create to follow a package-naming structure other than the default, you must include a pack-age statement in the source code. New packages must follow Java's hierarchical naming structure. This means that levels within the package naming structure should be sepa-rated from the package names in other levels by a period. This is a sample package state-ment for a multilevel package namespace:

```
package MyPackages.PackageSubName;
```

All classes belong to a package even if not explicitly declared. As usual in Java, what is not explicitly declared automatically gets default values. In this case, there is a default unnamed package to which all such packages belong. The package does not have an explicit name, and it is not possible for other packages to reference an unnamed pack-age. Therefore, no other package is able to reference most of the examples in this book as they are now. It is a good idea to place all nontrivial classes into packages.

Classes can only belong to one package and as such, class files can only have one package declaration. The package's declaration must occur as the first nonblank line in a Java source file (not including lines containing comments). Here is an example:

```
package technology;
class Computer {
    //body of class Computer
}
```

In this example the package name is technology. The class Computer is now consid-ered a part of this package. Including other classes in package technology is easy: Simply place an identical package line at the top of those source files, also. Because every class is generally placed in its own source file, every source file that contains classes for a particular package must include this line.

NOTE: The Java compiler only requires classes that are declared public to be put in a separate source file. Nonpublic classes can be put in the same source file. Although it is good programming practice to put each of these in its own source file, one package statement at the top of a file will apply to all classes declared in that file.

As mentioned previously, Java also supports the concept of package hierarchy. This is similar to the directory hierarchy found in many operating systems. This is done by specifying multiple names in a package statement separated by a period. In the following code, class Computer belongs to the package technology that is defined in the top-level package com:

```
package com.technology;
class Computer {
    //body of class Computer
}
```

This allows grouping of related classes into a package and then grouping related packages into a larger package. You can reference a member of another package by prepending the package name to the class name, such as:

```
com.technology.Computer {
    //body of class Computer
}
```

or

```
com.technology.Computer.promptForName();
```

In the second example, you make a call to a static method promptForName in class Computer. The class is stored in the com.technology package.

The Java interpreter requires that the class files be physically located in a directory hierarchy that matches the package hierarchy. This means the Computer.class file would need to be stored in com/technology/Computer.class, com\technology\Computer.class or com:technology:Computer.class on your UNIX, Windows or Mac filesystem respectively.

Take care when naming packages. If you rename a package, you must also rename the directory in which the class files are stored.

The CLASSPATH Environmental Variable

The Java interpreter must find all the referenced classes when running a Java application. By default Java looks in the base directory of the Java installation for the necessary JDK classes and the current directory for classes you've created. It is usually better when developing code to put your own classes someplace else.

An environmental variable named CLASSPATH is used to tell Java where the root of your package hierarchies are located. CLASSPATH contains a list of directories that Java will search for classes. The structure, syntax, and order of the listed directories are extremely important.

The structure within the named directories must match that of your packages. For example, if the root of your hierarchy is C:\java and you have a package called com.technology, Java will expect classes related to this package to be stored in the C:\java\com\technology directory.

The syntax of the directory list will vary according to the operating system being used. On UNIX systems CLASSPATH contains a colon-separated list of directory names. Under Windows, the list is separated by semicolon (;). The following is a CLASSPATH statement for a Windows system:

```
CLASSPATH=C:\java;C:\data\java
```

This tells the Java interpreter to look in the C:\java and C:\data\java directories for classes that are defined in packages you've created.

The order of the directory list represents the order in which Java searches for classes. In the previous example, the Java interpreter will search C:\java first. If a matching class name is found, Java will not search any further. If a matching class name isn't found, Java will search C:\data\java for the class.

When you set the CLASSPATH variable on your development system, you'll usually want to include the current working directory as well. Otherwise, you'll get an error when you try to compile programs that use classes defined in the current directory. On Windows, you add the current working directory to the CLASSPATH as follows:

```
CLASSPATH=.;C:\java;C:\data\java
```

Notice we've added .; to the beginning of the CLASSPATH. The . represents the current working directory.

Import Statements

In Java, core functions are in the java.lang package and are imported automatically. To access packages, classes, and objects that are not declared in this package library, you must explicitly import them using import statements. Import statements help to define and resolve the current namespace. They do this by allowing an imported package to be resolved using the name of its class component. If you do not use import statements, you must specify the full package reference before each class name in your source code.

Import statements should appear before other declarations in the source code and generally follow package statements if they are used. The idea behind import statements is to help Java find the appropriate methods and to avoid namespace conflicts. Keep in mind that if a class with the same name exists with two packages that you import, you will get a compile time error unless you specifically name the package as well as the class.

Java provides two ways to import classes. You can import only the class type you need by specifying an exact class in the import statement. In the following example, only the FileReader class is imported:

```
import java.io.FileReader;
```

To import multiple classes from a package, you use an asterisk as the class specifier, such as:

```
import java.io.*;
```

An asterisk in the last element of the import statement allows Java to import classes as necessary. This lets you dynamically add public types to the namespace.

While both techniques allow you to resolve the class FileReader to java.io.FileReader, the first method is much more efficient and can decrease compile time. It also eases the software maintenance burden, because programmers know the exact location of the class that is being imported. The reason for this is that Java can explicitly find the class to use rather than importing whole packages. Importing whole packages can increase the compilation time. However, it has no effect on the run time performance of the program.

Any place you can use a class name, you can use a fully qualified name. For example, when referencing the FileReader class, you could specify:

```
import java.io.FileReader;
class MyFileReader extends FileReader {
}
```

or you could specify:

```
class MyFileReader extends java.io.FileReader {
}
```

Package Naming Conventions

Packages can be named anything that follows the standard Java naming scheme. By convention, however, package names begin with lowercase letters to make it simpler to distinguish package names from class names when looking at an explicit reference to a class. This is why class names are, by convention, begun with an uppercase letter. For example, when using the following convention, it is immediately obvious that technology and com are package names and Computer is a class name. Anything following the class name is a member of that class:

```
technology.com.Computer.promptForName();
```

Java follows this convention for the Java internals and API as well. The System.out.println() method that has been used follows this convention. The package name is not explicitly declared because java.lang is always imported implicitly. System is the class name from package java.lang and it is capitalized. The full name of the method is:

```
java.lang.System.out.println();
```

Every package name must be unique to make the best use of packages. Naming conflicts that will cause runtime errors will occur if duplicate package names are present. It is not difficult to keep package names unique if a single individual or small group does the programming. Large-group projects must iron out package name conventions early in the project to avoid chaos.

Sun developed a convention that ensures package name uniqueness using a variation on domain names, which are guaranteed to be unique. This naming convention uses the domain name in a reverse manner. Following the naming convention, domain mycompany.com would prefix all package names with com.mycompany. This neatly solves the naming problem and generates a tree structure for all Java-class libraries.

Using Packages

As you know from the previous discussion, packages help you associate classes with a particular function. For example, the Abstract Window Toolkit package (java.awt) is used for building user interfaces. As another example, the Input/Output package (java.io) is used for reading from and writing to streams. The classes in a package may or may not be related in a class hierarchy. They are, however, related in purpose.

Packages have three effects on your object-oriented design. Packages

- enable you to define stricter access control
- make it easier to reuse common names
- collect classes so that they can be shared more easily between applications

Packages enable you to fine-tune how and when others can make use of your classes. By default, all of your classes can reference other classes in the same package, and all methods can invoke other methods and access variables in the same package. The keywords public and protected do not affect access between classes and members in the same package. The keyword private, however, does restrict access to the class that defines the private member.

With a package, you can fully qualify a class name so that Java knows where to look for it. This enables you to use the same class name as one defined in another package. That is, fully qualifying a class name enables you to reuse common class names, since you can specify where Java should look to find where these classes are defined.

For example, perhaps you've decided to use the class names Point and Rectangle in your own package called COM.Bluehorse.shapes. However, you also want to use the java.awt classes called Point and Rectangle. One way to proceed is to import the AWT classes, using the import statement at the top of your file:

```
import java.awt.Point;
import java.awt.Rectangle;
```

Whenever you want to refer to Java's Point or Rectangle class, you can do so directly, as in:

```
new Point(10, 10);
```

You can reference your own classes by fully qualifying them. For example, you could create a new instance of your own Point class like this:

```
new COM.Bluehorse.shapes.Point(10, 10);
```

Since classes within the same package are placed in their own directory, you can easily refer to the entire collection of classes and use them in another application, without worrying about whether you are importing extra baggage that belongs to application-specific classes. For example, you can import all the classes in a package named shapes by writing:

```
import COM.Bluehorse.shapes.*;
```

When you do this, you know that you are only getting the shapes classes—as opposed to, say, the shapes classes plus some application-specific classes. Only those classes in the shapes package are in the shapes directory.

> **TIP:** When placing a collection of classes into its own package, you should strip out the application-dependent aspects of these classes. In a good design, a package will contain application-independent classes that you can reuse in any number of applications.

Exercise 12.1

Given a package named COM.Company.Utilities, how would you import a class in this package named Calculator? What would the structure be for the directories and subdirectories that contained the Calculator class?

Exercise 12.2

Suppose you had a Circle class defined like this:

```
class Circle {
    double radius;
    double area() {
        return radius * radius * Math.PI;
    }
}
```

Place this class into a separate package. Add the appropriate access control keywords so that you can access this class from your default package and create a new Circle instance, assign your new instance a radius value, and display its area.

Exercise 12.3

What will happen when you first compile the file named Tree.java, and then compile the file named Forest.java, as presented below? If there is a problem, fix the code.

```
File Tree.java

package Flora;

public class Tree {
    protected int age;
}

File Forest.java
```

```
import Flora.Tree;

public class Forest {
   public static void main(String[] args) {
      Tree t = new Tree();
      System.out.println("The tree's age is " + t.age);
   }
}
```

Exercise 12.4

What will happen when you first compile the file named Tree.java, and then compile the file named Forest.java, as presented below? If there is a problem, fix the code.

```
File Tree.java

public class Tree {
   protected int age;
}

File Forest.java

public class Forest {
   public static void main(String[] args) {
      Tree t = new Tree():
      System.out.println("The tree's age is " + t.age);
   }
}
```

Creating a Package

To create a package, name the package at the top of the source file containing the package classes. Use the keyword package, followed by the name of the package.

A simple example of creating a package is:

```
package shapes;
//class definitions
```

The package keyword tells the Java compiler to assign the classes in that file to the named package—in this case, shapes.

TIP: You can have more than one file whose classes belong in the same package.

Package names determine a directory structure for compiled classes. For example, let's say we have two source files, Draw.java and Shapes.java. Draw.java contains an Applet subclass named Draw. Shapes.java defines two classes, Square and Circle. We assign the Square and Circle classes to the shapes package by using the package keyword. Figure 12-1 shows how Java would require the classes to be organized.

TIP: You can specify more levels of organization in your package by using subdirectories.

You specify each subdirectory using a dot (.), as in:

```
package Bluehorse.shapes;
```

If used with the classes we just discussed, this would require the directory structure shown in Figure 12-2.

This would allow us to collect other packages under the top-level directory Bluehorse. For example, the Bluehorse directory could have the subdirectories brushes, pens, and papers, in addition to shapes. The Java class libraries are organized using subdirectories, with the lang, util, io, and other packages organized under the java directory.

TIP: The Sun Java Development Kit and other environments contain options to automatically place your package classes into the correct directories and subdirectories when they are compiled. With the JDK, you can use the -d option when you compile.

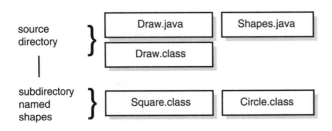

Figure 12-1 Organization of classes and packages in the file system

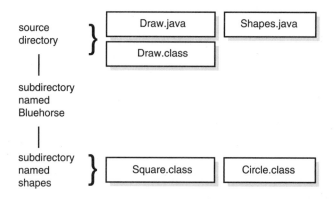

Figure 12-2   Arrangement of classes and packages in the file system, with subdirectories

   EXAM TIP: To use a class in a package other than the one in which it is defined, you must first import that class. You can import a class using the import statement, specifying the package the class is placed in.

To import a class named Circle in a package named Bluehorse.shapes, you can write:

```
import Bluehorse.shapes.Circle;
```

You can also import all of the classes in a package by using wildcard notation. Here's an example of importing all the classes in Bluehorse.shapes:

```
import Bluehorse.shapes.*;
```

And as you saw, you can also fully qualify the class name, so that Java knows where to find it when you reference it:

```
class SpecialCircle extends Bluehorse.shapes.Circle {
}
```

If you do not define a package for a source file, you can consider the classes in that file to be in the same "default" package.

Ordering of a Java Source File

You need to be able to distinguish legal and illegal orderings of top-level Java source file elements, including package declarations, import statements, public class declarations, and nonpublic class declarations. There are three basic entries that can be placed within a Java source file:

- A package definition.

- Any number of import statements.

- Any public and nonpublic classes and interfaces.

If you include a package declaration, this must be the first thing to appear in a source file. Any import statements come next; you can have as many import statements as you'd like. After the package and import statements, you can define any classes and interfaces that you'd like.

TIP: In Sun's JDK, you can only define one public class. What's more, if you do define a public class, the source file must be named after the class. For example, if you are defining a public class named Earth, then the source file it is defined in must be named Earth.java.

Other Java development environments do not have this restriction of one public class per source file.

Exercise 12.5

What's wrong with this class file?

```
import java.util.*;
import java.awt.*;
package myUtils;

public class Util {
    public double avg(double a, double b) {
        return (a + b)/2;
    }
}
```

Try compiling this file if you can't find the answer.

Exercise 12.6

Here is a small application to draw a square wherever the user clicks the mouse. When the user clicks in the applet, the applet detects this event and creates a new Square object, adding it to a Vector object. In the applet's paint() method, we enumerate through the Squares in the Vector and draw each one.

If you're not very familiar with graphical applications yet, don't worry too much about this exercise. If you feel comfortable with them, however, look over the code and then see if you can answer the questions that follow.

File Shape.Java

```
package COM.Bluehorse.Shapes;

import java.awt.*;

public abstract class Shape {
    Point loc;
    public abstract void draw(Graphics g);
}
```

File Square.java

```
package COM.Bluehorse.Shapes;

import java.awt.*;

public class Square extends Shape {
    public Square(int x, int y) {
        loc = new Point(x, y);
    }
    public void draw(Graphics g) {
        g.drawRect(loc.x, loc.y, 20, 20);
    }
}
```

File DrawApplet.java

```
import java.awt.*;
import java.awt.event.*;
import java.applet.Applet;
import COM.Bluehorse.Shapes.*;
import java.util.*;

public class DrawApplet extends Applet {

    Vector shapes = new Vector();

    public void init() {
        addMouseListener(new MouseHandler(this));
    }

    public void paint(Graphics g) {
        Square s;
        for (Enumeration e = shapes.elements(); e.hasMoreElements(); ) {
            s = (Square)e.nextElement();
            s.draw(this.getGraphics());
        }
```

```
        }
    }

    class MouseHandler extends MouseAdapter {

        DrawApplet applet;

        public MouseHandler(DrawApplet a) {
            applet = a;
        }

        public void mouseReleased(MouseEvent e) {
            applet.shapes.addElement(new Square(e.getX(), e.getY()));
            applet.repaint();
        }
    }
```

Here are some questions regarding access between classes in packages:

Is it possible for the mouseUp() method in DrawApplet to access the Square's loc field?

Is it possible for mouseUp() to access the Square's draw() method?

Inheritance

One of the more powerful concepts in an object-oriented language is inheritance. *Inheritance* is a methodology in which the code developed for one use can be extended for use elsewhere without having to make an actual copy of the code.

In Java, inheritance is done by creating new classes that are extensions of other classes. The new class is known as a subclass. The original class is known as a superclass. The subclass has all the attributes of the superclass, and in addition has attributes that it defines itself. A class can have only one superclass. This is known as *single inheritance*. However, a superclass can have multiple subclasses.

Declaring Inheritance

Declaring inheritance in classes is simply an extension of the class declarations rules discussed in the previous chapter. This is done with the extends keyword:

```
class ClassName extends AnotherClass {
    //body of class
}
```

The extends keyword immediately follows the class name. It is followed by the name of the superclass from which this class will inherit characteristics. There can be only one class name following the extends keyword.

As you may recall applets are declared as subclasses of java.applet.Applet. This declaration provides an applet with all its inherent characteristics. You don't need to code these characteristics because they are inherited from the superclass.

Let's use the apartment building analogy to demonstrate inheritance, starting with the class building:

```
public class Bldg {
    int numStories, totalSquareFeet, lotSize;
    String heatType;
    public String getHeatType () {
        return(heatType);
    }
}
```

In this simplistic version of a building class, variables for holding numStories, totalSquareFeet, and lotSize, and a method for obtaining the type of heating have all been declared. These are the characteristics that all buildings created using this class share.

Since we've created a basic building class, we can extend it to define more specific types of buildings. Here's an example class for an apartment building:

```
public class AptBldg extends Bldg {
    int numApts;
    Apt apt[];
    public int findVacatApt () {
        int i;
        for (i = 0; i < numApts; i++) {
            if (apt[i].isVacant() == true) {
                return(i);
            }
        }
        return(-1);
    }
}

public class Apt {
    boolean vacant;
    int aptNumber;
    public boolean isVacant() {
        return(vacant);
    }
}
```

In this example, two classes are declared: an apartment building class (AptBldg) and an apartment class (Apt). The apartment building class is declared using extends Bldg, which declares that AptBldg is a subclass of Bldg. By doing this, AptBldg inherits all the variables and methods declared in Bldg. AptBldg extends Bldg by declaring a variable for number of apartments and an array containing apartment objects. There is also a method that returns the first vacant apartment in the array of apartments.

The Apt class is a brand new class and does not extend any other classes. It declares two variables, vacant and aptNumber, as well as method isVacant, which can be used to determine if the apartment is vacant. The next step is to use the classes that are now declared.

Using Inheritance

It is now time to create a program for apartment managers. This program must be able to do things such as find an empty apartment. The classes declared previously are used in a new Java program that can do this:

```
public AptManager {
    public findEmptyApt (AptBldg aptBldg) {
        int AptNum;
        String heatType;
        AptNum = aptBldg.findVacantApt();
        if (AptNum > 0) {
            heatType = aptBldg.getHeatType();
            System.out.println("Apartment " + AptNum + "is available
for rent");
            System.out.println("Type of heat is" + heatType);
        }
    }
}
```

This example creates a method for finding an empty apartment. The method expects to be passed an apartment building object as an argument. The method then calls the findVacantApt method in the aptBldg object to locate a vacant apartment. If one is found, a call to the method getHeatType is made to determine the type of heat in the building. Both of these pieces of information are then printed out.

Notice that although findVacantApt is explicitly declared in AptBldg, the getHeat-Type method is not. It is instead declared in the Bldg class. Because AptBldg is declared a subclass of Bldg, it automatically inherits all of Bldg's methods, including getHeat-Type. By using inheritance we have saved the effort of having to recode the method for determining the heat type. If other subclasses of Bldg, such as school or office, were declared, they would also inherit this same method.

Another important characteristic of Java is that it avoids the "fragile superclass" problem of C++. With C++, a recompile of all subclasses must occur every time an upper level class is changed. Because Java is an interpreted language, no such recompile needs to take place. All superclass characteristics are passed down through inheritance. This is a great improvement over C++.

Interfaces

The need for an interface arose because Java only has single inheritance of implementation. This means that every class has exactly one superclass. If you want to inherit behavior from two classes, you just can't do it. To overcome this limitation, Java uses interfaces to bring in functionality from other classes.

Using Interfaces

An interface defines a set of abstract methods and class constants. In other words, as its name implies, an interface defines an interface, not an implementation. The implementation of an interface—that is, the behavior for the methods—is left to the class implementing the interface.

To understand why interfaces are used in Java, you must understand why Java uses single inheritance rather than multiple inheritance, and the key reason for using single inheritance is purely to eliminate complications that can arise when using multiple inheritance. For example, imagine this class situation, shown in Figure 12-3, that arises in languages that allow enable multiple inheritance.

If we invoke d's exam() method, and exam() invokes super.exam(), which method gets executed next—c's or b's? Maybe each gets executed once? What if each of these exam() methods invoked its super.exam() method—would that mean that a's exam() method gets executed twice?

In Java, this confusion is not possible, since a class can only have one superclass.

Even though multiple inheritance of implementation is not allowed, a design based on multiple inheritance can be very useful. For example, imagine you are designing a forms package. You would like the user to drag and drop TextField, Checkbox, and Choice objects onto a form. You would like to identify your subclasses of these java.awt

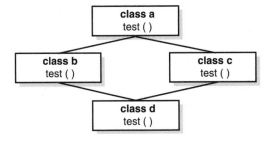

Figure 12-3   The multiple inheritance diamond

classes as being FormElements. In a multiple inheritance environment, you could design your classes like those in Figure 12-4.

In this design, your own form objects inherit behavior from FormElement. In Java, even though you cannot pass an implementation to a subclass of another class, you can still pass an interface specification to that class. The way you do that is by defining FormElement to be an interface. FormElement can still define a method, but instead of the java.awt subclasses inheriting an implementation, they only inherit a method signature. It is up to these subclasses to provide their own behavior for any methods defined by the interface. Figure 12-5 gives a sense of this relationship.

Defining Interfaces

You define an interface similar to a class that defines only abstract methods and class constants. However, you do not have to use the abstract keyword to define these things, since an interface assigns this keyword by default.

Here's an example of a FormElement interface:

```
public interface FormElement {
    public int TEXT = 1;
    public int CHOICE = 2;
    public boolean mustAnswer();
    public String getResponse();
}
```

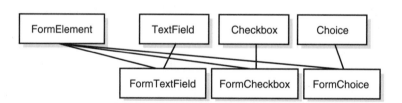

Figure 12-4 A form builder application design using multiple inheritance (You cannot do this in Java.)

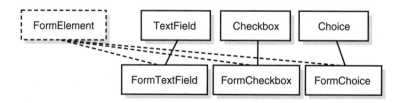

Figure 12-5 Inheriting an interface only

This interface defines two class constants, TEXT and CHOICE. It also defines two abstract methods, mustAnswer() and getResponse().

Here is how you might implement an interface in the FormTextField class.

```
public class FormTextField extends java.awt.TextField
    implements FormElement {

    public boolean mustAnswer() {
        return true;
    }
    public String getResponse() {
        return getText();
    }
}
```

Methods declared in an interface are implicitly abstract, which is why they are defined using a semicolon rather than a code block. Methods in an interface are also implicitly public. You do not need to declare them as either abstract or public. In fact, you are discouraged from doing so according to the JDK. With this in mind, we can rewrite the previous interface definition as:

```
public interface FormElement {
    public int TEXT = 1;
    public int CHOICE = 2;
    boolean mustAnswer();
    String getResponse();
}
```

Methods declared in an interface must not be declared as static or final. Static and final methods cannot be abstract. Additionally, methods declared in an interface must not be declared as strictfp, native, or synchronized. Those keywords describe implementation properties rather than interface properties.

Using the Cloneable Interface

There is no operator that allows you to make a direct copy of an object in memory. Instead, to make a copy of an object, you invoke its clone() method. The clone() method is defined in the Object class.

Not all classes allow their objects to be cloned. Only those that implement the Cloneable interface can be cloned. An interesting thing about the Cloneable interface is that it does not define any methods that must be implemented. At this point, you are probably wondering, so why define an interface at all? The answer is that defining your class as implementing an interface marks objects of that class as an instance of that interface. This means that we can use an interface as a kind of indicator of desired behavior.

The Java Virtual Machine does not call an object's constructor when you clone the object. A clone is simply an exact copy of the original. Before the Java runtime clones an object, it checks to see if the object's class implements the Cloneable interface. If it does, then the clone() method returns a clone of the object. Otherwise, the clone() method throws a CloneNotSupportedException.

Cloning an object can yield unintended side affects effects that are potentially dangerous. If an object is created that references another object, the clone of that object would reference the same object. The clone could make changes to the referenced object, which in turn would be reflected by the original object. For example, you create a clone of an object that is used to read and write data streams. The data stream opened by the original object is available to the clone, making it possible for the original and the clone to attempt conflicting operations on the stream. One could attempt to read from the stream while the other is writing to the stream. Or one could close the stream while the other is using the stream.

Because cloning can have unintended side effects, the clone() method is declared as protected in the Object class. This means the method must either be called from within a method defined by a class that implements the Cloneable interface or it must be explicitly overridden by that class so that it is public.

Since Object is defined in a different package than your own (Object is defined in java.lang), declaring clone() to be protected puts some restrictions on which objects can request a clone() of which other objects. An object can only request a clone of another object whose class is the same type or subclass of the object being cloned. The idea is to only enable a method to request a clone of an object whose class is in the same branch of the class hierarchy as itself.

Figure 12-6 provides an example object hierarchy that depicts cloning restrictions. First of all, all objects can clone themselves. Beyond that, some references to other object types are allowed. Here are some examples:

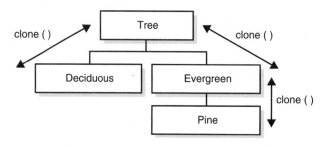

Figure 12-6   Restricting cloning to the same branch of a class hierarchy

- Pine objects can clone Evergreen or Tree objects.

- Evergreen objects can clone Tree objects.

- Deciduous objects can clone Tree objects.

This stops arbitrary objects, which have no relationship to each other, from cloning each other. For example, Deciduous objects cannot clone Evergreen objects, and no Tree object can clone a Forest object.

Exercise 12.7

What happens when you try to compile a Java source file containing the following code:

```
class Tree {
    protected int age;
}

class Pine extends Tree implements Cloneable {
    Pine() {
        age = 2;
    }
}

class Maple extends Tree {
    public static void main(String[] args) {
        Pine p1 = new Pine();
        Pine p2 = (Pine)p1.clone();
        System.out.println("Pine is " + p2.age);
    }
}
```

Answers to the Exercises

Exercise 12.1

You can import the class like this:

```
import COM.Company.Utilities.Calculator;
```

The directory structure starts with COM at the top level. A subdirectory of COM is Company. A subdirectory of Company is utilities. In the utilities directory, you'll find the Calculator class.

Exercise 12.2

You can modify Circle to place it into a package, like this:

```
package shapes;


public class Circle {

   public double radius;

   public double area() {
      return radius * radius * Math.PI;
   }
}
```

With everything public, classes outside of the package that Circle is defined in can now use the Circle class as before. Using Sun's JDK, if this is defined in a file named Circle.java, you can compile this by writing:

```
java -d . Circle.java
```

Here's how you can define a class to create a new Circle object:

```
import shapes.*;


class CircleTester {
   public static void main(String[] args) {
      Circle c = new Circle();
      c.radius = 10;
      System.out.println("area with radius = 10 is " + c.area());
   }
}
```

Exercise 12.3

The first file will compile fine, but when you try to compile Forest, the compiler will display a message indicating that Forest cannot access the protected field defined in Tree. A simple way to fix this problem is to make the age field public.

Another way is to define a public method that accesses the age field and returns its value. The Forest class can then invoke this public method from main().

Exercise 12.4

Both files will compile fine and you can execute Forest's main() method without a problem. It will access Tree's age field, even though it's protected, because Forest and Tree are in the same (default) package.

Exercise 12.5

A package declaration must come first in a source file, before any import statements or class definitions. The code presented in the exercise would cause a compile-time error.

Exercise 12.6

Is it possible for the mouseUp() method in DrawApplet to access the Square's loc field? No. Because loc is not defined with a public keyword, only those classes in the same package as the class defining loc can access this field.

Is it possible for mouseUp() to access the Square's draw() method? Absolutely. Both Square and draw() are defined with the public keyword, so any class in any package can invoke draw().

Could a subclass of DrawApplet, whose source is in the file DrawApplet.java, access DrawApplet's shapes field? No. shapes is private, so only DrawApplet itself can access this field.

Exercise 12.7

The compiler issues an error because Maple is not in the same branch of the class hierarchy as Pine, clone() is protected, and class Object, which defines clone(), comes from a different package.

Review Questions

1. What is the correct order and usage of statements in a source file?
   a. Zero or more package statements
      Any number of import statements
      public classes and interfaces
      nonpublic classes and interfaces
   b. One package statement
      Any number of import statements
      Any public and nonpublic classes and interfaces
   c. Zero or one package statement
      Any number of import statements
      Any public and nonpublic classes and interfaces
   d. One package statement
      One or more import statements
      Any public and nonpublic classes and interfaces

2. Java allows multiple inheritance of implementation through interfaces?
    a. True
    b. False

3. Specifying this line at the top of your source file:

```
package awt;
```

    a. results in a compile-time error because Java already defines an awt package.
    b. specifies that all of your classes in this file should go into Java's awt package.
    c. specifies that all of your classes in this file should go into your own awt package.
    d. imports all of the classes in your own awt package.

4. Given these two source files:

```
File FormQuestion.java
package forms;

public class FormQuestion {
    int type;
}

File Form.java
package forms;

class Form {
    int getType(FormQuestion question) {
        return question.type;
    }
}
```

    What is the outcome of compiling FormQuestion.java and then Form.java?
    a. Both compile successfully.
    b. Neither compile successfully.
    c. Only FormQuestion.java compiles.
    d. Only Form.java compiles.

5. Which of the following are true:
    a. If a public interface is declared in a source file, the interface must have the same name as the source file.
    b. If an import statement is included in a source file, the statement must appear as the first nonblank line.

c. If a package statement is included in a source file, the statement must appear as the first nonblank, noncomment line.

d. If a main() method is in a source file, it must appear on the first nonblank line.

Answers to Review Questions

1. c. A source file can contain a package statement followed by any number of import statements. The public and nonpublic classes and interfaces in the file must come after these statements. A source file doesn't have to have a package statement. However, if it does, there can be only one package statement.

2. b. False. It is true that interfaces allow objects to inherit behavior from multiple classes. However, Java only allows single inheritance.

3. c. The package keyword defines your own package for the classes in that file.

4. a. Both files compile successfully and are placed into the same package. Therefore, both classes can access each other and each other's members (as long as the accessed member is not private).

5. a and c. If a public interface is declared in a source file, the interface must have the same name as the source file. If a package statement is included in a source file, the statement must appear as the first nonblank line.

Passing Arguments to Programs

Objectives for This Chapter

- Identify correctly constructed declarations for the main() method.
- State the correspondence between index values in the argument array passed to a main method and command line arguments.
- Select specific command line elements from the arguments of the main() method using the correct array subscript value.
- Write HTML code to embed an applet in a Web page.
- Supply parameter values to the applet within the <applet> tag.
- Read the values of parameters specified in an <applet> tag and use them in an applet.

This chapter reviews how to invoke a Java program from the command line and pass parameters to the program. The exam has several questions that relate to creating a main() method and selecting arguments passed to main() from the command line. You'll also need to understand the arguments array.

Just as you can pass command-line arguments to a standalone application, you can also pass arguments to a Web-based applet. With foresight on the part of the programmer, this allows non-programmers to control the behavior of an applet. Applets are not required to have a main() method, and no questions on the exam directly address applets. However, you may find that a basic understanding of applets is useful and coverage of applet basics is exactly what you'll find in this chapter.

The main( ) Method

Unlike in C/C++ where you execute a file, in Java you run a program by passing a class name to the Java interpreter. When you invoke a standalone program, the Java runtime looks for that class' main() method. The main() method must be declared as a public, static, and void method that does not return a value and takes an array of String objects.

Here is the template for main():

```
public static void main(String[] args) {
  //add body of main here
}
```

If the Java interpreter does not find a main() method that follows the above format, the interpreter won't run the class.

 CAUTION: Some development environments, such as Metrowerks CodeWarrior, allow you to define a main() method that does not take any parameters. However, this is not the way things are done using the JDK, and the test is specific to the JDK.

The JDK will complain if you run a class whose main() method deviates from the standard declaration. The method must be static, since you have not yet created any instances of your class when you run your program. You cannot return a value to the operating system or Java interpreter. You cannot define a different argument. You can't even supply a subclass of String, because String is a final class and cannot be subclassed.

The exact order of the keywords public and static, and the String array definition is not strictly enforced. However, the *accepted order* for the keywords is to place public first, static second, and to define the String array using String[].

For example, this is also a valid main() method:

```
static public void main(String[] args) {
  //Not the normal way to declare main but not wrong either
}
```

However, the accepted way to write main() is:

```
public static void main(String[] args) {
  //The normal way to declare main
}
```

Command Line Arguments

Using the JDK, you can provide command line arguments for a standalone Java program. To do this, place the arguments after the program name when you invoke the Java interpreter.

For example, you can invoke a program called Flower, below, like this:

```
java Flower rose
```

This will pass the String "rose" to the main() method of the Flower class. The runtime will allocate a String array to the size of the number of command line arguments you supply (in this case, 1), allocate a String instance containing the command line argument, and place it into the array passed to main().

For example, invoking the following Flower class' main() method using the command above:

```
public class Flower {
    public static void main(String[] args) {
        System.out.println("My favorite flower is a " + args[0]);
    }
}
```

will result in the following output:

```
My favorite flower is a rose
```

Since this is an array, and since in the program we don't know for certain that the user has supplied a command line argument, we could get into trouble. We can't just go around accessing elements from an array beyond the bounds of an array. Java will throw an exception (ArrayIndexOutOfBoundsException). So, before using elements out of the args array in main(), it's a good idea to first check the length of the args array to make sure it contains what you think it contains. Here's a new version of the Flower class that does this in its main() method:

```
public class Flower {
    public static void main(String[] args) {
        if (args.length == 0)
            System.out.println("I like all flowers");
        else if (args.length == 1)
            System.out.println("My favorite flower is a " + args[0]);
        else {
            System.out.print("My favorite flowers are " + args[0]);
            for (int i = 1; i < args.length - 1; i++)
                System.out.print(", " + args[i]);
```

```
        System.out.println(" and " + args[args.length-1]);
      }
    }
  }
```

When run with commands like this:

```
java Flower
java Flower violet
java Flower violet roses daffodils
```

this prints:

```
I like all flowers
My favorite flower is a violet
My favorite flowers are violets, roses, and daffodils
```

Now that you've reviewed the basics of argument passing, lets take a closer look at the args array. As you know, the args array is used to access a program's command-line arguments. In the following example, three arguments are passed to the args array:

```
java Flower tulips daisies roses
```

The arguments are read into the args array as String objects. The tulips String would be accessed through args[0]. The daisies String would be accessed through args[1]. The roses String would be accessed through args[2]. Thus, while the size of the array in this example is 3, the array index goes from 0 to 2.

Exercise 13.1

Write a main() method that displays the command line arguments you pass to a program in reverse order.

When main( ) Ends

When main() ends, that may or may not be the end of the program. The JVM will run until the only remaining threads are daemon threads (meaning it will run until all of the user threads have died). If main() does not spawn any more threads, then the program will end when main() ends. However, if main() creates and starts a new thread, then even when main() comes to an end, the JVM may continue executing to support these other threads.

By default, a thread is a user thread if it was created by another user thread, and it is a daemon thread if it was created by another daemon thread. This means that, by default, all threads that you create in your program will be user threads.

If you create and display a user interface element from main(), such as a frame, your program will continue to run even after main() ends. This is because user interface elements have their own user thread associated with them to handle user input. Once the user closes this frame though, the program will end (if this is the last remaining user thread).

To explicitly set whether a thread is a user thread or a daemon thread, you can use the Thread method setDaemon() and pass it a boolean. To test whether a thread is a daemon thread or a user thread, you can use the Thread method isDaemon(), which returns an appropriate boolean.

Embedding an Applet in an HTML Page

First, we'll look at how you embed an applet in an HTML page. You've no doubt done this already in your Java career, but let's review this process briefly.

To run an applet, you need to embed a reference to the compiled applet in an HTML file. You can then view the HTML file in a Java-enabled Web browser, or in a development tool such as the JDK's appletviewer.

The simplest way to embed an applet within a Web page is to use the <applet> tag to. Here's a basic HTML file you can write to reference an applet (in this case, an applet with the compiled class file named Metric.class). It contains three keywords in the <applet> tag:

```
<html>
<head>
<title>Simple Applet</title>
</head>
<body>
<applet code="Metric.class" width=200 height=100>
</applet>
</body>
</html>
```

The code keyword identifies the compiled class file containing the applet. In this example, this file is relative to the IP address and directory containing the HTML file in which this reference is embedded. However, this value can also be an absolute path name, so that a Web page can contain an applet found anywhere on the Web.

TIP: If the applet is loaded relative to the page, there are two things that can change the base location. The first is if the HTML file itself contains a <base> tag-this tag specifies where to look for the applet class. The second is if the <applet> tag contains the codebase keyword. The codebase keyword is described in the next section.

The two other keywords you must have inside an <applet> tag are width and height. These specify the size of the screen, in pixels, that the browser or appletviewer should use to display the applet. The browser or appletviewer sizes the applet itself to the size indicated by these keywords. Be aware that because you are specifying the height and width in pixels, different screens will display the applet differently, according to their own, unique resolutions.

Passing Parameters to an Applet

The conventional way to pass a parameter to an applet is to use the <param> tag. Each <param> tag can only take one parameter, so you use one <param> tag per parameter. Parameter values can be retrieved by the applet as Strings, using methods defined in the Applet class. If you want to pass a different type of value, such as an int or a boolean, you must convert it from a String, most likely by using a wrapper class.

The <param> are placed between the <applet> and </applet> tags. The <param> tag uses two keywords: name, to name the parameter, and value, to give it a value. An example of the <param> tag is:

```
<html>
<head>
<title>Simple Applet</title>
</head>
<body>
<applet code="Metric.class" width=200 height=100>
<param name=state value=Hawaii>
</applet>
</body>
</html>
```

If you'd like a parameter value to contain spaces, you should place this value within quotes. For example, to supply a parameter value that's really two words, you can write:

```
<html>
<head>
<title>Simple Applet</title>
</head>
<body>
<applet code="Metric.class" width=200 height=100>
<param name=state value="North Carolina">
<param name=state value="South Carolina">
</applet>
</body>
</html>
```

However, it never hurts to include quotes, even for a single word, as in:

```
<html>
<head>
<title>Simple Applet</title>
</head>
<body>
<applet code="Metric.class" width=200 height=100>
<param name=state value="Washington">
<param name=state value="Oregon">
<param name=state value="California">
</applet>
</body>
</html>
```

Quoting the value part of fields is generally a good idea for HTML code and required for XHTML code.

Retrieving Parameters

You retrieve the value of a parameter using the getParameter() method defined by the Applet class. This method returns a String containing the value of the parameter or null if the parameter was not defined at all.

Most programmers don't realize that you can actually retrieve the parameters in the <applet> tag itself using getParameter(). Here's an example:

```
import java.applet.Applet;

public class Tag extends Applet {
  public void init() {
    System.out.println(getParameter("code"));
    System.out.println(getParameter("width"));
    System.out.println(getParameter("height"));
  }
}
```

Here's an HTML file we can use to run this applet:

```
<html>
<head>
<title>Simple Applet</title>
</head>
<body>
<applet code="Tag.class" width=200 height=100>
</applet>
</body>
</html>
```

The output from this program in the standard output is:

```
Tag.class
200
100
```

You can even put your own parameters right into the <applet> tag, rather than the <param> tag. For the sake of convention, you shouldn't do this, but it works. For example, if you run this program:

```
import java.applet.Applet;

public class Tag extends Applet {
  public void init() {
    System.out.println(getParameter("code"));
    System.out.println(getParameter("width"));
    System.out.println(getParameter("height"));
    System.out.println(getParameter("extra"));
  }
}
```

using this HTML file:

```
<html>
<head>
<title>Simple Applet</title>
</head>
<body>
<applet code="Tag.class" width=200 height=100 extra=country>
</applet>
</body>
</html>
```

the result in the standard output is:

```
Tag.class
200
100
Country
```

However, the reverse is not true. You cannot place a width value within a <param> tag, like this:

```
<applet code="Tag.class" height=100>
<param name=width value=200>
</applet>
```

If you do, the appletviewer or Web browser won't run the applet and will complain that the <applet> tag was not written properly.

Exercise 13.2

Write an init() method that checks for a parameter named button and creates a button with that name as its label. If no parameter is defined, give the button any label you'd like. Clicking on the button should write the button label to the standard output.

Customizing an Applet

To put this all together, the purpose of passing parameter values to an applet is to allow an applet to be used for many slightly different purposes. The applet will always do the same thing—for example, it might display text that runs across the page like a stock ticker, or display a sequence of images fast enough to animate them. However, with applet parameters, the specifics can change—the applet can display different text, and the applet can display different images for the animation.

This ability to customize enables you to reuse an applet without programming. As an example, here's an applet that can convert inches to centimeters. You can see what this looks like in Figure 13-1. Here's the code:

```java
import java.awt.*;
import java.applet.Applet;
import java.awt.event.*;

public class Metric extends Applet implements ActionListener {
    TextField tf;
    TextField tf2;

    double     convFactor;
    String     toUnits;
    String     fromUnits;

    public void init() {
        String factor = getParameter("factor");
        fromUnits = getParameter("from");
        toUnits = getParameter("to");
```

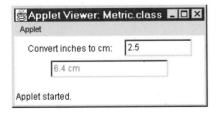

Figure 13-1   The metric applet with its default values

```
            if (fromUnits == null || toUnits == null || factor == null) {
                fromUnits = "inches";
                toUnits = "cm";
                convFactor = 2.56;
            } else {
                try {
                    convFactor = new Double(factor).doubleValue();
                } catch (NumberFormatException e) {
                    fromUnits = "inches";
                    toUnits = "cm";
                    convFactor = 2.56;
                }
            }

        add(new Label("Convert " + fromUnits + " to " + toUnits + ":"));

            tf = new TextField(10);
            add(tf);

            tf2 = new TextField(20);
            tf2.setEnabled(false);
            add(tf2);
            tf.addActionListener(this);
        }

        public void actionPerformed(ActionEvent e) {
            String s = tf.getText();
            try {
                double d = new Double(s).doubleValue();
                double result = d * convFactor;
                String toEntry = new Double(result).toString();
                tf2.setText(toEntry + " " + toUnits);
            } catch (NumberFormatException x) {
                tf2.setText("Please enter a number.");
                tf.setText("");
            }
            repaint();
        }
    }
```

If you run this applet using an HTML file that does not specify any parameter values, such as:

```
<html>
<head>
<title>Simple Applet</title>
</head>
<body>
<applet code="Metric.class" width=266 height=72>
</applet>
</body>
</html>
```

then you will see an applet that allows you to convert inches to centimeters. This applet will look like Figure 13-1 once you interact with it.

However, this applet can convert from any unit to any other unit, and it's a simple matter to let users know how to embed this conversion applet into their own HTML pages. All they have to do is provide three <param> tags. These tags should be named from, to, and factor, and their values control what the applet displays (the order of these tags does not matter). For example, when running the following HTML file:

```
<html>
<head>
<title>Simple Applet</title>
</head>
<body>
<applet code="Metric.class" width=266 height=72>
<param name=from value="miles">
<param name=to value="kilometers">
<param name=factor value="1.6">
</applet>
</body>
</html>
```

this applet appears like the screen shot in Figure 13-2 once you type in a number to convert.

Now, you're able to convert between miles and kilometers without any programming.

Answers to the Exercises

Exercise 13.1

```
class Reverse {
    public static void main(String[] args) {
        System.out.println("The parameters in reverse order are:");
        for (int i = args.length - 1; i >= 0; i--) {
```

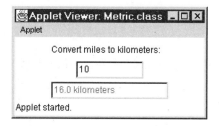

Figure 13-2 The metric applet customized for miles and kilometers

```
            System.out.print(args[i] + " ");
        }
        System.out.println("");
    }
}
```

If you run this program like this:

```
java Reverse My name is William
```

it will display

```
William is name My
```

Exercise 13.2

Here's the code:

```
import java.awt.*;
import java.awt.event.*;
import java.applet.*;

public class MyButtonApplet extends Applet {
    public void init() {
        String s = getParameter("button");

        if (s == null)
            s = new String("giraffe");

        add(new MyButton(s));
    }
}

class MyButton extends Button implements ActionListener {
    MyButton(String s) {
        super(s);
        addActionListener(this);
    }

    public void actionPerformed(ActionEvent e) {
        System.out.println(getLabel());
    }
}
```

When this runs with the following HTML file (where a <param> tag is not defined):

```
<html>
<head>
<title>Simple Applet</title>
</head>
<body>
<applet code="MyButtonApplet.class" width=230 height=100>
```

```
</applet>
</body>
</html>
```

This applet looks like Figure 13-3.

Clicking on the giraffe button writes the word "giraffe" to the standard output.

When you supply the following HTML file, however (where a <param> tag is now defined):

```
<html>
<head>
<title>Simple Applet</title>
</head>
<body>
<applet code="MyButtonApplet.class" width=230 height=100>
<param name=button value="elephant">
</applet>
</body>
</html>
```

Then the giraffe button is replaced with an elephant button, and clicking on this button writes the word "elephant" to the standard output.

Review Questions

1. Which of these defines a valid main() method?
   a. public static void main(String args[]) { }
   b. public static void main(String[]) { }
   c. public static void main(String[] args);
   d. public static void main(args) { }

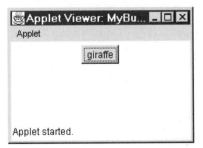

Figure 13-3   The default button in MyButtonApplet

2. How can you access the word "kiss" from the following invocation of main(): java lyrics a kiss is but a kiss
   a. args[0]
   b. args[2]
   c. args[4]
   d. args[5]
   e. args[6]
   f. b and e

3. The Java Virtual Machine will run until:
   a. main() ends
   b. the only threads left are user threads
   c. the only threads left are daemon threads
   d. a or c, whichever comes first

4. To specify a parameter in an <applet> tag named lastname that contains the value "Einstein," you could write:
   a. <param name=lastname value="Einstein">
   b. <param name=lastname value=Einstein>
   c. either a or b

5. To retrieve a parameter named lastname, you could write code for your applet that looked like:
   a. String s = getName("lastname");
   b. String s = parameter("lastname");
   c. String s = getParameter("lastname");

6. If you tried to read a parameter value and a parameter with that name was not defined in the <applet> tag:
   a. The runtime would throw an exception
   b. The parameter's value would be null
   c. The parameter's value would be an empty string

Answers to Review Questions

1. **a.** A String array can be defined by placing the square brackets after the variable name. The other possible main definitions are not valid.

2. **d.** The String array starts at 0. So, args[0] would be "a," args[1] would be "kiss," and so on, up to args[5], which is also "kiss." (Remember, lyrics is the name of the class to run.)

3. **c.** The JVM will run until all user threads die and the only threads left are daemon threads.

4. **c.** A parameter value can have quotes or not, depending on your preference. If the value contains spaces, however, it must be placed within quotes.

5. **c.** The method getParameter() retrieves a parameter value given a parameter name.

6. **b.** The method getParameter() returns null if a parameter with the given name is not defined.

Exceptions

Objectives for This Chapter

- Determine the flow of control for try, catch, and finally constructions when execution proceeds normally, when an exception is thrown and caught, and when an exception is thrown but is not caught.
- Declare a method that might throw unchecked exceptions.
- Specify which exceptions a method can throw.
- Identify which exceptions may be legitimately thrown from an overriding method in a subclass.
- Write code to create and throw an exception.

Java defines keywords and classes for exceptions, weaving exceptions right into the fabric of the language. You can throw exceptions to signal errors. By handling exceptions, you can separate control flow involving error processing from control flow that occurs when everything proceeds as expected. Exceptions are an extremely flexible way to report and respond to errors. We'll cover the basics as well as the advanced aspects of exceptions in this chapter as they relate to the test. For the exam, you'll need to be able to write code that makes proper use of exceptions and exception-handling clauses. You'll also need to be able to declare methods and override methods that throw exceptions.

Exception Basics

When you write a program, you need some way to report and handle errors. In a language such as C, the typical way to do this is with return codes. However, return codes have a number of down sides. First, you've got to remember to check them and know which "magic numbers" mean what. Second, checking return codes inevitably leads to mingling error processing with normal processing, making your code more difficult to read and understand. And third, methods must pass back return codes to report an error to *their* caller.

All of this error handling protocol must be managed and verified by the programmer. There is no formal mechanism in place to make sure the programmer has checked return codes correctly.

Java's exception reporting and handling gets away from these problems. First, the language itself requires methods to declare the methods they throw and to catch the exceptions a called method might throw, thereby formalizing exception handling. Along with this, exceptions are objects, not numbers, so their class names and any data they contain, such as strings, explains what they're all about without resorting to "magic numbers." Second, exception handling separates error processing from normal processing. Normal processing goes into a try block; error processing goes into a catch block. Finally, exceptions can be passed on to their caller by declaring a method using the appropriate keywords; the language takes care of this chore for you.

Working with Exceptions

The idea in exception handling is that you try to execute a block of code, you catch any exceptions that were thrown, and you finally (always) do some cleanup. The template to follow when invoking a method that might throw an exception is:

```
try {
  //do something here that might cause an exception
} catch (ExceptionType variable) {
  //handle the exception
} finally {
  //always do this
}
```

You can have multiple catch blocks, each catch block specifying its own Exception-Type in an order that always progresses from the most specific exception you want to catch to the superclasses for these exceptions that you want to catch. Attempting to catch the superclasses first results in a compile-time error. For example, placing a catch block with type Exception before a catch block with type IOException, results in a compile-time error.

NOTE: If you know C++, you might have always wondered what the big deal is with Java and exceptions—after all, there are exceptions in C++, too. The difference is that Java formalizes exceptions. In C++, exceptions are completely optional. In Java, you're forced to be very precise: methods must indicate which exceptions they throw in their declarations. Invoking methods that declare which exceptions they throw is not possible unless you catch these exception types. Java's insistence on a strict adherence to this protocol makes control flow for exceptions much more understandable and maintainable than when the exception policy is determined by individual programmers.

All exception types are subclasses of the built-in class Throwable, which places Throwable at the top of the exception class hierarchy. Immediately below Throwable are two subclasses that form the main branches in the hierarchy. These subclasses are Error and Exception.

The Error hierarchy describes internal errors that are not expected to be caught under normal circumstances in a program. Exceptions of type Error are used by Java to indicate errors having to do with the run-time environment itself. Stack overflow is an example of this type of error. There isn't much you can do when an error of this type occurs. These errors typically halt execution and the only thing you can do is to notify the user and try to terminate the program gracefully.

As a programmer, your focus will be on the Exception hierarchy. This class is used for exceptional conditions that programs should catch. This class is also used when you create your own custom exception types.

The Exception hierarchy also has two branches, which includes exceptions that derive from RuntimeException and those that do not. A RuntimeException occurs because you made a programming error and caused the program to perform an unacceptable action, such as division by zero, null pointer access, or invalid array indexing. Other exceptions occur because something bad happened, such as an I/O error or a malformed URL was used.

TIP: The name RuntimeException can be somewhat confusing. After all, the errors we are discussing all occur at run time. Essentially, any time a RuntimeException occurs, you made a mistake. An ArithmeticException occurred because you didn't test for zero before attempting to divide a value. A NullPointerException occurred because you didn't check to see if a variable was null before using it. An ArrayIndexOutOfBoundsException occurred because you didn't test the array index against the array bounds.

Uncaught Exceptions

Exceptions and Errors both inherit from class Throwable, which allows an object to be thrown using the throw keyword and caught using the catch keyword. Your programs should catch exceptions whenever possible. Uncaught exceptions halt execution and terminate your program.

To understand more about uncaught exceptions, let's look at one of the most common exceptions that can occur as an ArithmeticException. We can create an example that intentionally causes an ArithmeticException by attempting to divide by zero, such as:

```
class divZero {
    public static void main(String args[]) {
        int a = 0;
        int b = 100 / a;
    }
}
```

When Java detects the attempt to divide by zero, the run-time system constructs a new exception object and then throws the ArithmeticException exception. This causes execution of the divZero class to stop, and the program to terminate. Once an exception has been thrown, it must be caught by an exception handler and dealt with immediately. In this example, we didn't provide a handler, so the exception is caught by the default handler. The output of the default handler in this example would be:

```
java.lang.ArithmeticException: / by zero
    at divZero.main(divZero.java:4)
```

As you can see from the sample output, the default handler displays a string describing the exception that occurs, prints a track stack from the point at which the exception occurred, and then terminates the program. Here, the exception occurred in the main method of the divZero class, which was line 4 in the divZero.java file.

Checked and Unchecked Exceptions

Java methods can throw an exception if it encounters a situation it cannot handle. A method that might throw an exception should state this possibility in its method declaration. Here's an example from a method defined by Java's Thread class named sleep():

```
public static void sleep(long millis) throws InterruptedException
```

InterruptedException is a *checked* exception. This means any code invoking sleep() must be prepared to catch an InterruptedException. Checked exceptions must be

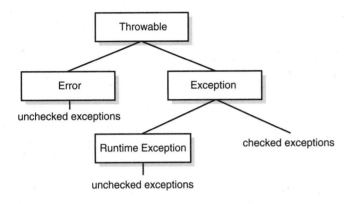

Figure 14-1 An exception hierarchy

caught (or rethrown—we'll get to that in a moment). Unchecked exceptions do not have to be caught. Whether a method is checked or unchecked depends on where the exception descends from in the class hierarchy.

Figure 14-1 provides a diagram to help you see where checked and unchecked exceptions fit into the class hierarchy. As you can see, instances of class Error are unchecked. Instances of RuntimeException and its subclasses are also unchecked. All other exception classes—namely, all other subclasses of class Exception—are checked.

You are not required to place calls to methods that throw unchecked exceptions in a try/catch block. However, it's often useful to do so anyway. For example, ArithmeticException is unchecked, but sometimes you want to handle this exception if it arises.

Using try, catch, and finally

Let's go back to the sleep() method whose definition I've provided above. If you want to invoke sleep(), you must place this call in a try/catch block, like so:

```
class A implements Runnable {
  Thread t;
  public static void main(String[] args) {
    A a = new A();
    a.go();
  }
  void go() {
    t = new Thread(this);
    t.start();
    try {
      System.out.println("try");
      t.sleep(1000);
    } catch(InterruptedException e) {
      System.out.println("catch");
```

```
        } finally {
            System.out.println("finally");
        }
    }
    public void run() {
        while(true) {
            // . . . infinite loop . . .
        }
    }
}
```

This example shows the try/catch/finally blocks in action. If everything works smoothly when we invoke sleep() and it does not throw an exception, then the messages try and finally appear in the standard output. Otherwise, if sleep() does throw an InterruptedException, the messages try, catch, and finally appear. If sleep() throws an unchecked exception, such as an ArithmeticException, the messages try and finally appear—because there is no catch clause defined for an ArithmeticException.

You always need a try block to use catch or finally. With a try block, you must use catch, finally, or both. You cannot use a try block on its own. Here's an example of using try and finally without a catch block at all:

```
try {
    if (result == 0) {
        doThis();
        return;
    } else {
        doThat();
        throw new MyException();
    }
} finally {
    alwaysDoThis();
}
```

The finally block is always executed when it's a matter of control flow. In other words, if you use a return statement or throw an exception, or if you try to use a break statement to branch around a finally block, your efforts to thwart the finally statement will be to no avail. (The exercises for this chapter do ask you to identify a sure-fire way of avoiding finally by invoking a certain system method, but as long as the issue is one of control flow, finally cannot be avoided.)

Exercise 14.1

Rewrite this algorithm from a C method to use Java's exception handling. Then write the code, using an array as the return value.

Method Name: Roots
Input: double a, double b, double c, and a pointer to an array of two double values
Output: a boolean indicating success or failure
Purpose: implements the quadratic equation

1. Find the value of $(b \times b) - (4 \times a \times c)$.

2. If this result is negative, there are no roots. Return false.

3. If a is negative, also return false.

4. Otherwise, calculate $(-b + \text{this value})$ divided by $2 \times a$. Also calculate $(-b - \text{this}$ value) divided by $2 \times a$. Place the results in the array reference by the pointer and return true.

Common Java Exceptions

It's useful to be familiar with the most common Java exceptions. These exception classes are defined in the package they are most associated with. For example, IOException is defined in java.io; MalformedURLException is defined in java.net. Here are some exceptions that you might see or have to handle from time to time.

Checked Exceptions

- **ClassNotFoundException (defined in java.lang)** Indicates that a class was called but could not be found. The class name is either incorrect or the class isn't available to the program.

- **IOException (defined in java.io)** Signals that an error occurred when reading from or writing to a file or network socket. You'll have to handle this kind of exception often when you use stream methods.

- **FileNotFoundException (defined in java.io)** When you access a file, you must be prepared to handle this exception. Remember, just because you create a File object does not mean that the file exists.

- **IllegalAccessException (defined in java.lang)** Occurs when you try to load in a class, but the currently executing method does not have access to the specified class. Can also occur when you try to create an instance of a class, but the current method does not have access to the appropriate zero-argument constructor.

- **InterruptedException (defined in java.lang)** When you put a thread to sleep or suspend a thread you've got to be ready to handle this exception; a sleeping thread or a suspended thread could be interrupted before its sleeping time elapses or before someone invokes resume() for the thread, in which case it will throw this exception.

- **MalformedURLException (defined in java.net)** When you create a URL, you must be prepared to handle this exception in case the URL string supplied is not valid.

Unchecked Exceptions

- **ArithmeticException (defined in java.lang)** Whenever an illegal math operation takes place, such as an integer divide by zero, the Java Virtual Machine throws this exception.

- **ArrayIndexOutOfBoundsException (defined in java.lang)** If you try to access an array with an illegal index value, this exception is thrown. The exception indicates that the index is either negative or greater than or equal to the size of the array.

- **ArrayStoreException (defined in java.lang)** If you try to store the wrong type of object in an array of objects, this exception occurs.

- **ClassCastException (defined in java.lang)** Indicates that the code has attempted to cast an object to a subclass of which it is not an instance.

- **EmptyStackException (defined in java.lang)** The exception is thrown by methods in the Stack class. If you try to retrieve an item from an empty stack, this exception occurs.

- **IllegalArgumentException (defined in java.lang)** If you try to pass an illegal or inappropriate argument to a method, this exception occurs.

- **InvalidParameterException (defined in java.lang)** If you try to pass an invalid parameter to a method, this exception occurs.

- **NullPointerException (defined in java.lang)** If you try to invoke a method using a null object reference, you'll see this exception. This exception can creep into your code when you least expect it. For example, you might have defined two method calls and expect methodOne() to return an object which you will use to invoke methodTwo(). However, if methodOne() returns null, attempting to invoke methodTwo() will throw a NullPointerException.

- **NumberFormatException (defined in java.lang)** If you are converting a String to a number, you've got to be prepared to handle this exception in case the String does not really represent a number.

- **StringIndexOutOfBoundsException (defined in java.lang)** Indicates an attempt to index outside the bounds of a string.

There are, of course, many more exceptions that you'll probably come across in your travels as a Java programmer. But these give you a feel for what you'll find.

Using Methods Defined by Exception and Throwable

The most common way to use exceptions is to simply identify the exception that occurred by its class type. Most programmers only check whether the exception's class is IOException, ArithmeticException, and so on, and perform error handling in a catch clause appropriate for that class type.

However, an exception is also a wealth of information. Exceptions can be created with a descriptive String that explains why the exception occurred. You can access this String using getMessage(), which is implemented in Throwable—the superclass of Exception.

You can also print the stack to the standard output or standard error. This can help with debugging so that you can see exactly where the exception was thrown. You can do this by invoking printStackTrace() for the exception.

Rethrowing an Exception

Let's look at the idea of rethrowing an exception. If you don't want to handle an exception yourself, you can let it go unhandled, meaning the exception will bubble up the call stack. Here's an example:

```
class A implements Runnable {
    Thread t;
    public static void main(String[] args) {
        A a = new A();
        a.go();
    }
    void go() {
        t = new Thread(this);
        t.start();
    }

    public void run() {
      try {
        doThis();
      } catch (InterruptedException e) {
        System.out.println("caught");
      }
    }

    void doThis() throws InterruptedException {
      t.sleep(2000);
    }
}
```

Notice that the method called doThis() is declared as throwing InterruptedException. A sleeping thread or a suspended thread could be interrupted before its sleeping time elapses or before someone invokes resume() for the thread, in which case it will throw InterruptedException. Even though doThis() does not handle InterruptedException, some method in the call stack above the call to sleep() has got to. So, the method run() handles this exception.

You can also declare the doThis() method as in the following code snippet to achieve the same effect:

```
void doThis() throws InterruptedException {
  try {
    t.sleep(2000);
  } catch (InterruptedException e) {
    throw e;
  }
}
```

This version of doThis() explicitly rethrows the exception.

 TIP: You can list more than one exception in the throws clause if you separate them with commas.

Exercise 14.2

Rewrite the following method so that instead of handling the exceptions itself, the method rethrows the exceptions, putting responsibility on the caller to handle the exceptions.

```
int doDivision(InputStream in) {
  try {
    int c = in.read();
    return 100/c;
  } catch (IOException x) {
    return 0;
  } catch (ArithmeticException x) {
    return 0;
  }
}
```

Which Exceptions a Method Can Throw

A method can throw the exceptions listed in its throws clause or subclasses of those exceptions. A method can also throw any unchecked exception, even if it is not declared in its throws clause. Here's an example of throwing a subclass of an exception class specified in the throws clause.

```java
import java.io.IOException;

class Throw {
    public static void main(String[] args) {
        Throw t = new Throw();
        try {
            t.test(4);
        } catch (Exception e) {
        }
    }

    void test(int i) throws Exception {
        if (i == 4)
            throw new IOException();
    }
}
```

The catch clauses must match the exceptions listed in the throws clause, but the test() method can throw any subclass of an exception listed in its throws clause.

Exceptions in an Overriding Method in a Subclass

For the exam, you'll need to identify what exceptions may be legitimately thrown from an overriding method in a subclass. While there's more on overriding methods in Chapter 9, we'll cover here how exceptions relate to overriding a method.

When you override a method, you must list those exceptions that the overriden code might throw. You can only list those exceptions, or subclasses of those exceptions, that are defined in the method definition you are inheriting from. (A method can also throw any unchecked exception, even if it is not declared in its throws clause.)

When you override a method in a subclass, you cannot add new exception types to those you inherit. You can choose to throw a subset of those exceptions listed in the method's superclass. However, a subclass further down the hierarchy cannot then re-list the exceptions dropped above it.

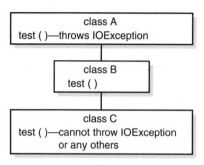

Figure 14-2 Class hierarchy of a method throwing an exception in the superclass

For example, suppose you have the hierarchy in Figure 14-2.

Class A defines a method named test(). Class B is a subclass of class A and overrides test(). Class C is a subclass of class B and also overrides test().

If class A indicates in its test() method that it throws an IOException, and class B does not, then class C cannot list IOException (or, in fact, any other exceptions if B does not also list any) in its throws clause.

In this example, the code will not compile. Even though the superclass, class A, lists IOException in its throws clause, class B does not. Since we create an instance of class B in main(), it is class B's exceptions that must match the catch clauses listed after the try:

```
import java.io.IOException;
class A {
  public static void main(String[] args) {
    B ref = new B();
    try {
      ref.test();
    } catch(IOException e) {
      // we can't catch something that's not thrown
    }
  }
  void test() throws IOException {
    throw new IOException();
  }
}
class B extends A {
  void test() {
  }
}
```

However, if we change main() so that it creates an instance of class A instead of class B, then this will compile and run fine.

This will also compile if the instance reference obj in main() is declared as type A. In that case, Java allows the possibility that this reference might really be of type A and the catch clause is fine.

If test() in class B invoked super.test(), then either test() in class B would have to indicate it throws an IOException, or the call to super.test() would have to be wrapped in a try-catch block.

Exercise 14.3

Take the above code and make the changes to it based on the possibilities listed above. First try to compile the code as is. Then, create an instance of class A; then declare the variable as class A. Finally, try to invoke test() in class A from class B using super. If the compiler complains at first, do what you have to do to get this working.

Creating and Throwing an Exception

For the example, you'll need to be able to write code to create and throw an exception. You can define your own exceptions simply by extending class Exception. Typically, the class type is all you need to distinguish your exception from the others.

You can add behavior to your exception or take advantage of methods already defined in Exception and Throwable. You can also supply a string to the constructor when you create your new exception; this string can contain text detailing why the error occurred. You can retrieve this string from the exception object using getMessage().

The methods in Exception and Throwable are discussed in the section, "What's Not on the Test."

To throw an exception, you simply create a new instance of the exception you want to throw and write it after a throw keyword. For example, to throw an exception named IllegalValueException (presumably a subclass of Exception), you can simply write:

```
throw new IllegalValueException();
```

As in the previous examples, the method that throws this exception must indicate it throws an exception of this type in its throws clause.

Exercise 14.4

Rewrite the quadratic equation exercise so that you throw your own exception type. Indicate the cause of the exception when you create it, and display this cause in an error message. You can use the answer for Exercise 14.1 as a starting point if you'd like.

Answers to the Exercises

Exercise 14.1

method name: Roots
input: double a, double b, double c
output: an array of two double values (an object in Java)
throws: ArithmeticException (could throw a new exception you defined yourself, called something like NoRootsException)
purpose: implements the quadratic equation

1. Find the value of b × b −4 × a × c

2. If this result is negative, there are no roots. Throw the exception declared as part of this method.

3. If a is negative, throw the same exception.

4. Otherwise, calculate (−b + this value) divided by 2 × a. Also calculate (−b − this value) divided by 2 × a. Place these results in a new double array and return this array.

Here's what this code might look like. It contains a main() method so that you can run it and test the method.

```
class Quad {
    public static void main(String[] args) {
        Quad q = new Quad();
        try {
            double[] answer = q.roots(1.2, 3.2, -4.0);
            System.out.println("The roots are " +
                answer[0] + ", " + answer[1]);
        } catch (NoRootsException x) {
            System.out.println("No roots exist");
        }
    }

    double[] roots(double a, double b, double c)
                throws NoRootsException {
        double[] result = new double[2];
        double temp = (b * b) - ( 4 * a * c);
        if (temp < 0)
            throw new NoRootsException();
        if (a < 0)
            throw new NoRootsException();
        temp = Math.sqrt(temp);
        result[0] = (- b + temp) / (2.0 * a);
        result[1] = (- b - temp) / (2.0 * a);
        return result;
```

```
      }

   }

class NoRootsException extends Exception { }
```

If you threw something like ArithmeticException, that's fine for what you reviewed up to this point in the chapter. However, in general, you should not throw an unchecked exception (which is what ArithmeticException is). By creating your own exception type, as this chapter discusses later, you can be very specific about what error occurred and you can make sure you throw a checked exception—an exception that must be handled.

Running the above Quad class' main() method yields the result:

The roots are 0.927443, −3.59411

To see an exception get thrown, try running with a equal to 0 or with b equal to 0 and a and c equal to something greater than 0.

Exercise 14.2

```
int doDivision(InputStream in) throws IOException,
ArithmeticException {
   int c = in.read();
   return 100/c;
}
```

Exercise 14.3

Here is the original code, this time with line numbers:

```
 1: import java.io.IOException;
 2:
 3: class A {
 4:  public static void main(String[] args) {
 5:     B ref = new B();
 6:     try {
 7:        ref.test();
 8:     } catch(IOException e) {
 9:        // we can't catch something that's not thrown
10:     }
11:  }
12:  void test() throws IOException {
13:     throw new IOException();
14:  }
15: }
16:
17: class B extends A {
18:  void test() {
19:  }
20: }
```

First, compile the code as is. The JDK will complain about line 8 and will display the messsage:

```
Exception java.io.IOException is never thrown in the body of the
corresponding try statement.
```

Then, create an instance of class A instead of class B. To do that, change line 5 to read:

```
A ref = new A();
```

Now the code will compile and run successfully when you run class A's main() method.

Next, try changing line 5 to read:

```
A ref = new B();
```

The code will still compile and run successfully when you run class A's main() method.

Then, leaving the code defined as above—declaring the variable to be of class A but creating an instance of class B—add after line 18:

```
super.test();
```

When you try to compile this, the compiler will complain about the line you just added (now line 19), and will say:

Exception java.io.IOException must be caught, or it must be declared in the throws clause of this method.

We can fix this—we have the technology. The simplest way to proceed is to indicate that test() as defined in class B also throws a java.io.IOException, just like test() in class A. So, we can change line 18 to read:

```
void test() throws IOException {
```

Now, we can compile and run this code just fine.

Exercise 14.4

Notice in this answer how NoRootsException must provide a constructor that passes the String argument to its superclass. This enables the new exception to be initialized with a string containing an explanation of what went wrong. This string can later be retrieved using getMessage().

```
class Quad {
   public static void main(String[] args) {
      Quad q = new Quad();
      try {
```

```
            // WORKS double[] answer = q.roots(1.2, 3.2, -4.0);
            // However,  the following produces an exception
            double[] answer = q.roots(1.2, 0.0, 2.1);
            System.out.println("The roots are " +
                answer[0] + ", " + answer[1]);
        } catch (NoRootsException x) {
            System.out.println("No roots exist: " + x.getMessage());
        }
    }

    double[] roots(double a, double b, double c)
                throws NoRootsException {
        double[] result = new double[2];
        double temp = (b * b) - ( 4 * a * c);
        if (temp < 0)
            throw new NoRootsException("negative square root");
        if (a < 0)
            throw new NoRootsException("divide by zero");
        temp = Math.sqrt(temp);
        result[0] = (- b + temp) / (2.0 * a);
        result[1] = (- b - temp) / (2.0 * a);
        return result;
    }

}

class NoRootsException extends Exception {
    NoRootsException(String s) {
        super(s);
    }
}
```

Review Questions

1. Why is this code illegal?

```
class A {
    public static void main(String[] args) {
        try {
            System.out.println("hello");
        }
    }
}
```

    a. You cannot have a try block without a catch and/or finally.

    b. Code that does not throw an exception cannot be in a try block.

    c. The method main() must always throw something if the try block is used without a catch.

2. Analyze the following code and pick the best analysis from the ones presented below.

```
class A {
    public static void main(String[] args) {
        method();
    }
    static void method() throws Exception {
        try {
            System.out.println("hello");
        } finally {
            System.out.println("good-bye");
        }
    }
}
```

    a. This code will compile and display both "hello" and "good-bye."

    b. This code will do everything in choice a, but Java will then halt the program and report that Exception was thrown but not handled.

    c. This code will not compile.

3. What appears in the standard output if you run this program?

```
class A {
    public static void main(String[] args) {
        method();
    }
    static void method() {
        try {
            System.out.println("hello");
        } finally {
            System.out.println("good-bye");
        }
    }
}
```

    a. "hello"

    b. "good-bye"

    c. "hello" followed by "good-bye"

4. What appears in the standard output if you run this program?

```
class A {
    public static void main(String[] args) {
        method();
    }
    static void method() {
        try {
            System.out.println("hello");
            return;
```

```
        } finally {
            System.out.println("good-bye");
        }
    }
}
```

a. "hello"

b. "good-bye"

c. "hello" followed by "good-bye"

5. What appears in the standard output if you run this program?

```
class A {
    public static void main(String[] args) {
        method();
    }
    static void method() {
        try {
            System.out.println("hello");
            System.exit(0);
        } finally {
            System.out.println("good-bye");
        }
    }
}
```

a. "hello"

b. "good-bye"

c. "hello" followed by "good-bye"

6. What is the result of invoking B first with no command-line argument, and then with the command line argument "throw?"

```
class B {
    public static void main(String[] args) {
        B b = new B();
        b.test(args);
    }

    void test(String[] args) {
        String s;

        if (args.length == 0)
            s = new String("don't throw");
        else
            s = args[0];

        try {
            method(s);
            System.out.println("no exception");
```

```
        } catch (MyException e) {
            System.out.println("caught");
        }
    }
    void method(String s) throws MyException {
        if (s.equals("throw"))
            throw new MyException();
        else
            return;
    }
}

class MyException extends Exception{}
```

    a. The program prints "no exception" two times in a row.

    b. First, the program prints "no exception." Then, the program prints "caught."

    c. The program prints "caught" two times in a row.

7. This question builds on Question 6, which defined a class called B. Given that class, why is it illegal to write a subclass of B like this?

```
class C extends B {

    public static void main(String[] args) {
        C c = new C();
        c.test(args);
    }

    void method(String s) {
        if (s.equals("yes"))
            throw new MyException();
        else
            return;
    }
}
```

    a. When you override a method, you must also indicate the exceptions the overridden method will throw.

    b. The subclass, C, cannot invoke test() without overriding it.

    c. A subclass cannot define main() if its superclass also defines main().

8. This question also builds on class B, defined in Question 6. Is it legal to write a subclass of B (and new subclass of Exception) like this?

```
class C extends B {

    public static void main(String[] args) {
        C c = new C();
```

```
        c.test(args);
    }

    void method(String s) throws AnotherException {
        if (s.equals("yes"))
            throw new AnotherException();
        else
            return;
    }
}

class AnotherException extends Exception {
}
```

    a. This code is legal.

    b. This code is illegal because AnotherException is not declared correctly.

    c. This code is illegal because the method you override cannot throw exceptions not declared by its ancestor's method.

9. This question also builds on class B, defined in Question 6. Is it legal to write a subclass of B (and a subclass of MyException) like this?

```
class C extends B {

    public static void main(String[] args) {
        C c = new C();
        c.test(args);
    }

    void method(String s) throws AnotherException {
        if (s.equals("yes"))
            throw new AnotherException();
        else
            return;
    }
}

class AnotherException extends MyException {
}
```

    a. This code is legal.

    b. This code is illegal because AnotherException is not declared correctly.

    c. This code is illegal because the method you override cannot throw exceptions not declared by its ancestor's method.

Answers to Review Questions

1. **a.** Let's look at the two other choices:

   - "Code that does not throw an exception cannot be in a try block." This is not true. You can have code that does not throw an exception within a try block. If you do, however you need a finally block following it.

   - "The method main() must always throw something if the try block is used without a catch." Again, this is not true because you can use a try block with a finally block. No exceptions have to be involved in that case.

2. **c.** This code will not compile. Exception must be handled in main(), or main() must indicate that it throws an Exception.

3. **c.** Both "hello" and "good-bye" will appear in the standard output.

4. **c.** Both "hello" and "good-bye" will appear in the standard output. Even though the code in try issues a return statement, the finally block is still executed.

5. **a.** Only the word "hello" appears in the standard output. Why doesn't "good-bye" appear? Because this is not a control flow issue. We go from writing "hello" to invoking a method named exit() in the System class. The exit() method exits to the system. We never return to this method to reach the finally block. (Sneaky, I know.)

6. **b.** Run this to see the results in the standard output.

7. **a.** The overridden method in class C should be declared as follows:

```
void method(String s) throws MyException {
    if (s.equals("yes"))
        throw new MyException();
    else
        return;
}
```

8. **c.** The method you override can only throw exceptions that have been declared by the ancestor's method.

9. **a.** This is legal. A method you override can throw any exception declared by its ancestor's method or any subclass of one of these exceptions. In this case, AnotherException has been defined as a subclass of MyException, which class B's method named method() declares it is capable of throwing.

CHAPTER 15

Multithreading

Objectives for This Chapter

- Write code to define, instantiate, and start new threads using both java.lang.Thread and java.lang.Runnable.
- Recognize conditions that might prevent a thread from executing.
- Write code using synchronized, wait, notify, and notifyAll to protect against concurrent access problems and to communicate between threads.
- Define the interaction between threads and between threads and object locks when executing synchronized, wait, notify, or notifyAll.

One of the most powerful aspects to Java is its capability to easily perform multiple tasks concurrently. Java builds multitasking into its keywords and into its core set of classes. Such foresight not only makes multitasking easier, as an add-on class library might in C, but it also makes multitasking platform-independent, object-oriented, and part of the language itself. Multitasking also helps make Java a natural language for the Internet. For example, your program can download a file in the background while running a Java applet in the foreground.

Java enables multitasking through the use of threads. Your program can create new instances of class Thread or subclasses of Thread to represent a thread of control. There is a thread life cycle that helps you keep track of what a thread is doing, there are keywords to coordinate among competing threads, and there are rules about scheduling threads and assigning priorities to them.

An Overview of Threads

Java builds multitasking right into its language keywords as well as into a core set of classes. Java represents a thread of execution using an instance of class Thread. Threads can run independently of each other, though they can also interact with each other. To help coordinate among threads, you can use the keyword synchronized.

A Java program runs until the only threads left running are *daemon* threads. The Java runtime consists of daemon threads that run your program. A Thread can be set as a daemon or user thread when it is created.

Thread States

In a standalone program, your class runs until your main() method exits—unless your main() method creates more threads. You can initiate your own thread of execution by creating a Thread object, invoking its start() method, and providing the behavior that tells the thread what to do. The thread will run until its run() method exits, after which it will come to a halt—thus ending its life cycle.

When the run() method returns, the thread is considered to be *dead*. A dead thread cannot be restarted. If you need to run the thread's task again, you must construct and start a new thread instance. Keep in mind though that the dead thread still exists as an object (either Thread or Runnable) but it doesn't run as a separate thread of execution.

Threads have other states as well. These states are:

- **Ready** When you create a thread, the thread doesn't run immediately. You must call the thread's start() method and afterward, the thread goes into a *ready* state where it waits for the scheduler to move it to the *running* state. A thread can also enter the ready state if after previously executing, it entered the *waiting* state and then became ready to resume its execution. A call to the yield() method can put a thread in the ready *state,* provided the thread scheduler allows the thread to yield. When monitors and synchronization are used, a thread may be in a waiting because the notify() or notifyall() method was called.

- **Running** When the thread scheduler allocates CPU time to a thread, it is in the *running* state. This means the thread is executing. The thread can be interrupted or otherwise leave this state.

- **Waiting** Threads can enter a *waiting* state for many different reasons. The thread may be waiting in input or it may be sleeping. The thread may have been interrupted or its execution may have been blocked. When monitors and synchronization are used, a thread may be in a waiting because the wait() method was called.

Each object has a lock that can be controlled by one thread only. The lock controls access to the object's synchronized code. Before a thread can access synchronized code, the thread must attempt to acquire the lock on the object. If the lock is currently available, meaning no other thread has the lock, the thread can obtain the lock and enter the ready state. While the thread has the lock on the object, no other synchronized methods may be invoked for that object. The lock is automatically released when the method completes execution and returns. The lock can also be released when a synchronized method executes wait(), yield(), or other methods that cause the thread to change from the running state.

If another thread has the lock, the thread has to wait on the lock. The thread then enters the waiting state until it can acquire the lock. When the thread acquires the lock, it moves from the waiting state to the ready state.

Thread Life Cycles

It's often useful to think of a thread as having a life cycle. Thread life cycle stages take the descriptive names "alive" (made up of two states, "running" "waiting"), and "dead." These stages are shown in Figure 15-1. We'll look at these stages, because this progression makes clearer what happens to a thread in a program.

Creating a new Thread instance puts the thread into the ready state. It's not alive until someone invokes the thread's start() method. The thread is then alive and will respond to the method isAlive() by returning true. The thread will continue to return true to isAlive() until it is dead, no matter whether it is in the running or waiting state.

You'll often see run() methods that loop forever, as in:

```
public void run() {
  while (true) {
    //do something continuously, like show an animation
  }
}
```

Does this mean this thread can never die? That its life cycle is different? No. Because other events can transition the thread out of its current state. Two ways you can keep a thread alive and transition it between running and waiting are

- **Putting it to sleep and waking it up**   When you put a thread to sleep(), you put it to sleep for a specified number of milliseconds. When this time has elapsed, the thread wakes up and continues with what it was doing. Putting a thread to sleep is a convenient way to slow down an animation. For example, rather than letting one frame move to the next in a blur, you could add a short pause to help the user keep up with the animation.

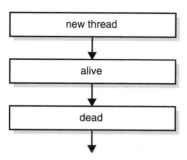

Figure 15-1 The thread life cycle

- **Pausing it and resuming it** Prior to JDK 1.2, you could use the stop(), suspend(), and resume() methods to control threads. The stop() method forcibly terminates a thread and puts it in the *dead* state. The suspend() method puts a thread in the waiting state and a subsequent call to resume allows the thread to return to the ready state where it can be scheduled to run. In JDK 1.2 and later, the stop(), suspend(), and resume()are deprecated.

These techniques both relate to one thread at a time; there is no communication between threads. You put one thread to sleep or wake it up; you pause one thread or resume that thread. Neither of these ways to control a thread are on the test. However, as always, the explanations for these methods are presented at the end of this chapter, because, as an expert, others will expect you to know them.

What is on the test is a third way to transition threads between running and waiting. However, unlike the two approaches listed above, this third way enables threads to interact with each other and provides some coordination between them. This third way uses the methods wait(), notify(), and notifyAll().

Thread Scheduling and Priorities

Threads have priorities. The thread with the highest priority is the one that Java runs. All the other threads have to wait. If more than one thread has the same highest priority, Java will switch between them.

If two threads are alive with the same highest priority, the JVM switches between them, usually quickly enough so that you never realize they are alternating execute-sleep-execute-sleep cycles. Java will switch between any number of threads with the same highest priority.

The priority numbers for threads falls between the range of Thread.MIN_PRIORITY and Thread.MAX_PRIORITY. The default priority, Thread.NORM_PRIORITY, is typically midway between these two. New threads take on the priority of the thread that spawned them.

You can explicitly set the priority of a thread using setPriority(), and you can get the priority of a thread using getPriority(). As you might expect, if a thread is currently executing and you use setPriority() to set a thread's priority to something less than it was before, the thread might stop executing, since there might now be another thread with a higher priority.

You can use priorities to help ensure that your program responds to the user as expected. For example, let's say you are implementing a special kind of Web browser. You can set the thread to read the Web page over the Internet at a lower priority than a thread that responds to the user clicking the stop button. This way, your browser is likely to respond immediately when the user clicks stop, rather than waiting until a large page is downloaded because the communication thread would not yield control.

CAUTION: The Java Virtual Machine determines when a thread can run based on its priority ranking, but that doesn't mean that a lower-priority thread will not run. This is important, because you should not rely on priorities to predict precisely what will occur in your program and when. For example, you should not rely on priorities to determine the correctness of an algorithm.

You don't have to rely on the Java Virtual Machine to switch between threads with the same priority. The currently executing thread can yield control by invoking yield(). If you invoke yield(), Java will pick a new thread to run. However, it is possible the thread that just yielded might run again immediately if it is the highest-priority thread.

Creating Threads With java.lang.Thread and java.lang.Runnable

When you invoke a thread's start() method, the Java runtime will invoke the Thread's run() method. However, the Thread class, by default, doesn't provide any behavior for run(). This thread will end quickly and will not have accomplished anything useful.

There are two ways to resolve this problem. You can subclass the Thread class and override the run() method, or you can implement the Runnable interface and indicate an instance of this class will be the thread's target.

Here's an example of each approach.

Subclassing Thread

You subclass threads to provide their behavior. When you subclass a Thread, you must override a method named run() to provide behavior for the thread.

Here's an example of a bouncing ball—it continuously reverses direction when it reaches the top or bottom of the screen. Figure 15-2 shows the ball somewhere in the middle of its travels up and down the applet.

Here's the applet:

```java
import java.awt.*;
import java.applet.Applet;
public class UpDown extends Applet {
    static int RADIUS = 20;
    static int X = 30;
    public int y = 30;
    public void init() {
        new BounceThread(this).start();
    }

    public void paint(Graphics g) {
        g.setColor(Color.blue);
        g.drawOval(X - RADIUS, y - RADIUS,
            2 * RADIUS, 2 * RADIUS);
    }
}

class BounceThread extends Thread {
    UpDown applet;
    int     yDir = +1;
```

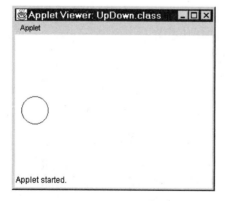

Figure 15-2 A screen snapshot of a bouncing ball

```
int     incr = 10;
int     sleepFor = 100;

BounceThread(UpDown a) {
   this.applet = a;
}

public void run() {
   while (true) {
      applet.y += (incr * yDir);
      applet.repaint();

      if (applet.y - UpDown.RADIUS < incr ||
         applet.y + UpDown.RADIUS + incr > applet.getSize().height)
         yDir *= -1;

      try {
         sleep(sleepFor);
      } catch (InterruptedException e) {
      }
   }
}
}
```

This applet creates a new thread and supplies a paint() method to draw a circle. The thread moves the circle's y value up and down, issuing a repaint and then going to sleep for 1/10 of a second. You'll learn about the sleep() method at the end of this chapter, but it should be fairly clear what it does: It puts a thread to sleep for a specified number of milliseconds. The thread reverses the direction it moves the ball's y value whenever the ball reaches the top or bottom of the applet's window. I've also taken the ball's (that is, the oval's) radius into account so that the ball appears to bounce off the inside edge of the applet.

TIP: The drawOval( ) method used by paint( ) draws an oval given the left and top of the oval, so I've offset where I draw the oval to take the radius into account.

Implementing Runnable

You can also implement the Runnable interface to provide the behavior of a thread. Here instead of creating a Thread subclass, you can write the code with only one class definition. You can accomplish this by implementing the Runnable interface and specifying the Java applet as the thread's target.

The Runnable interface defines one method that must be implemented: run(). A Thread can look to its target—an object whose class implements Runnable—to find its run() behavior.

When the thread needs to invoke its run() behavior, we can make certain the thread knows to look to its target object for the run() method.

Here's an example of the same bouncing ball, this time implemented using the Runnable interface instead of a Thread subclass:

```java
import java.awt.*;
import java.applet.Applet;

public class UpDown2 extends Applet implements Runnable {
    static int RADIUS = 20;
    static int X = 30;
    public int y = 30;
    Thread t;

public void init() {
    t = new Thread(this);
    t.start();
}

    public void paint(Graphics g) {
      g.setColor(Color.blue);
      g.drawOval(X - RADIUS, y - RADIUS,
        2 * RADIUS, 2 * RADIUS);
    }

    public void run() {
        int    yDir = +1;
        int    incr = 10;
        int    sleepFor = 100;

      while (true) {
         y += (incr * yDir);
         repaint();

         if (y - UpDown.RADIUS < incr ||
             y + UpDown.RADIUS + incr > getSize().height)
           yDir *= -1;

         try {
            t.sleep(sleepFor);
         } catch (InterruptedException e) {
         }
      }
   }
}
```

The Thread knows to look to its target because we have supplied a target object when we created the Thread instance. We did this in the init() method with the line:

```
t = new Thread(this);
```

In this case, we are indicating that the Applet object itself will be the target (that's why we used this). That's also why the Applet implemented the Runnable interface and supplied a run() method.

This version of UpDown is somewhat simpler than the first version. The run() method does not need to access the applet's instance or class variables through references anymore, since both run() and these variables are now defined in the same class definition. We do, however, have to keep track of the Thread instance, so that we can use this reference to invoke its sleep() method in run().

Exercise 15.1

Rewrite the following program to implement the Runnable interface rather than using a Thread subclass. This applet continually displays numbers in blue, one number per second. If the number is a prime, the applet displays the number in red.

Here is the code:

```
import java.awt.*;
import java.applet.Applet;

public class Ex1 extends Applet {
    Color       color = Color.red;
    int         candidate = 3;
    PrimeThread prime;

    public void init() {
        prime = new PrimeThread(this);
        prime.start();
    }

    public void paint(Graphics g) {
        g.setColor(color);
        g.drawString(new Integer(candidate).toString(), 30, 40);
    }

}

class PrimeThread extends Thread {
    Ex1 target;

    PrimeThread (Ex1 target) {
        this.target = target;
    }
```

```java
    public void run() {
        int candidate;
        for (candidate = 3; ; candidate++) {
            if (isPrime(candidate))
                target.color = Color.red;
            else
                target.color = Color.blue;

            target.candidate = candidate;
            target.repaint();

            try {
                sleep(1000);
            } catch (InterruptedException ie) {
            }
        }
    }

    public boolean isPrime(int number) {
        boolean isPrime = true;

        for (int i = 2; i < number - 1 && isPrime; i++) {
            if ( (number % i ) == 0)
                isPrime = false;
        }
        return isPrime;
    }
}
```

Monitors and Synchronization

For the exam, you'll need to be able to write code using synchronized threads that protect against concurrent access problems. You'll also need to be able to work with wait(), notify(), and notifyAll().

Understanding Synchronization

Working with concurrent threads sounds like a great idea, but we can create a many-headed monster if we're not careful. All these threads running about doing their own thing can get confusing, and threads might start to step on each others' toes. What if multiple threads need to change the same data? What if multiple threads each want to display something to the user? Will their efforts conflict with each other?

Here's an example of what might go wrong if a program doesn't use synchronization. Imagine an airline ticketing application. A ticket agent wants to assign a passenger to a seat. So he calls up a picture of a jet and looks at a map of the open seats. He looks for a minute or two until he spots a lovely window seat, 14A, then fills the passenger's request for a nice view and assigns the passenger to that seat.

In an application that uses only a single thread of execution, this works just fine. The ticket agent acts as the coordinator between multiple passengers who might request the same seat. For a multithreaded application, this has the potential for two passengers fighting over the same seat when they board the plane. (Perhaps you've seen this happening. Do you think their tickets were issued with a Java application? I think not.) The problem is that two separate threads might try to update the same data at once.

Here's a scenario. First, our ticket agent clicks a button to assign the passenger to the open seat. The thread of control used by this agent's program enters the method to update the seat. The method starts working with the data, finds the seat empty, and, having passed this test, is about to update the seat, when out of the blue . . . another ticket agent, working separately on another computer, oblivious of the first agent, does the same thing—clicks his button on his screen to assign his passenger to seat 14A. The thread of execution used by this second ticket agent interrupts the first thread (in this example) and performs its update. Then, the first thread regains access to the CPU and performs its update. Now, each agent has a ticket with that seat assignment. While the computer thinks only one person is assigned to the seat, each ticket agent has a printed ticket with an identical seat assignment.

To eliminate this type of problem, where one thread is interrupted in mid-step by another thread, Java provides a way to coordinate and synchronize between multiple threads. In fact, unlike other languages, Java builds this capability right into the language.

Each object and each class has a monitor. Threads can take temporary ownership of a monitor and release it later so that another thread can take temporary ownership of the same monitor. This is important as far as synchronizing between threads, because only one thread at a time can own a particular monitor.

By owning a monitor, a thread blocks all other threads from working with the other synchronized methods defined for an object or class that the monitor belongs to.

Let's take another look at the ticket reservation example and see what would have happened had the program used monitors. The first ticket agent clicks a button to assign a passenger to seat 14A. At this point, the program used by the first ticket agent would take control of the object's monitor that contained the method for updating the seat assignments—perhaps an instance of a class called SeatLayout or PassengerJet. Now, the second ticket agent clicks his button, but this time there's a slight delay. His thread wants to take control of the monitor, but the thread cannot—another thread already owns it. So the second ticket agent's thread waits.

The first thread checks the seat 14A, finds it open, and performs the update. Then it exits, releasing the monitor. Now the second thread can have its turn. It takes control of the monitor, but when it goes to check 14A before the update, it finds the seat is already taken (which is exactly what we want). Now the ticket agent can assign the passenger to a different seat, and all is well again.

The way that a method takes control of an object's monitor is by entering a block of code or a method that's defined using the keyword synchronized.

There are three types of code that can be synchronized:

- class methods

- instance methods

- any block of code within a method

To declare a method to be synchronized, use the keyword synchronized when declaring the method, as in:

```
synchronized boolean reserveSeat(SeatID id) {
   //method body goes here
}
```

Declaring a class method as synchronized is done similarly.

To declare a block of code as synchronized, use the keyword synchronized in front of that block. Then, in parentheses, indicate the object or the class whose monitor this code needs to acquire. Here's an example of synchronizing a block of code given an object reference:

```
boolean reserveSeat(SeatID id) {
   //method code can come before or after the synchronized block
   synchronized (currentPlane) {
     //synchronized code goes here . . .
   }

   //method code can come before or after the synchronized block
}
```

Using an object reference is appropriate in this example, where we only want one ticket agent assigning seats for a single plane—the plane they're currently working on— at one time.

TIP: Sometimes, it's appropriate to list a class after the synchronized keyword, such as when the code will change static data.

Using the synchronized keyword in a block of code takes the monitor from the class if it is a class method, or the object if it is an instance method. The synchronized keyword guarantees that only one thread at a time will execute that object's or class' code. If you have defined an instance method to be synchronized, any subclasses that override this method can be synchronized or not, according to their preference.

Synchronization stays in effect if you enter a synchronized method and call out to a nonsynchronized method. So, if a subclass overrides a nonsynchronized method and declares that method to be synchronized, the thread executing the synchronized method will continue to hold the monitor for an object, even if that method calls the nonsynchronized superclass' method using super. The thread only gives up the monitor after the synchronized method returns.

Exercise 15.2

Variables cannot take the synchronized keyword. That means that, in the code below, even though one thread might be in the middle of updateBalance(), another thread might still come along and read the balance.

However, you can provide accessor methods for a variable and make that accessor method synchronized. Rewrite the following class so that its variable is (in effect) synchronized by defining a synchronized accessor method.

```
class Account {
  double balance;
  synchronized void updateBalance(double amount) {
    balance += amount;
  }
}
```

Using wait( ), notify( ), and notifyAll( )

Synchronization stops bugs from occurring where one thread changes the state of an object that another thread had depended on to be stable. However, synchronization does nothing as far as communicating between threads. Sometimes, you need a way for one thread to be informed of what another thread is doing. For example, thread number 1 might be waiting for thread number 2 to calculate some result. When thread number 2 achieves this result, it should be able to notify thread number 1 that it found the result thread number 1 was waiting for.

Java builds a wait-notify mechanism into the Object class. By using the methods wait(), notify(), and notifyAll(), any thread can wait for some condition in an object to change, and any thread can notify all threads waiting on that object's condition that the condition has changed and that they should continue. A common scenario where this is useful is where one thread produces data for an object, and another thread is using the data in the object.

Here's a simple example of using wait() and notify(). The following applet, named ClickApplet, starts by creating a couple of ClickCanvas instances in its init() method. Each one of these special Canvas subclasses spawns a new thread in its constructor. The thread's run() method (supplied by ClickCanvas) waits on a condition. It starts waiting when it invokes wait(). The condition it's waiting to change is the boolean value defined in the applet named clicked.

As soon as clicked becomes true, the Canvas continues. How does the Canvas' thread know when the condition becomes true? The mouseDown() method in the applet, running in the user input thread, notifies the Canvas' thread that the condition has changed. It does this by invoking notify().

Here's the code.

```java
import java.awt.*;
import java.applet.*;
import java.awt.event.*;

public class ClickApplet extends Applet implements MouseListener   {

    boolean clicked;
    int counter;

    public void init() {
        add(new ClickCanvas(this));
        add(new ClickCanvas(this));
        addMouseListener(this);
    }

    public void mousePressed(MouseEvent e)
    {
        synchronized (this) {
            clicked = true;
            notifyAll();
        }
        counter++;
    }


    // stubbed methods from MouseListener interface
    public void mouseClicked(MouseEvent e) {}
    public void mouseReleased(MouseEvent e) {}
    public void mouseEntered(MouseEvent e) {}
    public void mouseExited(MouseEvent e) {}
}

class ClickCanvas extends Canvas implements Runnable{
    ClickApplet applet;
```

```
ClickCanvas(ClickApplet applet) {
    this.applet = applet;
    setBackground(Color.blue);
    setSize(30, 30);
    new Thread(this).start();
}

public void run() {
    while (true) {
        synchronized (applet) {
            while (!applet.clicked) {
                try {
                    applet.wait();
                }
                catch (InterruptedException x) {
                }
            }
            applet.clicked = false;
        }
        repaint(250);
    }
}

public void paint(Graphics g) {
    g.drawString(new Integer(applet.counter).toString(), 10, 20);
}
}
```

This applet counts the number of clicks the user makes in the applet. Of course, we could have simply made mouseDown() in the applet display the clicks and update the counter variable, but we want the above code to show how to coordinate between threads. Without wait() and notify() (or without a direct method call), there is no way for the ClickCanvas objects to know when to update their displays.

This applet exhibits some interesting behavior. Figure 15-3 shows what it looks like when it starts.

As the user starts clicking the applet, only one number in one ClickCanvas object updates at a time. Figures 15-4 and 15-5 are two screen shots showing successive clicks.

Why aren't both ClickCanvas objects updated at the same time? Why do they seem to leap-frog each other? Because we have only invoked notify(), rather than notifyAll().

When the waiting thread pauses, it relinquishes the object's monitor and waits to be notified that it should try to reacquire it. It does this with a call to wait(). Notice that we indicate which object we're waiting on. In this case, we're waiting on the applet. Since we keep the applet in an instance variable named applet in the ClickCanvas object, we can wait on the applet object by writing:

```
applet.wait();
```

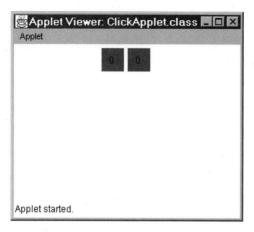

Figure 15-3   ClickApplet when it first appears in the appletviewer

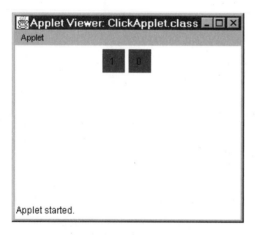

Figure 15-4   ClickApplet after the first click

Generally, wait() is placed inside of a while clause. The idea is that just because a thread wakes up, the condition it's waiting on has not necessarily changed. So, this condition should be rechecked and the thread should wait again if necessary.

You'll also notice two other things about the call to wait(). First, it is placed inside of a try-catch block. The wait() method might throw an InterruptedException, so the code must be prepared to handle that. Second, wait() is placed inside a synchronized block. The wait() and notify() methods can only be invoked from synchronized code. The

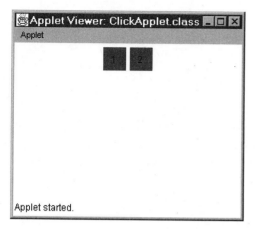

Figure 15-5 ClickApplet after the second click

monitor that the block or method acquires for synchronization must belong to the object that the thread will wait on. In fact, if you try to invoke wait() on an object without owning the object's monitor, the Java runtime will throw an IllegalMonitorStateException.

Placing the calls to wait() and notify() within synchronized code does two things. First, it guarantees that the currently executing code owns the monitor, so that this code can give it up in the call to wait() or notify(). Second, it helps ensure the contents of the object being used to determine when the conditions are stable. For example, since a while loop surrounds the wait() call, it's important that the condition doesn't change to false before the code escapes the while loop after a notify() call.

The notify() method wakes up one thread waiting to reacquire the monitor for the object. The thread it awakens is generally the one that has been waiting the longest. If you know you only have one thread waiting on a condition, you can to use notify(). Then, your application's behavior is predictable.

> **CAUTION:** Just because the thread that notify( ) awakens is generally the one that has been waiting the longest, you should not rely on this for your algorithm to work. It is not guaranteed to awaken the longest-waiting thread; it is only most likely to awaken that one.

If you have more than one thread (or if there is the potential to have more than one thread) waiting on a condition, you should use notifyAll() instead of notify(). The notifyAll() method wakes up all threads waiting to reacquire the monitor for the object.

Exercise 15.3

Rewrite the ClickApplet so that both threads are notified when the user clicks.

Managing Threads With Wait-Notify and Sleep

Prior to JDK 1.2, you could control a thread through pause(), resume(), and stop() methods. These methods were deprecated because they could cause problems in the code. For example, if you forcibly stop a thread, you can cause data corruption or even a deadlock condition in which the program freezes up. To avoid these and other pitfalls, these methods were deprecated in favor of other techniques. This doesn't mean you won't need to temporarily stop a thread from executing, or that you won't need to stop thread execution altogether. You'll still need to do this but you'll need to make use of the currently available methods to implement these behaviors safely. The new technique is to use a wait-notify-sleep mechanism.

To demonstrate the old and new methods, I've rewritten the bouncing ball program. The first version uses the deprecated pause(), resume(), and stop() methods. The second version uses wait(), notify(), and sleep().

Here's the first version using pause(), resume(), and stop():

```java
import java.awt.*;
import java.applet.Applet;

public class UpDown3 extends Applet {
    static int RADIUS = 20;
    static int X = 30;
    public int y = 30;
    BounceThread thread;

    public void init() {
        thread = new BounceThread(this);
    }

    public void start() {
      if (thread.isAlive())
        thread.resume();
      else
        thread.start();
      }

    public void stop() {
      thread.suspend();
    }

    public void destroy() {
      thread.stop();
    }
```

```
    public void paint(Graphics g) {
        g.setColor(Color.blue);
        g.drawOval(X - RADIUS, y - RADIUS,
            2 * RADIUS, 2 * RADIUS);
    }
}

class BounceThread extends Thread {
    UpDown applet;
    int     yDir = +1;
    int     incr = 10;
    int     sleepFor = 100;

    BounceThread(UpDown a) {
        this.applet = a;
    }

    public void run() {
        while (true) {
            applet.y += (incr * yDir);
            applet.repaint();

            if (applet.y - UpDown.RADIUS < incr ||
                applet.y + UpDown.RADIUS + incr >
                applet.size().height)
                yDir *= -1;

            try {
                sleep(sleepFor);
            } catch (InterruptedException e) {
            }
        }
    }
}
```

Here's the next version using wait(), notify(), and sleep():

```
import java.awt.*;
import java.applet.Applet;

public class UpDown4 extends Applet {
    static int RADIUS = 20;
    static int X = 30;
    public int y = 30;
    volatile BounceThread bounceThread;
    volatile boolean threadSuspended = true;

    public void init() {
        bounceThread = new BounceThread(this);
        bounceThread.start();
    }

    public void start() {
        if (bounceThread != null)
```

```
        {
          synchronized(bounceThread)
          {
            threadSuspended = false;
            bounceThread.notify();
          }
        }
      }

      public void stop() {
        threadSuspended = true;
      }

      public void destroy() {
        synchronized(bounceThread)
        {
          Thread t = bounceThread;
          bounceThread = null;
          t.notify();
        }
      }

      public void paint(Graphics g) {
        g.setColor(Color.blue);
        g.drawOval(X - RADIUS, y - RADIUS,
            2 * RADIUS, 2 * RADIUS);
      }
    }

    class BounceThread extends Thread {
      UpDown  applet;
      int     yDir = +1;
      int     incr = 10;
      int     sleepFor = 100;

      BounceThread(UpDown a) {
        this.applet = a;
      }

      public void run() {
        Thread currThread = Thread.currentThread();
        while (applet.bounceThread == currThread) {
          try {
            currThread.sleep(sleepFor);

            synchronized (this) {
              while (applet.threadSuspended &&
                  (applet.bounceThread ==
                  currThread))
                wait();
            }
          } catch (InterruptedException e) {
          }
```

```
        applet.y += (incr * yDir);
        applet.repaint();
        if (applet.y - UpDown.RADIUS < incr ||
            applet.y + UpDown.RADIUS + incr >
            applet.getSize().height)
            yDir *= -1;
    }
  }
}
```

Compare the two examples closely. For the exam, you'll need to be able to write code that uses wait(), notify(), and sleep(). Note also that both versions use a Thread subclass, but of course this would work just as well for the version that implements the Runnable interface. If the Web page containing the applet goes off-screen, the applet should stop, and that's what happens here. When the Web page comes back onscreen, the applet will start again.

Why a Thread Might Not Execute

For the exam, you'll need to be able to identify when conditions might prevent a thread from executing. Here is a list of reasons why a thread might be alive but still not run:

- The thread is not the highest priority thread and so cannot get CPU time.
- The thread has been put to sleep using the sleep() method.
- There is more than one thread with the same highest priority, and the Java Virtual Machine is switching between these threads; at the moment, the thread in question is awaiting CPU time.
- The thread is blocked. It is waiting for I/O call, or failed to get a monitor's lock and is waiting for the monitor's lock.
- The thread is waiting on a condition because someone invoked wait() for the thread. The thread waits for notify() or notifyAll().
- The thread has explicitly yielded control by invoking yield().

Exercise 15.4

Write four applets, each one illustrating a different aspect from the above list of reasons why a thread might not run.

Other Useful Thread Methods

Generally, a thread created by the user is a user thread. However, you can mark a thread as a daemon thread before you start it if you like by using setDaemon(). The Java Virtual Machine keeps running until all user threads have ended.

You can name threads using setName() or by supplying a name to the Thread's constructor. You can retrieve a thread's name using getName(). Naming a thread could be useful in identifying a particular thread if you are using more than one.

There is a static method named currentThread() that retrieves the currently executing thread. This allows you to put the current thread to sleep, for example, or to invoke some other method on it.

The join() method waits for a thread to die before continuing. You might use join() to stop execution until a thread has completed its task.

You can treat threads as a set by using a ThreadGroup. The ThreadGroup class defines most of the methods that affect individual threads. By assigning a thread to a ThreadGroup when you create the thread, you can then affect many threads at once.

Answers to the Exercises

Exercise 15.1

Here is one possible solution:

```
import java.awt.*;
import java.applet.Applet;

public class Ans1 extends Applet implements Runnable {
    Color        color = Color.red;
    int          candidate = 3;
    Thread       prime;

    public void init() {
        prime = new Thread(this);
        prime.start();
    }

    public void paint(Graphics g) {
        g.setColor(color);
        g.drawString(new Integer(candidate).toString(), 30, 40);
    }

    public void run() {
```

```
      for (candidate = 3; ; candidate++) {
         if (isPrime(candidate))
            color = Color.red;
         else
            color = Color.blue;

         repaint();

         try {
            prime.sleep(1000);
         } catch (InterruptedException ie) {
         }
      }
   }

   public boolean isPrime(int number) {
      boolean isPrime = true;

      for (int i = 2; i < number - 1 && isPrime; i++) {
         if ( (number % i ) == 0)
            isPrime = false;
      }
      return isPrime;
   }

}
```

A common mistake in making this conversion is to forget to write implements Runnable in the class definition. If you forget this part, the compiler will complain about not finding a constructor matching the way you are trying to create the thread. The issue here is that the Thread constructor that takes a target for the run() method takes an instance of Runnable. Remember, an object of a class that implements an interface is considered an instance of that class. You can think of it like this: instanceof will return true for a class that implements an interface. So, if you forget to define your class (your applet, in this case) as implementing the Runnable interface, it won't match one of the Thread's constructors.

Exercise 15.2

```
class Account {
   private double balance;

   synchronized double getBalance() {
      return balance;
   }

   synchronized void setBalance(double newBalance) {
      balance = newBalance;
   }
```

```
    synchronized void updateBalance(double amount) {
        setBalance(getBalance() + amount);
    }
}
```

With this rewrite, no other thread can access the balance field (unless it circumvents the accessor method protocol) when the updateBalance() method is in the middle of altering its value.

Exercise 15.3

Simply change the call to notify() to notifyAll(). The rest of the applet stays the same.

Exercise 15.4

Here are four programs that illustrate the first four items from this list:

• The thread is not the highest priority thread and so cannot get CPU time.

```
class Ex1504a {
    public static void main(String[] args) {
        MyThread t1 = new MyThread(1);
        MyThread t2 = new MyThread(2);

        t1.setPriority(Thread.MAX_PRIORITY);
        t2.setPriority(Thread.MIN_PRIORITY);

        t1.start();
        t2.start();
    }
}

class MyThread extends Thread {
    int id;
    MyThread(int id) {
        this.id = id;
    }

    public void run() {
        for (int i = 0; i < 100; i++)
            System.out.println("My id is " + id);
    }
}
```

In most cases, the output from this program is 100 lines of "My id is 1" and then, once that thread has completed, 100 lines of "My id is 2." However, keep in mind that the highest priority thread doesn't necessarily run first, which could mean that the output would change.

- The thread has been put to sleep using the sleep() method:

```
class Ex1504b {
    public static void main(String[] args) {
        MyThread t1 = new MyThread(1);
        MyThread t2 = new MyThread(2);

        t1.setPriority(Thread.MAX_PRIORITY);
        t2.setPriority(Thread.MIN_PRIORITY);

        t1.start();
        t2.start();
    }
}

class MyThread extends Thread {
    int id;
    MyThread(int id) {
        this.id = id;
    }

    public void run() {
        for (int i = 0; i < 100; i++) {
            if (id == 1 && i == 50) {
                try {
                    sleep(1000);
                } catch (InterruptedException x) {
                }
            }
            System.out.println("My id is " + id);
        }
    }
}
```

In most cases, the output from this program is 50 lines of My id is 1. Then, that thread goes to sleep, long enough (on my computer, at least) for the other thread to write out all of its lines (My id is 2). Then the first thread continues. With a shorter time, the sleeping thread would wake up and, with a higher priority than the currently running thread, get immediate access to the CPU and continue on. Again, keep in mind that the highest priority thread doesn't necessarily run first, which could mean that the output would change.

- There is more than one thread with the same highest priority, and the Java Virtual Machine is switching between these threads; at the moment, the thread in question is awaiting CPU time:

```
class Ex1504c {
    public static void main(String[] args) {
        MyThread t1 = new MyThread(1);
```

```
            MyThread t2 = new MyThread(2);

            t1.other = t2;
            t2.other = t1;

            t1.start();
            t2.start();
        }
    }

    class MyThread extends Thread {
        int id;
        MyThread other;
        MyThread(int id) {
            this.id = id;
        }

        public void run() {
            for (int i = 0; i < 100; i++) {
                System.out.println("My id is " + id);
            }
        }
    }
```

This program unpredictably alternates between displaying a few My id is 1 messages and then a few My id is 2 in the standard output.

- The thread has explicitly yielded control by invoking yield().

```
    class Ex1504d {
        public static void main(String[] args) {
            MyThread t1 = new MyThread(1);
            MyThread t2 = new MyThread(2);

            t1.other = t2;
            t2.other = t1;

            t1.start();
            t2.start();
        }
    }

    class MyThread extends Thread {
        int id;
        MyThread other;
        MyThread(int id) {
            this.id = id;
        }

        public void run() {
            for (int i = 0; i < 100; i++) {
                System.out.println("My id is " + id);
            }
```

```
      yield();
    }
  }
}
```

In most cases, this program displays all of the My id is 1 messages first, because it yields to the other thread. Once this thread's run() method is about to end, it runs the other thread, and it then displays all of its My id is 2 messages. Again, keep in mind that the highest priority thread doesn't necessarily run first, which could mean that the output would change.

Review Questions

1. If you would like to create a thread and supply a target that implements the Runnable interface, you can write:

   a. Thread t = new Thread(target);

   b. Thread t = new Thread(); t.target = target;

   c. Thread t = new Thread(); t.start(target);

2. Why might a thread be alive but not be the currently executing thread?

   a. It is the only thread currently running.

   b. It has been suspended.

   c. It has been resumed.

   d. It has been notified of some condition.

   e. All of the above.

3. What might make this method throw an exception (other than InterruptedException) when it runs (if anything)?

```
public void holdIt(Object ref) {
   synchronized (this) {
      try {
         ref.wait();
      } catch (InterruptedException x) {
      }
   }
}
```

   a. The call to wait() is not within a while loop.

   b. The holdIt() method must be synchronized.

   c. The current thread does not own the monitor it needs to invoke wait().

   d. nothing is wrong with this method definition—it will run fine and will not throw an exception.

4. If you have created two threads, one with a priority of Thread.MAX_PRIORITY and one with a normal, default priority, then which of these statements is true?
   a. The thread with the normal priority will definitely not run until the thread with the maximum priority ends.
   b. The thread with the normal priority will never run, even after the thread with the maximum priority ends.
   c. Neither of these statements is true.

5. The wait() method is defined in class:
   a. Thread
   b. Applet
   c. Object
   d. Runnable

6. You can set a thread's priority:
   a. When you first create the thread
   b. At any time after you create the thread
   c. Both of these

Answers to Review Questions

1. **a.** You must supply the target for the thread when you create it.

2. **b.** A suspended thread is not currently running and waits until it is resumed.

3. **c.** The code synchronizes on this, but then invokes wait() for ref, which might be a different object. If it were a different object, the call to wait() would cause Java to throw an IllegalMonitorStateException.

   To make this code hunky-dory, it could be written like this:

```
public void holdIt(Object ref) {
   synchronized (ref) {
      try {
         ref.wait();
      } catch (InterruptedException x) {
      }
   }
}
```

This time, the code synchronizes on the object ref, and then uses ref to invoke wait().

4. c. That's right. You should not rely on thread priorities for algorithm correctness. Even a thread with a lower priority may get some time to run. It will just get less time. But simply assigning one thread to the maximum priority and another thread to the minimum priority does not guarantee that the lower priority thread will not run. These priorities would just make one thread less likely to get access to the CPU, but it wouldn't stop it completely.

5. c. All Objects can respond to wait().

6. b. You can set a priority for a thread using setPriority(). There is no constructor that takes a thread priority.

Essential java.lang and java.util

Objectives for This Chapter

- Use wrapper classes to represent primitive values as objects.
- Write code using the following methods of the java.lang.Math class: abs(), ceil(), floor(), max(), min(), random(), round(), sin(), cos(), tan(), and sqrt().
- Identify legal operators for strings.
- Describe the significance of the immutability of String objects.
- Know the difference between the String and StringBuffer classes.
- Make appropriate selection of collection classes/interfaces to suit specified behavior requirements.

The java.lang and java.util packages are important parts of the Java language and, as you would expect, many exam questions pertain to these packages. This chapter focuses on the core aspects of java.lang and java.util that are identified with specific objectives in the exam, which includes wrapper classes for primitive data types, the java.lang.Math class, the java.lang.String class, and the java.util Collections API. You'll find separate chapters that cover other aspects of java.lang, such as exceptions, which are covered in Chapter 14, and threads, which are covered in Chapter 15. You'll also find limited discussion of java.util classes in other chapters.

Wrapper Classes

In Chapter 6, we covered Java's primitive data types. Primitive data types are not objects and cannot be subclassed. Primitive data types cannot be created or accessed with methods either. If you want to create or manipulate a primitive data type, you may want to wrap the primitive type with its corresponding wrapper class. Wrapper classes provide methods for working with, converting, and using the wrapped data types. The constructors for wrapped classes allow objects to be created and converted from primitive values or strings.

Table 16-1 shows corresponding wrapper classes for each of the eight primitive data types. Each of the wrapper classes is examined briefly in the sections that follow.

The Boolean Class

The Boolean class is a wrapper for boolean values. Key methods provided by the class are booleanValue(), getBoolean(), hashCode(), toString(), and valueOf(). These methods support type and class conversion.

The class has two constructors:

```
public Boolean(boolean value)
public Boolean(String s)
```

Thus, you can construct the class using an actual boolean value, such as:

```
boolean primitiveBool = false;
Boolean wrappedBool = new Boolean(primitiveBool);
```

Table 16-1   Primitive Data Types and Their Corresponding Wrapper Classes

Primitive Data Type	Wrapper Class
boolean	Boolean
byte	Byte
char	Character
double	Double
float	Float
int	Integer
long	Long
short	Short

Or you can pass the constructor a string that represents the value to be wrapped, such as:

```
Boolean wrappedBool = new Boolean("false");
```

The Character Class

The Character class is a wrapper for char values. The class provides many different methods for working with char values. You can use these methods to change case, to determine the type of value, and to perform class tests.

The class has one constructor:

```
public Character(char value)
```

Following this, you must construct the class using an actual char value, such as:

```
char primitiveChar = 'A';
Character wrappedChar = new Character(primitiveChar);
```

The Byte, Short, Integer, and Long Classes

The byte, short, int, and long primitive data types all have different wrapper classes. These classes provide methods for working with, testing, and converting the values. They also provide the MIN_VALUE and MAX_VALUE constants.

These classes all have two constructors, one that expects to be passed a primitive value and another that expects to be passed a String. You could construct these classes using primitive values as follows:

```
byte primitiveByte = 18;
Byte wrappedByte = new Byte(primitiveByte);
short primitiveShort = 12345;
Short wrappedShort = new Short(primitiveShort);
int primitiveInt = 9876543;
Integer wrappedInt = new Integer(primitiveInt);
long primitiveLong = 9997654321L;
Long wrappedLong = new Long(primitiveLong);
```

If you wanted to construct the classes from strings, you could use:

```
Byte wrappedByte = new Byte("18");
Short wrappedShort = new Short("12345");
Integer wrappedInt = new Integer("9876543");
Long wrappedLong = new Long("9997654321");
```

The Float and Double Classes

The Float and Double classes wrap the float and double primitive data types. These classes provide methods for working with, testing, and converting the values. They also provide the MIN_VALUE, MAX_VALUE, POSITIVIVE_INFINITY, and NEGATIVE_ INFINITY constants.

As with most other wrapper classes, the Float and Double classes have two constructors, one that expects to be passed a primitive value, and another that expects to be passed a String. To construct these classes using primitive values, you could use:

```
float primitiveFloat = 1.825F;
Float wrappedFloat = new Float(primitiveFloat);
double primitiveDouble = 1.825125125;
Double wrappedDouble = new Double(primitiveDouble);
```

To construct these classes using strings, you could use:

```
Float wrappedFloat = new Float("1.825F");
Double wrappedDouble = new Double("1.825125125");
```

Using Wrapper Classes

Wrapper classes can be used in many different ways, so lets review some of the basics which you'll need to know for the exam. When you use the string constructor for wrapper classes, all wrapper classes—with the exception of Boolean—will throw Number-FormatException if the string doesn't represent a valid value. Boolean doesn't throw this exception and instead, only wraps a value as true when you pass in the string "true". The Boolean class converts this string to lowercase for the comparison, so a string parameter of "tRuE" will work just as well.

After creating a wrapper class, you may need to extract the actual value. For example, if you created an Integer class and then needed to perform a calculation on the integer value, you would need to do this through the actual value. Each wrapper class has a method for performing this task. These methods are defined as follows:

```
public boolean booleanValue()
public byte byteValue()
public char charValue()
public double doubleValue()
public float floatValue()
public int intValue()
public long longValue()
public short shortValue()
```

The following code snippet shows how you could wrap an Integer and then extract its actual value for use in a calculation:

```
Integer i = new Integer("590");
Integer j = new Integer("150");
int k = i.intValue()*j.intValue();
```

All the wrapper classes except Character have a static method called valueOf(), which parses a string, constructs a wrapper of the same class type, and then returns the wrapper. For example, Integer.valueOf("405"), parses the value of the strings, constructs a wrapper of the Integer class, and then returns the wrapped value. You can then use the equals() method to check for equality of two wrappers. In the following example int1 and int2 are compared:

```
Integer int1 = new Integer("88995");
Integer int2 = new Integer("90110");
if (int1.equals(int2)) {
   System.out.println("The values are equal");
}
```

Exercise 16.1

Writes a standalone program that sets values for a Byte, Short, Integer, Long, Float, and Double. These values should be represented as strings to the wrapper class constructors. You should catch NumberFormatException if it occurs and display the error *Incorrect number format.*

Working with the Math Class

For the exam, you'll need to be able to write code that uses the static methods defined in the Math class. These static methods include abs(), ceil(), floor(), max(), min(), random(), round(), sin(), cos(), tan(), and sqrt(). Each of these methods is examined briefly in the sections that follow.

abs()

abs() returns the absolute value of a number. This method is overloaded with four versions: the argument can be a float, double, long, or int. The types byte and short are coerced to an int if they are used as arguments. This method returns the same type as the argument supplied.

ceil()

ceil() finds the next highest integer. The documentation says this method "returns the smallest (closest to negative infinity) double value that is not less than the argument and is equal to a mathematical integer." Let's unravel what this means with a simple example. Take a look at this program:

```
class M {
  public static void main(String[] args) {
      System.out.println(Math.ceil(9.01));
      System.out.println(Math.ceil(-0.1));
      System.out.println(Math.ceil(100));
      System.out.println(Math.ceil(Double.MIN_VALUE));
  }
}
```

When you run this, its output is:

```
10.0
-0.0
100.0
1.0
```

The value Double.MIN_VALUE is the smallest possible positive number that a variable of type double can hold. The ceil() method went up to 1. If the number is an integer to begin with, it returns that integer. Otherwise, it goes to the closest integer, counting up.

floor( )

floor() finds the next lowest integer. This method does the opposite of ceil(). Its documentation reads: "returns the largest (closest to positive infinity) double value that is not greater than the argument and is equal to a mathematical integer." Let's run the same program that we just ran, this time changing ceil() to floor():

```
class M2 {
public static void main(String[] args) {
    System.out.println(Math.floor(9.01));
    System.out.println(Math.floor(-0.1));
    System.out.println(Math.floor(100));
    System.out.println(Math.floor(Double.MIN_VALUE));
  }
}
```

The output is:

```
9.0
-1.0
100.0
0.0
```

max( )

max() finds the maximum between two values. max() is overloaded with versions for int, long, double, and float. This method simply returns the larger of the two values supplied.

min( )

min() finds the minimum between two values. min() is also overloaded with versions for int, long, double, and float. This method simply returns the smaller of the two values supplied.

random( )

random() returns a random number—a double value—between 0.0 and 1.0. You don't have nearly as much control over this random number as you do when you use the Random class and can seed the random number generator. If you want to seed the number or retrieve random numbers in different ranges, use the Random class.

round( )

This method finds the closest integer to a float-point number. There are versions of round() for double and float (of course, integer values don't need to be rounded).

For example, if you run this program:

```
class Round {
    public static void main(String[] args) {
        System.out.println(Math.round(9.01));
        System.out.println(Math.round(9.5));
        System.out.println(Math.round(-9.5));
        System.out.println(Math.round(-0.1));
        System.out.println(Math.round(100.0));
        System.out.println(Math.round(Double.MIN_VALUE));
    }
}
```

you get these results:

```
9
10
-9
0
100
0
```

EXAM TIP: As you can see, round( ) went up at .5 or above, and down when the number was less than .5. So, for 9.5, the number was rounded to 10. At −9.5, the number was rounded up to −9.

sqrt( )

sqrt() finds the square root of a number. If the argument is "not-a-number" (NaN) or less than zero, the result of sqrt() is NaN.

sin( )

sin() finds the sine of a number given the angle in radians. If it's been a while and you don't remember, there are *2*pi* radians in a circle. For example, *pi/2* radians equals 90 degrees.

cos( )

cos() finds the cosine of a number given the angle in radians.

tan( )

tan() finds the tangent of a number given the angle in radians.

Exercise 16.2

Using only the Math class, write a method that finds the maximum of two random numbers between 0 and pi. Then find the sine, cosine, and tangent of this number.

The String and StringBuffer Classes

For the exam, you'll need to be able to describe the significance of the immutability of strings. You'll also need to know how to declare strings and how to manipulate strings.

Java uses the String and StringBuffer classes to work with strings of characters. The String class supports immutable (or unchanging) strings. The StringBuffer class supports modifiable strings. Both strings and string buffers contain sequences of 16-bit Unicode characters.

String Operators

We'll get back to this notion of immutability in a moment, for now lets look at String operators. When used with Strings, the + operator creates a new String object that's a combination of the strings. For example:

```
String s = "hello," + " world";
```

results in the String s containing "hello, world." Strings also override the += operator, so that you can write:

```
String s = "hello,";
s += " world";
```

The + and += operators also work as you would hope when used with a String object and some other primitive data types, such as a number, boolean, or char. For example, when used with a number:

```
String s = "Nine to " + 5;
```

the + operator results in s being set to the String "Nine to 5."

The Immutability of Strings

At the beginning of the chapter, we told you Strings were unchangeable, yet as you've seen, you can indeed change strings. After all, you change the value of strings using the + and += operators. If you wanted to add two strings together, you would concatenate them with the + operator, such as:

```
String s1 = "Oh my";
s1 = s1 + " gosh";
```

The result of this operation is that s1 equals *Oh my gosh*, right? Well, yes and no—and this is where the whole notion of immutability comes into play. Strings created with the String class are read-only. When you add characters to a String object, say, using the + operator—the result is a new String object, not a modification of the original String object. While this behavior may seem a bit odd, there is a very good reason for handling strings in this manner.

In Java, every String literal, such as "Oh my," is represented by an instance of String. Java classes can have pools of strings. When a program containing a string literal is compiled, the compiler normally adds the String literal to an appropriate pool for the class. If the string literal already exists in the class, however, the compiler doesn't create a new copy and instead uses the existing literal from the pool. This is designed to save memory and cannot cause problems in the program because any time you modify a String the result is a new String.

Several interesting quirks result from this behavior and you should note these for the exam. The first important behavior is that String literals are placed in a class-specific pool. If you create additional literals with the same value as an existing literal, the new literal strings will point to the existing literal. Considering the following example:

```
String s1 = "Monday";
String s2 = "Monday";
```

Here, when you compile the program, the String literal "Monday" is placed into the pool of literal strings for the current class. When the compiler reads line 2, it checks the pool and finds an existing literal with this value and uses the existing value. So both s1 and s2 point to the same String literal in the class pool.

Another important behavior for strings occurs when you use the new String() constructor. If you've worked with strings, you know the String class has many constructors. The most basic constructor follows this format:

```
String stringName = "theString";
```

You can also construct a string explicitly by calling the constructor, such as:

```
String s1 = new String("Monday");
```

When a program containing this line is compiled, the String literal "Monday" is placed into the literal pool for the current class. Then when the new String() statement is executed at runtime, a new instance of String is constructed and returned. This new instance duplicates the String in the literal pool. Now you have two objects, one in the literal pool and another in the program's memory space. This uses memory unnecessarily.

Having two String objects with identical values can cause problems in your programs. To see how, consider the case where you are checking equality of strings. If string s1 is a String literal stored in the literal pool and string s2 is a string created at run-time, say by user input, the equality operator (==) will not return true when comparing the s1 and s2:

```
s1 = "Monday";
//s2 created by user response
if (s1 == s2) {
 //execute these statements
}
```

The objects are not the same and to successfully perform the comparison, you'd need to perform a comparison on the characters in the strings using the equals() method, such as:

```
s1 = "Monday";
//s2 created by user response
if (s1.equals(s2)) {
 //execute these statements
}
```

TIP: Because the equals( ) method must compare the actual characters in the Strings, the method is slower than the equality operator (==). If a program performs lots of string comparisons, using the equals( ) method, you may notice slow response time. To resolve this problem, you can use the intern (I) method of the String class to add a String to the literal pool. Once you do this, you can perform a comparison using the equality operator.

Methods of the String Class

The String class defines many methods. You should be familiar with these methods:

- **charAt( )** Returns the character at the index position passed to this method. The first character is at position 0. The last character is at position length() − 1. If you try to access a character outside the bounds of this String, this method will throw a StringIndexOutOfBoundsException. This method returns type char.

- **concat( )** Concatenates a given string onto the end of the String object responding to this method. Of course, since Strings are read-only, the string passed as an argument is not really appended to the original String. Instead, concat() returns a new String.

- **endsWith( )** Returns a boolean indicating whether the String passed as the parameter is at the end of the target String.

- **equals( )** Returns true if two String objects are the same lengths and contain the identical run of characters, taking case into account. String overrides the equals() method, which, by default, only returns true if the object references used with this method refer to the same underlying object. With String, completely different objects can make equals() return true.

- **equalsIgnoreCase( )** Returns true if two String objects are the same lengths and contain the identical run of characters, not taking case into account. In other words, with this method, a pair of corresponding characters are considered equal if the == operator returns true as they are; if the == operator returns true after they have both been made upper case; or if the == operator returns true after they have both been made lower case. When this method runs, Java makes characters upper or lower case using a static Character method called toUppercase() or toLowercase().

- **indexOf( )** Finds the first occurrence of a character or substring. The method returns the value −1 if it cannot find the character or substring; otherwise, the method returns the index where the character is.

- **lastIndexOf( )** Finds the last occurrence of a character or substring. The method returns the value −1 if it cannot find the character or substring; otherwise, the method returns the index where the substring starts.

- **length( )** Returns an int of the number of characters in this string.

- **replace( )** Returns a new string where all the occurrences of the first character passed as a parameter are replaced by the second parameter.

- **startsWith( )** Returns a boolean indicating whether the string passed as the parameter is at the beginning of the target String. The startsWith( ) method is also overloaded to start at an optional offset into the String.

- **substring( )** Returns a substring from the given String. There are two versions of this method. String substring(int beginIndex) returns a new string that is a substring of this string. The substring begins with the character at the specified index and extends to the end of this string. String substring(int beginIndex, int endIndex) returns a new string that is a substring of this string. The substring begins at the specified beginIndex and extends to the character at index endIndex −1.

- **toLowerCase( )** Returns a new String object representing the lower-case equivalent of the String. If the lower-case equivalent is not different from the original String, toLowerCase( ) returns the original object.

- **toString( )** You can override toString( ) in any class so that instances of that class return a String representation of themselves. This is useful when you want to place an object directly in an expression that calls for a String, such as an argument to System.out.println( ). For a String, toString( ) returns itself—the same object reference (of course, pointing to the same object) that was used to invoke this method.

- **toUpperCase( )** Returns a new String object representing the upper-case equivalent of the String. If the upper-case equivalent is not different from the original String, toUpperCase( ) returns the original string.

- **trim( )** Returns a new String object that cuts off the leading and trailing whitespace for the String for which this was invoked. Java considers whitespace to be any character with a code less than or equal to '\u0020.' The character '\u0020' is the space character.

- **valueOf( )** This static method is overloaded for the basic primitive data types, character arrays, and class Object. It returns a String representing the value of the data type. For example, a boolean might be true or false and a float might be 3.14. Objects return their value for toString( ).

Exercise 16.3

Write a standalone program that takes any number of command line parameters and displays the number of (naturally occurring) lowercase 'e' characters in all of them combined.

String Buffers

Java declares and manipulates objects of the StringBuffer class to handle most String operations. You can use the StringBuffer class directly as well with any of these constructors:

- **StringBuffer( )**   Constructs an empty string buffer.

- **StringBuffer(int length)**   Constructs an empty string buffer with a specified initial buffer length.

- **StringBuffer(String initialString)**   Constructs a string buffer from a String object.

Normally, you'll construct StringBuffer objects from String objects, so the constructor you'll use the most is the third one. Whenever you want to manipulate the contents of a string, you probably want to use a StringBuffer object instead of a String object. For example, if you want to read one character at a time from a source file or from the standard input and append the characters to what you've read so far, you would want to use a StringBuffer object instead of a String in most cases.

The append() and insert() methods of the StringBuffer class are overloaded to take every basic Java data type as well as character arrays and objects. This allows you to convert and append other objects and primitive data types to StringBuffer objects. You can also do some interesting things to the characters in a StringBuffer such as reversing the characters by invoking reverse(), or changing a particular character by using setCharAt().

StringBuffer does not inherit from String. If you want to use the string represented by a StringBuffer object as a parameter to a method, for example (such as println()), you have to obtain a String object from the StringBuffer object. You can do this by invoking toString().

The following example shows how you could construct and manipulate a String-Buffer object:

```
public class StringBufferTest {
  public static void main(String args[]) {
    StringBuffer strBuf = new StringBuffer("ABCDEFG");
    strBuf.reverse(); //now strBuf is "GFEDCBA"
    strBuf.reverse(); //now strBuf is "ABCDEFG"
```

```
        strBuf.insert(2, "-"); //now strBuf is "AB-CDEFG"
        strBuf.insert(5, "-"); //now strBuf is "AB-CD-EFG"
        strBuf.insert(8, "-"); //now strBuf is "AB-CD-EF-G"
        strBuf.setCharAt(2, '+'); //now strBuf is "AB+CD-EF-G"
        strBuf.setCharAt(5, '+'); //now strBuf is "AB+CD+EF-G"
        strBuf.setCharAt(8, '+'); //now strBuf is "AB+CD+EF+G"
        String str = strBuf.toString();
        System.out.println(str);
    }
}
```

Exercise 16.4

Both the String class and the StringBuffer class have equals() methods. Given what you know about the equals() method and these classes, what will be the output from the following snippet of code and why?

```
StringBuffer strBuf = new StringBuffer("12345");
String str = strBuf.toString();
if (str.equals(strBuf)) {
 System.out.println(str);
}
```

Rewrite the example to produce output of "not equals" if there is no output.

Collections

The Collection classes and interfaces are an important part of the exam. For the exam, you'll need to determine which collection classes/interfaces should be used in a given situation. These situations are based on meeting specific behavior requirements, such as the requirement for storing data elements that must not appear more than once in the data store or the requirement to have a set of key values to lookup or index stored data.

The Collection classes and interfaces are often referred to as a framework. The reason they are called a framework is that each class is designed with a common behavior. Each implementation of a class builds off this framework and can optimize its own functionality as necessary. These functions include searching, synchronizing, and storing data.

Overview of the Collections API

Before taking a look at how you can use the Collections API, we'll provide a brief summary of the available classes and interfaces. Table 16-2 provides a summary of pre-JDK 1.2 collection classes and interfaces.

Table 16-2 Collection Classes and Interfaces

Type/Name	Description
	Interface
Enumeration	Provides methods for stepping through an ordered set of objects or values. This interface has been replaced by the Iterator interface in the JDK 1.2 Collection API.
	Class
BitSet	A growable set of bits. Each bit is represented by a Boolean value and can be indexed like an array or vector.
Dictionary	This provides abstract functions used to store and retrieve objects using key-value pairs. Any object can be used as a key or value. This class is an abstract superclass of Hashtable.
Hashtable	Implements a Hashtable data structure that indexes and stores the objects in a dictionary using hash codes as the keys. This class does not allow the null value to be stored.
Properties	A subclass of Hashtable that can be read from and written to a stream. The class enables you to specify default values to be used if a key is not found in the table.
Stack	Implements a last-in, first-out (LIFO) stack. Objects can be pushed onto the stack and popped off the stack. You can also peek at the last item on the stack without taking it off the stack.
Vector	An expandable array of objects with a clear order. You can add, delete, and insert elements into vectors. In JDK 1.2, this class implements the List interface and extends the AbstractList class.

In JDK 1.2 and later, maps are replacing dictionaries as a means to associate keys with values. Because of this, you should use map-related classes and interfaces instead of the Dictionary, Hashtable and Properties classes.

Table 16-3 summarizes the JDK 1.2 Collection interfaces. As you examine the table, note that four basic types of interfaces are defined: collections, lists, sets and maps.

Table 16-4 summarizes the Collection classes for JDK 1.2. These classes obtain their basic behavior from their related interface and the AbstractCollection class.

Table 16-3 JDK 1.2 Collection Interfaces

Type/Name	Description
Collection	Implements an unordered group of objects. Collections are sometimes referred to as bags because they allow duplicates and don't place constraints on the type or order of elements.
Comparator	Provides a basic mechanism for comparing the elements of a collection.
Iterator	Provides a basic mechanism for iterating through the elements of a collection. Replaces Enumeration.
List	Extends the Collection interface to implement an ordered collection of objects. This ordered list can be indexed and it can contain duplicate values.
ListIterator	Extends the Iterator interface to support iteration of lists.
Map	Provides basic functions to store and retrieve data using key values. The key values must be unique.
Map.Entry	An inner interface of Map that specifies methods for working with a key-value pair.
SortedMap	A Map whose elements are sorted in ascending order.
Set	Extends the Collection interface to implement a finite set. Sets do not allow duplicate values. Simple sets do not have a specific order. Some sets allow the null value but if they do, the value can only occur once.
SortedSet	A Set whose elements are sorted in ascending order.

Table 16-4 JDK 1.2 Collection Classes

Type/Name	Description
Arrays	Provides static methods for searching, sorting, and converting arrays to lists.
Collections	Provides static methods for searching, sorting, and manipulating objects that implement the Collection interface.
AbstractCollection	Provides a basic implementation of the Collection interface and is in turn extended by other classes.
AbstractList	Extends AbstractCollection and provides the basic implementation of the List interface.
AbstractSequentialList	Extends the AbstractList and provides functionality for sequentially accessing a list (instead of randomly accessing the list).

Type/Name	Description
LinkedList	Extends AbstractSequentialList and implements a doubly linked list. A linked list is a list in which each element references the next element. A doubly linked list is a list in which each element references the previous and the next element.
ArrayList	Extends AbstractList and implements a resizable array.
AbstractSet	Extends AbstractCollection and provides the basic implementation of the Set interface.
HashSet	Extends AbstractSet and implements a set of key-value pairs. The class uses hash tables for storage and doesn't allow duplicate values. You can't use the null value either.
TreeSet	Extends AbstractSet and implements a sorted binary tree that supports the SortedSet interface. You can't have duplicate values in a TreeSet.
AbstractMap	Extends AbstractCollection and provides the basic implementation of the Map interface.
HashMap	Extends AbstractMap and implements a map of key-value pairs. The class uses hash tables for storage and doesn't allow duplicate values. You can use the null value.
TreeMap	Extends AbstractMap and implements a sorted binary tree that supports the SortedMap interface.
WeakHashMap	Extends AbstractMap and implements a map with weak keys. An entry in the hash table is automatically removed when its key is garbage-collected.

Collection API Essentials

As you've seen, the Collection API provides an extensive set of classes and interfaces. For the exam, you don't need to memorize every facet of this API. You do, however, need to be able to select an appropriate collection class or interface to suit specified behavior. If you plot out the behavior of these classes and interfaces, you find four fundamental types:

- **Collections**   Simple collections can be unordered and don't have any restrictions. You can use any type of object and you can have multiple occurrences of an object. The Collection interface supports methods for adding, removing, counting, and checking items in a collection.

- **Lists**   Lists are ordered collections that allow multiple occurrences of an object. The order can be the natural order or the order in which the objects are added to the collection. Because the list is ordered, its objects can be indexed. The ListIterator interface provides methods for iterating through the elements of a list. Abstract lists can be accessed randomly, through an array, through a link list, or through doubly linked list.

- **Sets** Sets are collections that do not allow duplicate values. Some sets allow the null value but if they do, the value can only occur once. The AbstractSet and HashSet classes create sets that aren't ordered. The TreeSet class creates sets that are ordered through a binary tree.

- **Maps** Maps are collections that use a set of values to look up or index stored data. With maps, you can search on a key field. Key fields values must be unique. In JDK 1.2, maps replace dictionaries as the preferred technique to associate keys with values. The AbstractMap, HashMap, and WeakHashMap classes create maps that aren't ordered. The TreeMap class creates maps that are ordered through a binary tree.

The way values are stored using the fundamental types is equally as important. If you examine the storage techniques used, you'll find values are stored using one of these techniques:

- **Arrays** Arrays provide storage for ordered items with unique values. You can use arrays when you have a fixed number of elements with specific values. The array ordering makes it difficult to add and remove elements in the array. If an array is full, you'll need to create a new array and copy the contents of the current array before you can add elements. Arrays don't provide a special search mechanism.

- **Linked lists** Linked lists provide storage for ordered items that don't have to have unique values. You can easily add and remove values from the linked list. The size of a linked list can grow dynamically. Linked lists can grow dynamically because each element points to the next (and sometimes the previous) element. However, accessing linked lists is slower than accessing arrays. Linked lists don't provide a special search mechanism.

- **Trees** Trees provide storage for items that are sorted in ascending order. With trees, you can easily add and remove elements as long as the order of the tree is maintained. Trees with elements distributed evenly can be searched more efficiently than linked lists and arrays.

- **Hash tables** In a hash tables, each item is represented with a key-value pair. The key must be a unique identifier for the item being stored. Using the key, you can quickly and efficiently find items in the hash table. Using a hash table results in some additional overhead, which occurs when calculating hash values. Hash tables are best suited to large data sets.

Answers to the Exercises

Exercise 16.1

One possible solution for Exercise 16.1 is as follows:

```
public class MyStrings {
  public static void main(String args[]) {
    try {
      Byte wrappedByte = new Byte("18");
      Short wrappedShort = new Short("12345");
      Integer wrappedInt = new Integer("9876543");
      Long wrappedLong = new Long("9997654321");
      Float wrappedFloat = new Float("1.825F");
      Double wrappedDouble = new Double("1.825125125");
    }
    catch (NumberFormatException e) {
      System.out.println("Incorrect number format");
    }
  }
}
```

Exercise 16.2

```
void exercise() {
      double d1 = Math.random() * Math.PI;
      double d2 = Math.random() * Math.PI;
      double m = Math.max(d1, d2);
      System.out.println(Math.sin(m));
      System.out.println(Math.cos(m));
      System.out.println(Math.tan(m));
   }
```

Exercise 16.3

```
class ECounter {
   public static void main(String[] args) {
     String s;
     int index;
     int ecount = 0;
     for (int i = 0; i < args.length; i++) {
        s = args[i];
        index = 0;
        while ( (index = s.indexOf('e', index)) != -1) {
           index++;
           ecount++;
        }
     }
     System.out.println("There are " + ecount + " e's.");
   }
}
```

Exercise 16.4

The example doesn't produce any output. Although the StringBuffer object and the String object have the same contents, they are different objects. You can compare a string to a string or a string buffer to a string buffer. However, you cannot compare a string to a string buffer or vice versa.

Because the example produces no output, you should have rewritten the code snippet to produce the output "not equals." One possible solution is as follows:

```
StringBuffer strBuf = new StringBuffer("12345");
String str = strBuf.toString();
if (str.equals(strBuf)) {
 System.out.println(str);
} else
  System.out.println("not equals");
```

Review Questions

1. What Math methods, invoked like this:

```
Math.method(x);
```

would return the value −5 given the value of x to be −4.5?
   a. round()
   b. ceil()
   c. floor()
   d. a, b, and c
   e. a and c

2. What is possible output from invoking

```
Math.random();
```

   a. 132.93
   b. 0.2154
   c. 29.32E10
   d. all of the above

3. To find the square root of a number, you can use the Math method:
   a. srt()
   b. sqrt()
   c. squareRoot()

4. Given this line of code

```
String s = "Penguin";
```

what will be assigned to c if you execute

```
char c = s.charAt(6);
```

    a. 'n'

    b. 'i'

    c. nothing will be assigned because charAt() will respond with a StringIndex-OutOfBoundsException.

5. What do you expect the output to be for the following program?

```java
class Str {

    public static void main(String[] args) {
        String s = "Hi!";
        String t = "Hi!";
        if (s == t)
            System.out.println("equals");
        else
            System.out.println("not equals");
    }
}
```

    a. "equals"

    b. "not equals"

6. What do you expect the output to be for the following program?

```java
class StrQ6 {
    public static void main(String[] args) {
        String s = "Hi!";
        String t = new String(s);
        if (s == t)
            System.out.println("equals");
        else
            System.out.println("not equals");
    }
}
```

    a. "equals"

    b. "not equals"

7. What do you expect the output to be for the following program?

```
class StrQ7 {
    public static void main(String[] args) {
        String s = "HELLO";
        String t = s.toUpperCase();
        if (s == t)
            System.out.println("equals");
        else
            System.out.println("not equals");
    }
}
```

    a. "equals"

    b. "not equals"

8. Imagine the following lines of code:

```
String s = "Hello,";
String t = s;
s += " world";
if (s == t)
    System.out.println("equals");
else
    System.out.println("not equals");
```

What gets written to the standard output?

    a. "equals"

    b. "not equals"

9. In the following example you create an instance of the StringBuffer class, then you call the append() method of the StringBuffer:

```
StringBuffer strBuf = new StringBuffer("12345");
strBuf.append("6789");
```

After executing line two, does strBuf still reference the same object instance?

    a. Yes

    b. No

10. If you need to store multiple data elements in a data store, which class/interface would you use if searching is a priority and you have a unique key field?

    a. List

    b. Set

    c. Map

    d. Vector

    e. Collection

11. If you need to store multiple data elements that must not appear more than once in the data store, which class/interface would you use if searching is not a priority?
    a. List
    b. Set
    c. Map
    d. Vector
    e. Collection

12. Which of the following can store duplicate elements?
    a. List
    b. Set
    c. Map
    d. Collection

13. When you want to associate keys with values and you are using JDK 1.2, which of the following classes are preferred?
    a. Dictionary
    b. HashTable
    c. Properties
    d. HashMap
    e. TreeMap

14. Can a null value be added to a Set?
    a. Yes, but not with the HashSet class.
    b. Yes, but only with the AbstractSet class.
    c. Yes, but only with the TreeSet class.
    d. Yes
    e. No

Answers to Review Questions

1. **c.** Only floor() will go to the next lower number. Both round() and ceil() go higher—to −4.

2. **b.** Math.random() yields a result between 0.0 and 1.0.

3. **b.** (I made up the other method names).

4. **a.** The first index position is 0, so charAt(6) results in the 7th character in the string, which is 'n'.

5. **a.** The strings are equal. String "Hi!" is created as a String literal in the literal pool. Both String s and String t point to this String literal.

6. **b.** The strings are not equal. The first string is created as a String literal in the literal pool. At runtime, the second string is constructed as a new instance.

7. **a.** Surprised? The method toUpperCase() returns the original string if the parameter is already in upper case. Hence the == operator yields true in this example.

8. **b.** After these three lines of code execute, it might seem that we have modified the object reference s, and that t and s are still equivalent object references. However, this is not the case. The += operator creates a new String object. The variables t and s now contain different references. The words "not equals" are written to the standard output.

9. **a.** The StringBuffer class is read-write. Because of this, the example modifies the existing StringBuffer object.

10. **c.** A map supports searching on a key field as long as the key values are unique.

11. **b.** A set rejects duplicate entries so if you want to ensure data elements only appear one this is the best choice. We could have used a map also. However, because searching isn't a priority, the best choice is b.

12. **a, c,** and **d.** Lists, maps and collections can have duplicate elements. Keep in mind that while maps can have duplicated values, they cannot have duplicated keys.

13. **d** and **e.** Maps are replacing dictionaries as the preferred way to associate keys with values. Both HashMap and TreeMap are maps.

14. **a.** A null value can be added to most sets as long as the value only occurs once. With the HashSet class, however, null values are not allowed.

java.io

Objectives for This Chapter

- Construct "chains" of InputStream and OutputStream objects using the subclasses of FilterInputStream and FilterOutputStream.

- Identify valid constructor arguments for FilterInputStream and FilterOutputStream subclasses.

- Read, write, and update files using FileInputStream, FileOutputStream, and RandomAccessFile objects.

- Write code that uses objects of the classes InputStreamReader and OutputStreamWriter to translate between Unicode and either platform default or ISO 8859-1 character encoding.

- Describe the permanent effects on the file system of constructing and using FileInputStream, FileOutputStream, and RandomAccessFile objects.

- Navigate the file system using the File class.

Java defines a wide variety of classes and methods in its java.io package that you can use to read from and write to streams of data. What is a stream? A stream is an ordered sequence of bytes that have a source or a destination. Destinations or sources can be files or Internet resources, for example.

There are different kinds of streams in Java. Some streams are associated with files and make it easy to read from or write to a file. Some streams can be chained together so that each type of stream adds its own processing to the bytes as they pass through the stream.

The java.io Package

The top-level classes in the java.io package—InputStream and OutputStream, FilterInputStream and FilterOutputStream, FileInputStream and FileOutputStream, File, and RandomAccessFile—are all classes you should know about. Here's a quick review of these classes.

There are four pairs of classes and interfaces to understand. Once you grasp where these are in the class hierarchy for the I/O classes, the rest of the classes fall into place. These four pairs of classes and interfaces are

- InputStream and OutputStream
- FilterInputStream and FilterOutputStream
- DataInput and DataOutput
- Reader and Writer

Each of the class and interface pairs is examined in the sections that follow.

InputStream and OutputStream

At the top level of the input/output hierarchy are the classes InputStream and OutputStream. These are abstract classes and define basic methods for working with streams of data, such as read(), write(), and skip(). They also declare a close() method to close the stream. Creating the object opens the stream.

These classes declare a few other methods. For example, InputStream declares a method called available() that tests to see whether any bytes are available to be read. OutputStream also declares a method called flush() which writes any bytes in a buffer to the stream.

Figure 17-1 provides an overview of InputStream and OutputStream. Individual subclasses of InputStream implement the read() method for reading one byte at a time.

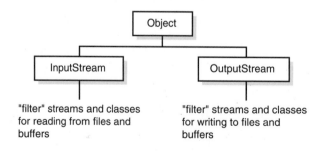

Figure 17-1   InputStream and OutputStream are at the top level.

Individual subclasses of OutputStream implement the write() method for writing one byte at a time.

Subclasses of these top-level abstract classes include classes for reading and writing to files, buffers, byte arrays, and more. These are not on the test, so don't panic.

FileInputStream and FileOutputStream are used to read from and write to a file. FileOutputStream will also create the file you write to. We have supplied examples of using FileInputStream and FileOutputStream later in this chapter.

In addition to FilterInputStream and FilterOutputStream, there are some direct subclasses of InputStream and OutputStream that you can instantiate. The additional InputStream subclasses are

- **ByteArrayInputStream**   Allows you to use byte arrays rather than a file as an input stream.

- **ObjectInputStream**   Allows you to read data from an object.

- **PipedInputStream**   Allows you to associate an output file with an input file. Then you can read data from a PipeInputStream and write the data to a PipedOutputStream.

- **SequenceInputStream**   Enables you to read from a sequence of files. The class reads from the first file until it comes to the end, then reads the second and so on.

- **StringBufferInputStream**   Allows you to read from a StringBuffer as you would from a file.

The additional OutputStream subclasses are

- **ByteArrayOutputStream**   Allows you to use byte arrays rather than a file as an output stream.

- **ObjectOutputStream**   Allows you to write data to an object.

- **PipedOutputStream**   Allows you to associate an input file with an input file. Then you can write data to a PipeOutputStream and read the data from a PipedInputStream.

FilterInputStream and FilterOutputStream

Filter streams do things with the bytes read from or written to another stream. The Filter stream classes are subclasses of InputStream and OutputStream. While some subclasses of InputStream and OutputStream can be used by themselves, FilterInputStream, FilterOutputStream, and their subclasses are used with other stream objects.

When you create a Filter stream, you must specify the stream to which it will attach. You do this by passing an instance of InputStream or OutputStream, as appropriate (depending on if you are creating a FilterInputStream or a FilterOutputStream), to the constructor. The Filter streams do not define a no-args constructor. This means they must be chained in some way—a Filter stream must reference either another Filter stream or an InputStream or OutputStream. (All Filter streams descend from either InputStream or OutputStream.)

A Filter stream processes a stream of bytes in some way. By "chaining" multiple Filter streams, you can add multiple filters to a stream of bytes. You can chain together as many Filter streams as you like. Each Filter stream in the chain continues adding processing to the bytes read from or written to a resource.

TIP: The first Filter stream in a chain must be associated with some underlying file or other resource to be created in the first place. After the first Filter stream is created, other Filter streams can attach to that first Filter stream.

Figure 17-2 shows where the File streams and the Filter streams fit into the I/O hierarchy we started earlier.

Both FilterInputStream and FilterOutputStream have several subclasses. The FilterInputStream subclasses are

- **BufferedInputStream** Invoking a read method for a BufferedInputStream fills up the buffer and returns bytes from this buffer to the program doing the reading.

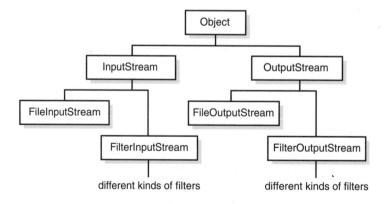

Figure 17-2 File streams and Filter streams

- **CheckedInputStream**   Maintains a checksum of the data being read. The check-sum can then be used to verify the integrity of the input data.

- **DataInputStream**   Expects a data input stream which can be a file input stream, a pipe, or another type of input stream. You can pass in an input stream, read the data, and return an appropriate value. This class allows reading of primitive data types.

- **DigestInputStream**   Creates a transparent stream that updates an associated message digest using the bits going through the stream. To complete the message digest computation, call a digest method after reading the stream.

- **InflaterInputStream**   Implements a stream filter for uncompressing data in the "deflate" compression format. It is also used as the basis for other decompression filters, such as GZIPInputStream, ZipInputStream, and JarInputStream.

- **PushbackInputStream**   Allows you to push back or unread 1 byte. This is useful when you want to read an indefinite number of data bytes that are delimited by a particular byte value and then after reading the terminating byte push back so that the next read operation on the input stream will reread the byte that was pushed back.

The FilterOutputStream subclasses are

- **BufferedOutputStream**   Enables you to write bytes to a buffer. Once the buffer is filled, the contents are written to the designated output stream.

- **CheckedOutputStream**   Maintains a checksum of the data being written. The checksum can then be used to verify the integrity of the output data

- **DataOutputStream**   Expects you to pass in an output stream. Then when you write data, it converts the output to bytes and writes them to the output stream. This class allows writing of primitive data types.

- **DeflaterOutputStream**   Implements an output stream filter for compressing data in the "deflate" compression format. It is also used as the basis for other types of compression filters, including GZIPOutputStream, ZipOutputStream, and JarOutputStream.

- **DigestOutputStream**   Creates a transparent stream that updates an associated message digest using the bits going through the stream. To complete the message digest computation, call a digest method after writing the stream.

- **PrintStream**   Provides print() and println() methods for the basic primitive data types as well as Object, String, and character arrays.

DataInput and DataOutput

DataInput and DataOutput are interfaces that declare methods for reading and writing Java's primitive data types—byte, short, int, long, float, double, char, and Boolean. It is up to the classes that implement this interface to supply the specific methods that fulfill these contracts. There are three classes that implement the DataInput and DataOutput interfaces: DataInputStream, DataOutputStream, and RandomAccessFile.

Figure 17-3 shows where the DataInputStream, DataOutputStream, and RandomAccessFile classes are in the I/O class hierarchy and their connection to the DataInput and DataOutput interfaces. It is important to note that while DataInput-Stream and DataOutputStream know how to work with Java data types, FileInput-Stream only knows how to read individual bytes.

TIP: Notice that RandomAccessFile implements both DataInput and DataOutput methods. RandomAccessFile objects can read from and write to files. That's why RandomAccessFile does not inherit from FileInputStream or FileOutput-Stream — it can do both (and remember, Java does not allow multiple inheritance of implementation).

With these three cornerstones of the I/O hierarchy (InputStream and OutputStream, the Filter streams, and the DataInput and DataOutput interfaces), you can begin to make sense of the other I/O classes.

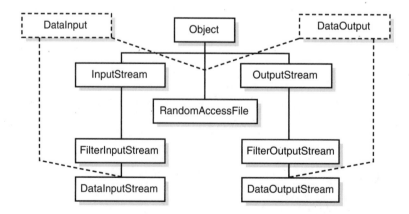

Figure 17-3   Classes that implement the DataInput and DataOutput interfaces

Reader and Writer

The InputStream and OutputStream classes and their subclasses support 8-bit characters. With internationalization and localization initiatives, JDK 1.2 needed a way to read and write streams using 16-bit Unicode characters. The answer is the Reader and Writer classes.

The Reader class is similar to the InputStream class. It is the root of an input class hierarchy and it includes subclasses for buffering and filtering input. Beyond this, the Reader class also supports pipes. Because the Reader class supports Unicode, it is the preferred way to read files in JDK 1.2 and later.

The Reader class has six direct subclasses. These subclasses are

- **BufferedReader** Supports buffered character input. Its LineNumberReader subclass keep track of line numbers while reading buffered input.

- **CharArrayReader** Enables Java to read a character input stream from a character buffer.

- **FilterReader** An abstract class that provides basic filtering for character input streams. Its PushBackReader subclass provides a filter that enables characters to be pushed back onto the input stream.

- **InputStreamReader** Reads character from an input stream, automatically converting between streams of bytes and sequences of Unicode characters. Its FileReader subclass provides basic functionality for reading a file given a file path or File handle.

- **PipedReader** Reads characters from a pipe. Pipes are used in thread communication.

- **StringReader** Reads characters from a string.

The Writer class has seven direct subclasses. These subclasses are

- **BufferedWriter** Supports buffered character output.

- **CharArrayWriter** Allows Java to write a character output stream from a character buffer.

- **FilterWriter** An abstract class that provides basic filtering for character output streams.

- **OutputStreamReader** Writes characters to an output stream, automatically converting between sequences of Unicode characters and streams of bytes. Its FileWriter subclass provides basic functionality for writing to a file given a file path or File handle.

- **PipedWriter**   Writes characters to pipes.
- **PrintWriter**   Supports platform-independent character printing.
- **StringWriter**   Writes characters to a string.

The abstract Reader superclass provides a read() method that can be used to read character input. This method has three constructors:

- **int read( ) throws IOException**   Reads a single character by returning the next char or—1 if at the end of the input. The char is stored in the low-order 16 bits of the int return value.
- **int read(char[ ] cbuf) throws IOException**   Reads an array of characters and returns the number of chars read or—1 if at the end of the input.
- **int read(char[ ] cbuf, int off, int len) throws IOException**   Reads len characters using the given offset into the character buffer array and returns the number of chars read or—1 if at the end of the input.

The abstract Writer superclass provides a write() method which can be used to write character output. This method has five constructors:

- **int write(int c) throws IOException**   Writes a single character. The char is stored in the low-order 16 bits of c.
- **int write(String s) throws IOException**   Writes the String s.
- **int write(char[] cbuf) throws IOException**   Writes an array of characters.
- **int write(char[] cbuf, int off, int len) throws IOException**   Writes len characters using the given offset into the character buffer array.
- **int write(String s, int off, int len) throws IOException**   Writes len characters using the given offset into String s.

All readers and writers inherit from the Reader or Writer superclass so they also support the read() and write() methods shown here.

Working with Files

With the File class you can create, delete and rename files. You can work with file names in a platform-independent way, test to see if a file exists, and find information about a file node. You can also create directories and temporary files.

You can create a File object using one of three constructors. These constructors take a:

- String containing a path name
- String containing a path name and a String containing a file name
- File representing a path and a String containing a file name

The sections that follow examine the key methods of the File class.

 TIP: The File class defines a static variable named **separatorChar** that contains the platform-dependent path separator — a back-slash for Windows, a colon for the Mac, and a forward-slash for UNIX. You can use this character to write platform-independent code that navigates the file system.

Testing to See if a File Exists

Just because you can create a File object, it doesn't mean the file or directory exists. To test to see if a File object refers to an existing file, you can invoke exists(), which returns true or false.

Finding Information about a File Node

The methods canRead() and canWrite() return Boolean values that indicate whether the application can read from or write to the file. For example, a stand-alone application might be able to write to a file, while an applet, because of security restrictions, may not.

Another useful method is lastModified(). This method returns a platform-dependent value you can use to determine whether a particular file was created before or after another.

Deleting and Renaming Files

While you cannot create files using the File class or a File object, you can use File methods to make a permanent change to the file system. For example, you can delete and rename files. Invoke delete() to delete a file. This method returns a Boolean indicating success or failure. Invoke rename() to rename a file, and supply a File object that embodies the new name.

Creating Directories

You can also create directories using File. You can invoke the method mkdir() to create a directory specified by the File object. This method also returns a Boolean indicating success or failure.

Navigating the File System

You can use the method getParent() to retrieve a String containing the name of the parent directory.

The methods getPath() and getName() return the directory structure for this File object and the file's name, respectively.

The method getAbsolutePath() returns the absolute path if this File object represents an absolute path.

CAUTION: If you use getAbsolutePath() and the File object does not represent an absolute path, this method makes one up. It returns the name of the current user directory with the filename concatenated to it.

Creating Files

To create a file using the File object, you create an instance of File and then invoke the createNewFile() method. This method returns true if the file can be created, false if the file already exists. The following example creates a file called A.txt in the current directory:

```
import java.io.*;
class A {
    public static void main(String[] args) throws Exception {
        File f = new File("A.txt");
        if (!f.createNewFile()) {
            System.out.println("A.txt already exists.");
        }
    }
}
```

Files can also be created with FileOutputStream and RandomAccessFile. Here's a basic example of using a FileOutputStream to create a file, although this program does not do anything with the file it creates.

```
import java.io.*;
class B {
    public static void main(String[] args) throws Exception {
        FileOutputStream out = new FileOutputStream("A.test");
        out.close();
    }
}
```

If you ran this program, you would see a file named "A.test" in the same directory as the program. Because you are working with a stream, you must close the stream when you are finished working with it. This is handled with the close() method.

Exercise 17.1

Write a stand-alone program that takes a command line parameter and, after ensuring the file does not exist, create a file with that name.

Creating Temporary Files

You can use the File objects createTempFile() method to create temporary files. The method has two constructors:

```
public static File createTempFile(String prefix, String suffix)
public static File createTempFile(String prefix, String suffix,
File directory)
```

The first constructor creates a file with the file name given as the prefix and the file extension given as the suffix. With this constructor, the file is created in the current directory. The second constructor allows you to set the directory location as the third argument.

The following code snippet will create a file named ≅MyApp*n*.tmp where n is a number that is generated during the call to createTempFile():

```
void createTempFile() {
    try {
        File tempFile = File.createTempFile("~MyApp", ".tmp");
        tempFile.deleteOnExit();
    } catch (IOException ioe) {
        System.out.println("Error creating temporary file!");
    }
}
```

Note the use of the deleteOnExit() method of the File object. The call to dele-teOnExit() will ensure the temporary file is deleted when the JVM exits.

Streams

Input and output streams are an important part of file handling. You can use these streams to work with data files containing binary information and text files using a character encoding. You can also use streams to apply filters to manipulate the data or text in different ways.

Sequencing Stream Filters

FilterInputStream and FilterOutputStream enable you to read from and write to streams using filters. Filter streams are used to process a stream of bytes in some way. By sequencing multiple Filter streams, you can add multiple filters to a stream of bytes. You can link as many Filter streams as you like with each filter adding processing to the bytes read from or written to a resource.

You can attach to resource in several different ways. One way is to attach directly to a file as shown in this example:

```
FileInputStream fileIn = new FileInputStream("record.dat");
```

Here the input stream looks for a file in the current directory that is named record.dat. You could also attach the stream to a File object, such as

```
File f = new File("record.dat");
FileInputStream fileIn = new FileInputStream(f);
```

As with the abstract InputStream and OutputStream classes, FilterInputStream and FilterOutputStream only support reading and writing bytes and byte arrays from files. You can read bytes using an input stream or write bytes using an output stream. Here is an example that reads bytes from an input stream:

```
File f = new File("record.dat");
FileInputStream fileIn = new FileInputStream(f);
byte b = fileIn.read();
```

Through a DataInputStream you can read other data types, such as

```
DataInputStream dataIn = stream;
double s = dataIn.readDouble();
```

stream is a placeholder for the actual sequence of streams from which DataInput-Stream is created. The reason you must create a data input stream from another stream is that DataInputStream has no methods for retrieving data from files. Similarly, DataOutputStream has no methods for writing data to files. Instead of accessing files directly, DataInputStream is used to assemble bytes into more useful data types and DataOutputStream is used to break down values into bytes. The actual reading and writing of bytes is handled by FileInputStream and FileOutputStream.

To make use of file data or to write data to files, you have to combine streams by feeding an existing stream to the constructor of another stream. For example, to read numbers from the record.dat file, you must first create a FileInputStream and then pass this stream to the constructor of a DataInputStream.

```
FileInputStream fileIn = new FileInputStream("record.dat");
DataInputStream dataIn = new DataInputStream(fileIn);
double s = dataIn.readDouble();
```

DataInputStream will now access the data from the record.dat file using the FileInputStream.

As discussed previously, there are many filters that can be used. These filters are made available through FilterInputStream and FilterOutputStream. The way you sequence filters is extremely important. If you want stream B to use the methods of stream A and still be able to use the methods of stream B, you must attach stream B after you attach stream A. For example, if you wanted a buffered data stream, you would attach the data stream in the following sequence for reading:

FileInputStream → BufferedInputStream → DataInputStream

But would use the reverse sequence for buffered writing:

DataOutputStream → BufferedOutputStream → FileOutputStream

Here is an example that constructs a buffered data stream for reading:

```
DataInputStream dataIn = new DataInputStream
    (new BufferedInputStream(
        new FileInputStream("record.dat")));
```

DataInputStream is last in the chain of constructors so that you can use its methods and allow it to use buffered reading.

Another important stream is a pushback stream, which was briefly discussed previously in the chapter. PushbackInputStream is used to perform a preliminary read of a byte and push the input stream back so that the character can be reread. You can create a pushed back input stream as follows:

```
PushbackInputStream pushbackIn = new PushbackInputStream
    (new BufferedInputStream(
        new FileInputStream("record.dat")));
```

You can then perform a preliminary read of the next byte:

```
int b = pushbackIn.read();
```

Afterward, you could push back the byte using:

```
pushbackIn.unread(b);
```

Or you could only push back the byte if the character read doesn't match what is expected, such as:

```
if (b != '=') pushbackIn.unread(b);
```

The PushbackInputStream supports several utility methods. You'll find methods for reading and unreading bytes, checking availability of bytes, skipping bytes, and closing files. You'll also find a method that allows you to test for the support of the mark() and reset() methods, which are inherited from FilterInputStream. The complete list of methods supposed is

- **read( )**   Reads a byte or array of bytes that can be pushed back.
- **unread( )**   Pushes back a byte or an array of bytes by copying it to the front of the pushback buffer.
- **available( )**   Returns the available number of bytes that can be read from the input stream without blocking.
- **skip( )**   Skips over and discards n number of bytes.
- **markSupported( )**   Returns true if the input stream supports the mark and reset methods, false if it does not.

As you can see from the list of supported methods, PushbackInputStream does not support methods for reading data types. If you need to read data types other than bytes and be able to push back to the stream, you'll need to chain the data stream with a pushback stream. Because pushback streams use buffering, the sequence of streams looks like this:

```
DataInputStream dataIn = new DataInputStream(
    pushbackIn = new PushbackInputStream(
        new BufferedInputStream(
            new FileInputStream("record.dat")))));
```

Exercise 17.2

Create a data input stream that can be used to read numbers from a compressed Zip file.

Reading and Writing Data Streams

Data streams make it easy to read or write the result of computations. DataInputStream supports methods for reading all the basic data types and a few encoded character types. These methods include:

- **int read(byte[ ] b)**   Reads arrays of bytes where b is the buffer into which the data is read.
- **int read(byte[ ] b, int off, int len)**   Reads arrays of bytes where b is the buffer into which the data is read, off is the start offset of the data, and len is the maximum number of bytes to read.

- **boolean readBoolean( )**   Reads boolean values (1 byte expected).
- **byte readByte( )**   Reads a signed 8-bit byte (1 byte expected).
- **int readUnsignedByte( )**   Reads an unsigned 8-bit byte (1 byte expected).
- **char readChar( )**   Reads a Unicode character (2 bytes expected).
- **double readDouble( )**   Reads doubles (8 bytes expected).
- **float readFloat( )**   Reads floats (4 bytes expected).
- **void readFully(byte[ ] b)**   Reads all the bytes in a stream where b is the buffer into which the data is read.
- **int readInt( )**   Reads ints (4 bytes expected).
- **long readLong( )**   Reads longs (8 bytes expected).
- **short readShort( )**   Reads signed 16-bit values (2 bytes expected).
- **int readUnsignedShort( )**   Reads unsigned 16-bit values (2 bytes expected).
- **String readUTF( )**   Reads a Unicode character string encoded in Java's modified UTF-8 format.

DataOutputStream provides methods for writing data types and some encoded character formats. These methods include:

- **void write(int b)**   Writes the specified byte b to the output stream.
- **void write(byte[ ] b, int off, int len)**   Writes an array of bytes where b is the array, off is the offset to start at, and len is the number of bytes to write.
- **void writeBoolean(boolean b)**   Writes booleans as a 1-byte value.
- **void writeByte(byte b)**   Writes a byte as a 1-byte value
- **void writeBytes(String s)**   Writes a string as a sequence of bytes.
- **void writeChar(char c)**   Writes a Unicode character as a 2-byte value, high byte first.
- **void writeChars(String s)**   Writes a string of Unicode characters as a sequence of characters. Each character written as a 2-byte value, high byte first.
- **void writeDouble(double d)**   Converts a double to a long and then writes as 8-byte value, high byte first.
- **void writeFloat(float f)**   Converts a float to an int and then writes as a 4-byte value, high byte first.
- **void writeInt(int i)**   Writes ints as 4-byte values, high byte first.

- **void writeLong(long l)**   Writes longs as 8-byte values, high byte first.

- **void writeShort(short s)**   Writes shorts as 2-byte values, high byte first.

- **void writeUTF(String s)**   Writes a string as a sequence of UTF-8 encoded characters using Java's modified format.

When reading and writing values, it is important to keep in mind that Java always writes the high byte first when multibyte values are being used. This technique may be different than the technique the operating system uses to write files. For example, Pentium processors typically store values with the least significant or low byte first rather than the most significant or high byte first. On the other hand, SPARC processors use the same technique as Java where the high byte is written first.

Methods that deserve further attention are readUTF and writeUTF. These methods are designed to work with Java's modified UTF-8 encoding. With this encoding technique, all characters in the range '\u0001' to '\u007F' are represented by a single byte with bits 0 through 7. A pair of bytes represents the null character '\u0000' and characters in the range '\u0080' to '\u07FF'. The low order byte holds bits 0 through 5 and the high order byte holds bits 6 through 10. Characters in the range '\u0800' to '\uFFFF' are represented by three bytes. The low order byte holds bits 0 through 5. The next byte holds bits 6 through 11, and the high order byte holds bits 12 through 15.

Writing values using the modified UTF-8 encoding has several consequences. It means:

- 7-bit ASCII values are written as 1 byte with an additional bit (the top bit being 0)

- 16-bit Unicode characters with the top 5 bits 0 and null are written as 2-byte sequences.

- All other 16-bit Unicode characters are written as 3-byte sequences.

 TIP: Keep in mind that this section is focusing primarily on techniques used to work with data streams. Java supports other techniques for working with encoded text streams and these techniques are discussed later in the chapter.

Encoded Text Streams

For the exam, you'll need to be able to write code that uses InputStreamReader and OutputStreamWriter to translate between Unicode and either platform default or ISO 8859-1 character encoding. You'll also need to be able to distinguish between conditions under which platform default encoding conversion should be used and conditions under which a specific conversion should be used.

In a perfect world, everything would be written in Unicode and we'd have an easy time working with data files. Unfortunately, we don't live in a perfect world and Java's standard encoding technique (Unicode) may not be what you need to read from or write to files. In fact, most operating environments use an encoding other than Unicode as their default encoding. For example, on Windows, the standard encoding is ISO 8859-1 encoding, also referred to as ISO Latin-1.

To work with various character encoding, Java uses a set of stream filters. The filter classes descend from the abstract Reader and Writer classes. For input stream conversion, you'll use InputStreamReader to turn an input stream containing bytes that use a specific encoding into a reader that produces Unicode characters. For output stream conversion, you'll use OutputStreamWriter to turn a stream of Unicode characters into a stream of bytes that use a specific encoding. The following example creates an input reader that reads keys entered at the console and converts them to Unicode:

```
InputStreamReader in = new InputStreamReader(System.in);
```

Because an encoding is not specified, the reader assumes the normal character encoding for the system is used. You can also specify the encoding and the constructor for this is

```
InputStreamReader(InputStream in, String enc)
```

where enc describes the encoding scheme that you want to use, such as

```
InputStreamReader in = new InputStreamReader
    (new FileInputStream("record.txt"), "8859_1");
```

In the previous example, the string "8859_1" tells the reader to use the ISO 8859-1 character encoding.

Every implementation of Java is required to support the following encoding shown in Table 17-1. Other encoding is supported on a per platform basis.

Because most programmers will at one time or another want to attach a reader or writer to a file, there is a pair of convenience classes for this purpose. They are FileReader and FileWriter. The reader definition

```
FileReader in = new FileReader("record.txt");
```

is the same as

```
InputStreamReader in = new InputStreamReader
    (new FileInputStream("record.txt"));
```

Table 17-1 Required Character Encoding Support for Java

Character Encoding	Description
US-ASCII	7-bit ASCII encoding, which is (ISO646-US).
ISO-8859-1	ISO Latin-1.
UTF-8	8-bit Unicode Transformation Format.
UTF-16BE	16-bit Unicode Transformation Format, big-endian byte order (meaning the high order bits are stored first).
UTF-16LE	16-bit Unicode Transformation Format, little-endian byte order (meaning the low order bits are stored first).
UTF-16	16-bit Unicode Transformation Format, byte order specified by a mandatory initial byte-order mark (either order accepted on input, big-endian used on output).

The writer definition

```
FileWriter out = new FileWriter("record.txt");
```

is the same as

```
OutputStreamWriter out = new OutputStreamWriter
   (new FileOutputStream("record.txt"));
```

The complete list of FileReader and FileWriter constructors are as follows:

- **FileReader(File file)**   Creates a new FileReader, given the File to read from.

- **FileReader(FileDescriptor fd)**   Creates a new FileReader using the FileDescriptor to read from.

- **FileReader(String fileName)**   Creates a new FileReader using the name of the file to read from.

- **FileWriter(File file)**   Constructs a FileWriter object using a File object.

- **FileWriter(FileDescriptor fd)**   Constructs a FileWriter object associated with a file descriptor.

- **FileWriter(String fileName)**   Constructs a FileWriter object using the name of the file to write to.

- **FileWriter(String fileName, boolean append)**   Constructs a FileWriter object using a file name with a Boolean indicating whether or not to append data. If you append data, you write to the end of the file. If you don't append data, you write to the beginning of the file.

As you examine the constructors, you should note that there aren't any constructors that set the encoding. This means the default character encoding for the operating system is assumed and used for reading and writing. To set a specific encoding, you must use InputStreamReader or OutputStreamWriter.

Writing To and Reading From Files

You can read, write, and update files using Reader, FileOutputStream, and RandomAccessFile objects. Here's another program that does just that:

```java
import java.io.*;
class FileReadWrite {
    static String fileName = "A.test";
    public static void main(String[] args) {
        try {
            FileOutputStream out = createFile();
            writeFile(out);
            readFile();
        } catch (IOException io) {
            System.out.println(io.getMessage());
        }
    }
    static FileOutputStream createFile() throws IOException {
        File f = new File(fileName);
        FileOutputStream out = new FileOutputStream(f);
        return out;
    }
    static void writeFile(FileOutputStream out) throws IOException
    {
        DataOutputStream ds = null;
        try {
            ds = new DataOutputStream(out);
            ds.writeBytes("hello!");
        } finally {
            if (ds != null)
                ds.close();
        }
    }
    static void readFile() throws IOException {
        BufferedReader br = null;
        try {
            File f = new File(fileName);
            FileReader in = new FileReader(f);
            br = new BufferedReader(in);
            String s = br.readLine();
```

```
                    System.out.println(s);
            } finally {
               if (br != null)
                   br.close();
            }
         }
      }
```

This example consists of three static methods in addition to main(). The first, create-File(), creates a new file and returns a FileOutputStream object so that we can write to it. The second, writeFile(), attaches a type of Filter stream—a DataOutputStream—to the FileOutputStream object, and uses the methods defined by DataOutputStream to write to our stream. The third, readFile(), creates a FileReader handle to the file, attaches a BufferedReader to it, and then uses the methods in BufferedReader to read from it.

Notice that we close the file very deliberately by placing the close() call inside a finally block so that it is always executed, even if one of the methods in the try block throws an exception. We also check to make sure the Filter object was created (in fact, the compiler insists upon it) before invoking close().

 CAUTION: Creating a FileOutputStream object creates the appropriate file. What if the file already exists? In that case, FileOutputStream recreates the file and writes to it again. (That is, FileOutputStream replaces the existing file.)

To append to a file instead of overwriting it, you need to use a RandomAccessFile object. RandomAccessFiles are described in the next section.

Exercise 17.3

Write a program that writes your phone number to a file. Don't write a String—write an int containing your seven digit number.

Random Access Files

RandomAccessFile objects do two things: they allow you to open a file as read-only or read/write, and they allow you to write to any location in the file, not just the beginning. The downside of using a RandomAccessFile is that it does not inherit from Input-Stream or OutputStream. This means that you cannot use them in a chain, for example, with the Filter stream classes.

RandomAccessFile does at least implement the DataInput and DataOutput interfaces, so it does support all of the methods for reading and writing Java's primitive data
types. When you create a RandomAccessFile, you'll supply a mode as the second argument. This mode is a String that can be either "r" for read or "rw" for read/write. (The
first argument is either a String containing the path and file name, or a File object.)

You can determine where the file pointer currently is, in bytes, by invoking getFile-
Pointer(). The 0th byte is the first position in the file.

You can set the file pointer with seek(), passing this method the number of bytes to
offset. And you can determine the length of the file with length().

Here's an example of appending to a file rather than overwriting it, as would happen
if we used FileOutputStream in place of RandomAccessFile in the program that follows:

```java
import java.io.*;
class Ran {
    static String fileName = "Ran.test";

    public static void main(String[] args) {
        try {
            sayHello();
            appendHi();
            readGreeting();
        } catch (IOException x) {
            System.out.println(x.getMessage());
        }
    }

    public static void sayHello() throws IOException {
        DataOutputStream ds = null;
        try {
            File f = new File(fileName);
            FileOutputStream out = new FileOutputStream(f);
            ds = new DataOutputStream(out);
            ds.writeBytes("hello!");
        } finally {
            if (ds != null)
                ds.close();
        }
    }

    public static void appendHi() throws IOException {
        RandomAccessFile out = null;
        try {
            File f = new File(fileName);
            out = new RandomAccessFile(f, "rw");
            out.seek(out.length());
            out.writeBytes(" hi!");
        } finally {
            if (out != null)
                out.close();
```

```
        }
    }

    public static void readGreeting() throws IOException {
        RandomAccessFile in = null;
        try {
            File f = new File(fileName);
            in = new RandomAccessFile(f, "r");
            String s = in.readLine();
            System.out.println(s);
        } finally {
            if (in != null)
                in.close();
        }
    }
}
```

The output from this program is a file named Ran.test that contains the following:

```
hello! hi!
```

In addition, this program also writes these contents to the standard output.

If we used a FileOutputStream instead if a RandomAccessFile in the sayHi() method, the file would simply contain:

```
hi!
```

because "hello!" would have been overwritten. But we were able to append using a RandomAccessFile because RandomAccessFile objects don't recreate the file if it already exists, and we can set the file pointer exactly where we want it—in this case, to the end of the file.

You can also see that the first time we wrote to the file we used a FileOutputStream. It was only when we wanted to append that we needed a RandomAccessFile. We created the RandomAccessFile object using "rw" the first time, because we wanted to write to it. The second time, in readGreeting(), we used "r," because we only wanted to read from the file.

Also, notice how we used readLine() to read from the file. This method is declared in the DataInput interface, which RandomAccessFile implements.

 NOTE: As with the earlier example of working with files, we wrapped the close() call inside a finally block so that the file is always closed when we're done with it.

File Descriptors

There is one more way to create a FileOutputStream object, and that's by using a constructor that takes a FileDescriptor object. FileDescriptors represent an existing, open file. A FileDescriptor object is a handle to the open file, but it does not have any methods you can use other than a method called valid() that returns true if the file it represents exists and is open.

You can get a FileDescriptor object by invoking a FileOutputStream's or RandomAccessFile's getFD() method. It is sometimes necessary to use a FileDescriptor if you want to create another stream to an existing stream.

Here's the idea. You have an existing stream and you want to create another stream object that references the same underlying file. However, streams do not supply a method that allows you to retrieve the name of the underlying file. Nor do they supply a method that allows you to retrieve a File object for the underlying file. However, FileOutputStream and RandomAccessFile do supply the magical getFD() method.

So, if you do not know the File object or the filename the stream refers to, you must use the FileDescriptor object returned by getFD() to create your new stream.

(You can also create a new RandomAccessFile using a FileDescriptor.)

Exercise 17.4

Finish this program to first write the numbers 1, 3, and 5 to a file, leaving gaps for the even numbers. Then on a second pass, write the numbers 2 and 4 in the proper places. Use the method declared by the DataOutput interface called writeBytes() to write out a String for "2" and "4" as appropriate.

```java
import java.io.*;
class Gaps {
    public static void main(String[] args) throws Exception {
        File f = new File("Gaps.test");
        RandomAccessFile out = new RandomAccessFile(f, "rw");
        out.writeBytes("1 3 5");
        System.out.println("len is " + out.length());

        // Supply the missing code here to write out "2" and "4"
        // in the gaps in the character "1 3 5" already written to
        // the file.

        out.close();
    }
}
```

Using Buffered Readers to Read Text Input

You've seen BufferedReader in previous examples. You use BufferedReader to read data in text format. When you want to process text input, BufferedReader is really your only option. BufferedReader has two constructors:

- **BufferedReader(Reader in)**   Creates a buffering character-input stream that uses a default-sized input buffer.

- **BufferedReader(Reader in, int sz)**   Creates a buffering character-input stream that uses an input buffer of the specified size.

The BufferedReader methods that you may want to use include:

- **void close( )**   Closes the stream.

- **void mark(int readAheadLimit)**   Marks the present position in the stream.

- **boolean markSupported( )**   Determines whether the stream supports the mark() operation, which it does.

- **int read( )**   Reads a single character.

- **int read(char[] cbuf, int off, int len)**   Reads characters into a portion of an array.

- **String readLine( )**   Reads a line of text.

- **boolean ready( )**   Specifies whether this stream is ready to be read.

- **void reset( )**   Resets the stream to the most recent mark.

- **long skip(long n)**   Skips n number of characters.

To use a BufferedReader, you must combine the reader with an input source, such as:

```
BufferedReader in = new BufferedReader
    (new FileReader("record.txt"));
```

You can read files in several different ways. You can read a single character or an array of characters using read. You can read an entire line of characters using readLine. The key to readLine is that each line must end with an end of line sequence. The read and readLine methods return null when no more input is available. Because of this, a typical code snippet to read the contents of a file looks like this:

```
BufferedReader in = new BufferedReader
    (new FileReader("record.txt"));

String s;
while ((s = in.readLine()) != null)
```

```
{
    //work with the file contents here
}
```

The FileReader class automatically converts bytes to Unicode characters. For other input sources, you'll need to use the InputStreamReader. InputStreamReader does not provide convenience methods to convert bytes to Unicode characters. If you created an InputStreamReader as shown in this example:

```
BufferedReader in = new BufferedReader
    (new InputStreamReader(System.in));
```

you would need to read a string first from the file and then convert it to the format you need. In this example, you read a line from the file and convert the string read to a float:

```
String s = in.readLine();
float f = Float.parseFloat(s);
```

Using Print Writers to Write Text Output

Print writers provide a convenient way to write to data to text files. Using a print writer, you can print strings and numbers in text format. Print writers are created using the PrintWriter class attached to a FileWriter, such as:

```
PrintWriter out = new PrintWriter
    (new FileWriter("record.txt"));
```

or by combining a print writer with an output stream, such as:

```
PrintWriter out = new PrintWriter
    (new FileOutputStream("record.txt"));
```

PrintWriter has four constructors:

- **PrintWriter(OutputStream out)**   Create a new PrintWriter, without automatic line flushing, from an existing OutputStream. This means println() methods will not flush the output buffer.

- **PrintWriter(OutputStream out, boolean autoFlush)**   Create a new PrintWriter from an existing OutputStream with line flushing set as you specify. If autoflush is true, println() methods will flush the output buffer.

- **PrintWriter(Writer out)**   Create a new PrintWriter, without automatic line flushing. This means println() methods will not flush the output buffer.

- **PrintWriter(Writer out, boolean autoFlush)** Create a new PrintWriter with line flushing set as you specify. If autoflush is true, println() methods will flush the output buffer.

You cannot use print writers to write raw bytes. You can only use text. Additionally, print writers always use buffered writing. Using the PrintWriter constructors, you can turn automatic flushing of the buffer on or off.

To write to a PrintWriter, you use the print() and println() methods. These methods work exactly as they do with System.out. print() sends values to the output stream. println() sends values to the output stream followed by an end of line character. The end of line sequence used is the default for the system as determined by calling System.getProperty("line.separator"). For Windows systems, the end of line character is \r\n, for Unix systems, \n, and for Mac systems, \r.

To get a better understanding of PrintWriter, consider the following example:

```
PrintWriter out = new PrintWriter
    (new FileOutputStream("record.txt"));

String name = "William R. Stanek";
String address = "123 Main St.";
String city = "Seattle";
String state = "WA";
String zipcode = "97232";

out.print(name + ':' + address + ' ');
out.print(city + ', ' + state + ' ');
out.println(zipcode + ';');
```

This writes

```
William R. Stanek: 123 Main St. Seattle, WA 97232;
```

to the stream out. The characters are then converted to bytes and are stored in the record.txt file. The println method adds the correct end of line character for the operating system. Since the autoflush mode isn't set, the writer uses the default without automatic line flushing. This means the call to println doesn't automatically flush the buffer. You'll need to specifically flush the buffer with a call to flush(). When you are finished writing to the file, you can close it by calling close().

The main PrintWriter methods that you'll use are

- **boolean checkError( )** Flushes the stream and checks its error state. Returns true if a formatting or output error occurred.

- **void close( )** Closes the stream.

- **void flush( )**   Flushes the stream.

- **void print(boolean b)**   Prints a Boolean value in text format.

- **void print(char c)**   Prints a Unicode character.

- **void print(char[ ] s)**   Prints an array of Unicode characters.

- **void print(double d)**   Prints a double-precision floating-point number in text format.

- **void print(float f)**   Prints a floating-point number in text format.

- **void print(int i)**   Prints an integer in text format.

- **void print(long l)**   Prints a long integer in text format.

- **void print(Object obj)**   Prints an object by printing the string resulting from toString.

- **void print(String s)**   Prints a Unicode string.

- **void println( )**   Prints a Unicode string followed by a line terminator. Flushes the stream if the stream is set to autoflush mode.

- **void write(char[ ] buf)**   Writes an array of Unicode characters.

- **void write(char[ ] buf, int off, int len)**   Write a portion of an array of Unicode characters starting at the offset off and continuing for the number of characters specified by len.

- **void write(int c)**   Writes a single Unicode character.

- **void write(String s)**   Writes a Unicode string.

- **void write(String s, int off, int len)**   Writes a portion of a Unicode string starting at the offset off and continuing for the number of characters specified by len.

Answers to the Exercises

Exercise 17.1

```
import java.io.*;
class NewFile {
  public static void main(String[] args) {
    if (args.length != 1) {
      System.out.println("Supply a file name.");
      System.exit(1);
    }
    try {
```

```
                    File f = new File(args[0]);
                    if (!f.createNewFile())
                        System.out.println(args[0] + " already exists.");
                } catch (IOException io) {
                    System.out.println(io.getMessage());
                }
            }
        }
```

Exercise 17.2

You can create a data input stream that can be used to read compressed Zip files in several ways. One of those ways is

```
DataInputStream dataIn = new DataInputStream
    (ZipIn = new ZipInputStream
        (new FileInputStream("record.zip")));
```

You could also write

```
ZipInputStream zipIn = new ZipInputStream(new
FileInputStream("record.zip"));
DataInputStream dataIn = new DataInputStream(zipIn);
```

Exercise 17.3

```
import java.io.*;
class Phone {
    static String fileName = "Phone.test";
    public static void main(String[] args) {
      try {
         FileOutputStream out = createFile();
         writeFile(out);
      } catch (IOException io) {
         System.out.println(io.getMessage());
      }
    }
    static FileOutputStream createFile() throws IOException {
        File f = new File(fileName);
        FileOutputStream out = new FileOutputStream(f);
        return out;
    }
    static void writeFile(FileOutputStream out) throws IOException
{
        DataOutputStream ds = null;
        try {
           ds = new DataOutputStream(out);
           ds.writeInt(5551212);
        } finally {
           if (ds != null)
              ds.close();
```

```
        }
    }
}
```

Exercise 17.4

```
import java.io.*;
class Gaps {
    public static void main(String[] args) throws Exception {
        File f = new File("Gaps.test");
        RandomAccessFile out = new RandomAccessFile(f, "rw");
        out.writeBytes("1 3 5");
        System.out.println("len is " + out.length());

        out.seek(1);
        out.writeBytes("2");
        out.seek(3);
        out.writeBytes("4");
        out.close();
    }
}
```

Review Questions

1. What are valid parameters for the FilterInputStream constructor?
   a. No parameter
   b. InputStream
   c. File
   d. RandomAccessFile
   e. DataInput
   f. All of the above
   g. a and b

2. To create a file you can use an instance of class:
   a. File
   b. RandomAccessFile
   c. FileOutputStream
   d. Any of these
   e. b and c

3. To create a new directory, you can use an instance of class:
   a. File
   b. RandomAccessFile
   c. FileOutputStream
   d. Any of these
   e. b and c

4. What will the result be of executing the following program?

```java
import java.io.*;
class B {
   public static void main(String[] args) {
      try {
         File f = new File("B.test");
         FileOutputStream out = new FileOutputStream(f);
      } catch (IOException io) {
         System.out.println(io.getMessage());
      }
   }
}
```

   a. It will throw an IOException which will be caught.
   b. It will run fine, but no file will result because nothing was written to it.
   c. It will run fine, the file "B.test" will exist after it runs, and the file's size will be 0.

5. If file is an instance of a RandomAccessFile and whose underlying file length is greater than 0, the line:

```java
file.seek(file.length()-1);
```

   will:
   a. position the file pointer at the end of the file (after the last character)
   b. position the file pointer just before the last character
   c. cause seek() to throw an IOException

6. You can attach a FilterOutputStream object to:
   a. An underlying file
   b. Another FilterOutputStream object
   c. A FilterInputStream object
   d. All of these
   e. a or b

7. To delete a file, you can use an instance of class:
   a. FileOutputStream
   b. RandomAccessFile
   c. File

Answers to Review Questions

1. **b.** Only objects of type InputStream are valid parameters to pass to create a new FilterInputStream object.

2. **d.** As of JDK 1.2, the File object can be used to create a file as well as FileOutput-Stream and RandomAccessFile.

3. **a.** The File class contains a method called mkdir() that will create a new directory.

4. **c.** This is valid code and will run fine, creating an empty file called "B.test."

5. **b.** You can position the file pointer at the end of the file by setting it to file.length().

6. **e.** A FilterOutputStream can be attached to any OutputStream subclass. This includes other filter streams as well as file streams.

7. **c.** You can use the delete() method defined in File to delete a file.

java.awt: Graphics and Components

Objectives for This Chapter

- Implement the paint() method for Component classes.
- Describe the flow of control between the methods repaint() and update().
- Use the following methods of the Graphics class: drawString(), drawLine(), drawRect(), drawImage(), drawPolygon(), drawArc(), fillRect(), fillPolygon(), and fillArc().
- Use Graphics methods in paint() and obtain a Graphics object from an Image.
- Construct graphical elements, including text areas, text fields, and lists.
- List the classes in the java.awt package that are valid arguments to the add() methods and those that are not valid.

"Graphical user interfaces" is a big topic. Entire books have been written on Java's Abstract Windowing Toolkit (AWT), which is the name of the package containing the classes you use to build graphical user interfaces. In this chapter, we'll review the basics of the AWT package as well as the advanced aspects you'll be expected to know for the exam.

Until now, this book has, for the most part, separated issues of Java programming from issues relating to the user interface. To help make Java programming snippets clear, we have mostly used character-mode, stand-alone programs—as opposed to graphical programs or Web-based applets—to illustrate Java programming. In this chapter, we'll look exclusively at the classes and techniques of building graphical applications.

The Abstract Windowing Toolkit (AWT)

If you want to create a graphical user interface for your Java program, you've got to work with the java.awt package, referred to familiarly as AWT. This class library defines a slew of platform-independent classes that represent user interface elements. Table 18-1 provides an overview of some of the key classes you'll use.

Table 18-1   Key AWT Classes

Class	Description
Area	Encapsulates an arbitrarily-shaped area.
BorderLayout	The border layout manager. The border layout uses five regions. Each region is identified by a corresponding constant: NORTH, SOUTH, EAST, WEST, and CENTER.
Button	Creates a push button control.
Canvas	Represents a blank rectangular area of the screen onto which you can draw or from which your can trap input events from the user.
CardLayout	The card layout manager. The card layout treats each component in the container as a card. The container itself acts as a stack of cards and only one card is visible at a time.
Checkbox	Creates a check box control.
CheckboxGroup	Creates a group of check box controls.
Choice	Creates a pop-up list.
Color	Used to manage the default RGB color space or arbitrary color spaces created for the application.
Component	An abstract superclass for non-menu AWT components, including buttons, check boxes, and scroll bars.
Container	A subclass of Component that can hold other components.
Cursor	Encapsulates the bitmap representation of the mouse cursor.
Dialog	A top-level window with a title and a border that is typically used to take some form of input from users.
Dimension	Specifies the dimensions of an object with width and height values.
FileDialog	Creates a window from which a file can be selected.
FlowLayout	The flow layout manager. A flow layout positions components left to right, top to bottom.
Font	Represents fonts.

Class	Description
FontMetrics	Encapsulates information about the rendering of a font.
Frame	Creates a window with a title and border.
Graphics	The abstract base class for all graphics contexts that allow you to draw onto components. The class encapsulates the state information needed for basic rendering operations.
GraphicsDevice	Describes a graphic device such as a screen or printer.
GraphicsEnvironment	Describes the collection of GraphicsDevice object and Font objects available to an application on a particular platform.
GridBagConstraints	Specifies constraints for components that are laid out using the GridBagLayout class.
GridBagLayout	The grid bag layout manager. A grid bag layout is a flexible layout that aligns components vertically and horizontally, without requiring that the components be of the same size.
Image	Encapsulates graphical images.
Insets	Encapsulates the borders of a container.
Label	Creates a label that displays a single line of read-only text.
List	Creates a list from which the user can choose. Lists are similar to the standard Windows list box.
Menu	Creates a pull-down menu that is deployed from a menu bar.
MenuBar	Creates a menu bar onto which menus can be placed. A menu bar must be bound to a frame by calling the setMenuBar method of the associated Frame object.
MenuComponent	The abstract superclass of all menu-related components.
MenuItem	Creates a menu item.
MenuShortcut	Assigns a keyboard shortcut for a menu item.
Panel	The simplest container class, which provides space in which an application can attach any other component including other panels.
Point	Encapsulates a point representing a location along an x/y coordinate space.
Polygon	Encapsulates a polygon, which is a closed, two-dimensional region within a coordinate space.
PopupMenu	Implements a menu, which can be dynamically popped up at a specified position within a component.

(continued)

Table 18-1   Key AWT Classes *(continued)*

Class	Description
Rectangle	Encapsulates a rectangle.
Scrollbar	Creates a scroll bar control.
ScrollPane	Implements a container that provides horizontal and/or vertical scroll bars for another component.
SystemColor	Encapsulates the colors of GUI objects on a system.
TextArea	Creates a multiline region that displays text. It can be set to allow editing or to be read-only.
TextComponent	A superclass for TextArea and TextField.
TextField	Creates a text component that allows for the editing of a single line of text.
Toolkit	The abstract superclass implemented by the AWT. Subclasses of Toolkit are used to bind the various components to particular native toolkit implementations.
Window	Creates a window without a frame, menu bar, or title.

As you can see, there are many useful AWT classes. For ease of reference, I like to divide the AWT classes into three categories:

- Components, which are the things the user interacts with. Subclasses of Component include Button, Checkbox, Choice, List, TextField, and TextArea.

- Containers, which are special types of Components that contain and arrange other Components.

- Other helper classes, such as Graphics, Color, and classes implementing Layout-Manager, all of which are used by Components and Containers to draw and place things on the screen.

We'll talk about Components and Containers in this chapter. You'll find a discussion of layout managers in Chapter 19. Naturally, this is not an exhaustive investigation into the AWT—I only dwell on core classes and concepts. However, with all the information discussed here, you'll still gain a very thorough understanding of the AWT.

AWT Essentials

AWT defines windows according to a class hierarchy. The two most common windows are those derived from Frame and Panel. Frame is the window used most commonly by

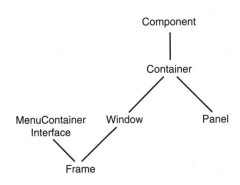

Figure 18-1   The class hierarchy for Panel and Frame

applications. Panel is the window used most commonly by applets. Most of the functionality of the Frame and Panel classes is derived from their parent classes as depicted in Figure 18-1.

As Figure 18-1 shows, the Component class is at top of the AWT class hierarchy. Component is an abstract superclass from which all the user interface elements that are displayed on the screen and interface with the user are derived. Component defines dozens of methods for handling events, positioning the window, sizing the window, and updating the display. The Component object is also responsible for setting and getting the foreground color, the background color, and fonts.

The Container class is a subclass of Component that is used to hold other components. Components added to a container are tracked in a list and the order of that list defines the front-to-back stacking order of components within the container. If no index is specified when adding a component to a container, it will be added to the end of the list. This means it is placed at the back of the stacking order. Containers are responsible for laying out any components that they contain. Container layout is handled using the layout managers discussed in Chapter 19.

The Panel class is a concrete subclass of Container. This class is used to implement containers and derives nearly all its functionality from the Container class. A panel provides space in which a program can attach any other component, including other panels. A panel doesn't contain a title bar, menu bar, or border. Panel is also the superclass for Applet. When screen output is directed to an applet, it is drawn on the surface of a Panel object.

The Window class creates a top-level window that is not contained within any other object. Windows sit directly on the desktop. In most cases, you won't create Window objects directly. Instead, you'll use a subclass of Window, such as Frame.

The Frame class creates window with a title bar and border. Typically, frame windows are used with applications and not with applets. In fact, if you create a frame window from within an applet, a warning is displayed that tells the user the window was generated by an applet rather than an application. This warning is necessary to maintain security. Otherwise, a frame window generated by an applet may be used to gather sensitive information without the user knowing that they aren't working with a locally run application.

Applets and AWT

Java's Applet class is defined in the package java.applet, not in java.awt. However, the Applet class is a user interface component. Applet descends from Panel. This means that Applets can do everything Panels can do (that is, they can contain a user interface), plus a little bit more.

That "little bit more" involves interacting with Web browsers. There are four life-cycle methods that the browser (or appletviewer if you're running in a development environment) invokes at different stages of your applet's life.

- When the Applet instance is first instantiated, Java invokes the applet's init() method.

- When the Web page containing the applet is about to appear, Java invokes the applet's start() method.

- When the Web page is about to be replaced with another page, Java invokes the applet's stop() method.

TIP: Java can alternately call an applet's start() and stop() methods as the Web page containing the applet appears and is removed from the Web browser's display.

- When the Web page is removed from the browser's cache and the applet instance is about to go away, Java invokes the applet's destroy() method.

You can override any of these methods to support your own applet's behavior. Typically, you would create a user interface in init(), pause and resume threads in start() and stop(), and halt threads in destroy().

The paint( ) Method

The runtime environment tells every Component (and, naturally, every Container, because Container is a subclass of Component) when it is time to make something appear on the screen—that is, when to redraw. The runtime environment will tell a

Component to redraw when it is dirty, when it has first appeared on the screen, when it is resized or its Container is resized, when something else on the screen (such as an overlapping window) that was covering the Component has gone away, or when the programmer has explicitly requested a redraw.

Java tells your Component to redraw by invoking its paint() method. The paint() method takes one parameter: an instance of class Graphics. You can use this instance to perform low-level drawing operations. We'll take a look at the Graphics class in just a moment.

The method declaration for paint() is:

```
public void paint(Graphics g)
```

You should put all of your drawing code into paint(), and no more than your drawing code. You want paint() to execute as quickly as possible. Don't put calculations into paint(), for example, or other things that will slow down the actual painting.

Repainting

If you want to explicitly repaint a component, you should not call paint() directly. Instead, you should invoke your component's repaint() method.

The repaint() method is overloaded. The no-args version of repaint() does not cause your user interface to repaint right away. In fact, when repaint() returns, your component has not yet been repainted: you've only issued a request for a repaint. However, there is another version of repaint() that requests the component be repainted within a certain number of milliseconds.

The repaint() method will cause AWT to invoke a component's update() method. AWT passes a Graphics object to update()—the same one that it passes to paint(). We'll cover the Graphics class in a moment. (For now, we're just getting the progression of repaint calls straight.)

> **NOTE:** The Graphics object that AWT hands to update() and paint() is different every time the Component is repainted. When Java repaints on its own, such as when the user resizes an applet, the AWT does not invoke update()—it just calls paint() directly.

The update() method does three things in this order:

1. Clears the background of the object by filling it with its background color.

2. Sets the current drawing color to be its foreground color.

3. Invokes paint(), passing it the Graphics object it received.

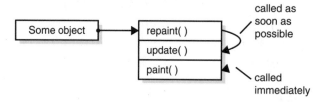

Figure 18-2 The Sequence of repaint( ), update( ), and paint( )

Figure 18-2 shows the sequence you should ingrain in your memory.

paint( ) and the Graphics Class

The paint() method takes an instance of the Graphics class. This object is a graphics context, platform-specific but with a platform-independent interface, allows you to draw on which screen.

The Graphics class defines lots of abstract methods for low-level drawing operations, such as drawing graphic primitives like lines and ovals, and setting drawing modes and colors. These abstract methods make the Graphics class an abstract class. Subclasses of Graphics implement the specific instructions that allow the graphics context to draw onto onscreen components or offscreen images. Most likely, you'll never see these Graphics subclasses, and you shouldn't care. They are platform-specific and depend on the operating environment your application is running in.

For example, running this program on Windows NT

```
import java.applet.Applet;
import java.awt.Graphics;

public class Gr extends Applet {
    public void paint(Graphics g) {
        System.out.println(g.getClass().getName());
    }
}
```

writes this class name to the screen:

```
sun.awt.windows.Wgraphics
```

This program yields a different result when run on a Mac or under Solaris.

You can't draw directly to this specific class anyway, so it doesn't really matter what it is. Besides, all you care about as a Java programmer is the Graphics interface. That's what Java does well—hides the implementation of the specifics to let you concentrate on your application's design.

Smoother Graphics

What this code does is eliminate the call to fill the background in the background color. This eliminates the flash. If you sometimes want to perform the normal behavior, you can put a test in the update() method, and under normal conditions invoke your super-class' version of update(), but when you are just switching to a new image, you can branch to your flicker-free code.

There are a number of ways you can make your painting occur faster and more smoothly than by following what Java does by default. One of these ways is by overriding a method called update(). Even though all your drawing code goes into paint(), Java actually invokes update() first, due to a call to repaint(). The repaint() method invokes update() as soon as it can, which means that repaint() often returns before Java invokes update() and paint().

The update() method does three things:

- Clears the Component of any drawing it contains (that is, it refreshes the background by redrawing the background in the background color).

- Sets the current drawing color of the Component to be the Component's foreground color.

- Invokes the Component's paint() method.

Because update() first clears the background, you'll sometimes find that your application flickers in a very unattractive way. To avoid this poor effect, you can override the normal update() method. For example, imagine you are flipping between images in your applet and each image is the same size. If you allowed the standard update() to paint() sequence to occur each time you display a new image, the background of the image would "flash" and become the same color as the background before being replaced by the new image.

In your override, you can just call paint() directly, after setting the current foreground color:

```
public void update(Graphics g) {
    g.setColor(getForeground());
    paint(g);
}
```

What this code does is eliminate the call to fill the background in the background color. This eliminates the flash. If you sometimes want to perform the normal behavior, you can put a test in the update() method, and under normal conditions invoke your superclass' version of update(), but when you are just switching to a new image, you can branch to your flicker-free code.

Drawing Using a Graphics Object

Because Graphics is abstract, you cannot create a Graphics instance directly by invoking its constructor. When you draw inside of paint(), the AWT hands you a Graphics object to use. If you want to draw outside of paint(), you can get a Graphics object in one of two ways:

- If you already have some other Graphics object, you can create a copy of it using the create() method defined by Graphics.

- If you have a component and want a Graphics object for it, you can invoke the component's getGraphics() method.

Graphics objects have a state, which includes its drawing color, paint mode, font, and clipping region. You can get and set any of these values. The update() method and the paint() method are handed an instance of the Graphics class. The Graphics instance you receive in paint() is tied to the component responding to the paint() method. This means that any drawing you do using the Graphics class appears in the component.

The Graphics methods use pixels as their units of measurement. Coordinates are also relative to the Component or Container they're displayed in. Horizontal (x) coordinates are measured from the left. Vertical (y) coordinates are measured from the top.

So, if a method calls for a baseline or corner point, you should supply measurements for that point as the number of pixels from the left and top edge of the window it is used in. Pixels are defined as int values.

Graphics defines many methods for drawing. Most of these methods draw in the current foreground color. The following are some common Graphics methods you might use in paint().

drawString( )

This method draws the characters in a String object into the display. This method takes three parameters: String object (or string literal) to display and the baseline for the first character (the x and y coordinates for the first character).

Here is a classic example of using drawString() to create the "Hello, world" applet. The bottom, left of the "H" in "Hello, world" is at the x and y coordinates, which in this case is x=80, y=30.

```
import java.awt.*;
import java.applet.*;

public class Str extends Applet {
   public void paint(Graphics g) {
      g.drawString("Hello, world!", 80, 30);
   }
}
```

The result looks like Figure 18-3.

drawLine( )

This method takes four parameters: the x, y location of the starting point, and the x, y location of the line's ending point. Here's an example of drawing a tic-tac-toe board.

```
import java.awt.*;
import java.applet.*;

public class Tic extends Applet {
   public void paint(Graphics g) {
      g.drawLine(60, 5, 60, 175);
      g.drawLine(120, 5, 120, 175);
      g.drawLine(5, 60, 175, 60);
      g.drawLine(5, 120, 175, 120);
   }
}
```

The display looks like Figure 18-4.

drawRect( ), fillRect( )

These methods draw a rectangle. The method drawRect() draws the outline of a rectangle; fillRect() draws a solid rectangle. Each of these methods takes four parameters: the top, left corner of the rectangle, and the width and height of the rectangle. The left and

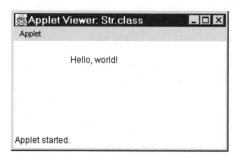

Figure 18-3   Using drawString()

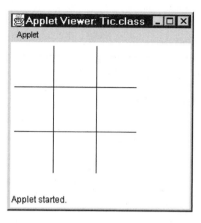

Figure 18-4 Using drawLine()

right edges of the rectangle are at x and x + width respectively. The top and bottom edges of the rectangle are at y and y + height respectively.

Here's an example of drawing a variety of rectangles:

```
import java.awt.*;
import java.applet.*;

public class Rect extends Applet {
   public void paint(Graphics g) {
      g.drawLine(60, 5, 60, 175);
      g.drawLine(120, 5, 120, 175);
      g.drawLine(5, 60, 175, 60);
      g.drawLine(5, 120, 175, 120);
      g.fillRect(80, 80, 20, 20);
   }
}
```

This code displays as shown in Figure 18-5.

 TIP: The drawOval( ) and fillOval( ) are very similar to drawRect( ) and fillRect( ), except these draw ovals inside the rectangle defined by corresponding parameters to drawRect( ) and fillRect( ).

drawPolygon( ), fillPolygon( )

You can draw a shape with any number of sides using drawPolygon() or fillPolygon(). Each of these methods is overloaded. One version takes an array of x and y coordinates

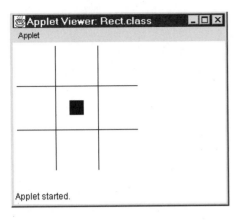

Figure 18-5   Using fillRect()

(int values) and the number of elements to use in the arrays. A second version takes a
Polygon instance, which defines the x and y arrays as part of its instance data.

For example, the following code draws a wacky, five-sided shape:

```
import java.awt.*;
import java.applet.*;

public class Poly extends Applet {
    public void paint(Graphics g) {
        int[] xArray = {20, 60, 90, 70, 30};
        int[] yArray = {50, 4, 45, 90, 70};
        g.fillPolygon(xArray, yArray, 5);
    }
}
```

Figure 18-6 shows what this code produces.

Notice how the last point connects back to the first.

drawArc( ), fillArc( )

These methods draw or fill an arc starting at a particular angle and moving counter-
clockwise for the number of degrees you define. The 3 o'clock position is 0 degrees.

To draw an arc, you supply the:

- arc's top, left corner as an x, y coordinate (similar to how you define a rectangle's
  top, left corner)

- width and height of the arc (again, similar to how you define the width and height
  of an oval)

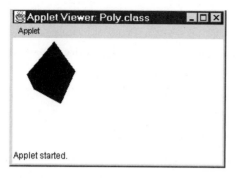

Figure 18-6 Using fillPolygon()

- start angle

- number of degrees to move along the arc (the end angle is start angle + arc angle)

For example, to draw the arc shown in Figure 18-7, you could write the following code:

```
import java.awt.*;
import java.applet.*;

public class Arc1 extends Applet {
    public void paint(Graphics g) {
        g.drawArc(20, 20, 150, 50, 0, 90);
    }
}
```

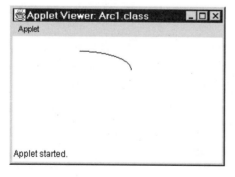

Figure 18-7 Using drawArc( )

Notice that the x, y coordinates 20, 20 indicate the top, left of the bounding box of the arc. (Imagine continuing the arc so that it creates an oval. The left and top of the oval are at x=20, y=20.) Also, notice that 0 degrees is at the 3 o'clock position, and that we're moving counter-clockwise 90 degrees (one-quarter of the way around the oval).

You can also move in the negative direction, if you wish, so that you're moving clockwise around the oval, rather than counter-clockwise.

drawImage( )

This method is overloaded to allow you a great deal of control over the way an image is displayed. The minimum parameters you need to supply are:

- An image to draw. This is an instance of the Image class.

- The x and y positions where the left and top corner of the image should appear.

- An image observer that communicates with the graphics system. This object helps notify the graphics system when the image is ready to be drawn—such as when it has been fully loaded over the Internet, for example.

There are also versions of drawImage() that specify a background color in which to draw transparent pixels (for example, when using a GIF image where you can define a particular pixel color to be transparent), and that specify height and width values for squeezing or stretching an image to fit a particular region.

The drawImage() methods you may use include:

- abstract boolean drawImage(Image img, int x, int y, ImageObserver observer)
  Draws an image with its upper-left corner specified by x and y. The specified ImageObserver monitors the image while it loads.

- abstract boolean drawImage(Image img, int x, int y, int width, int height, Color bgcolor, ImageObserver observer)
  Draw an image with its upper-left corner specified by x and y, scaling it to fit the specified width and height and using the background color bgcolor for transparent pixels. The specified ImageObserver monitors the image while it loads.

- abstract boolean drawImage(Image img, int x, int y, int width, int height, ImageObserver observer)
  Draw an image with its upper-left corner specified by x and y, scaling it to fit the specified width and height. The specified ImageObserver monitors the image while it loads.
  To actually draw an image, you need to obtain an image object. We'll discuss that next.

Exercise 18.1

Write an applet to display a solid circle that fits perfectly inside the outline of a square.

The Image Class

The JDK features direct support for GIF and JPEG images. You can work with these images in several different ways. One way would be to create a blank image. Another would be to obtain an image from a file stored at a local or remote location. After you obtain an image, display the image onscreen.

Creating a Blank Image

You can create an Image object, typically for use for as an offscreen buffer, by invoking the Component method createImage(). The createImage() method has two forms:

- **Image createImage(ImageProducer producer)**   Returns an image created by the specified image producer, which is an object of a class that implements the Image-Producer interface.

- **Image createImage(int width, int height)**   Returns a blank offscreen image that has the specified width and height.

The second form on the method is the one most commonly used. It creates a new image of the given width and height. If you're using this new Image object as an off-screen buffer for rendering graphics that will appear in the Component object you're creating it from, you'll probably want to set this Image object's size to the same width and height as your component.

Here is an example that creates an empty image:

```
Canvas c = new Canvas();
Image myImage = c.createImage(300, 300);
```

Loading or Transferring an Image

Instead of creating an Image object using an Image constructor, you can obtain an image, typically by downloading it over the Internet by specifying a URL. (Of course, the URL can be a local URL.) You can retrieve an image and obtain an Image object by invoking a method of the Applet class named getImage(). The method has two forms:

- **Image getImage(URL url)**   Returns an Image object that encapsulates the image found at the specified URL. The URL must specify an absolute location.

- **Image getImage(URL url, String name)** Returns an Image object that encapsulates the image found at the specified URL and has the specified name.

Here's the idea behind getImage( ): when this method returns, you have an Image object, but the data for the image is not necessarily immediately available. That is, this method returns right away, even if the image resource is located over the Internet on a Web server and must be downloaded.

When you invoke the Graphics method drawImage(), the image download begins. The object you specify as an ImageObserver keeps the Java graphics system up-to-date on the state of the download. When the ImageObserver sees that the download is complete, it notifies the graphics system that it can draw the image in its entirety. We'll talk more about ImageObserver in a moment.

Once you create or obtain an image, you can display it using the drawImage() method of the Graphics class. Here's a sample applet that loads and displays an image based on a file name supplied in a parameter:

```java
import java.awt.*;
import java.applet.*;

public class GetDisplayImage extends Applet {
    Image img;

    public void init() {
        img = getImage(getDocumentBase(), getParameter("image"));
    }

    public void paint(Graphics g) {
        g.drawImage(img, 0, 0, this);
    }

}
```

The applet code for the source would look like this:

```html
<applet code="gdImage"  width=300 height=300>
    <param name="image" value="myimage.gif">
</applet>
```

In the example, an Image object is created by calling getImage with a URL loaded relative to the result of getDocumentBase() and a file name supplied through a parameter called image. The document base is the URL of the HTML page containing the applet. When the applet runs, the init() method is called, which starts the loading of the image. Onscreen, you would see the image as it loads because the applet's ImageObserver calls paint() every time additional image data arrives.

A better way to implement the applet would be to have the ImageObserver monitor the progress of the download and then display the image when the download is complete. Your applet could then do other things in the meantime.

Using an ImageObserver

ImageObserver is an interface. This interface is defined in the java.awt.image package. The Component class implements this interface, so any Component (such as the Applet itself) can be used as an ImageObserver. ImageObserver only implements one method: imageUpdate(). Using an ImageObserver allows you to perform other tasks while an image is being downloads. For example, you could show a progress indicator.

The imageUpdate() method has the form:

```
public boolean imageUpdate(Image img, int flags,
                           int x, int y,
                           int width, int height)
```

The ImageUpdate() method is called whenever information about an image which was previously requested becomes available. The method should return true if further updates are needed or false if the required information has been acquired. The image being tracked is passed in using the img parameter.

Various constants are combined to form the flags argument, which indicates what information about the image is now available. The contents of the flags argument can change the interpretation of the x, y, width, and height parameters. The flags are

- **ALLBITS** The file transfer/download is now complete and all bits for the image are available. The parameters x, y, width, and height are not used.

- **FRAMEBITS** A complete frame that is part of a multiframe image has arrived. This frame can be displayed. The parameters x, y, width, and height are not used.

- **SOMEBITS** Additional pixels needed to draw the image have become available. The parameters x, y, width, and height specify the rectangle containing the new pixels.

- **WIDTH** The width parameter in the applet tag is valid and contains the width of the image.

- **HEIGHT** The height parameter in the applet tag is valid and contains the height of the image.

- **PROPERTIES** The properties of the image can now be obtained using the get-Property( ) method of the Image object.

- **ERROR**   An error occurred while obtaining the image. The image is incomplete and cannot be displayed. Also sets the ABORT flag. No further image data will be received.

- **ABORT**   The transfer/download was aborted before it was complete. If an error has not occurred, accessing the image data will restart the download of the image.

The Applet class inherits the imageUpdate() method from the Component class and uses this method to repaint images as they are loaded. You can override this method in your class to change that behavior.

Two examples using the imageUpdate() method follow. The first example paints the image as it is downloaded to provide smooth updating. It handles file not found errors by examining the flags parameter for the ABORT flag. If this flag is found, the error variable is set to true and then repaint() is called to paint the entire applet. Here is the source:

```
public boolean imageUpdate(Image img, int flags,
                           int x, int y,
                           int width, int height) {

    if ((flags & SOMEBITS) !=0) {
        //received additional data but not all data
        //paint new pixels smoothly
        repaint(x, y, width, height);

    } else if ((flags & ABORT) !=0) {
        //error occurred, probably file not found
        //repaint whole applet and set error variable
        error = true;
        repaint();
    }

    return (flags & (ALLBITS|ABORT)) == 0;
}
```

The next example using the imageUpdate() method waits until the image download is complete before painting into the applet. This causes the image to display in its entirety after a short delay. The source for this example is:

```
public boolean imageUpdate(Image img, int flags,
                           int x, int y,
                           int width, int height) {

    if ((flags & ALLBITS) !=0) {
        //received all data
        //paint entire image smoothly
        repaint();
```

```
    } else if ((flags & (ABORT|ERROR)) !=0) {
        //error or abort occurred, probably file not found
        //repaint whole applet and set error variable
        error = true;
        repaint();
    }

    return (flags & (ALLBITS|ABORT|ERROR)) == 0;
}
```

Exercise 18.2

Create an applet that loads an image using an ImageObserver. The applet should accept the image filename using a parameter set in the applet's param tag. The background for the applet should be set to white. The image should be displayed only when the download is complete. If an error occurs when downloading the applet, "Error: Image Not Found" should be displayed in place of the image.

You can also create an Image object, typically for use for as an offscreen buffer, by invoking the Component method createImage(). This method creates a new image to the given width and height. If you're using this new Image object as an offscreen buffer for rendering graphics that will appear in the Component object you're creating it from, you'll probably want to set this Image object's size to the same width and height as your component.

After you have the Image object, you can obtain its Graphics object to use to draw to it by invoking its getGraphics() method.

Working with Frame Windows

The types of windows you'll create most often are those derived from Frame. You will use it to create top-level or child windows for applications and to create child windows in applets.

Constructing the Frame

Frame windows have a title bar and border. Frame has four constructors, only two of which you'll use in most cases. The constructors you'll use are

- **Frame( )** Constructs a new Frame object without a title.
- **Frame(String title)** Constructs a new Frame object with the specified title.

New frame windows aren't visible initially and do not have specific dimensions either. You must set the window size after it has been created. Afterward, you can display the frame window.

Sizing the Frame

To set the dimensions of a frame window, you use the setSize() method. This method is inherited from the Component class and has two forms:

- **void setSize(Dimension d)**   Sets the size of the frame so that it has the width and height of the Dimension object passed in the method call.

- **void setSize(int width, int height)**   Sets the size of the frame so that the width is width and the height is height.

Regardless of whether you use a Dimension object or set a specific width and height, the dimensions are specified in terms of pixels. To obtain the current size of a frame, you can use the getSize() method. This method returns the current size of the frame contained within the width and height of a Dimension object. The getSize method has two forms:

- **Dimension getSize( )**   Returns the size of the frame in the form of a Dimension object.

- **Dimension getSize(Dimension rv)**   Stores the width/height of this component in a named Dimension object and then returns the object. If the object is null, it is created.

Both getSize() methods are useful for getting the current width and height of a frame. You'll use the latter constructor when you want to avoid allocating a new Dimension object on the heap.

After a frame is created, it will not be visible until you call setVisible(). setVisible has the form:

```
public void setVisible(boolean b)
```

where b is the flag that determines whether the frame is visible. The frame is visible if the argument to this method is true. Otherwise, the frame is hidden.

Setting the Frame Title

Another aspect of a frame that you can easily manipulate is the title. The title can be set when the frame is created using the Frame(String title) constructor. It can also be set or changed later using the setTitle() method. This method has the general form:

```
void setTitle(String title)
```

where title is the new title for the frame.

Closing the Frame Window

Any program that creates a window must also be able to remove the window from the screen when it is closed. You do this by calling setVisible(false) when the program inter- cepts a window-close event. This means your program must implement the window- Closing() method of the WindowListener interface. This interface is implemented with the WindowAdapter class.

A sample adapter class that implements the windowClosing method is shown in the following example:

```
import java.awt.event.*;

class MyWindowAdapter extends WindowAdapter {
   SimpleFrame simpleFrame;
   public MyWindowAdapter(SimpleFrame simpleFrame) {
      this.simpleFrame = simpleFrame;
   }
   public void windowClosing(WindowEvent we) {
      simpleFrame.setVisible(false);
   }
}
```

Creating a Frame Window in An Application

While it is possible to create a window by creating an instance of the Frame object, you usually won't do this. A Frame object created in this manner doesn't have the function- ality you need to perform advanced tasks, such as receiving or processing events. Because of this, you will usually create a subclass of Frame. Once you do this, you can override the methods and event handling of the Frame object to achieve the necessary behavior.

Extending the Frame class is easy. Here's an example:

```
class SimpleFrame extends Frame {
    SimpleFrame(String "My Window Frame") {
    }
}
```

Most of the time, you'll want the frame to implement a WindowListener interface so that events, such as the windows-close event can be handled. You can use a WindowAdapter to do this. The WindowAdapter class implements the WindowListener interface and adds several methods for opening, activating, and closing windows based on events. In the following example, the MyWindowAdapter class implements the windowClosing method, calling setVisible(false) to close the window:

```
class MyWindowAdapter extends WindowAdapter {
    SimpleFrame simpleFrame;
    public MyWindowAdapter(SimpleFrame simpleFrame) {
        this.simpleFrame = simpleFrame;
    }
    public void windowClosing(WindowEvent we) {
        simpleFrame.setVisible(false);
    }
}
```

Once you create the adapter class, you can update the Frame class to use the adapter as shown in the following example:

```
class SimpleFrame extends Frame {
    SimpleFrame(String "My Window Frame") {
        MyWindowAdapter adapter = new MyWindowAdapter(this);
        addWindowListener(adapter);
    }
```

Now that you can define a Frame class and implement the WindowListener interface, you can create an object of the SimpleFrame class. This causes the frame window to come into existence, but it will not be visible initially. You must make it visible by calling setVisible(true). When created, the frame window is given a default width and height. You can set the dimensions explicitly by calling setSize. These functions could be implemented in an application method, such as main. Here's an example:

```
public static void main(String args[]) {
    Frame f;
    f = new SimpleFrame("My Frame Window");
    f.setSize(300, 300);
    f.setVisible(true);
}
```

The complete frame example comes together as follows:

```
import java.awt.*;
import java.awt.event.*;

class SimpleFrame extends Frame {
    SimpleFrame(String title) {
        super(title);
        MyWindowAdapter adapter = new MyWindowAdapter(this);
        addWindowListener(adapter);
    }
    public static void main(String args[]) {
        Frame f;
        f = new SimpleFrame("My Frame Window");
        f.setSize(300, 200);
        f.setVisible(true);
    }
    public void paint(Graphics g) {
        g.drawString("Application Frame: Testing...", 15, 100);
    }
}

class MyWindowAdapter extends WindowAdapter {
    SimpleFrame simpleFrame;
    public MyWindowAdapter(SimpleFrame simpleFrame) {
        this.simpleFrame = simpleFrame;
    }
    public void windowClosing(WindowEvent we) {
        simpleFrame.setVisible(false);
    }
}
```

Creating a Frame Window in An Applet

You can create frame windows in applets as well as applications. First, create a subclass of Frame and then override the standard applet methods as necessary, such as init(), start(), stop(), and paint(). Afterward, implement the windowClosing method of the WindowListener interface. As before, you can use a WindowAdapter to do this.

The following example creates a subclass of Frame called MySimpleAppletFrame. A window of this subclass is instantiated within the init() method of AppletFrame. MySimpleAppletFrame calls the Frame's constructor, which causes a standard frame window to be created with the title specified. The start() and stop() methods of the applet are overridden so that they show and hide the child window upon starting and stopping respectively. Because of this, the window is displayed when the applet is viewed and removed when the applet is stopped.

```
import java.awt.*;
import java.awt.event.*;
import java.applet.*;

class MySimpleAppletFrame extends Frame {
    MySimpleAppletFrame(String title) {
        super(title);
        MyWindowAdapter2 adapter = new MyWindowAdapter2(this);
        addWindowListener(adapter);
    }
    public void paint(Graphics g) {
        g.drawString("Applet Frame: Testing...", 15, 100);
    }
}

class MyWindowAdapter2 extends WindowAdapter {
    MySimpleAppletFrame mySimpleAppletFrame;
    public MyWindowAdapter2(MySimpleAppletFrame
                   mySimpleAppletFrame) {
        this.mySimpleAppletFrame = mySimpleAppletFrame;
    }
    public void windowClosing(WindowEvent we) {
        mySimpleAppletFrame.setVisible(false);
    }
}

public class MyAppletFrame extends Applet {
    Frame f;
    public void init() {
        f = new MySimpleAppletFrame("My Frame Window");
        f.setSize(300,200);
        f.setVisible(true);
    }
    public void start() {
        f.setVisible(true);
    }
    public void stop() {
        f.setVisible(false);
    }
    public void paint(Graphics g) {
        g.drawString("Applet Window", 15, 100);
    }
}
```

How Java Arranges Components Within Containers

Creating a frame window and drawing a text string on it is fine, but at some point you'll probably want to create buttons, check boxes, and other standard user interface elements that the user can click, check, and so on. All of Java's user interface components are subclasses of the Component class.

We'll look at examples of creating Component objects in a moment. First, though, it's useful to know how you will arrange these Component objects in your application's display.

You add Component objects to Container objects using add(). The Container object knows how to contain objects and arrange the objects it contains.

First, you will probably have a Container object of some kind that will contain a Component. For example, a Window is a Container. Perhaps this Window object is referred to by the object reference window.

Second, you create a Component object, such as a Button, TextField, Checkbox, and so on. Let's say you assign the object reference for a Component object to a variable named component.

The way you add the component to the window is to write:

```
window.add(component);
```

Keep in mind that Container inherits from Component. Hence, Containers can contain Component objects as well as other Container objects.

The Component Class, Subclasses, and Methods

In this section, we'll create Component objects. The Component objects we'll look at in this section are TextArea, List, and TextField.

As you examine these components, keep in mind that they can be added directly to an applet's panel without the need of an additional container. The reason for this, as stated earlier, is that Panel is a superclass for Applet, which means any screen output directed at the applet is drawn to the surface of the related Panel object.

TextArea

A TextArea object provides a window for the user to type into. When you create a TextArea object, you specify the number of lines that the text window can contain, and the number of columns of text it will contain. The number of columns that a TextArea (or TextField) object can contain is only approximate.

There are five constructors for TextArea. The two you'll use the most specify the number of rows and columns for the TextArea. Their format is:

```
TextArea(int numRows, int numCols);
TextArea(String text, int numRows, int numCols);
```

You may also want to use the constructor introduced with Java 1.1. These constructors take a string, number of rows, number of columns, and an integer describing any scroll bars desired in the TextArea. The constructor format is:

```
TextArea(String text, int numRows, int numCols, int scrollbars);
```

The other constructors are the no-args constructor and a constructor that simply takes a String parameter—the text to display in the TextArea object. Displaying a TextArea constructed without specifying the number of rows and columns will probably give you results you don't want, since the TextArea has not been sized properly.

Here's an example of a TextArea object that displays three rows of text and up to ten columns:

```java
import java.awt.*;
import java.applet.*;

public class TA1 extends Applet {
    public void init() {
        add(new TextArea(3, 10));
    }
}
```

This applet looks like what's shown in Figure 18-8 when it is first run.

Figure 18-9 shows what happens as you start typing into the TextField.

Even though the TextArea was only set to three rows and ten columns, the user typed more text than could fit into this space. The TextArea displays little scroll bars when this happens so the user can get to the rest of the text. In this case, the user typed a speech

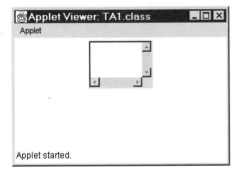

Figure 18-8   A TextArea set to three rows and ten columns

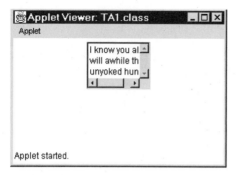

Figure 18-9   Typing into the TextArea set to three rows and ten columns

from Henry IV, Part 1: "I know you all, and will awhile uphold the unyoked humor of your idleness."

If you want a TextArea (or a TextField) object to be used only to display text (if you want the user to be unable to edit the text in this object), you can invoke the method setEditable() and pass a value of false as the parameter.

TextField

A TextField object also provides a window for the user to type into, but it only allows the user to type one line. When you create a TextField object, you specify the number of columns in the TextField.

As with TextArea, you can also construct a TextField without specifying the number of columns. Again, this is probably not something you will want to do, because then you will not be in control of the size of the TextField.

Here is an example of creating a TextField that is 20 columns wide:

```
import java.awt.*;
import java.applet.*;

public class TF1 extends Applet {
    public void init() {
        add(new TextField(20));
    }
}
```

Figure 18-10 shows what this looks like.

Unlike with a TextArea, if you type more characters than can fit within the width of the TextField, no scroll bars appear. However, you can still use the arrow keys on the keyboard to move to the front or end of the text.

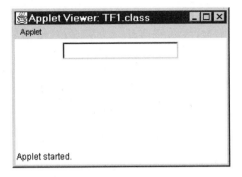

Figure 18-10   A TextField that is 20 columns wide

List

A List object presents a list of Strings that the user can select from. When you create a List, you indicate the number of lines the List will show at one time. If there are more items in the List than can be displayed, scroll bars appear to the right of the List so the user can scroll through the rest of the choices. You can also indicate whether the user may make multiple selections or just a single selection.

To create a List object containing a certain number of rows, use this constructor:

```
List(int numRows, boolean multipleSelections);
```

You can populate the List by invoking add(). For example, to create a List that shows five items at a time and allows the user to select multiple types of fish, you can write:

```
import java.awt.*;
import java.applet.Applet;

public class L1 extends Applet {
    public void init() {
        List l = new List(5, true);
        l.add("trout");
        l.add("salmon");
        l.add("snapper");
        l.add("bass");
        l.add("tuna");
        l.add("halibut");
        l.add("swordfish");
        add(l);
    }
}
```

This applet looks like Figure 18-11 when it first appears.

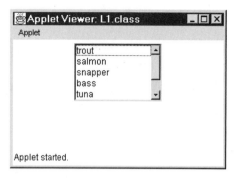

Figure 18-11   A list displayed in an applet

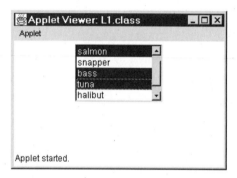

Figure 18-12   The user interacting with a list that allows multiple selections

As the user interacts with it and selects multiple fish, the list might look like Figure 18-12.

Exercise 18.3

Create and display a TextArea object that contains the text "To Whom It May Concern." The TextArea should be large enough to dash off a small note to someone. (You can decide what's large enough.)

Key Component Methods

You'll find that component objects have a lot of common methods. Some of the key methods are setEnabled(), setVisible(), getSize(), setSize(), setForeground(), and set-Background(). We looked briefly at some of these methods earlier in the chapter. Now we'll provide some additional examples for when these methods are used with components. As you'll see, they behave much as they do with containers, such as Frame.

setEnabled

You can use the setEnabled() method to make a component selectable or not by the user. Let's say you had two buttons that you wanted to make mutually exclusive. You could use setEnabled(true) and setEnabled(false) to turn them on and off—to make them selectable or not selectable—by the user. Here's an example:

```
import java.applet.Applet;
import java.awt.*;
import java.awt.event.*;

public class Toggle extends Applet {
    Button start, stop;
    public void init() {
        start = new Button("start");
        stop = new Button("stop");
        start.addMouseListener(new ButtonToggler(start, stop));
        stop.addMouseListener(new ButtonToggler(stop, start));

        start.setEnabled(true);
        stop.setEnabled(false);
        add(start);
        add(stop);
    }
}

class ButtonToggler extends MouseAdapter {
    Button otherButton;
    Button myButton;

    public ButtonToggler(Button myButton, Button otherButton) {
        this.myButton = myButton;
        this.otherButton = otherButton;
    }

    public void mouseClicked(MouseEvent me) {
        myButton.setEnabled(false);
        otherButton.setEnabled(true);
    }
}
```

getSize and setSize

The getSize() method retrieves the size of a Component. This method returns a Dimension object, which has two fields: width and height. The setSize() method sets the size of a Component and can be used to set the initial component size as well as to resize the component. Although two resize() methods are defined, these are deprecated in JDK 1.1 and later.

Components that are within a Layout Manager that automatically sizes the Components they contain should not call setSize() directly. Instead, the Layout Manager should take care of sizing the Component appropriately.

setVisible

The setVisible() method makes a Component visible or invisible. A boolean parameter indicates whether to show the Component (if the parameter is true) or hide the Component (if the parameter is false).

One common place to use setVisible() is when you create a stand-alone graphical application. Typically, your top-level Container is a Frame. To make the Frame appear, you've got to invoke it's setVisible() method. Here's an example of using both setSize() and setVisible() to make a Frame take up space and appear on the screen:

```
import java.awt.*;

public class Fr extends Frame {
    public static void main(String[] args) {
        Fr fr = new Fr();
        fr.setSize(220, 100);
        fr.setVisible(true);
    }
}
```

Figure 18-13 shows what this simple program looks like when you run it.

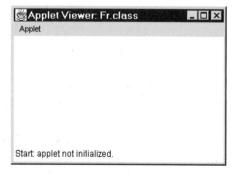

Figure 18-13   A simple frame

setForeground and setBackground

The setForeground() and setBackground() methods are used to set the foreground and background color of a Component. These methods each take one parameter, an instance of class Color.

The Color class defines a whole bunch of static constants that contain instances of class Color already initialized to common colors. Each constant is named after the color. To use red, for example, you can access Color.red. To use blue, you can access Color.blue. The colors Java makes available through the Color class are black, blue, cyan, dark gray, gray, green, light gray, magenta, orange, pink, red, white, and yellow.

Now, what if you want a different color? No problem. You can mix your own color out of red, green, and blue elements by creating a new Color instance and supplying the red, green, and blue values in the constructor. For example, you can use the constructor with this signature:

```
Color(int red, int green, int blue);
```

The red, green, and blue values range from 0 to 255. If all are set to 0, you get black. If all values are set to 255, you get white.

The Color class provides methods to convert between red, green, blue and hue, saturation, and brightness if you'd rather work with the latter system. There are also methods for getting the red, green, and blue portions of a color. For example, to set the foreground color to green for a Component referenced by the variable component, you can write:

```
component.setForeground(Color.green);
```

Answers to the Exercises

Exercise 18.1

```
import java.awt.*;
import java.applet.*;

public class Drawing extends Applet {
    public void paint(Graphics g) {
        g.drawRect(5, 5, 50, 50);
        g.fillOval(5, 5, 50, 50);
    }
}
```

Exercise 18.2

Here's one way the applet could be implemented:

```java
import java.awt.*;
import java.applet.*;

public class DisplayImage extends Applet {
    Image img;
    boolean error = false;

    public void init() {
        setBackground(Color.white);
        img = getImage(getDocumentBase(), getParameter("image"));
    }

    public void paint(Graphics g) {
        if (error) {
            Dimension d = getSize();
            g.setColor(Color.blue);
            g.fillRect(0, 0, d.width, d.height);
            g.setColor(Color.black);
            g.drawString("Error: File Not Found", 10, d.height/2);
        } else {
            g.drawImage(img, 0, 0, this);
        }
    }

    public void update(Graphics g) {
        paint(g);
    }

    public boolean imageUpdate(Image img, int flags,
                               int x, int y,
                               int width, int height) {

        if ((flags & ALLBITS) !=0) {
            //received all data
            //paint entire image smoothly
            repaint();

        } else if ((flags & (ABORT|ERROR)) !=0) {
            //error or abort occurred, probably file not found
            //repaint whole applet and set error variable
            error = true;
            repaint();
        }

        return (flags & (ALLBITS|ABORT|ERROR)) == 0;
    }
}
```

Exercise 18.3

```
import java.awt.*;
import java.applet.*;

public class ToWhom extends Applet {
    public void init() {
        add(new TextArea("To Whom It May Concern", 10, 30));
    }
}
```

Review Questions

1. You should place all of your low-level graphics rendering code into:
   a. update()
   b. paint()
   c. init()
   d. repaint()

2. The AWT passes your paint() method an instance of class:
   a. Thread
   b. Applet
   c. Graphics
   d. Component

3. Given a Graphics object in the variable g, the method call:

```
g.DrawRect(0, 10, 30, 40);
```

   a. draws the outline of a rectangle that is centered at x=0, y=10, and is 30 pixels wide and 40 pixels height.
   b. draws the outline of a rectangle whose top, left corner is at x=0, y=10, and whose bottom, right corner is at x=30, y=40.
   c. fills a rectangle with the foreground color where the rectangle's left edge is 0, top is 10, width is 30, and height is 40.
   d. draws the outline of a rectangle where the rectangle's left edge is 0, top is 10, width is 30, and height is 40.

4. Here is some partial code for a main() method:

```
Frame f = new Frame("My frame");
f.setSize(100, 100);
```

What line of code could you add to make this new Frame object appear on the screen?

a. f.appear();

b. f.setForeground();

c. f.setVisible();

d. f.enable();

5. The Graphics class has a coordinate system with an origin at

a. the center of the space

b. the bottom left corner of the space

c. the top left corner of the space

d. a user-configurable coordinate system

6. The Code:

```
new List(10, true);
```

a. creates a new list that is ten columns wide and accepts multiple selections.

b. creates a new list that is ten rows tall and accepts multiple selections.

c. creates a new list that can contain no more than ten entries and accepts multiple selections.

d. creates a new list that is ten rows tall and only enables one entry to be selected at a time.

Answers to Review Questions

1. **b.** All low-level drawing code should go into your paint() method.

2. **c.** You can use the Graphics object to perform low-level drawing operations.

3. **d.** The template is: drawRect(left edge, top edge, width, height)

4. **c.** The setVisible() method makes a component appear.

5. **a.** The Graphics class has a coordinate system with an origin at the top left of the space.

6. **b.** The first parameter is the number of rows to display without scrolling; the second parameter indicates whether or not to allow multiple selections.

java.awt: Layout

Objectives for This Chapter

- Identify AWT classes that determine layouts for components with a container.
- Change the layout scheme associated with a Container instance.
- Identify the effects of layout classes.
- State strategies to achieve a dynamic resizing of a Component.
- Distinguish between methods invoked by the user thread and those normally invoked by AWT.

In this chapter, we'll look at layout managers. For the exam, you'll need to know how to write code using the layout manager classes of java.awt. You'll also need to be able to distinguish the responsibilities of layout managers from those of containers.

Components and Layout Managers

The fact that Containers contain Components is all well and good, but how do Containers arrange the Components within them? The answer is that they hand off this chore to a layout manager. Each Container has exactly one layout manager. The layout manager determines how to arrange the Components within a Container.

Layout Manager Essentials

Whenever the Container or a Component within a Container changes in a way that might mean the layout needs to be updated—such as when the Container first appears on the screen, if new Components are added to a Container, if the Components within a Container change size, or if the Container itself is resized—the AWT invokes the Container's invalidate() method, followed shortly later by validate(). The validate() method in turn invokes that Container's layout() method. The Container's layout() method, however, does not figure out what to do on its own. This method asks its Container's layout manager what to do by calling the layout manager's layoutContainer() method. The layoutContainer() method takes the Container as an argument.

What is a layout manager, exactly? Any class that implements the LayoutManager interface. Java's five layout managers all inherit directly from class Object, but they implement the LayoutManager interface, which defines five abstract methods:

- addLayoutComponent()
- layoutContainer()
- minimumLayoutSize()
- preferredLayoutSize()
- removeLayoutComponent()

You will probably never invoke any of these methods directly, even if you implement your own layout manager instead of using one of the five that come with Java. (You'll usually find that one of Java's five layout managers works just fine.)

Instead of invoking a layout manager's methods yourself, Java's default Container methods invoke them for you at the appropriate times. Table 19-1 shows the connection between Container and layout manager methods.

Using Layout Managers

Each type of Container comes with a default Layout Manager. We'll discuss the different ones in this section. Later, you'll review what the default Layout Managers are for the different Containers, and you'll review how to change the Layout Manager for a Container.

The five different layout managers are the classes FlowLayout, BorderLayout, GridLayout, CardLayout, and GridBagLayout.

FlowLayout

A FlowLayout object arranges components left to right and top to bottom, centering each line as it goes. As new components are added to a Container with a FlowLayout, the FlowLayout positions each component on the same line as the previous one until

Table 19-1   Container and Layout Manager Methods

Container Methods	Layout Manager Methods
add()	addLayoutComponent()
doLayout()	layoutContainer()
getMinimumSize()	minimumLayoutSize()
getPreferredSize()	preferredLayoutSize()
remove()/removeAll()	removeLayoutComponent()

the next component will not fit given the width of the Container. Then, the FlowLayout centers that row, starts a new row, and begins adding components to the new row. A FlowLayout lets each component be its preferred size and does not change the size of a component. (The same is not true for other Layout Managers, as we'll review shortly.)

The FlowLayout lets the component be its preferred size even if the component cannot fit in the width or height provided. For example, if a label or button contains text that makes it too wide to display in the Container, the component will be on its own row, and you'll see only the centered portion that fits in the Container's width.

Here's some code that illustrates this:

```
import java.awt.*;
import java.applet.*;

public class Fit extends Applet {
    public void init() {
        add(new Label("Romeo, Romeo, wherefore art thou, Romeo?"));
    }
}
```

This places a very long label into an applet. However, if the HTML file that embeds this applet looks like this:

```
<applet code=Fit.class width=50 height=50>
</applet>
```

then the label won't be fully seen. The applet will look like Figure 19-1.

If a Container using a FlowLayout is resized, all of the components inside it might need to be rearranged. This might very well mean the components end up in a different relationship to each other, depending on what now fits on each row. Where a text field, button, and choice might have been on the same row at first, resizing the Container to be smaller might force each component to be placed on its own row.

Figure 19-1   A label that doesn't fit in the width of the applet

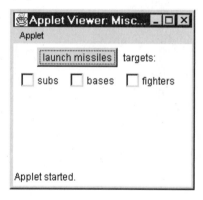

Figure 19-2   An applet that uses a FlowLayout to arrange components

Figure 19-2 shows an example of a bunch of components first arranged one way, and then, when the applet is resized, Figure 19-3 shows how they look after the FlowLayout has rearranged them.

Here's the code for this applet:

```
import java.awt.*;
import java.applet.*;

public class MiscComponents extends Applet {
    public void init() {
```

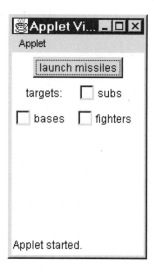

Figure 19-3   Resizing an applet that uses a FlowLayout

```
        add(new Button("launch missiles"));
        add(new Label("targets: "));
        add(new Checkbox("subs"));
        add(new Checkbox("bases"));
        add(new Checkbox("fighters"));
    }
}
```

FlowLayouts are particularly useful for arranging a series of buttons to create a kind of menu, where each button is placed after the one before it.

BorderLayout

BorderLayout objects arrange components according to the directions North, South, East, and West. There's also an area for Center, which includes any space left over from the other regions.

Each region can contain a component. The component at North gets positioned at the top of the container, and the component at South gets positioned at the bottom of the container. The layout manager forces the North and South components to be exactly as wide as the container.

The border layout is not affected by the order in which you add components. Instead, you must specify the region to which you are adding a component. As you know, you add elements to a container using the add() method. With border layout, an overloaded version of add is used. This version of the add method form takes two parameters: first the component being added and then the Object. Proper use of the border layout manager requires the second parameter to be a String object.

The BorderLayout class defines constants that you can use for this purpose. These constants are defined to be strings. The five constants are

- BorderLayout.NORTH
- BorderLayout.SOUTH
- BorderLayout.EAST
- BorderLayout.WEST
- BorderLayout.CENTER

Components are rarely allowed to be their preferred size in a BorderLayout. If the Container is smaller than the components' preferred sizes, the components are squeezed. If the Container is larger, the components are stretched. For example, Figure 19-4 shows five Button objects arranged in a Container that uses a BorderLayout. This picture gives a better sense of the regions of a BorderLayout than words do. Notice that the North and South regions stretch horizontally across the screen, whereas the East and West regions are positioned between the North and South regions.

Here's the code for this picture:

```
import java.awt.*;
import java.applet.*;

public class Five extends Applet {
    public void init() {
```

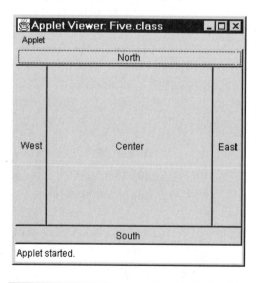

Figure 19-4   Five buttons in a BorderLayout

```
        setLayout(new BorderLayout());
        add(new Button("North"), BorderLayout.NORTH);
        add(new Button("South"), BorderLayout.SOUTH);
        add(new Button("East"), BorderLayout.EAST);
        add(new Button("West"), BorderLayout.WEST);
        add(new Button("Center"), BorderLayout.CENTER);
    }
}
```

BorderLayout objects also have another limitation: you cannot display more than one component in a particular region. If you do add more than one to a region, only the last component you add will appear. For example, if you try to add three Checkbox objects (though three buttons, three labels—three of anything have the same result) to the North region" of a BorderLayout, like this:

```
import java.applet.Applet;
import java.awt.*;

public class BorderOver extends Applet {
    public void init() {
        setLayout(new BorderLayout());

        add(new Checkbox("mouse"), BorderLayout.NORTH);
        add(new Checkbox("dog"), BorderLayout.NORTH);
        add(new Checkbox("cat"), BorderLayout.NORTH);
    }
}
```

the result is that only the last component is displayed, as shown in Figure 19-5.

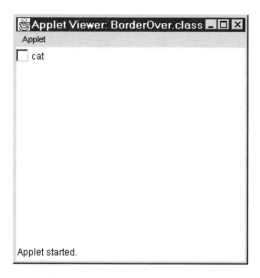

Figure 19-5   In a BorderLayout, only the last component added to a region is displayed.

So what is a BorderLayout good for? Unlike a FlowLayout, a BorderLayout is useful for making certain that components keep the same relationship to each other, even if the applet is resized. They also are excellent at arranging components along the top and bottom of a Container, which a FlowLayout cannot do.

If you want to show more than one component in a particular region of a Border-Layout, you can nest another Container inside the first Container. For example, to place three buttons at the top of a Container and three at the bottom, you can place each set of three inside their own Container using a FlowLayout, and then place the two Containers inside the one using the BorderLayout. The code might look like this:

```
import java.applet.Applet;
import java.awt.*;
public class Border extends Applet {
    public void init() {
        Panel p;

        setLayout(new BorderLayout());

        p = new Panel();
        p.add(new Button("dog"));
        p.add(new Button("cat"));
        p.add(new Button("mouse"));
        add(p, BorderLayout.NORTH);

        p = new Panel();
        p.add(new Button("steak"));
        p.add(new Button("tuna"));
        p.add(new Button("cheese"));
        add(p, BorderLayout.SOUTH);
    }
}
```

which would result in the display in Figure 19-6.

North and South components can be stretched horizontally—they fill up the space from the left to the right edge of the Container. East and West components can be stretched vertically—they fill up the space from the top of the South area to the bottom of the North area.

Adding a component to the center of the BorderLayout will make that component take up whatever space is left over in the center (if any). A Center component can be stretched both horizontally and vertically. The Center includes regions of the Border-Layout that are not used. For example, if nothing is placed in the East or West, then the Center stretches all the way from the left edge of the Container to the right edge.

So which components can be stretched? Well, here's a partial list of the "stretchable" versus the "nonstretchable" components:

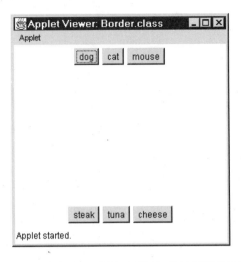

Figure 19-6 Panels within a BorderLayout

- **stretchable** Button, Label, TextField
- **nonstretchable** Checkbox

In the following example, each component is placed within a different region of an applet that uses a BorderLayout. You can see the effect of stretching or not stretching based on the type of component.

Here's the code for this example:

```
import java.awt.*;
import java.applet.*;

public class Stretch extends Applet {
    public void init() {
        setLayout(new BorderLayout());
        add(new Button("East"), BorderLayout.EAST);
        add(new Label("West"), BorderLayout.WEST);
        add(new TextField("North"), BorderLayout.NORTH);
        add(new Checkbox("South"), BorderLayout.SOUTH);
    }
}
```

The result is shown in Figure 19-7. Each component fills up its region of the screen, except for the checkbox in the south.

If you don't want the components right on top of each other, one of the constructors for BorderLayout allows you to specify the horizontal and vertical gaps that should be placed around the regions of the layout.

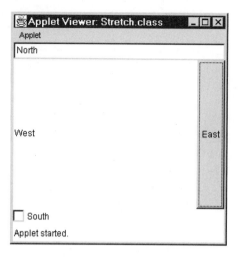

Figure 19-7 In a BorderLayout, different components stretch or don't stretch depending on their type.

GridLayout

GridLayout objects allow you to specify a rectangular grid in which to place the components. Each cell in the grid is the same height as the other cells, and each width is the same width as the other cells. Components are stretched both vertically and horizontally to fill the cell. The size of the cells is determined according to how many cells are requested in the Container given the Container's size.

When a GridLayout is first constructed, you must specify how many rows and how many columns the grid will have. Components are added to the GridLayout left to right and top to bottom. If more components are added than there are columns, the Grid-Layout keeps the same number of rows but adds the necessary number of columns.

For example, the following program causes the applet to be displayed with all six buttons on the same row:

```
import java.applet.Applet;
import java.awt.*;

public class GridOver extends Applet {
    public void init() {
        setLayout(new GridLayout(1, 2));

        add(new Button("mouse"));
        add(new Button("dog"));
        add(new Button("cat"));
```

```
        add(new Button("elephant"));
        add(new Button("monkey"));
        add(new Button("giraffe"));
    }
}
```

This looks like what's shown in Figure 19-8.

Changing the GridLayout to be created with two rows and two columns (instead of one row and two columns) makes GridLayout arrange the Button objects in two rows and three columns, like that shown in Figure 19-9.

As with a BorderLayout, if you don't want the components right on top of each other, one of the constructors for GridLayout allows you to specify the horizontal and vertical gaps that should be placed around the cells of the layout.

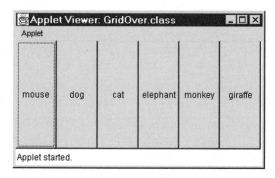

Figure 19-8   A GridLayout arranging buttons in one row

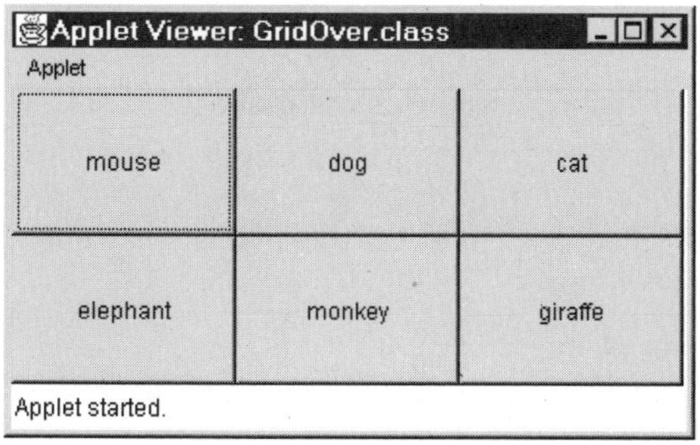

Figure 19-9   A GridLayout Arranging Buttons in 2 rows

Other Types of Layout Managers

Other types of layout managers that you can use include CardLayout and GridBag Layout.

CardLayout

You can use CardLayout to present different screens to a user based on a stack of cards metaphor. You can flip to the first, next, or last card using methods defined by Card-Layout. You can also go directly to a particular card, as long as you've named it, using a method named show().

GridBagLayout

You saw how the GridLayout arranges components in a strict grid where each row and each column are the same size. Components can only occupy one cell.

GridBagLayout is much more complicated than that, and also much more flexible. With GridBagLayout, your rows and columns don't have to all be the same size. Also, each component can occupy more than one cell.

Default Layout Managers

Since a Container class always has one layout manager associated with it, Container classes are defined with a default layout manager. These defaults are shown in Table 19-2.

You can change a Container's layout manager to use a different kind by invoking set-Layout(). One common technique is to create the new layout manager and set it at the same time, as in:

```
f.setLayout(new FlowLayout());
```

This creates a new FlowLayout object and assigns it as the layout manager for a Container object referenced by the variable f.

Table 19-2 Containers and Their Default Layout Managers

Container	Default Layout Manager
Frame	BorderLayout
Panel	FlowLayout
Dialog	BorderLayout
Window	BorderLayout

Exercise 19.1

Arrange two buttons that read "yes" and "no" at the bottom of an applet. Your applet should look something like what's in Figure 19-10.

TIP: Here's a hint: Making an applet look like this involves placing the buttons within their own Container, such as a Panel, and then placing the Panel into the applet. You'll see why if you try to place the buttons directly into the applet.

Answers to the Exercises

Exercise 19.1

To place Components such as buttons along the bottom of an applet, you need a BorderLayout. However, to place two Buttons side by side, as in this applet, you need a FlowLayout. The trick here is to place the two Buttons inside a Panel. The default layout for a Panel is a FlowLayout. Then, you can place the Panel into the applet and replace the applet's layout manager to be a BorderLayout. That way, you can place this Panel containing the two Buttons at the bottom of the applet.

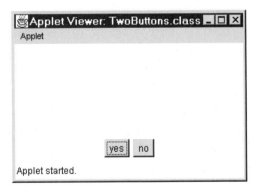

Figure 19-10 Two buttons in an applet

Here's a solution:

```java
import java.awt.*;
import java.applet.*;

public class TwoButtons extends Applet {
    public void init() {
        Panel p = new Panel();
        p.add(new Button("yes"));
        p.add(new Button("no"));

        setLayout(new BorderLayout());

        add(BorderLayout.SOUTH, p);
    }
}
```

Review Questions

1. Which layout manager positions each component on the same line as the previous one until the next component will not fit given the width of the Container, and then starts a new row, centering each component added to the new row?

    Select the one right answer.
    a. BorderLayout
    b. FlowLayout
    c. GridLayout
    d. CardLayout
    e. GridBagLayout

2. A component will automatically be resized vertically, but not horizontally, when it is placed in which region of a BorderLayout?

    Select the one right answer.
    a. North or South
    b. East or West
    c. Center
    d. North, South, or Center
    e. any region

3. What will the user interface look like in an applet given the following init() method?

```java
public void init() {
    setLayout(new BorderLayout());
```

```
        add(BorderLayout.EAST, new Button("Click Me!"));
    }
```

Select the one right answer.
   a. Nothing will appear in the applet.
   b. A button will appear in the applet set in the exact center.
   c. A button will appear on the left side of the applet.
   d. A button will appear on the right side of the applet.
   e. A button will fill the entire applet.

4. To place a button at the bottom of a container, no matter how the user resized the container, it would be simplest to use what type of layout manager?
   a. BorderLayout
   b. GridLayout
   c. FlowLayout
   d. GridbagLayout

5. To add a component (referenced by comp) to the center of a container (referenced by cont) using a BorderLayout, you can write:
   a. comp.add(BorderLayout.CENTER, cont);
   b. comp.add(cont, BorderLayout.CENTER);
   c. cont.add(BorderLayout.CENTER, comp);
   d. cont.add(comp, BorderLayout.CENTER);

Answers to Review Questions

1. **b.** A FlowLayout arranges components in this way.

2. **b.** East and West can resize a component vertically to the width of the Container.

3. **d.** A button will appear on the right side of the applet (really, try it).

4. **a.** With a BorderLayout, you could add the component to the "South" region and that's where it would stay.

5. **c and d.** add() is defined as a Container method. Although the placement of the component is usually the first parameter, there is an overloaded method that allows it to be the second parameter.

java.awt: Event Handling

Objectives for This Chapter

- Describe the event-handling model in Java.
- Identify important events in the AWTEvent hierarchy.
- Add a Listener to a component's list of event listeners.
- Identify the important Listener interfaces.
- Implement a Listener interface.
- State the difference between low-level and semantic events.
- Extend an Adapter class.

Events are an important part of the Java language. When users interact with a component, AWT notifies the component's listeners (if any) of the events they're interested in. You can register your object as a listener interested in particular events by using methods such as addMouseListener() to get mouse events, or addActionListener() to get action events. There is a different method corresponding to the different types of events. Objects that listen for events must conform to an interface appropriate for those events. Java defines a number of Listener interfaces you can implement in your own classes.

For the exam, you'll need to be able to write code that implements listener classes and extract information from the related events to determine the affected component, mouse position, nature, and time of the event. You'll also need to be able to state the event class for any specified event listener interface in the java.awt.event package.

Event Classes

The Java packages define many different event classes that represent specific types of events. EventObject, which is at the top of the event hierarchy, is actually defined in java.util, not in java.awt. This is to make events more generic and not necessarily tied to the AWT. However, all of the events dispatched by AWT's components use event classes that are subclasses of AWTEvent, which is in java.awt.

The hierarchy of EventObject and AWTEvent classes that you'll work with is as follows:

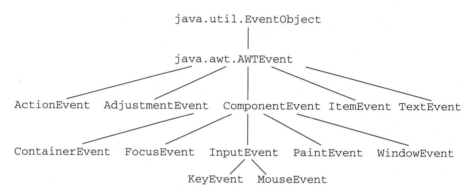

What the hierarchy doesn't show are event classes that you won't use regularly. These event classes are InputMethodEvent and InvocationEvent.

The java.util.EventObject class is very basic. It only implements two methods. The key method you'll be interested in is getSource(), which returns the object that originated an event. java.awt.AWTEvent is a subclass of java.util.EventObject and the superclass of all AWT event classes. The key method that you should know about is getID(), which returns the ID of an event. The event ID is an int that specifies the type of event, such as a button or mouse click.

Subclasses of AWTEvent represent various types of events. These are

- **ActionEvent**   An event generated by the activation of components.
- **AdjustmentEvent**   An event generated by adjustment of adjustable components, such as moving a scrollbar.
- **ComponentEvent**   A high-level event generated by manipulation of a component.
- **ContainerEvent**   An event generated when components are added to or removed from containers.
- **InputEvent**   A high-level event generated by an input device.
- **ItemEvent**   An event generated when an item is selected from a choice, check box, or list.

- **KeyEvent**   An event generated by the keyboard.

- **MouseEvent**   An event generated by the mouse.

- **PaintEvent**   An event generated when components are painted.

- **TextEvent**   An event generated when text components are modified.

- **WindowEvent**   An event generated by window activity, such as minimizing or maximizing a window.

The AWTEvent objects your event handlers receive are tailored to the type of event they represent. The AWT does not notify your event handler of every event that occurs over a component. Instead, AWT informs your event handler only about the events it is interested in.

Listening for Events

You must explicitly indicate which objects should handle specific events that occur in a particular component. You set up event handlers by telling a component which object will listen for the events it's interested in.

For example, let's say you have placed a button in your user interface, and you want your application to know when the user clicks this button. You need to perform the following steps in your code:

1. Define a class that implements a Listener interface. There are a variety of Listener interfaces, each one representing different types of events. For example, there's a MouseMotionListener that declares methods for handling mouse movements; there's a FocusListener that declares methods for reacting to a component acquiring or losing the focus.

2. Create an instance of this class.

3. Tell the component whose events you are interested in, which types of events you are interested in, and which object will handle those events. You do this by invoking a method called addABCListener() and passing it the instance of your Listener class. There are different addABCListener() methods, where "ABC" in the method name is replaced by the type of listener you're adding to the component's list of listeners. So, to add an instance of MouseMotionListener called myMouseMotionListener to a component's list of listeners, you would write:

```
myComponent.addMouseMotionListener(myMouseMotionListener);
```

To get a flavor for this, here's a simple applet that draws scribbles by handling the MouseListener and MouseMotionListener events. This program could also use an inner class to handle the events, rather than having the applet itself implement these interfaces. Or, it could define a separate class that only handled the events related to scribbling. Another possibility is for it to enable certain events and handle them directly without going through this Listener interface at all (we won't discuss that approach in this chapter). Let's start with this example and improve upon its design as we progress through this chapter.

```java
import java.awt.*;
import java.awt.event.*;
import java.applet.Applet;

public class Scribble extends Applet
    implements MouseMotionListener, MouseListener
{
    private int x;
    private int y;

    public void init() {
        addMouseListener(this);
        addMouseMotionListener(this);
    }

    public void mousePressed(MouseEvent e) {
        x = e.getX();
        y = e.getY();
    }

    public void mouseDragged(MouseEvent e) {
        Graphics g = getGraphics();
        int newX = e.getX();
        int newY = e.getY();
        g.drawLine(x, y, newX, newY);
        x = newX;
        y = newY;
    }

    // Left-over methods from the interfaces.
    public void mouseMoved(MouseEvent e) { }
    public void mouseClicked(MouseEvent e) { }
    public void mouseReleased(MouseEvent e) { }
    public void mouseEntered(MouseEvent e) { }
    public void mouseExited(MouseEvent e) { }
}
```

Figure 20-1 shows what this looks like after a user has interacted with this applet for a bit.

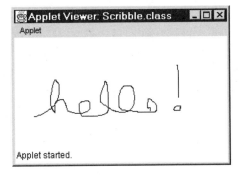

Figure 20-1   Using the scribble applet

NOTE: As you can see, this applet doesn't remember the drawing the user has performed, so if the applet is resized, the paint( ) operation will make the scribble vanish like shaking an Etch-a-Sketch.™

In this example, we imported java.awt.event, which contains all of the event classes we need. Notice how we had to implement stubs for mouseMoved(), mouseClicked(), mouseReleased(), mouseEntered(), and mouseExited(). We did not care about these events but were forced to implement them anyway. Why? Because the MouseListener and MouseMotionListener interfaces define all of these abstract methods. Sure, all we care about is mousePressed() and mouseDragged(), but if we didn't implement the others, our Applet subclass would be abstract.

Creating empty stubs seems like a waste of effort—if you are creating a class that only handles events, it is. There is a way around this problem; we'll look at that short-cut in a few pages. First, let's look at the Listener interfaces in more detail.

The Listener Interfaces

The previous program showed a way to detect mouse events. What other types of Listener interfaces are there?

The Listener interfaces are all defined in java.awt.event. They are presented here in alphabetical order. I've also listed the methods that you must define if you implement one of these interfaces. You can refer to this list if you would like to implement one of these interfaces and the methods you can use to add an instance of the listener.

ActionListener

ActionListener is implemented by objects that handle ActionEvent events. Common AWT classes that use ActionListeners are Button, List, and TextField. These components use ActionListener to recognize when they are acted upon, such as when a button is pressed or when a list item is double-clicked. Its interface and add methods are

Interface Method

- public void actionPerformed(ActionEvent e)

Add Method

- *obj*.addActionListener(ActionListener l)

AdjustmentListener

AdjustmentListener is implemented by objects that handle AdjustmentEvent events. The most common AWT class to implement an AdjustmentListener is the Scrollbar class. Scroll bars used AdjustmentListeners to recognize when the scroll bar is manipulated. Its interface and add methods are

Interface Method

- public void adjustmentValueChanged(AdjustmentEvent e)

Add Method

- *obj*.addAdjustmentListener(AdjustmentListener l)

ComponentListener

ComponentListener is implemented by objects that handle ComponentEvent events. Components implement this listener to recognize when they are hidden, moved, resized, or shown. Its interface and add methods are

Interface Methods

- public void componentHidden(ComponentEvent e)
- public void componentMoved(ComponentEvent e)
- public void componentResized(ComponentEvent e)
- public void componentShown(ComponentEvent e)

Add Method

- *obj*.addComponentListener(ComponentListener l)

ContainerListener

ContainerListener is implemented by objects that handle ContainerEvent events. Containers implement this interface to recognize when a component is added to or removed from a container. Its interface and add methods are

Interface Methods

- public void containerAdded(ContainerEvent e)
- public void containerRemoved(ContainerEvent e)

Add Method

- *obj*.addContainerListener(ContainerListener l)

FocusListener

FocusListener is implemented by objects that handle FocusEvent events. The listener is used to recognize when a component gains or loses keyboard focus, such as what happens when a user clicks in an input field so that she can type text or clicks out of a field after typing text. Its interface and add methods are

Interface Methods

- public void focusGained(FocusEvent e)
- public void focusLost(FocusEvent e)

Add Method

- *obj*.addFocusListener(FocusListener l)

ItemListener

ItemListener is implemented by objects that handle ItemEvent events. Common AWT classes that use ItemListeners are Checkbox, Choice, and List. These components use ItemListener to recognize when one of their items has been selected or deselected. MenuItem components also use ItemListener to recognize when a checkable menu item is selected or deselected.

The interface and add methods for ItemListener are

Interface Method

- public void itemStateChanged(ItemEvent e)

Add Method

- *obj*.addItemListener(ItemListener l)

KeyListener

KeyListener is implemented by objects that handle KeyEvent events. The listener is used to recognize when a key is pressed, released, or typed. Its interface and add methods are

Interface Methods

- public void keyPressed(KeyEvent e)
- public void keyReleased(KeyEvent e)
- public void keyTyped(KeyEvent e)

Add Method

- *obj*.addKeyListener()

MouseListener

MouseListener is implemented by objects that handle MouseEvent events. The listener is used to recognize when the mouse is clicked, enters a component, exits a component, or is released. Its interface and add methods are

Interface Methods

- public void mouseClicked(MouseEvent e)
- public void mouseEntered(MouseEvent e)
- public void mouseExited(MouseEvent e)
- public void mousePressed(MouseEvent e)
- public void mouseReleased(MouseEvent e)

Add Method

- *obj*.addMouseListener(MouseListener l)

MouseMotionListener

MouseMotionListener is implemented by objects that handle MouseMotionEvent events. The listener is used to recognize when the mouse is moved or dragged. Its interface and add methods are

Interface Methods

- public void mouseDragged(MouseEvent e)
- public void mouseMoved(MouseEvent e)

Add Method

- *obj*.addMouseMotionListener(MouseMotionListener l)

TextListener

TextListener is implemented by objects that handle TextEvent events. The listener is used to recognize when a text value has changed. TextArea and TextField are the most common AWT classes that use TextListeners. Its interface and add methods are

Interface Methods

- public void textValueChanged(TextEvent e)

Add Method

- *obj*.addTextListener(TextListener l)

WindowListener

WindowListener is implemented by objects that handle WindowEvent events. The listener is used to recognize when a window is opened, closed, activated, deactivated, iconified, or de-iconified. Its interface and add methods are

Interface Methods

- public void windowActivated(WindowEvent e)
- public void windowClosed(WindowEvent e)
- public void windowClosing(WindowEvent e)
- public void windowDeactivated(WindowEvent e)
- public void windowDeiconified(WindowEvent e)

- public void windowIconified(WindowEvent e)
- public void windowOpened(WindowEvent e)

Add Method

- *obj*.addWindowListener(WindowListener l)

Implementing a Listener Interface

You've already seen an example of an applet implementing a Listener interface. However, you can also define a class specifically for handling an event. Here's a trivial example so that you can see the mechanics of it. You'll see fuller examples in the exercises.

In this applet, we create a button named "Click me!" We also define a class called OurClickHandler that implements the MouseListener interface. In the applet's init() method, we add an instance of this class to the button's list of listeners by calling addMouseListener(). Then, when the user clicks this button, AWT routes all mouse events, including mouseClicked(), to our instance of OurClickHandler. There, we write a simple message to the standard output. Here's the code:

```java
import java.awt.*;
import java.awt.event.*;
import java.applet.Applet;

public class ClickApplet extends Applet {
    public void init() {
        Button b = new Button("Click me!");
        b.addMouseListener(new OurClickHandler());
        add(b);
    }
}

class OurClickHandler implements MouseListener {
    public void mouseClicked(MouseEvent e) {
        System.out.println("button clicked");
    }

    // Left-over interface methods.
    public void mousePressed(MouseEvent e) { }
    public void mouseReleased(MouseEvent e) { }
    public void mouseEntered(MouseEvent e) { }
    public void mouseExited(MouseEvent e) { }
}
```

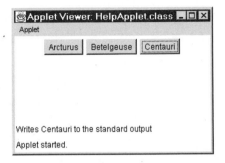

Figure 20-2   The context-sensitive help applet

Exercise 20.1

Create an applet that contains context-sensitive help messages. Do this in an applet that places three buttons along the top of the interface. These buttons should write their names to the standard output when clicked. You can use any names you'd like for the buttons.

Place a label at the bottom of the applet. Whenever the user moves the mouse cursor over one of the buttons, display a simple message containing a few words in the label at the bottom of the applet that explains what will happen if the user clicks the button. As an example, your applet might look like Figure 20-2.

Semantic and Low-Level Events

It's convenient to separate the different types of events into two categories. You can think of these as semantic and low-level events. There are three types of semantic events: action events, item events, and adjustment events.

Let's take a look at the different AWT components and see which semantic events they fire under what circumstances.

ActionEvent

AWT sends an ActionEvent object to any registered ActionListener objects when the user

- clicks a button
- hits the Enter key when typing in a text field

- selects a menu item
- double-clicks a list item

AdjustmentEvent

AWT sends an AdjustmentEvent object to any registered AdjustmentListener objects when the user

- scrolls up, down, left, or right using a scroll bar
- scrolls up, down, left, or right using a scroll pane

ItemEvent

AWT sends an ItemEvent object to any registered ItemListener objects when the user

- selects an item in a list
- selects an option from a choice box
- selects a menu item from a checkbox menu item
- clicks a checkbox

AWTEvent Subclasses

So far, we've breezed over the AWTEvent subclasses so that you could see the overall architecture of event handling. You know that you must implement a Listener interface if you are interested in a particular event, and you must register an instance of the class implementing this Listener interface as an event listener with the user interface component whose events you want to handle.

Now, let's back up just a bit and review the AWTEvent subclasses that AWT will pass your event handlers. Java defines AWTEvent subclasses for different categories of events. For example, the MouseEvent class is used when the user

- clicks down on the mouse
- releases the mouse
- moves the mouse into or out of a component

If you need to identify which particular event occurred based on the MouseEvent object alone, you use an int id field to determine this. You would invoke the object's getId() method and then use constants defined in MouseEvent to identify the event. In this example, the constants you would check include MOUSE_CLICKED, MOUSE_PRESSED, MOUSE_RELEASED, MOUSE_ENTERED, and MOUSE_EXITED. Different AWTEvent subclasses have their own constants. Many of these constants are presented in the section below on the AWTEvent subclasses. You can also review the APIs for a complete list. However, you generally won't need to do this. You can, instead, simply supply the appropriate event method and let AWT invoke this method for you.

As you would expect, you will use methods in the AWTEvent subclasses to get specific information about the event. I have listed some of the important methods and constants for each type of event.

AWTEvent

This is the root of all AWT events and is defined in java.awt. All of its subclasses are located in java.awt.event.

ActionEvent

- getModifiers() returns an int whose bits match whether the user had selected the Shift, Alt or Control keys when the user generated this event.

- The constants ALT_MASK, CTRL_MASK, META_MASK, and SHIFT_MASK can be used with the | operator with getModifiers() to determine whether any of these special modifier keys were pressed when the user generated this event.

AdjustmentEvent

- getAdjustable() retrieves the object where this event originated. This object will be an instance of a class that implements the Adjustable interface.

- getValue() returns the current value in this adjustment event.

ComponentEvent

- getComponent() returns the component that triggered this event.

ContainerEvent

- getChild() returns a child component object.

- getContainer returns the container object.

- The constants COMPONENT_ADDED and COMPONENT_REMOVED are useful to help you keep track of when components have been added to or removed from a container.

FocusEvent

This class simply defines some new constants (such as FOCUS_GAINED and FOCUS_LOST).

InputEvent

- getModifiers() returns an int representing the bit values that determine whether the user pressed the ALT, CONTROL, or SHIFT keys when the user generated this event.

- getWhen() returns the time stamp for this event.

ItemEvent

- getItem() returns the item where the event occurred.

- getItemSelectable() returns the object whose class implements the ItemSelectable interface where this event occurred.

- getStateChange() returns either SELECTED or DESELECTED, depending on whether the user just selected or deselected the item.

KeyEvent

- getKeyCode() returns an int value representing a key on the keyboard. This key may or may not generate a character—for example, the letter "a" does, but the F1 key does not.

- getKeyChar() returns a char of the character typed.

MouseEvent

- getClickCount() returns the number of times the user clicked the mouse to generate this event (that is, was this a double-click? A triple-click?).

- getX() returns the x coordinate of the mouse event.

- getY() returns the y coordinate of the mouse event.

- These constants identify the event type: MOUSE_CLICKED, MOUSE_PRESSED, MOUSE_RELEASED, MOUSE_ENTERED, and MOUSE_EXITED.

PaintEvent

Even though AWT passes this type of event to components, you should normally not listen for this type of event. Instead, you should override paint().

TextEvent

- Defines the constant TEXT_VALUE_CHANGED.

WindowEvent

- getWindow() returns the window that generated this event.

Exercise 20.2

Write an applet that contains three text fields. These text fields should have a white background when the user is not interacting with them. Each text field should turn red when the user is about to enter data, and each should turn yellow if the user types an exclamation point (!). Once the use has finished typing, the text field should become white again.

Implement this by creating a special class that updates the text field's colors. This class should not be a subclass of TextField. Your application might look like that shown in Figure 20-3.

Extending Adapter Classes

Sometimes it's not very convenient to implement a Listener interface. As you saw with the Scribble applet, you'll find that there are a number of methods that are simply stubs

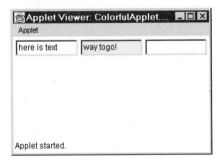

Figure 20-3 An applet with colorful text fields

and do nothing but clutter up your source code. Rather than creating useless no-op methods, you can extend a Java class that has already done this.

There's an Adapter class to match most of the available interfaces. Each Adapter class defines no-op stubs for the methods declared in the corresponding interface. For reference, here is the complete list of the Adapter classes:

- **ComponentAdapter**   Implements the ComponentListener interface and handles ComponentEvent events.

- **ContainerAdapter**   Implements the ContainerListener interface and handles ContainerEvent events.

- **FocusAdapter**   Implements the FocusListener interface and handles FocusEvent events.

- **KeyAdapter**   Implements the KeyListener interface and handles KeyEvent events.

- **MouseAdapter** Implements the MouseListener interface and handles MouseEvent events.

- **MouseMotionAdapter**   Implements the MouseMotionListener interface and handles MouseMotionEvent events.

- **WindowAdapter**   Implements the WindowListener interface and handles WindowEvent events.

Extending an Adapter class only makes sense when the object that will listen for and handle the event has no other responsibilities. If you want your applet to handle the event, as in the Scribble example, then it must implement the appropriate Listener interface, since Java does not have multiple inheritance of implementation.

Exercise 20.3

Rewrite Exercise 20.2 using an adapter class rather than implementing more than one listener interface. If possible, eliminate the need to write no-op stubs.

Answers to the Exercises

Exercise 20.1

```
import java.awt.*;
import java.awt.event.*;
import java.applet.Applet;
```

```java
public class HelpApplet extends Applet {
    public void init() {
        Button b;
        Panel p = new Panel();
        setLayout(new BorderLayout());

        HelpLabel label = new HelpLabel();

        b = new Button("Arcturus");
        b.addMouseListener(label);
        p.add(b);

        b = new Button("Betelgeuse");
        b.addMouseListener(label);
        p.add(b);

        b = new Button("Centauri");
        b.addMouseListener(label);
        p.add(b);

        add("North", p);
        add("South", label);
    }
}

class HelpLabel extends Label implements MouseListener {

    public void mouseEntered(MouseEvent e) {
        Button b = (Button)(e.getComponent());
        String s = "Writes " + b.getLabel() +
                   " to the standard output";
        setText(s);
    }

    public void mouseClicked(MouseEvent e) {
        Button b = (Button)(e.getComponent());
        System.out.println(b.getLabel());
    }

    // Left-over MouseListener methods.
    public void mousePressed(MouseEvent e) { }
    public void mouseReleased(MouseEvent e) { }
    public void mouseExited(MouseEvent e) { }

}
```

Exercise 20.2

```java
import java.awt.*;
import java.awt.event.*;
import java.applet.Applet;
```

```
public class ColorfulApplet extends Applet {
    public void init() {
        for (int i = 0; i < 3; i++) {
            TFHandler tfHandler = new TFHandler();
            TextField tf = new TextField(10);
            tf.addFocusListener(tfHandler);
            tf.addKeyListener(tfHandler);
            add(tf);
        }
    }
}

class TFHandler implements FocusListener, KeyListener {

    public void focusGained(FocusEvent e) {
        e.getComponent().setBackground(Color.red);
    }

    public void focusLost(FocusEvent e) {
        e.getComponent().setBackground(Color.white);
    }

    public void keyTyped(KeyEvent e) {
        if (e.getKeyChar() == '!')
            e.getComponent().setBackground(Color.yellow);
    }

    // Left-over Listener events.
    public void keyPressed(KeyEvent e) { }
    public void keyReleased(KeyEvent e) { }
}
```

Exercise 20.3

The import statements and the Applet class are the same as Exercise 20.2. Here is the new event handler.

```
class TFHandler extends KeyAdapter implements FocusListener {

    public void focusGained(FocusEvent e) {
        e.getComponent().setBackground(Color.red);
    }

    public void focusLost(FocusEvent e) {
        e.getComponent().setBackground(Color.white);
    }

    public void keyTyped(KeyEvent e) {
        if (e.getKeyChar() == '!')
            e.getComponent().setBackground(Color.yellow);
    }

}
```

Review Questions

1. Given an object named myHandler whose class implements the FocusListener interface, how can you tell a component named component that myHandler should receive all focus events?

   a. component.add(myHandler);

   b. component.addListener(myHandler);

   c. addFocusListener(component, myHandler);

   d. component.addFocusListener(myHandler);

2. Which messages will appear in the standard output whenever the user clicks the button named "Click me!" given the following code?

```
import java.awt.*;
import java.awt.event.*;
import java.applet.Applet;

public class ClickExample extends Applet {
    public void init() {
        Button b = new Button("Click me!");
        b.addMouseListener(new OurClickHandler());
        add(b);
    }
}

class OurClickHandler implements MouseListener {
    public void actionPerformed(ActionEvent e) {
        System.out.println("button action");
    }

    public void mouseClicked(MouseEvent e) {
        System.out.println("button clicked");
    }

    // Left-over interface methods.
    public void mousePressed(MouseEvent e) { }
    public void mouseReleased(MouseEvent e) { }
    public void mouseEntered(MouseEvent e) { }
    public void mouseExited(MouseEvent e) { }
}
```

   a. "button action"

   b. "button clicked"

   c. both "button action" and "button clicked"

   d. neither of these messages

3. If you need to create a class that will handle keystrokes as the user types, and if your new class will not need to extend any other class, you can:
   a. extend KeyAdapter to427 implement your new class
   b. implement KeyListener
   c. implement ActionListener
   d. either a or b
   e. either a, b, or c

4. AWT generates an action event for all of the following situations, except:
   a. The user clicks a list item
   b. The user clicks a button
   c. The user types text into a text field and hits enter
   d. The user selects a menu item

5. To identify when the user has closed a window, you can implement which Listener interface?
   a. MouseListener
   b. ActionListener
   c. WindowListener
   d. all of these

Answers to Review Questions

1. **d.** Use component.addFocusListener() to register the listener.

2. **b.** The message "button action" does not appear because the code never registers the instance of MyClickHandler as one of the button's ActionListeners (also, it does not declare that it implements the ActionListener interface).

3. **d.** Either extending KeyAdapter or implementing KeyListener are probably your best choices. An action event is only generated for a text field (for example) when the user hits Enter, and so is not best suited for processing keystrokes as the user types.

4. **a.** The user must double-click a list item to generate an action event. Single clicking a list item causes AWT to generate an item event.

5. **c.** WindowListener interface defines methods called windowClosing() and windowClosed() that you can override to detect when the user has closed a window.

Sun Certified Programmer Practice Exam 1

Practice Exam Number 1

Here are the rules:

Allow 120 minutes to complete this exam. You should turn off the telephone, go someplace where you won't be disturbed, check the time on your watch, and begin. Don't bring any books with you, because you won't have them during the test. You can take breaks, but don't look anything up. You can have a piece of scratch paper and a pen or pencil, but you can't have any crib sheets!

If you get at least 36 questions right, you've hit the 61% mark, and you've passed. Good luck!

Questions

1. Given the following class definition:

```
class A {
   protected int i;
   A(int i) {
      this.i = i;
   }
}
```

which of the following would be a valid inner class for this class?

Select all valid answers.

a.

```
class B {
}
```

b.

```
class B extends A {
}
```

c.

```
class B {
    B() {
        System.out.println("i = " + i);
    }
}
```

d.

```
class B {
    class A {
    }
}
```

e.

```
class A {
}
```

2. What statements are true concerning the method notify() that is used in conjunction with wait()?

Select all valid answers.
   a. If there is more than one thread waiting on a condition, only the thread that has been waiting the longest is notified.
   b. If there is more than one thread waiting on a condition, there is no way to predict which thread will be notified.
   c. Notify() is defined in the Thread class.
   d. It is not strictly necessary to own the lock for the object you invoke notify() for.
   e. Notify() should only be invoked from within a while loop.

3. Given the following class:

```
class Counter {
    public int startHere = 1;
    public int endHere = 100;
    public static void main(String[] args) {
        new Counter().go();
    }
    void go() {
        // A
        Thread t = new Thread(a);
        t.start();
    }
}
```

what block of code can you replace at line A above so that this program will count from startHere to endHere?

Select all valid answers.

   a.

```
Runnable a = new Runnable() {
    public void run() {
        for (int i = startHere; i <= endHere; i++) {
            System.out.println(i);
        }
    }
};
```

   b.

```
a implements Runnable {
    public void run() {
        for (int i = startHere; i <= endHere; i++) {
            System.out.println(i);
        }
    }
};
```

   c.

```
Thread a = new Thread() {
    public void run() {
        for (int i = startHere; i <= endHere; i++) {
            System.out.println(i);
        }
    }
};
```

4. What is written to the standard output given the following statement?

```
System.out.println(4 | 7);
```

Select the one right answer.

a. 4

b. 5

c. 6

d. 7

e. 0

5. Given the following class:

```
class Counter {
    public static void main(String[] args) {
        Thread t = new Thread(new CounterBehavior());
        t.start();
    }
}
```

which of the following is a valid definition of CounterBehavior that would make Counter's main() method count from 1 to 100, counting once per second?

Select the one right answer.

a. This class is an inner class to Counter:

```
class CounterBehavior {
    for (int i = 1; i <= 100; i++);
        try {
            System.out.println(i);
            Thread.sleep(1000);
        } catch (InterruptedException x) {}
    }
}
```

b. This class is an inner class to Counter:

```
class CounterBehavior implements Runnable {
    public void run() {
        for (int i = 1; i <= 100; i++);
            try {
                System.out.println(i);
                Thread.sleep(1000);
            } catch (InterruptedException x) {}
        }
    }
}
```

   c. This class is a static inner class to Counter:

```
static class CounterBehavior implements Runnable {
    public void run() {
        try {
            for (int i = 1; i <= 100; i++) {
                System.out.println(i);
                Thread.sleep(1000);
            }
        } catch (InterruptedException x) {}
    }
}
```

6. Given the following class definition:

```
class A {
    public int x;
    private int y;
    class B {
        protected void method1() {
        }
        class C {
            private void method2() {
            }
        }
    }
}
class D extends A {
    public float z;
}
```

    what can method2() access directly, without a reference to another instance?

    Select all valid answers.
    a. The variable x defined in A
    b. The variable y defined in A
    c. method1 defined in B
    d. The variable z defined in D

7. You have an 8-bit file using the character set defined by ISO 8859-8. You are writing an application to display this file in a TextArea. The local encoding is already set to 8859-8. How can you write a chunk of code to read the first line from this file? You have three variables accessible to you:

- **myfile** is the name of the file you want to read

- **stream** is an InputStream object associated with this file

- **s** is a String object

Select all valid answers.

a.

```
InputStreamReader reader = new InputStreamReader(stream, "8859-8");
BufferedReader buffer = new BufferedReader(reader);
s = buffer.readLine();
```

b.

```
InputStreamReader reader = new InputStreamReader(stream);
BufferedReader buffer = new BufferedReader(reader);
s = buffer.readLine();
```

c.

```
InputStreamReader reader = new InputStreamReader(myfile, "8859-8");
BufferedReader buffer = new BufferedReader(reader);
s = buffer.readLine();
```

d.

```
InputStreamReader reader = new InputStreamReader(myfile);
BufferedReader buffer = new BufferedReader(reader);
s = buffer.readLine();
```

e.

```
FileReader reader = new FileReader(myfile);
BufferedReader buffer = new BufferedReader(reader);
s = buffer.readLine();
```

8. How can you write a line of code for an applet's init() method that determines how wide the applet is?

Select all valid answers.

a.

```
int width = this.getY();
```

b.

```
int width = this.getSize().w;
```

c.

```
int width = getSize();
```

d.

```
int width = getSize().w;
```

e.

```
int width = getWidth();
```

9. For a variable width font, how "wide" is a TextField created using the expression:

```
new TextField(20)
```

Select the one right answer.
   a. 20 times the average of all the characters in the font used for this TextField object
   b. 20 times the width of the letter M
   c. 20 times the width of the letter a
   d. 20 inches
   e. 20 picas

10. Given this interface definition:

```
interface A {
    int method1(int i);
    int method2(int j);
}
```

which of the following classes implement this interface and is not abstract?

Select all valid answers.
   a.

```
class B implements A {
    int method1() { }
    int method2() { }
}
```

   b.

```
class B {
    int method1(int i) { }
    int method2(int j) { }
}
```

c.

```
class B implements A {
    int method1(int i) { }
    int method2(int j) { }
}
```

d.

```
class B extends A {
    int method1(int i) { }
    int method2(int j) { }
}
```

e.

```
class B implements A {
    int method2(int j) { }
    int method1(int i) { }
}
```

11. Given the following code:

```
import java.awt.*;
import java.awt.event.*;
public class MyApplet extends java.applet.Applet {
    public void init() {
        Button b = new Button("Button1");
        b.addMouseListener(new ClickHandler());
        add(b);
    }
    class ClickHandler extends MouseAdapter {
        public void mouseClicked(MouseEvent evt) {
            // A
        }
    }
}
```

insert a line of code at the time of the MouseClick event. Note that the value output should be with respect to the component, which handled the event.

Fill in the blank.

12. Given the same code as in question 11, how can you write a line of code at A that will place the Button object into a variable named mybutton that is already defined to be a reference to a Button object?

Fill in the blank.

13. Which Listener interface can you implement to be able to respond to the user hitting the enter key after typing into a TextField object?

    Fill in the blank.

14. What is written to the standard output as the result of executing the following statements?

```
Boolean b1 = new Boolean(true);
Boolean b2 = new Boolean(true);
if (b1 == b2)
    if (b1.equals(b2))
        System.out.println("a");
    else
        System.out.println("b");
else
    if (b1.equals(b2))
        System.out.println("c");
    else
        System.out.println("d");
```

    Select the one right answer.

    a. a

    b. b

    c. c

    d. d

15. Which Listener interfaces can you add to a TextArea object?

    a. TextListener

    b. ActionListener

    c. MouseMotionListener

    d. MouseListener

    e. ComponentListener

16. What appears in the standard output if the method named problem() in the code below throws an instance of class Exception when the method named trythis() is invoked?

```
public void trythis() {
    try {
        System.out.println("1");
        problem();
    } catch (RuntimeException x) {
        System.out.println("2");
        return;
    } catch (Exception x) {
```

```
        System.out.println("3");
        return;
    } finally {
        System.out.println("4");
    }
    System.out.println("5");
}
```

Select all valid answers.

a. "1"

b. "2"

c. "3"

d. "4"

e. "5"

17. What is the type of the Event object passed to the mouseDragged() method defined in a class that implements java.awt.event.MouseMotionListener (that is, what is the class name for the argument)?

Fill in the blank.

18. Examine the following switch block:

```
char mychar = 'c';
switch (mychar) {
    default:
    case 'a': System.out.println("a"); break;
    case 'b': System.out.println("b"); break;
}
```

Which of the following questions are definitely true?

Select all valid answers.

a. This switch block is illegal, because only integers can be used in the switch statement.

b. This switch block is fine.

c. This switch block is illegal, because the default statement must come last.

d. When this code runs, nothing is written to the standard output.

e. When this code runs, the letter "a" is written to the standard output.

19. What keyword must appear in a method declaration (followed by the name of the exception) when that method might cause an exception to be thrown and that method does not handle the exception?

Fill in the blank.

20. Which statements accurately describe the following line of code?

```
String[][] s = new String[10][];
```

Select all valid answers.
a. This line of code is illegal.
b. s is a two-dimensional array containing ten rows and ten columns.
c. s is an array of ten arrays.
d. Each element in s is set to "".
e. Each element in s is uninitialized and must be initialized before it is referenced.

21. What will happen if you try to compile and run the following class?

```
class Test {
    static int myArg = 1;
    public static void main(String[] args) {
        int myArg;
        System.out.println(myArg);
    }
}
```

Select the one right answer.
a. This code compiles and displays 0 in the standard output when run.
b. This code compiles and displays 1 in the standard output when run.
c. This code does not compile because you cannot define a local variable named the same as a static variable.
d. This code does not compile because the local variable is used before it is initialized.

22. Which declarations for the main() method in a stand-alone program are NOT valid?

Select all valid answers.
a.

```
public static void main()
```

b.

```
public static void main(String[] string)
```

c.

```
public static void main(String args)
```

   d.

```
static public int main(String[] args)
```

   e.

```
static void main(String[] args)
```

23. Which of the following identifiers are illegal?

   Select all valid answers.
   a. #_pound
   b. _underscore
   c. 5Interstate
   d. Interstate5
   e. _5_

24. If the user invokes a standalone application by typing:

```
java YourApp 1 2 3
```

   and the main() method defines its String[] parameter as args, how can you access
   the number 2 using args?

   Fill in the blank.

25. Which interface implementations can you add as listeners for a TextField object?

   Select all valid answers.
   a. ActionListener
   b. FocusListener
   c. MouseMotionListener
   d. WindowListener
   e. ContainerListener

26. What must be true for the RunHandler class so that instances of RunHandler can
   be used as written in the code below:

```
class Test {
   public static void main(String[] args) {
      Thread t = new Thread(new RunHandler());
      t.start();
   }
}
```

   Select all valid answers.

    a. RunHandler must implement the java.lang.Runnable interface.

    b. RunHandler must extend the Thread class.

    c. RunHandler must provide a run() method declared as public and returning void.

    d. RunHandler must provide an init() method.

27. To determine if you can invoke addContainerListener() for a component referenced using a variable named c, which expression(s) can you evaluate that will give you a true or false answer to this question?

Select all valid answers.

    a.

```
c == Container
```

    b.

```
c.equals(Class.Container)
```

    c.

```
c instanceof Container
```

    d.

```
c instanceof Component
```

    e.

```
c implements Container
```

28. Write a statement for a constructor that invokes the no-args, default constructor in its superclass.

Fill in the blank.

29. What is written to the standard output given the following statement?

```
System.out.println(4 & 7);
```

Select the one right answer.

    a. 4

    b. 5

    c. 6

    d. 7

    e. 0

30. What will the following block of code write to the standard output when it is executed?

```
int i = 3;
int j = 0;
double k = 3.2;
if (i < k)
   if (i == j)
      System.out.println(i);
   else
      System.out.println(j);
else
   System.out.println(k);
```

Select the one right answer.

a. 3

b. 0

c. 3.2

d. none of these

31. How can you use the String method indexOf() to determine which position the letter 'C' is in given this String?

```
String s = "ABCDE";
```

Write a complete statement in your answer, but you do not have to assign *value* you retrieve to another variable.

Fill in the blank.

32. Given that the variable g references a valid Graphics object, what does the following statement do?

```
g.fillRect(2, 3, 10, 20);
```

Select all valid answers.

a. Draw the outline of a rectangle in the current background color.

b. Draw the outline of a rectangle in the current foreground color.

c. Fill in a rectangle using the current background color.

d. Fill in a rectangle using the current foreground color.

e. Fill in a rectangle in black.

33. Describe the following applet.

```
import java.applet.Applet;
import java.awt.event.*;
```

```
import java.awt.*;
public class MyApplet extends Applet {
    Button b1, b2;
    public void init() {
        ActionListener a = new ActionListener() {
            public void actionPerformed(ActionEvent evt) {
                if (evt.getSource() == b1) {
                    b1.setEnabled(false);
                    b2.setEnabled(true);
                } else {
                    b1.setEnabled(true);
                    b2.setEnabled(false);
                }
            }
        };
        b1 = new Button("1");
        b1.addActionListener(a);
        add(b1);
        b2 = new Button("2");
        b2.addActionListener(a);
        add(b2);
    }
}
```

Select all valid answers.

a. Nothing appears in the applet.

b. One button appears in the applet but does nothing.

c. Two buttons appear in the applet.

d. When the user clicks a button, nothing happens.

e. When the user clicks a button, it becomes disabled.

f. When a user clicks a button, the other button becomes enabled.

34. Which of the following are true for the setBackground() method defined for the Graphics class?

Select all valid answers.

a. Takes an integer value

b. Takes an instance of class Color

c. Takes an instance of a Component subclass

d. Sets the drawing mode for the associated Component object

e. Sets the drawing color for the associated Component object

f. Changes the background color for the associated Component object

35. What does the following program do when it is run with the command?

```
java Mystery Mighty Mouse
class Mystery {
```

```
    public static void main(String[] args) {
        Changer c = new Changer();
        c.method(args);
        System.out.println(args[0] + " " + args[1]);
    }
    static class Changer {
        void method(String[] s) {
            String temp = s[0];
            s[0] = s[1];
            s[1] = temp;
        }
    }
}
```

Select the one right answer.

a. This program causes an ArrayIndexOutOfBoundsException to be thrown.

b. This program runs but does not write anything to the standard output.

c. This program writes "Mighty Mouse" to the standard output.

d. This program writes "Mouse Mighty" to the standard output.

36. What happens when you try to compile and run the following program?

```
class Mystery {
    String s;
    public static void main(String[] args) {
        Mystery m = new Mystery();
        m.go();
    }
    void Mystery() {
        s = "constructor";
    }
    void go() {
        System.out.println(s);
    }
}
```

Select the one right answer.

a. This code will not compile.

b. This code compiles but throws an exception at runtime.

c. This code runs but nothing appears in the standard output.

d. This code runs and "constructor" in the standard output.

e. This code runs and writes "null" in the standard output.

37. What can you write at the comment //A in the code below so that this program writes the word "running" to the standard output?

```
class RunTest implements Runnable {
    public static void main(String[] args) {
```

```
        RunTest rt = new RunTest();
        Thread t = new Thread(rt);
        //A
    }
    public void run() {
        System.out.println("running");
    }
    void go() {
        start(1);
    }
    void start(int i) {
    }
}
```

Select all valid answers.

a.

```
System.out.println("running");
```

b.

```
rt.start();
```

c.

```
rt.go();
```

d.

```
rt.start(1);
```

38. What order can you place the following pieces of a source file in so that the source
file will compile without errors or warnings?

```
//A
import java.applet.*;
//B
class Helper {
}
//C
package myclasses;
//D
public class MyApplet extends java.applet.Applet {
}
```

Select all valid answers.
a. A, B, C, D
b. A, C, B, D
c. C, A, B, D

    d. C, A, D, B

    e. C, B, A, D

39. Analyze these two consecutive lines of code.

```
float f = 3.2;
int i = f;
```

    Select all valid answers.

    a. This code would not compile.

    b. This code would compile and i would be set to 3.

    c. The second line could compile if it were written instead as:

```
int i = (byte)f;
```

    d. The first line could compile if it were written instead as:

```
float f = 3.2F;
```

40. Construct an array of three String objects containing the strings "a," "b," and "c" using the { } notation. Call the String by the variable name s.

    Fill in the blank.

41. What is the final value of temp in this sequence?

```
long temp = (int)3.9;
temp %= 2;
```

    a. 0

    b. 1

    c. 2

    d. 3

    e. 4

    Select the one right answer.

42. Analyze this line of code:

```
if (5 & 7 > 0 && 5 | 2) System.out.println("true");
```

    Select the one right answer.

    a. This line of code will not compile.

    b. This code will compile but nothing will appear in the standard output.

    c. This code will compile and write the word "true" in the standard output.

43. Create a List object that allows multiple selections and displays five rows at a time. Start by writing:

```
List l =
```

in your answer.

Fill in the blank.

44. What will the user interface look like in an applet given the following init() method?

```
public void init() {
    setLayout(new BorderLayout());
    add(BorderLayout.EAST, new Button("hello"));
}
```

Select the one right answer.
a. Nothing will appear in the applet.
b. A button will appear in the applet set in the exact center.
c. A button will appear on the left side of the applet.
d. A button will appear on the right side of the applet.
e. A button will fill the entire applet.

45. Choose all true statements about the paint() method defined in the Component class:

Select all valid answers.
a. It is protected.
b. It takes an instance of class Graphics.
c. It is static.
d. It is invoked automatically whenever you minimize and then maximize a component, such as a window.
e. There is also a version that takes an int.

46. Given this ActionListener:

```
class HandleClick implements ActionListener {
    public void actionPerformed(ActionEvent evt) {
        // A
    }
}
```

what line of code can you write at A that will make a component referenced by c disappear from the display?

Fill in the blank.

47. Analyze the following code:

```
class WhatHappens implements Runnable {
   public static void main(String[] args) {
      Thread t = new Thread(this);
      t.start();
   }
   public void run() {
      System.out.println("hi");
   }
}
```

Select the one right answer.

a. This program does not compile.

b. This program compiles but nothing appears in the standard output.

c. This program compiles and the word "hi" appears in the standard output, once.

d. This program compiles and the word "hi" appears continuously in the standard output until the user hits CONTROL-C to stop the program.

48. What is wrong with the following code?

```
final class First {
   private int a = 1;
   int b = 2;
}
class Second extends First {
   public void method() {
      System.out.println(a + b);
   }
}
```

Select all valid answers.

a. You cannot invoke println() without passing it a String.

b. Since a is private, no classes other than First can access it.

c. Second cannot extend First.

d. final is not a valid keyword for a class.

49. Analyze the following two classes.

```
class First {
   static int a = 3;
}
final class Second extends First {
   void method() {
      System.out.println(a);
   }
}
```

Select the one right answer.

a. Class First compiles, but class Second does not.

b. Class Second compiles, but class First does not.

c. Neither class compiles.

d. Both classes compile, and if method() is invoked, it writes 3 to the standard output.

e. Both classes compile, but if method() is invoked, it throws an exception.

50. Why won't the following class compile?

```
class A {
    private int x;
    public static void main(String[] args) {
        new B();
    }
    class B {
        B() {
            System.out.println(x);
        }
    }
}
```

Select the one right answer.

a. Class B tries to access a private variable defined in its outer class.

b. Class B cannot be accessed from a static context.

c. Class B's constructor must be public.

51. Analyze the following code.

```
void looper() {
  int x = 1;
one:
  while (x <= 10) {
two:
  System.out.println(++x);
  if (x != 5)
     break two;
  }
}
```

Select all valid answers.

a. This code compiles.

b. This code does not compile.

c. This method writes the number 0 to the standard output.

d. This writes the numbers 1 and 2 to the standard output.

e. This writes the numbers 3 to the standard output.

    f. This writes the number 4 to the standard output.

    g. This writes the numberws 5 through 9 to the standard output.

    h. This writes the number 10 to the standard output.

52. What appears in the standard output when the method named testing is invoked?

```
void testing() {
one:
two:
   for (int i = 0; i < 3; i++) {
three:
      for (int j = 10; j < 30; j+=10) {
         System.out.println(i + j);
         if (i > 2)
            continue one;
      }
   }
}
```

Select all valid answers.

    a. 10 and 20

    b. 11 and 21

    c. 12 and 22

    d. 13 and 23

    e. 30, 31, 32, and 33

53. What will the result be for the following block of code when it is executed?

```
int i = 3;
int j = 0;
float k = 3.2F;
long m = -3;
if (Math.ceil(i) < Math.floor(k))
   if (Math.abs(i) == m)
      System.out.println(i);
   else
      System.out.println(j);
else
   System.out.println(Math.abs(m) + 1);
```

Select the one right answer.

    a. 3

    b. 0

    c. −3

    d. 4

    e. none of these

54. The ISO code for the language you are interested in is 8859-5. Assume you have a stream in a variable named mystream that's associated with a file generated in this 8-bit character set. If the default conversion to Unicode in your environment is for the encoding 8859-1, how can you create a new instance of InputStreamReader that will perform the conversion from ISO 8859-5 to Unicode, automatically? (Start by writing the keyword new.)

Fill in the blank.

55. What is written to the standard output as the result of executing the following statements?

```
Boolean b1 = new Boolean(true);
Boolean b2 = new Boolean(true);
Object obj1 = (Object)b1;
Object obj2 = (Object)b2;
if (obj1 == obj2)
    if (obj1.equals(obj2))
        System.out.println("a");
    else
        System.out.println("b");
else
    if (obj1.equals(obj2))
        System.out.println("c");
    else
        System.out.println("d");
```

Select the one right answer.

a. a

b. b

c. c

d. d

56. What will the user interface look like in an applet given the following init() method?

```
public void init() {
    setLayout(new BorderLayout());
    add(new Button("hello"));
}
```

Select the one right answer.

a. Nothing will appear in the applet.

b. A button will appear in the applet set in the exact center.

c. A button will appear in the applet along the top and centered horizontally.

d. A button will appear in the top left corner.

57. What expressions are true concerning the following lines of code?

```
int[] arr = {1, 2, 3};
for (int i=0; i < 2; i++)
    arr[i] = 0;
```

Select all valid answers.

a. arr[0] == 0

b. arr[0] == 1

c. arr[1] == 1

d. arr[2] == 0

e. arr[3] == 0

58. What will happen if you try to compile and execute B's main() method?

```
class A {
    int i;
    A(int i) {
        this.i = i * 2;
    }
}
class B extends A {
    public static void main(String[] args) {
        B b = new B(2);
    }
    B(int i) {
        System.out.println(i);
    }
}
```

Select the one right answer.

a. The instance variable i is set to 4.

b. The instance variable i is set to 2.

c. The instance variable i is set to 0.

d. This code will not compile.

59. Which best describes the user interface of an applet given the following init() method:

```
public void init() {
    setLayout(new BorderLayout());
    add(BorderLayout.NORTH, new TextField(10));
    add(BorderLayout.CENTER, new Button("help"));
}
```

Select all valid answers.

a. The TextField object will be placed at the top of the applet and will be ten columns wide.

   b. The Button object will be centered in the applet and will be just large enough to contain the text "help."

   c. The Button object will be centered in the applet and will start at the left edge of the applet, fit just under the TextField object above it, and extend to the right and bottom edge of the applet.

   d. The TextField object will be placed along the top of the applet and will stretch from the left edge to the right edge.

   e. The placement of the Button object and the TextField object depends on the overall size of the applet.

60. Which of the following statements about try, catch, and finally are true?

   Select all valid answers.

   a. A try block must always be followed by a catch block.

   b. A try block can be followed either by a catch block or a finally block, or both.

   c. A catch block must always be associated with a try block.

   d. A finally can never stand on its own (that is, without being associated with try block).

   e. None of these are true.

Answers to Exam Questions

  1. **a** and **c.** Instantiating an inner class doesn't imply anything about constructors of the outer class, unless the inner class is derived from the outer class. Thus, both a and c are valid options.

  2. **b.** b is the only correct answer. a, c, and d are definitely false. For e, one common construct is to invoke wait() in a while loop, but it is not necessary to invoke notify() or wait() in a while loop.

  3. **a** and **c.** b is definitely not correct. a and c are anonymous inner classes that implement Runnable.

  4. **d.** The value of 4 | 7 can be seen clearly as binary digits:

100 |
111
——
111
or 7.

5. **c.** c is the only correct answer. A static inner class can be instantiated from static methods of the enclosing class. b is not correct because the inner class is needed in main(), where there is no instance of the enclosing class (Counter).

6. **a, b,** and **c.** d is not correct—an inner class cannot access a variable in a subclass of an enclosing class without a reference to it.

7. **a, b,** and **e.** The other answers won't compile because InputStreamReader cannot accept a file.

8. **e.** The other answers are either partial answers or won't compile.

9. **a.** Variable width fonts are based on the average of the letters when specifying the width.

10. **c** and **e.** c and e are the only correct answers. b is a concrete class, but it does not implement the interface.

11.

```
System.out.println(evt.getX());
```

12.

```
mybutton = (Button)evt.getComponent();
```

13. ActionListener

14. **c.** b1 and b2 are different objects but the Boolean class overrides the equals() test to return true if the two objects being compared have the same Boolean value.

15. **a, c, d,** and **e.** b is not correct, because you cannot add an ActionListener to a TextArea. (You can add an ActionListener to a TextField, however.)

16. **a, c,** and **d.** Note that even with a return statement at the end of the catch block, the finally block is still executed.

17. MouseEvent

18. **b** and **e.** b and e are both correct. It is perfectly valid to put the default case first. Since there is no break statement at the end of the default, the 'a' case is always run if there is no match for 'a' or 'b'.

19. throws

20. **c.** c is the only correct answer. The entries in an array of objects all are set to null if no explicit value is given.

21. **d.** Even though there is a static variable named myArg, the local variable takes precedence.

22. **b.** a, c, d, and e are not valid. b is the only valid declaration (even though we've used the parameter name string rather than the usual args).

23. **a and c.** a and c are illegal. Note that e is legal: a variable can start with an under-score. Therefore, a variable does not have to contain any letters at all.

24.

```
args[1]
```

25. **a, b, and c.** The answers d and e are not valid for TextField objects.

26. **a and c.** a and c are the correct answers. The answer b is an option, but it does not have to be so—RunHandler could extend Thread, which would then indicate that it implements the Runnable interface—but it does not need to extend Thread to implement Runnable.

27. **c.** c is the only correct answer.

28.

```
super();
```

29. **a.** The value of 4 & 7 can be seen clearly as binary digits:
    100 &
    111
    ——
    100
    or 4.

30. **b.** b is correct.

31.

```
s.indexOf('C');
```

32. **d.** d is the only correct answer. There is a method called drawRect() that draws the outline of a rectangle.

33. **c, e, and f.** c, e, and f all describe this applet accurately.

34. **b and f.** b and f are the correct answers.

35. **d.** The method in the inner class changes the entries in the array, because objects are passed by reference (nonobjects are passed by value).

36. **e.** Note that there is no real constructor: what appears to be a constructor is really a method, because it specifies a return type (void). A real constructor does not have a return type. Hence, s is never initialized, and so null appears in the standard output.

37. **a.** a is the only correct answer.

38. **c and d.** c and d are correct. The package statement must come first, and import second. After that, classes can be declared in any order. (There can only be one public class per source file.)

39. **a, c, and d.** The default value for a floating-point number is a double. Since a double is greater precision than a float, a floating-point constant assigned to a float data type must be cast or specified as a float by appending the number with an F.

40.

```
String s = {"a", "b", "c"};
```

41. **b.** temp is truncated to 3. The result of 3 % 2 is 1.

42. **a.** The problem is in 5 | 2. An if() expression must resolve to true or false.

43.

```
List l = new List(5, true);
```

44. **d.** Try it and see.

45. **b.** b is the only correct answer.

46.

```
c.setVisible(false);
```

47. **a.** This code does not compile because there is no this variable in the static main() method to pass to the Thread's constructor.

48. **b and c.** b and c are both correct.

49. **d.** This code is perfectly fine, and Second can access the static variable in its superclass.

50. b. This could be made to compile by making class B static, or by creating class B from an instance method.

51. b. This code does not compile. Because the label two: is not associated with a loop.

52. a, b, and **c.** a, b, and c are all correct.

53. d. Math.floor(3.2) is 3, so the first if() expression yields false, taking us to the final else clause.

54.

```
new InputStreamReader(mystream, "8859-5");
```

55. c. Why? Because even though we've cast the Boolean objects to be of type Object, the method invoked still goes to the actual object type, which is Boolean. So, as is the case here, equals() will return true in the case of Boolean objects assigned to the same Boolean value.

56. b. The button appears centered in the Applet. Try it.

57. a. a is the only correct answer.

58. d. Because B's constructor implicitly calls A's no-args constructor, and such a constructor is not defined.

59. c and d. Both c and d are correct.

60. b, c, and **d.** A try block does not need to be followed by a catch block—as long as it is followed by a finally block, so answer a is not correct.

Sun Certified Programmer Practice Exam 2

Practice Exam Number 2

Here are the rules:

Allow 120 minutes to complete this exam. You should turn off the telephone, go someplace where you won't be disturbed, check the time on your watch, and begin. Don't bring any books with you, because you won't have them during the test. You can take breaks, but don't look anything up. You can have a piece of scratch paper and a pen or pencil, but you can't have any crib sheets!

If you get at least 36 questions right, you've hit the 61 percent mark, and you've passed. Good luck!

Questions

1. In the following example you create an instance of the StringBuffer class, then you call the append() method of the StringBuffer:

```
StringBuffer strBuf = new StringBuffer("ABC");
strBuf.append("DEF");
```

After executing line two, does strBuf still reference the same object instance? Yes or no.

2. If you want to associate keys with values and you are using JDK 1.2, which of the following classes is preferred:
   a. Dictionary
   b. HashTable
   c. Properties
   d. HashMap
   e. TreeMap

3. Which of the following classes can store duplicate elements/keys:
   a. List
   b. Set
   c. Map
   d. Collection

4. If you need to store multiple data elements that must not appear more than once in the data store, which class/interface would you use if searching is not a priority:
   a. List
   b. Set
   c. Map
   d. Vector
   e. Collection

5. Which of the following class definitions defines a legal abstract class?

   Select all right answers.

   a.

   ```
   class Animal {
     abstract void growl();
   }
   ```

   b.

   ```
   abstract Animal {
     abstract void growl();
   }
   ```

   c.

   ```
   class abstract Animal {
     abstract void growl();
   }
   ```

d.

```
abstract class Animal {
  abstract void growl();
}
```

e.

```
abstract class Animal {
  abstract void growl() {
    System.out.println("growl");
  }
}
```

6. For an object to be a target for a Thread, that object must be of type:

   Fill in the blank.

7. What is the proper way of defining a class named Key so that it cannot be sub-classed?

   Select the one right answer.

   a.

```
class Key { }
```

   b.

```
abstract final class Key {   }
```

   c.

```
native class Key { }
```

   d.

```
class Key {
  final;
}
```

   e.

```
final class Key { }
```

8. What modes are legal for creating a new RandomAccessFile object?

   Select all valid answers.
   a. "w"
   b. "r"
   c. "x"
   d. "rw"
   e. "xrw"

9. Given the following code:

```
class Tester {
  public static void main(String[] args) {
    CellPhone cell = new CellPhone();
    cell.emergency();
  }
}

class Phone {
  final void dial911() {
    //code to dial 911 here
  }
}

class CellPhone extends Phone {
  void emergency() {
    dial911();
  }
}
```

   What will happen when you try to compile and run the Tester class?

   Select the one right answer.
   a. The code will not compile because Phone is not also declared as final.
   b. The code will not compile because you cannot invoke a final method from a subclass.
   c. The code will compile and run fine.
   d. The code will compile but will throw a NoSuchMethodException when Tester is run.
   e. Phone and CellPhone are fine, but Tester will not compile because it cannot create an instance of a class that derives from a class defining a final method.

10. Which assignments are legal?

    Select all valid answers.
    a. long test = 012;
    b. float f = −412;

c. int other = (int)true;

d. double d = 0x12345678;

e. short s = 10;

11. Given this class definition:

```
abstract class Transaction implements Runnable { }
class Deposit extends Transaction {
  protected void process() {
    addAmount();
  }
  void undo(int I) {
    System.out.println("Undo");
  }
}
```

what will happen if we attempted to compile the code?

Select the one right answer.

a. This code will not compile because the parameter i is not used in undo().

b. This code will not compile because there is no main() method.

c. This code will not compile because Deposit must be an abstract class.

d. This code will not compile because Deposit is not declared public.

e. Everything will compile fine.

12. Which exceptions might wait() throw?

Fill in the blank.

13. Which of the following represents an octal number?

Select all that apply.

a. 0x12

b. 320

c. 032

d. (octal)2

e. 12

14. What will appear in the standard output when you run the Tester2 class?

```
class Tester2 {
  int var;
  Tester(double var) {
    this.var = (int)var;
  }
  Tester(int var) {
    this("hello");
  }
```

```
    Tester(String s) {
      this();
      System.out.println(s);
    }
    Tester() {
      System.out.println("good-bye");
    }
    public static void main(String[] args) {
      Tester t = new Tester(5);
    }
}
```

Select the one right answer.

a. nothing

b. "hello"

c. 5

d. "hello" followed by "good-bye"

e. "good-bye" followed by "hello"

15. Write a line of code to use the String's substring() method to obtain the substring "lip" from a String instance named s that is set to "tulip."

Fill in the blank.

16. What are the range of values for a variable of type short?

Select the one right answer.

a. -2^7 to 2^7-1

b. 0 to 2^8;

c. -2^{16} to $2^{15}-1$

d. -2^{15} to $2^{15}-1$

e. $-2^{15}-1$ to 2^{15}

17. What will happen when you try to compile and run the following program?

```
class Car {
  int milesPerGallon;
  int index;
  Car(int mpg) {
    milesPerGallon = mpg;
    index = 0;
  }
  Car() {
  }
  public static void main(String[] args) {
    int index;
    Car c = new Car(25);
    if (args.length > 0)
      if (args[index].equals("Hiway"))
```

```
        c.milesPerGallon *= 2;
      System.out.println("c.milesPerGallon:   " + c.milesPerGallon);
  }
}
```

Select the one right answer.

a. The code compiles and displays "mpg: 50" if the command-line argument is "Hiway." If the command-line argument is not "Hiway," the code displays "mpg: 25."

b. The code compiles and displays "mpg: 50" if the command-line argument is "Hiway." If the command-line argument is not "Hiway," the code throws an ArrayIndexOutOfBoundsException.

c. The code does not compile because the automatic variable named index has not been initialized.

d. The code does not compile because milesPerGallon has not been initialized.

e. The code does not compile because the no-args constructor is not written correctly.

18. What will happen when you compile and run this program:

```
class Array {
  public static void main(String[] args) {
    int length = 100;
    int[] d = new int[length];
    for (int index = 0;index < length; index++)
      System.out.println(d[index]);
  }
}
```

Select the one right answer.

a. The code will not compile because the int[] array is not declared correctly.

b. The code will compile but will throw an IndexArrayOutOfBoundsException when it runs and nothing will appear in the standard output.

c. The code will display the numbers 0 through 99 in the standard output, and then throw an IndexOutOfBoundsException.

d. The code will compile but the println() method will throw a NoSuchMethodException.

e. This code will work fine and display the number 0, 100 times in the standard output.

19. What is the result of attempting to compile and run the following class?

```
class Ar {
  public static void main(String[] args) {
    int[] seeds = new int[3];
```

```
       for (int i = 0; i < seeds.length; i++) {
         System.out.println(i);
       }
     }
   }
```

Select all valid answers.

a. 0

b. 1

c. 2

d. 3

e. The program does not compile because the seeds array is not initialized.

20. What method name can you use from the applet to read a String passed to an applet via the <param> tag? (Supply the method name only, without parameters.)

Fill in the blank.

21. Given these class definitions:

```
class Superclass { }
class Subclass1 extends Superclass { }
```

and these objects:

```
Superclass a = new Superclass();
Subclass1 b = new Subclass1();
```

which of the following explains the result of the statement:

```
a = b;
```

Select the one right answer.

a. Illegal at compile time

b. Legal at compile time but possibly illegal at runtime

c. Definitely legal at runtime

22. Given these class definitions:

```
class Superclass { }
class Subclass1 extends Superclass { }
class Subclass2 extends Superclass { }
```

and these objects:

```
Superclass a = new Superclass();
Subclass1 b = new Subclass1();
Subclass2 c = new Subclass2();
```

which of the following explains the result of the statement:

```
b = (Subclass1)c;
```

Select the one right answer.
a. Illegal at compile time
b. Legal at compile time but possibly illegal at runtime
c. Definitely legal at runtime

23. How can you use the escape notation \u to set the variable c, declared as a char, to the Unicode character whose value is hex 0x30A0?

Fill in the blank.

24. Which operators are overloaded for String objects?

Select all valid answers.
a. −
b. +=
c. >>
d. &
e. None of these

25. How can you change the break statement below so that it breaks out of both the inner and middle loops and continues with the next iteration of the outer loop?

```
outer: for (int x = 0; x < 3; x++) {
  middle: for (int y = 0; y < 3; y++) {
    inner: for (int z = 0; z < 3; z++) {
      if (arr(x, y, x) == targetValue)
        break;
    }
  }
}
```

Select the one right answer.
a. break inner;
b. break middle;
c. break outer;
d. continue;
e. continue middle;

26. Given this code snippet:

```
try {
  tryThis();
```

```
    return;
} catch (IOException x1) {
    System.out.println("exception 1");
    return;
} catch (Exception x2) {
    System.out.println("exception 2");
    return;
} finally {
    System.out.println("finally");
}
```

what will appear in the standard output if tryThis() throws a NumberFormat-Exception?

Select the one right answer.
a. Nothing
b. "exception 1" followed by "finally"
c. "exception 2" followed by "finally"
d. "exception 1"
e. "exception 2"

27. Given these class definitions:

```
class Superclass { }
class Subclass1 extends Superclass { }
```

and these objects:

```
Superclass a = new Superclass();
Subclass1 b = new Subclass1();
```

which of the following explains the result of the statement:

```
b = a;
```

Select the one right answer.
a. Illegal at compile time
b. Legal at compile time but possibly illegal at runtime
c. Definitely legal at runtime

28. Given these class definitions:

```
class Superclass { }
class Subclass1 extends Superclass { }
```

and these objects:

```
Superclass a = new Superclass();
Subclass1 b = new Subclass1();
```

which of the following explains the result of the statement:

```
b = (Subclass1)a;
```

Select the one right answer.

a. Illegal at compile time

b. Legal at compile time but possibly illegal at runtime

c. Definitely legal at runtime

29. To invoke read() from an InputStream subclass, you must handle what type of exception?

Fill in the blank.

30. Imagine there are two exception classes called Exception1 and Exception2 that descend from the Exception class. Given these two class definitions:

```
class First {
  void test() throws Exception1, Exception2 { . . . }
}
class Second extends First {
  void test() { . . . }
}
```

create a class called Third that extends Second and defines a test() method. What exceptions can Third's test() method throw?

Select all valid answers.

a. Exception1

b. Exception2

c. No checked exceptions

d. Any exceptions declared in the throws clause of the Third's test() method.

31. Given this code snippet:

```
double a = 90.7;
double b = method(a);
System.out.println(b);
```

if this snippet displays 90 in the standard output, what Math method did method() invoke?

Select all valid answers.

a. abs

b. min

c. floor

d. round

e. ceil

32. Given this code snippet:

```
double a = 14.9;
double b = method(a);
System.out.println(b);
```

if this snippet displays 15 in the standard output, what Math method(s) could method() have invoke?

Select the one right answer.
a. ceil() and round()
b. floor() and round()
c. ceil() only
d. floor() only
e. round() only

33. What methods does Java define in the Math class specifically for trigonometric calculations?

Select all valid answers.
a. cos
b. asin
c. tan
d. sin
e. angle

34. What String instance method would return true when invoked like this:

```
a.method(b);
```

where a = "GROUNDhog" and b = "groundHOG?"

Select the one right answer.
a. equals
b. toLowerCase
c. toUpperCase
d. equalsIgnoreCase
e. None of the above

35. What access control keyword should you use to allow other classes to access a method freely within its package, but to restrict classes outside of the package from accessing that method?

Select all valid answers.

a. public

b. protected

c. private

d. Do not supply an access control keyword.

36. What does the following code do?

```
File f = new File("hello.test");
FileOutputStream out = new FileOutputStream(f);
```

Select the one right answer.

a. Creates a new file named "hello.test" if it does not yet exist. It also opens the file so you can write to it and read from it.

b. Creates a new file named "hello.test" if it does not yet exist. The file is not opened.

c. Opens a file named "hello.test" so that you can write to it and read from it, but does not create the file if it does not yet exist.

d. Opens a file named "hello.test" so that you can write to it but cannot read from it.

e. Creates an object that you can now use to create and open the file named "hello.test," and write to and read from the file.

37. Which expressions are illegal?

Select all valid answers.

a. (true & true)

b. (4 & 5)

c. (int myInt = 0 > 3)

d. float myFloat = 40.0;

e. boolean b = (boolean)99;

38. Which label name(s) are illegal?

Select all valid answers.

a. here:

b. _there:

c. this:

d. that:

e. 2to1odds:

39. What keyword, when used in front of a method, must also appear in front of the class?

Fill in the blank.

40. What letters get written to the standard output with the following code?

```
class Unchecked {
  public static void main(String[] args) {
    try {
      method();
    } catch (Exception e) {
    }
  }

  static void method() {
    try {
      wrench();

      System.out.println("a");
    } catch (ArithmeticException e) {
      System.out.println("b");
    } finally {
      System.out.println("c");
    }
    System.out.println("d");
  }

  static void wrench() {
    throw new NullPointerException();
  }
}
```

Select all valid answers.

a. "a"

b. "b"

c. "c"

d. "d"

e. None of these

41. What happens if the file "Ran.test" does not yet exist and you attempt to compile and run the following code?

```
import java.io.*;

class Ran {
  public static void main(String[] args) throws IOException {
    RandomAccessFile out = new RandomAccessFile("Ran.test", "rw");
    out.writeBytes("Ninotchka");
  }
}
```

Select the one right answer.

a. The code does not compile because RandomAccessFile is not created correctly.

b. The code does not compile because RandomAccessFile does not implement the writeBytes() method.

c. The code compiles and runs but throws an IOException because "Ran.test" does not yet exist.

d. The code compiles and runs but nothing appears in the file "Ran.test" that it creates.

e. The code compiles and runs and "Ninotchka" appears in the file "Ran.test" that it creates.

42. If you supply a target object when you create a new Thread, as in:

```
Thread t = new Thread(targetObject);
```

what test of instanceof does targetObject have to pass for this to be legal?

Select the one right answer.

a. targetObject instanceof Thread

b. targetObject instanceof Object

c. targetObject instanceof Applet

d. targetObject instanceof Runnable

e. targetObject instanceof String

43. What appears in the standard output when you run the Dots class?

```
import java.io.*;

class Dots {
  Thread t;
  public static void main(String[] args) throws Exception {
    Dots d = new Dots();
    d.t = new DotThread();
  }

  public void init() {
    t.start();
    t = new DashThread();
    t.start();
  }
}

class DotThread extends Thread {
  public void run() {
    for (int index = 0; index < 100; index++)
```

```
          System.out.println(".");
      }
  }

  class DashThread extends Thread {
    public void run() {
      for (int index = 0; index < 100; index++)
        System.out.println("-");
    }
  }
```

Select the one right answer.
a. nothing
b. 100 dots
c. 200 dots
d. 100 dashes (−)
e. 100 dots (.) and 100 dashes(−)

44. When you invoke repaint() for a Component, the AWT package calls which Component method?

Select the one right answer.
a. repaint
b. update
c. paint
d. draw
e. show

45. How can you test whether an object referenced by ref implements an interface named MyInterface? Replace *your test here* with this test:

```
if (your test here) {
  System.out.println("ref implements MyInterface");
```

Fill in the blank.

46. What does the following line of code do?

```
TextField tf = new TextField(30);
```

Select the one right answer.
a. This code is illegal; there is no such constructor for TextField.
b. Creates a TextField object that can hold 30 rows, but because it is not initialized to anything, it will always be empty.

c. Creates a TextField object that can hold 30 columns, but because it is not initialized to anything, it will always be empty.

d. Creates a TextField object that can hold 30 rows of text.

e. Creates a new TextField object that is 30 columns of text.

47. Given these code snippets:

```
Boolean b1 = new Boolean(true);
Boolean b2 = new Boolean(true);
```

Which expressions are legal Java expressions that return true?

Select all valid answers.

a. b1 == b2

b. b1.equals(b2)

c. b1 & b2

d. b1 | b2

e. b1 && b2

f. b1 || b2

48. which LayoutManager arranges components left to right, then top to bottom, centering each row as it moves to the next?

Select the one right answer.

a. BorderLayout

b. FlowLayout

c. GridLayout

d. CardLayout

e. GridBagLayout

49. A component will automatically be resized horizontally, but not vertically, when it is placed in which region of a BorderLayout?

Select the one right answer.

a. North or South

b. East or West

c. Center

d. North, South, or Center

e. Any region

50. How can you place three Components along the bottom of a Container?

Select the one right answer.

   a. Set the Container's LayoutManager to be a BorderLayout and add each Component to the "South" of the Container.

   b. Set the Container's LayoutManager to be a FlowLayout and add each Component to the Container.

   c. Set the Container's LayoutManager to be a BorderLayout; add each Component to a different Container that uses a FlowLayout, and then add that Container to the "South" of the first Container.

   d. Use a GridLayout for the Container and add each Component to the Container.

   e. Do not use a LayoutManager at all and add each Component to the Container.

51. What will happen when you attempt to compile and run the following program by passing the test class to the Java interpreter?

```
class test {
  public static void main() {
    System.out.println("hello");
  }
}
```

Select the one right answer.

   a. The program does not compile because main() is not defined correctly.

   b. The program compiles but when you try to run it the interpreter complains that it cannot find the main() method it needs to run.

   c. The program compiles but you cannot run it because the class is not declared as public.

   d. The program compiles and runs without an error but does not display anything in the standard output.

   e. The program compiles and displays "hello" in the standard output when you run it.

52. How would you make the background color red for a Panel referenced by the variable p?

Fill in the blank.

53. What is the result of invoking main() for the classes D and E?

```
class D {
  public static void main(String[] args) {
    String s1 = new String("hello");
```

```
      String s2 = new String("hello");
      if (s1.equals(s2))
        System.out.println("equal");
      else
        System.out.println("not equal");
  }
}

class E {
  public static void main(String[] args) {
    StringBuffer sb1 = new StringBuffer("hello");
    StringBuffer sb2 = new StringBuffer("hello");
    if (sb1.equals(sb2))
      System.out.println("equal");
    else
      System.out.println("not equal");
  }
}
```

elect the one right answer.

a. D: equal; E: equal

b. D: not equal; E: not equal

c. D: equal; E: not equal

d. D: not equal; E: not equal

e. Nothing appears in the standard output for either class.

54. What method from Java can you use to hide a Component from a user interface display?

Select all right answers.

a. disable

b. setVisible(false)

c. remove

d. delete

e. unhook

55. Which statements about garbage collection are true?

Select all valid answers.

a. You can directly free the memory allocated by an object.

b. You can directly run the garbage collector whenever you want to.

c. The garbage collector informs your object when it is about to be garbage collected.

d. The garbage collector reclaims an object's memory as soon as it becomes a candidate for garbage collection.

e. The garbage collector runs in low-memory situations.

56. If you'd like to change the size of a Component, you can use the method:

Select the one right answer.
a. size
b. resize
c. area
d. setSize
e. dimension

57. The setForeground() and setBackground() methods are defined in class:

Select the one right answer.
a. Graphics
b. Container
c. Component
d. Object
e. Applet

58. How many bits are used to maintain a char data type?

Fill in the blank.

59. The && operator works with which data types?

Select all valid answers.
a. int
b. long
c. double
d. boolean
e. float

60. To place a 1 in the high-bit of an int named ref that's set to 0x00000001, you can write:

Select the one right answer.
a. ref >> 31;
b. ref >>= 31;
c. ref << 31;
d. ref <<= 31;

Answers to Exam Questions

1. **Yes.** The StringBuffer class is read-write. Because of this, the example modifies the existing StringBuffer object.

2. **d** and **e.** Maps are replacing dictionaries as the preferred way to associate keys with values. Both HashMap and TreeMap are maps.

3. **a** and **d.** Only lists and collections can have duplicate elements. Maps can have duplicate values but cannot have duplicate keys.

4. **b.** A set rejects duplicate entries so if you want to ensure data elements only appear once, then this is the best choice. We could have used a map also. However, because searching isn't a priority, the best choice is b.

5. **d.** An abstract class is defined using the keyword abstract in front of the class keyword and almost always defines at least one abstract method. An abstract class does not have to define an abstract method. If there are no abstract methods in an abstract class, then any subclasses of the abstract class can be instantiated (as long as they are not, in turn, defined using the abstract keyword).

6. "Runnable." Only classes that implement the Runnable interface (and so are of type Runnable) can be targets of threads.

7. **e.** Use the final keyword in front of the class to make the class unable to be subclassed.

8. **b** and **d.** Only "r" and "rw" are legal modes for a RandomAccessFile.

9. **c.** This code is perfectly fine.

10. **a, b, d,** and **e.** The other tries to cast a boolean to an int, which is illegal.

11. **c.** Since the superclass is abstract and implements Runnable, but does not supply a run() method, the subclass must supply run() or also be declared abstract.

12. "InterruptedException" or "IllegalMonitorException"

13. **c.** An octal number in Java is preceded by a 0.

14. **e.** There are three constructors that come into play. First, the constructor that takes an int is invoked. This invokes the constructor that takes a String. This invokes the no-args constructor, which displays "good-bye." Then, the constructor that takes a String displays "hello."

15. "s.substring(2, 5)" or "s.substring(2)"

16. **d.** A short is a signed 16-bit number, so the correct answer is $(-2\char`^15$ to $2\char`^15-1)$. The range of integer types goes from -2(number of bits -1) to 2(number of bits -1) -1.

17. **c.** Even though there is an instance variable named index defined in the Car class, the local or automatic variable named index takes precedence. Since automatic variables do not have a default value, this code will not compile because it is uninitialized when we attempt to access the element in the args array.

18. **e.** There's nothing wrong with this code. 100 zeroes will appear in the standard output.

19. **a, b,** and **c.** The elements in arrays are initialized to their default values: 0, 0.0, null, false, or \u0000, depending on the data type.

20. "getParameter"

21. **c.** Assigning a subclass type to a superclass type is perfectly legal and will run fine at runtime.

22. **a.** You cannot assign an object to a sibling object reference, even with casting.

23. "c = '\u30A0';" You can set a char to a Unicode sequence by matching the template \udddd, where dddd are four hexadecimal digits representing the Unicode character you want.

24. **b.** Only + and += are overloaded for String objects.

25. **b.** Changing the break statement to break middle will break out of the loop named using the label middle and continue with the next iteration of the outer loop. The statement continue outer would also have this effect.

26. **c.** NumberFormatException will be handled in the catch clause for Exception. Then, regardless of the return statements, the finally clause will be executed before control returns to the calling method.

27. **a.** An explicit cast is needed to assign a superclass type to a subclass type.

28. **b.** If the object contained in a is not actually a Subclass1 object, the assignment will cause Java to throw a ClassCastException. That would be the case in the code in this example.

29. "IOException" or "java.io.IOException"

30. **c.** A method in a subclass cannot add new exception types that it might throw. Since its superclass, Second, does not define any exceptions in its test() method, Third can't either.

31. **c.** The Math method floor() finds the integer closest to but less than the parameter to floor(). The methods round() and ceil() would both result in 91, and min() and max() both require two parameters.

32. **a.** Both ceil() and round() will produce 15 from 14.9. The floor() method yields 14.

33. **a, b, c,** and **d.** The methods Java defines for trig operations include sin(), asin(), cos(), and tan().

34. **d.** The method equalsIgnoreCase() would return true for the two Strings a and b in the question.

35. **d.** This is the default access control for methods and member variables.

36. **a.** The first line creates a File object that represents the file. By creating a FileOutputStream, you create the file if it does not yet exist, and open that file for reading and writing.

37. **c, d,** and **e.** You cannot assign an integer to a boolean—not even with casting. Also, the default type for a floating-point literal is double, and you cannot assign a double to a float without casting.

38. **c** and **e.** this is a reserved word, so it cannot be used as an identifier (such as a label). 2to1odds starts with a number, so it is also invalid as an identifier.

39. "abstract"

40. **c.** Only the "c" from finally gets written out. The exception thrown doesn't match the exception caught, so the catch block is not executed. Control returns to the caller after finally to see if there is a catch block there to handle this unchecked exception. If there is not (as is the case here), execution comes to an end.

41. **e.** This code compiles and runs fine. RandomAccessFile implements the DataOutput interface, so it does implement writeBytes(), among others. RandomAccessFile creates the file if it does not yet exist.

42. **d.** The target object for a Thread must implement Runnable, which means it will pass the test:

targetObject instanceof Runnable

43. **a.** The thread with start() method is never invoked. (This is not an applet, so init() is not automatically invoked.)

44. **b.** The AWT invokes update() for the Component, which invokes paint() in its default behavior.

45. "ref instanceof MyInterface"

46. **e.** TextField defines a constructor that takes the number of columns, as shown in the example. TextField objects can have their text updated at any time, including long after they're created.

47. **b.** The first yields false, and the others are not legal Java expressions (this is a wrapper type we're using here).

48. **b.** A FlowLayout arranges components in this way.

49. **a.** North and South only can resize a component horizontally, to the width of the Container.

50. **c.** Complicated as it might seem, this is the best way to accomplish this goal. First, you set the Container's LayoutManager to be a BorderLayout. Then, you create an intermediate Container and add each Component to this new Container that uses a FlowLayout. Finally, you add that Container to the "South" of the original Container.

51. **b.** The program will compile fine. However, the Java interpreter specifically looks for a main() method declared as public and static, that returns no value, and that takes an array of String objects as its parameter.

52. "p.setBackground(Color.red);"

53. **c.** The StringBuffer class does not override equals(). Hence, this class returns false when passed two different objects.

54. **b.** The setVisible(false) removes a Component from the display.

55. **b and c.** e is not a correct answer because you can explicitly run the gc regardless of the amount of memory your system has available.

56. **d.** setSize() is the correct method.

57. **c.** These are Component methods. (The setColor() method is defined in the Graphics class.)

58. "16"

59. **d.** The && operator combines two boolean expressions.

60. **d.** The << operator shifts the bits the given number of places to the left.

Sun Certified Programmer Practice Exam 3

Practice Exam Number 3

Here are the rules:

Allow 120 minutes to complete this exam. You should turn off the telephone, go someplace where you won't be disturbed, check the time on your watch, and begin. Don't bring any books with you, because you won't have them during the test. You can take breaks, but don't look anything up. You can have a piece of scratch paper and a pen or pencil, but you can't have any crib sheets!

If you get at least 36 questions right, you've hit the 61 percent mark, and you've passed. Good luck!

Questions

1. Given the following class definition:

```
class A {
   public int x;
   private int y;
   class B {
      public int z;
      protected void method1() {
```

```
          private void method2() {
          }
          class C {
             private void method3() {
             }
          }
       }
    }
    float z;
```

what can method3() access directly, without a reference to another instance?

Select all valid answers.

a. The variable x defined in A

b. The variable y defined in A

c. The variable z defined in B

d. method1 defined in B

e. method2 defined in B

2. You created a file using the character set defined by UTF-16. You are writing an application that stores data in the file. The local encoding is set to ISO 8859-8 by default. How can you write a chunk of code to write to the file? You have three variables accessible to you:

- myfile is the name of the file you want to write.

- stream is an InputStream object associated with this file.

- s is a String object.

Select all valid answers.

a.

```
FileOutputStream stream = new FileOutputStream(myFile);
OutputStreamWriter out = new OutputStreamWriter(stream);
out.write(s);
```

b.

```
OutputStreamWriter out = new OutputStreamWriter
   (new FileOutputStream(myFile, "UTF-16"));
out.write(s);
```

c.

```
OutputStreamWriter out = new OutputStreamWriter
   (new FileOutputStream("UTF-16", myFile));
out.write(s);
```

d.

```
FileOutputStream stream = new FileOutputStream(myFile);
OutputStreamWriter out = new OutputStreamWriter(stream, "UTF-16"));
out.write(s);
```

e.

```
OutputStreamWriter out = new OutputStreamWriter(myfile, "UTF-16"));
out.write(s); stream,
```

3. How can you write a line of code for an applet's init() method that determines how wide the applet is?

Select all valid answers.
   a. int width = this.getY();
   b. int width = this.getSize().w;
   c. int width = getSize();
   d. int width =getSize().w;
   . **e.** int width = getWidth();

4. For a variable width font, how wide is a TextField created using the expression:

```
new TextField(20)
```

Select the one right answer.
   a. 20 times the average of all the characters in the font used for this TextField object
   b. 20 times the width of the letter M
   c. 20 times the width of the letter a
   d. 20 inches
   e. 20 picas

5. Given this interface definition:

```
interface A {
    int method1(int i);
    int method2(int j);
}
```

which of the following classes implement this interface and is not abstract?

Select all valid answers.

a.

```
class B implements A {
    int method1() { }
    int method2() { }
}
```

b.

```
class B {
    int method1(int i) { }
    int method2(int j) { }
}
```

c.

```
class B implements A {
    int method1(int i) { }
    int method2(int j) { }
}
```

d.

```
class B extends A {
    int method1(int i) { }
    int method2(int j) { }
}
```

e.

```
class B implements A {
    int method2(int j) { }
    int method1(int i) { }
}
```

6. Given the following code:

```
import java.awt.*;
import java.awt.event.*;
public class MyApplet extends java.applet.Applet {
    public void init() {
        Button b = new Button("Button1");
        b.addMouseListener(new ClickHandler());
        add(b);
    }
    class ClickHandler extends MouseAdapter {
        public void mouseClicked(MouseEvent evt) {
            // A
```

```
        }
    }
}
```

what line of code at A writes the mouse's horizontal location to the standard output at the time of the event? Note that the value output should be with respect to the component which handled the event.

Fill in the blank.

7. Given the same code as in question 11, how can you write a line of code at A that will place the Button object into a variable named mybutton that is already defined to be a reference to a Button object?

Fill in the blank.

8. Which Listener interface can you implement to be able to respond to the user hitting the enter key after typing into a TextField object?

Fill in the blank.

9. What is written to the standard output as the result of executing the following statements?

```
Boolean b1 = new Boolean(true);
Boolean b2 = new Boolean(true);
if (b1 == b2)
    if (b1.equals(b2))
        System.out.println("a");
    else
        System.out.println("b");
else
    if (b1.equals(b2))
        System.out.println("c");
    else
        System.out.println("d");
```

Select the one right answer.

a. a

b. b

c. c

d. d

10. Which Listener interfaces can you add to a TextArea object?

a. TextListener

b. ActionListener

   c. MouseMotionListener

   d. MouseListener

   e. ComponentListener

11. What appears in the standard output if the method named problem() in the code below throws an instance of class Exception when the method named trythis() is invoked?

```
public void trythis() {
    try {
        System.out.println("1");
        problem();
    } catch (RuntimeException x) {
        System.out.println("2");
        return;
    } catch (Exception x) {
        System.out.println("3");
        return;
    } finally {
        System.out.println("4");
    }
    System.out.println("5");
}
```

Select all valid answers.

   a. "1"

   b. "2"

   c. "3"

   d. "4"

   e. "5"

12. What is the type of the Event object passed to the mouseDragged() method defined in a class that implements java.awt.event.MouseMotionListener (that is, what is the class name for the argument)?

Fill in the blank.

13. Examine the following switch block:

```
char mychar = 'c';
switch (mychar) {
    default:
    case 'a': System.out.println("a"); break;
    case 'b': System.out.println("b"); break;
}
```

Which of the following questions are definitely true?

Select all valid answers.

a. This switch block is illegal, because only integers can be used in the switch statement.

b. This switch block is fine.

c. This switch block is illegal, because the default statement must come last.

d. When this code runs, nothing is written to the standard output.

e. When this code runs, the letter "a" is written to the standard output.

14. What keyword must appear in a method declaration (followed by the name of the exception) when that method might cause an exception to be thrown and that method does not handle the exception?

Fill in the blank.

15. Which statements accurately describe the following line of code?

```
String[][] s = new String[10][];
```

Select all valid answers.

a. This line of code is illegal.

b. s is a two-dimensional array containing ten rows and ten columns

c. s is an array of ten arrays.

d. Each element in s is set to "".

e. Each element in s is uninitialized and must be initialized before it is referenced.

16. What will happen if you try to compile and run the following class?

```
class Test {
    static int myArg = 1;
    public static void main(String[] args) {
        int myArg;
        System.out.println(myArg);
    }
}
```

Select the one right answer.

a. This code compiles and displays 0 in the standard output when run.

b. This code compiles and displays 1 in the standard output when run.

c. This code does not compile because you cannot define a local variable named the same as a static variable.

d. This code does not compile because the local variable is used before it is initialized.

17. Which declarations for the main() method in a stand-alone program are not valid?

Select all valid answers.
   a. public static void main()
   b. public static void main(String[] string)
   c. public static void main(String args)
   d. static public int main(String[] args)
   e. static void main(String[] args)

18. Which of the following identifiers are illegal?

Select all valid answers.
   a. #_pound
   b. _underscore
   c. 5Interstate
   d. Interstate5
   e. _5_

19. If the user invokes a stand-alone application by typing:

```
java YourApp 1 2 3
```

and the main() method defines its String[] parameter as args, how can you access the number 2 using args?

Fill in the blank.

20. Which interface implementations can you add as listeners for a TextField object?

Select all valid answers.
   a. ActionListener
   b. FocusListener
   c. MouseMotionListener
   d. WindowListener
   e. ContainerListener

21. What must be true for the RunHandler class so that instances of RunHandler can be used as written in the code below:

```
class Test {
   public static void main(String[] args) {
      Thread t = new Thread(new RunHandler());
      t.start();
   }
}
```

Select all valid answers.
  a. RunHandler must implement the java.lang.Runnable interface.
  b. RunHandler must extend the Thread class.
  c. RunHandler must provide a run() method declared as public and returning void.
  d. RunHandler must provide an init() method.

22. To determine if you can invoke addContainerListener() for a component referenced using a variable named c, which expression(s) can you evaluate that will give you a true or false answer to this questions?

Select all valid answers.
  a. c == Container
  b. c.equals(Class.Container)
  c. c instanceof Container
  d. c instanceof Component
  e. c implements Container

23. Write a statement for a constructor that invokes the no-args, default constructor in its superclass.

Fill in the blank.

24. What is written to the standard output given the following statement:

```
System.out.println(4 & 7);
```

Select the one right answer.
  a. 4
  b. 5
  c. 6
  d. 7
  e. 0

25. What will the following block of code write to the standard output when it is executed?

```
int i = 3;
int j = 0;
double k = 3.2;
if (i < k)
    if (i == j)
        System.out.println(i);
    else
        System.out.println(j);
else
    System.out.println(k);
```

Select the one right answer.

a. 3

b. 0

c. 3.2

d. None of these

26. How can you use the String method indexOf() to determine which position the letter 'C' is in given this String:

```
String s = "ABCDE";
```

Write a complete statement in your answer, but you do not have to assign *value* you retrieve to another variable.

Fill in the blank.

27. Given that the variable g references a valid Graphics object, what does the following statement do?

```
g.fillRect(2, 3, 10, 20);
```

Select all valid answers.

a. Draw the outline of a rectangle in the current background color.

b. Draw the outline of a rectangle in the current foreground color.

c. Fill in a rectangle using the current background color.

d. Fill in a rectangle using the current foreground color.

e. Fill in a rectangle in black.

28. Describe the following applet.

```
import java.applet.Applet;
import java.awt.event.*;
import java.awt.*;
public class MyApplet extends Applet {
    Button b1, b2;
    public void init() {
        ActionListener a = new ActionListener() {
            public void actionPerformed(ActionEvent evt) {
                if (evt.getSource() == b1) {
                    b1.setEnabled(false);
                    b2.setEnabled(true);
                } else {
                    b1.setEnabled(true);
                    b2.setEnabled(false);
                }
            }
        };
        b1 = new Button("1");
```

```
        b1.addActionListener(a);
        add(b1);
        b2 = new Button("2");
        b2.addActionListener(a);
        add(b2);
    }
}
```

Select all valid answers.

a. Nothing appears in the applet.

b. One button appears in the applet but does nothing.

c. Two buttons appear in the applet.

d. When the user clicks a button, nothing happens.

e. When the user clicks a button, it becomes disabled.

f. When a user clicks a button, the other button becomes enabled.

29. The method setBackground() defined for the Graphics class:

Select all valid answers.

a. takes an integer value.

b. takes an instance of class Color.

c. takes an instance of a Component subclass.

d. sets the drawing mode for the associated Component object.

e. sets the drawing color for the associated Component object.

f. changes the background color for the associated Component object.

30. What does the following program do when it is run with the command?

```
java Mystery Mighty Mouse

class Mystery {
    public static void main(String[] args) {
        Changer c = new Changer();
        c.method(args);
        System.out.println(args[0] + " " + args[1]);
    }
    static class Changer {
        void method(String[] s) {
            String temp = s[0];
            s[0] = s[1];
            s[1] = temp;
        }
    }
}
```

Select the one right answer.

a. This program causes an ArrayIndexOutOfBoundsException to be thrown.

b. This program runs but does not write anything to the standard output.

    c. This program writes "Mighty Mouse" to the standard output.

    d. This program writes "Mouse Mighty" to the standard output.

31. What happens when you try to compile and run the following program?

```
class Mystery {
    String s;
    public static void main(String[] args) {
        Mystery m = new Mystery();
        m.go();
    }
    void Mystery() {
        s = "constructor";
    }
    void go() {
        System.out.println(s);
    }
}
```

Select the one right answer.

    a. This code will not compile.

    b. This code compiles but throws an exception at runtime.

    c. This code runs but nothing appears in the standard output.

    d. This code runs and writes "constructor" in the standard output.

    e. This code runs and writes "null" in the standard output.

32. What can you write at the comment //A in the code below so that this program writes the word "running" to the standard output?

```
class RunTest implements Runnable {
    public static void main(String[] args) {
        RunTest rt = new RunTest();
        Thread t =new Thread(rt);
        //A
    }
    public void run() {
        System.out.println("running");
    }
    void go() {
        start(1);
    }
    void start(int i) {
    }
}
```

Select all valid answers.

    a. System.out.println("running");

    b. rt.start();

    c. rt.go();

    d. rt.start(1);

33. What order can you place the following pieces of a source file in so that the source file will compile without errors or warnings?

```
//A
import java.applet.*;
//B
class Helper {
}
//C
package myclasses;
//D
public class MyApplet extends java.applet.Applet {
}
```

Select all valid answers.

 a. A, B, C, D

 b. A, C, B, D

 c. C, A, B, D

 d. C, A, D, B

 e. C, B, A, D

34. Analyze these two consecutive lines of code:

```
float f = 3.2;
int i = f;
```

Select all valid answers.

 a. This code would not compile.

 b. This code would compile and i would be set to 3.

 c. The second line could compile if it were written instead as:

```
int i = (byte)f;
```

 d. The first line could compile if it were written instead as:

```
float f = 3.2F;
```

35. Construct an array of three String objects containing the strings "a," "b," and "c" using the { } notation.

Call the String by the variable name s.

Fill in the blank.

36. What is the final value of temp in this sequence?

```
long temp = (int)3.9;
temp %= 2;
```

a. 0

b. 1

c. 2

d. 3

e. 4

Select the one right answer.

37. Analyze this line of code:

```
if (5 & 7 > 0 && 5 | 2) System.out.println("true");
```

Select the one right answer.

a. This line of code will not compile.

b. This code will compile but nothing will appear in the standard output.

c. This code will compile and write the word "true" in the standard output.

38. Create a List object that enables multiple selections and displays five rows at a time. Start by writing:

```
List l =
```

in your answer.

Fill in the blank.

39. What will the user interface look like in an applet given the following init() method?

```
public void init() {
    setLayout(new BorderLayout());
    add("East", new Button("hello"));
}
```

Select the one right answer.

a. Nothing will appear in the applet.

b. A button will appear in the applet set in the exact center.

c. A button will appear on the left side of the applet.

d. A button will appear on the right side of the applet.

e. A button will fill the entire applet.

40. Choose all true statements about the paint() method defined in the Component class:

Select all valid answers.

a. It is protected.

b. It takes an instance of class Graphics.

c. It is static.

d. It is invoked automatically whenever you minimize and then maximize a component, such as a window.

e. There is also a version that takes an int.

41. Given this ActionListener:

```
class HandleClick implements ActionListener {
    public void actionPerformed(ActionEvent evt) {
        // A
    }
}
```

what line of code can you write at A that will make a component referenced by c disappear from the display?

Fill in the blank.

42. Analyze the following code:

```
class WhatHappens implements Runnable {
    public static void main(String[] args) {
        Thread t = new Thread(this);
        t.start();
    }
    public void run() {
        System.out.println("hi");
    }
}
```

Select the one right answer.

a. This program does not compile.

b. This program compiles but nothing appears in the standard output.

c. This program compiles and the word "hi" appears in the standard output, once.

d. This program compiles and the word "hi" appears continuously in the standard output until the user hits CONTROL-C to stop the program.

43. What is wrong with the following code?

```
final class First {
    private int a = 1;
    int b = 2;
}
class Second extends First {
    public void method() {
        System.out.println(a + b);
    }
}
```

Select all valid answers.

a. You cannot invoke println() without passing it a String.

b. Because a is private, no classes other than First can access it.

c. Second cannot extend First.

d. final is not a valid keyword for a class.

44. Analyze the following two classes.

```
class First {
   static int a = 3;
}
final class Second extends First {
   void method() {
       System.out.println(a);
   }
}
```

Select the one right answer.

a. Class First compiles, but class Second does not.

b. Class Second compiles, but class First does not.

c. Neither class compiles.

d. Both classes compile, and if method() is invoked, it writes 3 to the standard output.

e. Both classes compile, but if method() is invoked, it throws an exception.

45. Why won't the following class compile?

```
class A {
   private int x;
   public static void main(String[] args) {
      new B();
   }
   class B {
      B() {
          System.out.println(x);
      }
   }
}
```

Select the one right answer.

a. Class B tries to access a private variable defined in its ouer class.

b. Class A attempts to create an instance of B when there is no current instance of class A.

c. Class B's constructor must be public.

46. Analyze the following code.

```
void looper() {
    int x = 0;
one:
    while (x < 10) {
two:
        System.out.println(++x);
        if (x > 3)
            break two;
    }
}
```

Select all valid answers.

a. This code compiles.

b. This code does not compile.

c. This method writes the number 0 to the standard output.

d. This method writes the numbers 1 and 2 to the standard output.

e. This method writes the number 3 to the standard output.

f. This method writes the number 4 to the standard output.

g. This method writes the numbers 5 through 9 to the standard output.

h. This method writes the number 10 to the standard output.

47. What appears in the standard output when the method named testing is invoked?

```
void testing() {
one:
two:
    for (int i = 0; i < 3; i++) {
three:
        for (int j = 10; j < 30; j+=10) {
            System.out.println(i + j);
            if (i > 2)
                continue one;
        }
    }
}
```

Select all valid answers.

a. 10 and 20

b. 11 and 21

c. 12 and 22

d. 13 and 23

e. 30, 31, 32, and 33

48. What will the result be for the following block of code when it is executed?

```
int i = 3;
int j = 0;
float k = 3.2F;
long m = -3;
if (Math.ceil(i) < Math.floor(k))
    if (Math.abs(i) == m)
        System.out.println(i);
    else
        System.out.println(j);
else
    System.out.println(Math.abs(m) + 1);
```

Select the one right answer.

a. 3

b. 0

c. −3

d. 4

e. none of these

49. The ISO code for the language you are interested in is 8859-5. Assume you have a stream in a variable named mystream that's associated with a file generated in this 8-bit character set. If the default conversion to Unicode in your environment is for the encoding 8859-1, how can you create a new instance of InputStreamReader that will perform the conversion from ISO 8859-5 to Unicode, automatically? (Start by writing the keyword new.)

Fill in the blank.

50. What is written to the standard output as the result of executing the following statements?

```
Boolean b1 = new Boolean(true);
Boolean b2 = new Boolean(true);
Object obj1 = (Object)b1;
Object obj2 = (Object)b2;
if (obj1 == obj2)
    if (obj1.equals(obj2))
        System.out.println("a");
    else
        System.out.println("b");
else
    if (obj1.equals(obj2))
        System.out.println("c");
    else
        System.out.println("d");
```

Select the one right answer.

a. a

b. b

c. c

d. d

51. What will the user interface look like in an applet given the following init() method?

```
public void init() {
    setLayout(new BorderLayout());
    add(new Button("hello"));
}
```

Select the one right answer.

a. Nothing will appear in the applet.

b. A button will appear in the applet set in the exact center.

c. A button will appear in the applet along the top and centered horizontally.

d. A button will appear in the top left corner.

52. What expressions are true concerning the following lines of code?

```
int[] arr = {1, 2, 3};
for (int i=0; i < 2; i++)
    arr[i] = 0;
```

Select all valid answers.

a. arr[0] == 0

b. arr[0] == 1

c. arr[1] == 1

d. arr[2] ==0

e. arr[3] == 0

53. What will happen if you try to compile and execute B's main() method?

```
class A {
    int i;
    A(int i) {
        this.i = i * 2;
    }
}
class B extends A {
    public static void main(String[] args) {
        B b = new B(2);
    }
    B(int i) {
```

```
        System.out.println(i);
      }
    }
```

Select the one right answer.

a. The instance variable i is set to 4.

b. The instance variable i is set to 2.

c. The instance variable i is set to 0.

d. This code will not compile.

54. Which best describes the user interface of an applet given the following init() method:

```
public void init() {
    setLayout(new BorderLayout());
    add(BorderLayout.NORTH, new TextField(10));
    add(Borderlayout.CENTER, new Button("help"));
}
```

Select all valid answers.

a. The TextField object will be placed at the top of the applet and will be 10 columns wide.

b. The Button object will be centered in the applet and will be just large enough to contain the text "help."

c. The Button object will be centered in the applet and will start at the left edge of the applet, fit just under the TextField object above it, and extend to the right and bottom edge of the applet.

d. The TextField object will be placed along the top of the applet and will stretch from the left edge to the right edge.

e. The placement of the Button object and the TextField object depends on the overall size of the applet.

55. Which of the following statements about try, catch, and finally are true?

Select all valid answers.

a. A try block must always be followed by a catch block.

b. A try block can be followed either by a catch block or a finally block, or both.

c. A catch block must always be associated with a try block.

d. A finally can never stand on its own (that is, without being associated with try block).

e. None of these are true.

56. Given the following class definition:

```
class A {
    protected int i;
    A(int i) {
        this.i = i;
    }
}
```

Which of the following would be a valid inner class for this class?

Select all valid answers.

a.

```
class B {
}
```

b.

```
class B extends A {
}
```

c.

```
class B {
    B() {
        System.out.println("i = " + i);
    }
}
```

d.

```
class B {
    class A {
    }
}
```

e.

```
class A {
}
```

57. What statements are true concerning the method notify() that is used in conjunction with wait()?

Select all valid answers.

a. If there is more than one thread waiting on a condition, only the thread that has been waiting the longest is notified.

b. If there is more than one thread waiting on a condition, there is no way to predict which thread will be notified.

    c. Notify() is defined in the Thread class.

    d. It is not strictly necessary to own the lock for the object you invoke notify() for.

    e. Notify() should only be invoked from within a while loop.

58. Given the following class:

```
class Counter {
    public int startHere = 1;
    public int endHere = 100;
    public static void main(String[] args) {
        new Counter().go();
    }
    void go() {
        // A
        Thread t = new Thread(a);
        t.start();
    }
}
```

what block of code can you replace at line A above so that this program will count from startHere to endHere?

Select all valid answers.

    a.

```
Runnable a = new Runnable() {
    public void run() {
        for (int i = startHere; i <= endHere; i++) {
            System.out.println(i);
        }
    }
};
```

    b.

```
a implements Runnable {
    public void run() {
        for (int i = startHere; i <= endHere; i++) {
            System.out.println(i);
        }
    }
};
```

    c.

```
Thread a = new Thread() {
    public void run() {
        for (int i = startHere; i <= endHere; i++) {
            System.out.println(i);
```

```
        }
    }
};
```

59. What is written to the standard output given the following statement:

```
System.out.println(4 | 7);
```

Select the one right answer.

a. 4

b. 5

c. 6

d. 7

e. 0

Given the following class:

```
class Counter {
    public static void main(String[] args) {
        Thread t = new Thread(new CounterBehavior());
        t.start();
    }
}
```

which of the following is a valid definition of CounterBehavior that would make Counter's main() method count from 1 to 100, counting once per second?

Select the one right answer.

a. This class is an inner class to Counter:

```
class CounterBehavior {
    for (int i = 1; i <= 100; i++);
        try {
            System.out.println(i);
            Thread.sleep(1000);
        } catch (InterruptedException x) {}
    }
}
```

b. This class is an inner class to Counter:

```
class CounterBehavior implements Runnable {
    public void run() {
        for (int i = 1; i <= 100; i++);
            try {
                System.out.println(i);
                Thread.sleep(1000);
            } catch (InterruptedException x) {}
```

```
          }
      }
  }
```

     c. This class is a static inner class to Counter:

```
static class CounterBehavior implements Runnable {
    public void run() {
        try {
            for (int i = 1; i <= 100; i++) {
                System.out.println(i);
                Thread.sleep(1000);
            }
        } catch (InterruptedException x) {}
    }
}
```

Answers to Exam Questions

1. **a, b, c, d,** and **e.** All the answers are correct. An inner class can access the variables and methods of an enclosing class no matter what their access control (even private).

2. **d.** The OutputStreamWriter parameters should be an output stream and the encoding to use.

3. **e.** The other answers are either partial answers or won't compile.

4. **a.** Variable width fonts are based on the average of the letters when specifying the width.

5. **c** and **e.** c and e are the only correct answers. b is a concrete class all right, but it does not implement the interface.

6. System.out.println(evt.getX());

7. mybutton = (Button)evt.getComponent();

8. ActionListener

9. **c.** b1 and b2 are different objects, but the Boolean class overrides the equals() test to return true if the two objects being compared have the same boolean value.

10. **a, c, d,** and **e.** b is not correct, because you cannot add an ActionListener to a TextArea. (You can add an ActionListener to a TextField, however.)

11. **a, c,** and **d.** Note that even with a return statement at the end of the catch block, the finally block is still executed.

12. MouseEvent

13. **b** and **e.** It is perfectly valid to put the default case first. Since there is no break statement at the end of the default, the 'a' case is always run if there is no match for 'a' or 'b.'

14. throws

15. **c.** c is the only correct answer. The entries in an array of objects all are set to null if no explicit value is given.

16. **d.** Even though there is a static variable named myArg, the local variable takes precedence.

17. **b.** a, c, d, and e are not valid. b is the only valid declaration (even though we've used the parameter name string rather than the usual args).

18. **a** and **c.** a and c are illegal. Note that e is legal: a variable can start with an under-score. Therefore, a variable does not have to contain any letters at all.

19. args[1]

20. **a, b,** and **c.** The answers d and e are not valid for TextField objects.

21. **a** and **c.** a and c are the correct answers. The answer b is an option, but it does not have to be so—RunHandler could extend Thread, which would then indicate that it implements the Runnable interface—but it does not need to extend Thread to implement Runnable.

22. **c.** c is the only correct answer.

23. super();

24. **a.** The value of 4 & 7 can be seen clearly as binary digits:
100 &
111
—
100
or 4

25. **b.** b is correct.

26. s.indexOf('C');

27. **d.** d is the only correct answer. There is a method called drawRect()0 that draws the outline of a rectangle.

28. **c, e,** and **f.** c, e, and f describe this applet accurately.

29. **b** and **f.** b and f are the correct answers.

30. **d.** The method in the inner class changes the entries in the array, because objects are passed by reference (nonobjects are passed by value).

31. **e.** Note that there is no real constructor: what appears to be a constructor is really a method, because it specifies a return type (void). A real constructor does not have a return type. Hence, s is never initialized, and so null appears in the standard output.

32. **a.** a is the only correct answer.

33. **c** and **d.** c and d are correct. The package statement must come first, and import second. After that, classes can be declared in any order. (There can only be one public class per source file.)

34. **a, c,** and **d.** The default value for a floating-point number is a double. Since a double is greater precision than a float, a floating-point constant assigned to a float data type must be cast or specified as a float by appending the number with an F.

35. String[] s = {"a", "b", "c"};

36. **b.** temp is truncated to 3. The result of 3 % 2 is 1.

37. **a.** The problem is in 5 | 2. An if() expression must resolve to true or false.

38. List l = new List(5, true);

39. **d.** Try it and see!

40. **b.** b is the only correct answer.

41. **c.** setVisible(false);

42. **a.** This code does not compile because there is no this variable in the static main() method to pass to the Thread's constructor.

43. **b** and **c.** b and c are both correct.

44. **d.** This code is perfectly fine, and Second can access the static variable in its superclass.

45. **b.** This could be made to compile by making class B static, or by creating class B from an instance method.

46. **b.** This code does not compile! Because the label two: is not associated with a loop.

47. **a, b,** and **c.** a, b, and c are all correct.

48. **d.** Math.floor(3.2) is 3, so the first if() expression yields false, taking us to the final else clause.

49. new InputStreamReader(mystream, "8859-5");

50. **c.** Why? Because even though we've cast the Boolean objects to be of type Object, the method invoked still goes to the actual object type, which is Boolean. So, as is the case here, equals() will return true in the case of Boolean objects assigned to the same boolean value.

51. **b.** The button appears centered in the Applet. Try it!

52. **a.** a is the only correct answer here.

53. **d** is correct because B's constructor implicitly calls A's no-args constructor, and such a constructor is not defined.

54. **c** and **d.** Both c and d are correct.

55. **b, c,** and **d.** A try block does not need to be followed by a catch block—as long as it is followed by a finally block, so answer a is not correct.

56. **a** and **c.** Instantiating an inner class doesn't imply anything about constructors of the outer class, unless the inner class is derived from the outer class. Thus, both a and c are valid options.

57. **b.** b is the only correct answer. a, c, and d are definitely false. For e, one common construct is to invoke wait() in a while loop, but it is not necessary to invoke notify() or wait() in a while loop.

58. **a** and **c.** b is definitely not correct. a and c are anonymous inner classes that implement Runnable.

59. **d.** The value of 4 | 7 can be seen clearly as binary digits:

    100 |

    111

    —

    111

    or 7

60. **c.** c is the only correct answer. A static inner class can be instantiated from static methods of the enclosing class. b is not correct because the inner class is needed in main(), where there is no instance of the enclosing class (Counter).

PART II

Studying for
The Developer's Exam

Developer Exam Roadmap

In this chapter, we'll introduce the topics covered in the Sun Certified Developer exam for Java 2 Platform (Exam number 310-027). The Developer exam consists of two parts:

• Programming assignment

• Short-answer essay exam

The programming assignment asks you to develop part of an application. The short-answer essay exam asks you questions about the coding assignment.

A Quick Overview

As shown in Figure 24-1, your path to developer certification starts with taking the Programmer exam. This is exam number 310-025. If you pass, you can proudly call yourself a Sun Certified Java Programmer. To get started on the path to becoming a Sun Certified Java Developer, you must purchase the programmer assignment, exam number CX-310-252A, from Sun Educational Services. In the United States, you can purchase an assignment by calling 1-800-422-8020. Outside the United States, check out the Web site at **http://suned.sun.com/** for additional phone numbers.

After you purchase the assignment, you will be notified that you can download the programming assignment. Notification should take place within 24-hours after payment. The assignment is obtained from Sun's My Certification database. You log on to the My Certification database (**http://www.galton.com/~sun/**) using the student ID assigned by Sylvan Prometric when you took the Programmer exam. You'll create a password the first time you log in.

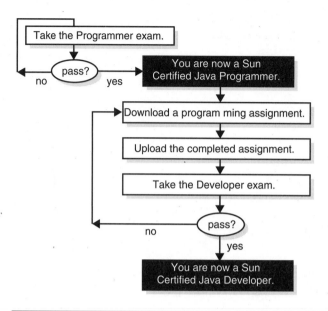

Figure 24-1 The steps to developer certification

Once logged on, you can download the programming assignment that must be completed as part of Developer certification. The programming assignment consists of a complete set of specifications that you must implement. Some code is already completed for you. You can do the assignment as your schedule allows, and upload it to the My Certification database after you have finished. You will later receive a message confirming receipt of the assignment.

Sun does not review your assignment until you complete the essay examination. Prior to taking the exam, you must call Sun and buy a voucher (or buy or get a voucher from your company, which has in turn purchased a voucher through Sun). Afterward you can register for the test by calling Sylvan Prometric. Their number is 1-800-795-3926. Or you can register online at **www.2test.com.** The essay exam consists of 5 to 10 short-answer questions regarding the assignment. These questions ask you to justify your design choices.

Concepts You Should Know Before Getting Started

The Sun Certified Developer exam is designed to test your knowledge of Java software development. You'll need to be intimately familiar with the Java language and the Java 2

API to complete and pass the assignment. The specific concepts and technologies covered by the exam include

- Client-server application design
- Interface design
- Error handling
- Event handling
- I/O streams
- Java Swing
- JDBC
- Multithreading
- Object serialization
- RMI
- TCP/IP networking
- javadoc

The remaining chapters in this part of the book provide an overview of key concepts that haven't been covered previously. For specifics on multithreading, error handling, event handling, I/O streams, and object serialization, you should refer to Chapters 15, 14, 20, 17, and 11 respectively.

The Programming Assignment

The programming assignment is the first part of the exam. Once you've paid for it, you'll be notified that you have permission to download the programming assignment from the Sun Educational Services Database. In the programming assignment Jar file, you'll find the following:

- A document that introduces the assignment and provides an index
- Source code that serves as a starting point for the assignment
- A flat text data file that you must convert into the required format for use in the assignment

These files contain different programs and assignments for different candidates. The idea is that multiple candidates won't be able to collaborate because of this. The instructions provided in the documentation leave gaps intentionally so that candidates must make and document design decisions. The programming assignment requires the following features:

- A graphical user interface for viewing information
- Communications functionality to connect the user interface with the database
- Extensions to the database to support a more flexible search and record-locking mechanism
- Network server functionality for the database systems
- Data conversion to prepare a flat text file for use in the database

The instructions you'll see from Sun are a bit more specific, such as:

1. Write an application program in Java. The application requires the following:

   A. A graphical user interface demonstrating good principles of design

   B. A network connection, using a specified protocol, to connect to an information server which supplies the data for display in the user interface

   C. A network server, which connects to a previously specified Java database

   D. A database, created by extending the functionality of a previously written piece of code, for which only limited documentation is available

2. List a number of the main choices to be made during the implementation of the above.

3. List a number of the main advantages and disadvantages of each of those choices.

4. Briefly justify choices made in terms of the comparison of design and implementation objectives with the advantages and disadvantages of each.

Feedback on passing the Developer programming assignment and exam is not immediate, because there are no absolute right or wrong answers. The programming is graded based on a set of criteria that includes good object-oriented design, documentation, efficiency, and style. Follow the directions that come with the programming assignment as exactly as possible.

While the examiner does grade the assignment for correct operation, the actual grade you receive is based on many factors. These factors are graded on a point system with a total of 155 points possible. The factors and the possible points include the following:

- Overall ease of use and user-friendliness of the assignment (15 points).

- Clarity and maintainability of the design and implementation. The code should be designed so that it can be easily understood and modified without requiring global changes (7 points).

- Consistent and logical approach to the design implementation in which the best algorithms are used and the solution is well thought out (20 points).

- Consistent coding style, naming conventions, and indentation (15 points).

- Documentation of nonobvious aspects of source code and not excessively commenting obvious aspects of code; use of Javadoc source documentation, user documentation, and a README file (6 points).

- Extensions to the database to support standard, flexible search algorithm (8 points).

- Implements proper error-handling in the server and network interface (6 points).

- Layout of the user interface with proper use of graphical user interfaces and proper implementation of event handling (20 points).

- Object-oriented design with appropriate use of standard elements and design patterns (6 points).

- Proper use of record locking in the database (15 points).

- Proper use of thread-safe design in the server and network interface (8 points).

- Satisfies the data conversion requirements (10 points).

- Use of standard classes and interfaces from the Java 2 API rather than custom classes and interfaces (5 points).

- Use of standard Java exception handling facilities and the ability to communicate errors to users without the program exiting abnormally (10 points).

As you work through the assignment, you'll want to refer to this list periodically. Although the exact weighting of a specific point may change over time, the relative importance of various points should remain consistent.

The programming assignment and exam are graded by professionals outside of Sun —consultants in the business of providing high-level Java services. Sun Educational Services doesn't want to be accused of having a vested interest in who passes and fails, so they send this job out. However, if there's a borderline case, the exam might go back into JavaSoft. JavaSoft engineers will then grade the assignment and test and act as a moderator.

Sun will contact you to let you know the results. You should allow 30 days for the grading to be completed.

The Essay Exam

You should sign up for the essay exam once you have completed and uploaded your programming assignment. You must be sure you pass the automated tests based on the test harness, because you'll fail immediately if you submit code that fails the test harness. There are instructions in the programming assignment that explain how to write your code so that the test harness can interact with it and perform its tests.

The essay exam consists of five to ten short-answer essay questions. You have 90 minutes to answer them. These questions ask you to discuss what you did on the programming assignment and to justify your design decisions. There are no absolute right or wrong answers. The people grading your assignment and the exam will look for your understanding of the issues involved.

As with the Programmer certification, the written portion of the Developer certification is administered on PCs by a company called Sylvan Prometric. They have test centers all over the United States and the world. When you show up, you sign in, you identify yourself by showing two forms of ID (one with a picture, and both with signatures), and then you take the test at your scheduled time.

You can't bring any paper into or out of the testing room. They don't want you taking a crib sheet in with you or writing out test questions during the test. (Of course, after you leave the testing area, you can try to recall as many questions as possible. However, be aware that the tests are copyrighted, so you can't publish the questions, make copies of them, and so on.)

You also can't bring in any pagers or cellular phones. After all, in this day and age, it would be a simple matter to have your local Java guru talk you through the test.

Even though you can't take any paper in with you, the people at Sylvan Prometric do give you either some scratch paper or a small marker board and a marker to help you work out answers.

Your answers should be clear, concise, and well thought out. You'll need to justify your answers based on the assignment, so you should thoroughly review everything you've done on the assignment before taking the essay exam. When you complete the exam, you won't know whether you've passed or not (although you might have a good feel for how things went). You'll be notified by Sun when the grading is completed.

How to Sign Up For and Take the Exams

You must call Sun and buy a voucher (or buy or get a voucher from your company, which has in turn purchased a voucher through Sun). The idea behind the voucher system is that your company may offer free vouchers or at a discount if they are encouraging you to become certified.

The main number for Sun Educational Services in the United States is 1-800-422-8020. Listen to the options from the phone menu and make sure you tell them what test you want to sign up for. Outside the United States, check out the Web site at **http://suned.sun.com/** for additional phone numbers.

The good people at Sun will ask for a credit card to pay for the voucher. You have to wait for the voucher to arrive before you can sign up for the test. They send the vouchers by FedEx, so you'll get any vouchers by the next business day. Once you get it, don't misplace it—it's like money. You can't replace them and if you drop it on the street, that's that. Someone can pick it up and go take a Java test.

The voucher is supposed to be good for up to one year after you purchase it. However, mine came with an expiration date set to seven months after the purchase. Voucher expiration dates cannot be extended. However—here's the loophole—after you sign up for a testing appointment, you can extend the appointment for up to one year.

You may have your voucher, but you're not done yet. You've still got to register for the test. You can do this by calling Sylvan Prometric. Their number is 1-800-795-EXAM. (I know, I hate dialing by letters, too: their number in numbers is 1-800-795-3926.)

You'll have to give them your Social Security number for identification, and they'll ask you some questions, such as which company you're with, your phone number, and your address. Then they'll schedule you for a test.

When they schedule you, they'll find a time that's convenient for you to visit one of their testing centers. You need to be there on time, because you can't stay past your stop time—the computer will shut off! What they do is distribute the test electronically to the test center you'll be at. According to a person I spoke with at Sylvan, you must be there when the test is ready to go.

If you miss your schedule time, and if they can fit you in the next day and that's what you want, they'll do their best to accommodate you. The only possible problem might be that a space is not available at the test center closest to you.

Just so that your friendly neighborhood Java expert doesn't show up in your place as a ringer, you need to bring two forms of ID, one of which must be a photo ID.

If you want to postpone for some reason—if you're panicking or you just plum can't make it—you can do so until the day before the test.

How to Acquire the Programming Assignment for the Developer Test

After you've taken and passed the Programmer exam, you can obtain the programming assignment that's part of Developer certification. You obtain the assignment by

downloading it from the My Certification database. Go to: **http://www.galton.com/**
~sun/ and enter your last name and Social Security number (which is your Sylvan student ID). You should allow at least a week after passing the exam for Sylvan to let Sun
know that you passed, and for Sun to update their server. Until then, the server will say
"User not found." Don't worry; the records will be updated as soon as they can get to
them. If you've allowed a week to go by and it really looks like the server is not being
updated, you can call the main numbers at Sun Educational Services, explain the situation, and they'll patch you through to someone who can help you.

After your record has been updated, entering your last name and student ID will
bring you to a screen that displays your current status in the testing cycle. If you have
passed the Programmer exam, you'll see a button on the bottom of the screen that says
"Download assignment." Go ahead and click that for instructions on how to access the
assignment.

Once you've downloaded the archive file that contains the assignment, you'll see a
new button back on the page you just came from. This button reads "Upload assignment." When you're all done, you'll come back here, click this button, and upload your
work to Sun.

You'll get a number of files, including a PostScript document, a Word for Windows
document, and an RTF (Rich Text Format) document, all containing the same instructions. There are .gif images that show some design diagrams, as well as a number of
source and class files that you'll use as part of your programming assignment.

The first thing you should do, even before reading the documents, is to make backups of everything. The test is customized for you, and you need to be able to get back
to what you downloaded if something goes wrong, or if you want to start over again.

Only after you complete this programming assignment and sign up for the Developer exam can you submit your assignment for grading. You submit the assignment by
uploading it through the download Web site.

All of the programming assignments are marked very carefully and it takes time to
ensure the quality and consistency of this process.

Strategies for Approaching
the Developer Assignment

First and foremost, give yourself time—a few days, if not a week or more. The assignment is long and complicated. Think about the issues. Read the design document two,
three, or four times. Print it out and mark it up. Make sketches.

After you've thought about the design for a while, create the user interface. Seeing a user interface can make the assignment more tangible. This is especially true if you feel overwhelmed. You'll begin to realize which pieces have to connect with which other pieces. What's more, it's comforting to have part of it done and working.

Look over the source code that comes with the assignment. That can really help you figure out what is already done for you and what you've got to write yourself.

One of the wonderful things about this assignment is a test harness that's distributed with the assignment. You can run this test harness to see if your program is working well enough to submit. Passing the test harness can go a long way to making you feel comfortable with your work.

Make backups of the database files before you start testing, because, depending on your particular version of the assignment, you might start changing things.

Developing with Java

Objectives for This Chapter

- Indent your code according to common practice.
- Comment only the nonobvious lines.
- Use consistent coding style.
- Handle errors appropriately.
- Use javadoc-style comments.
- Define abstract classes where appropriate.
- Use interfaces where appropriate.
- Arrange classes into packages.
- Create well-defined APIs for your classes.

At this point, you've reviewed all of the basics of the Java language. If you've already taken the Sun Certified Java Programmer test and passed, congratulations. If you've tried the test and failed, use the experience to focus your studying on those areas you were least certain about. Use this book's objectives to help you, and work through all the exercises. Make up your own test questions based on the samples in this book and what you can remember from the exams. Sometimes you'll come up with a question that you stump yourself with. Now is the time to do so, because you can look up the answer and write programs to verify your answers—before you get into the testing room. The fun part comes after you've passed the Programmer exam. After you've fought through the first test, it's time become a Sun Certified Java Developer.

Developer certification involves two stages: completing a programming assignment (which is really the heart of it), and then answering questions about your design. Because the programming assignment is the focus, the chapters in this section concentrate on the skills you need to complete this assignment. In this part of the book, you'll work on expanding your basic programming knowledge and learning how to implement what you know to write sophisticated programs.

The assignment is graded partly on good object-oriented programming techniques, especially concerning clarity of design. It's important to use abstract classes, interfaces, and packages correctly. The person who grades your programming assignment gives you points based on your programming style and the comments you supply. This does not mean you should provide a page of comments for each method you write—far from it. It means you must program in the style that your grader expects. This chapter will show you what that is.

Styles and Conventions

Every programmer knows how to indent code so that all code in a block is easy to spot. Regardless of how many spaces you indent compared to the next programmer, your main objective, whatever your style, is to be consistent.

Beware of some integrated development environments (IDEs) with their own code editors. Some of these automatically indent code for you, and you're probably apt to use the tab key in these editors. That's fine, but take a look at your code using a plain ASCII editor at some point. You might find that what looks good in the editor with your IDE doesn't look so hot with another editor. If this is the case, you might want to think about changing your tabs to spaces and making sure that no matter what editor the examiners use to view your program, it's going to look the way you intended.

Identifiers

Again, you can use any style you would like, but be consistent. A common practice is to make your class names start with a capital letter and your variable and method names start with a lower-case letter. Usually, identifiers that are really multiple words—like "max value" and "the applet"—start with a small letter but have a capital at the start of each word, such as maxValue and theApplet.

Another common practice is to make constants—usually defined as public static final—all upper-case and connect words with an underscore, as in MAX_VALUE and THE_APPLET.

Names also are usually selfdocumenting. Unless it's a temporary variable, you might want to use descriptive names like maxValue instead of m, for example. However, it's common to name temporary variables (such as loop indexes or nested user interface objects such as panels) with just a letter or two.

TIP: If you have a style you're comfortable with now, don't change it just for this programming assignment. If you do, it might cause you to inadvertently mix styles, and that's what you're trying to avoid.

Comments

Most programmers hate documentation. If you do too, this next piece of advice might not apply to you. I am one of those who like comments; I feel the more, the better. However, be aware: you'll lose points if you put in excessive comments. In particular, you should not comment lines that essentially document themselves. You should only include comments for those lines that are tricky or not immediately obvious.

Error Handling

Sometimes it's easy to fall into a trap in which you let your application take a guess at what to do, even when it encounters an unexpected situation. For example, consider these switch-case statements:

```
switch (userSelection) {
  case MOVE: moveItem(); break;
  case DELETE: deleteItem(); break;
}
```

What if userSelection is not equal to either MOVE or DELETE? Should you do nothing? Or perhaps you should add a default case:

```
switch (userSelection) {
  case MOVE: moveItem(); break;
  case DELETE: deleteItem(); break;
  default: editItem();
}
```

In this case, what you should do depends on whether userSelection is supposed to absolutely, positively equal either MOVE or DELETE. If it is but doesn't equal either one, then this is a very serious problem. You may even want to throw an exception:

```
switch (userSelection) {
  case MOVE: moveItem(); break;
  case DELETE: deleteItem(); break;
  default: throw
    new UserSelectionException("Should be move or delete");
}
```

NOTE: We have assumed there is a class defined for this application called UserSelectionException.

It might be tempting to throw an unchecked exception rather than make your own exception class. For example, you might think you could throw NumberFormatException or ArithmeticException if a number is not in the right format or if you are about to divide by 0. The problem is that you should never throw an unchecked exception from your own code. As we reviewed in Chapter 14, you should only throw checked exceptions—exceptions which must be caught.

Another problem with throwing a generic, unchecked exception is that it does not fully identify the application-specific problem. Perhaps the problem with the number not being in the right format is a protocol error. It might make better sense to create a new class called ProtocolException and throw that when an error arises. By supplying a message for this object before you throw it, your exception handler can display this message to help with debugging.

When you handle the error, also give some thought about what it is you would like to do in your catch block. Should you print out a debugging message, end the application, or take a guess as to what to do? You might want to do something differently each time, but similar problems should be handled in similar ways. Remember your credo: be consistent.

Java's Documentation Problem

In C/C++, documentation is often placed into header files. This is because a header file contains the function definitions and variables shared by more than one program in an application. Since this file is shared by any program that needs it, the header file is the right place to put these comments. A great advantage of this approach is that a developer can distribute only the binary files for the actual program to keep the implementation hidden or the developer can distribute the header files as well as the binary files to provide all the public documentation for the binary files, as well as means for using them.

This approach does not even begin to work in Java. Why? Because there are no header files. There are no declarations of methods separate from their implementation (unless you've defined an interface or abstract method). All methods are implemented where they are declared. This might appear to mean that distributing documentation concerning how to use a Java package would run the risk of one of two extremes:

- Distribute the source code that contains the in-line documentation for the public classes, variables, and methods.

- Keep the documentation in separate files, far away from the original source, and potentially fall out of sync with the code.

Happily, the JDK provides relief from both of these port choices by supplying a special utility called javadoc. This utility pulls out the important information concerning your classes, variables, and methods, and automatically generates great-looking documentation. The advantage of this approach is that you can run javadoc whenever you want and generate new documentation that reflects the current state of your code.

javadoc

When you run javadoc and pass it the name of a class or package, javadoc generates documentation in HTML format for all of your public classes, and your public and protected variables and methods.

You're no doubt familiar with the HTML format that javadoc generates, because this is the same format that the API files are published in. Javadoc creates an HTML file for each class. Each HTML file lists the fields, the constructors, and then the methods for a class. Javadoc also places a class hierarchy at the top of the HTML file and provides an index to the fields, constructors, and methods after that. All you have to do to generate this documentation is run the command javadoc and place the resulting HTML files into the same directory as the API files for the JDK.

Javadoc will generate four types of files:

- **packages.html** A listing of each package you generated documentation for and the class they contain.

- **AllNames.html** An alphabetical index of all of your method and variable names.

- **tree.html** A listing of all of the classes you've generated documentation for and where these fit into the class hierarchy, going all the way back to java.lang.Object.

- **classname.html** Documentation for that class.

Naturally, all of these files contain hypertext links to the classes, methods, and variables they refer to, including Java's own classes.

Helping javadoc

In addition to the two common ways of writing a comment:

```
//everything to the end of the line is a comment
```

and

```
/* everything in here is a comment */
```

java also defines a special third way:

```
/** everything in here is a javadoc comment */
```

By default, this special javadoc comment only has meaning before a public class, or before a public or protected variable or method. You can see javadoc-style comments for private variables or methods if you use the -private option when you run javadoc. With a javadoc comment, you can help javadoc to document your code. For example, here is a simple class definition:

```
public class PrimeNumber {
   private int number;
   private boolean primeVal;

   public int getNumber() {
     return number;
   }
   public void setNumber(int num) {
     number = num;
   }
   public boolean isPrime() {

   /* code to test number */

   return primeVal;

   }
}
```

Javadoc will automatically generate the documentation shown in Figure 25-1 and Figure 25-2 (these show the top half and bottom half of a Web browser displaying the file that javadoc generated).

This is fine as far as it goes. What you'd really like to do is add some of your own comments to this documentation. By adding documentation to this class using special javadoc comments, like this:

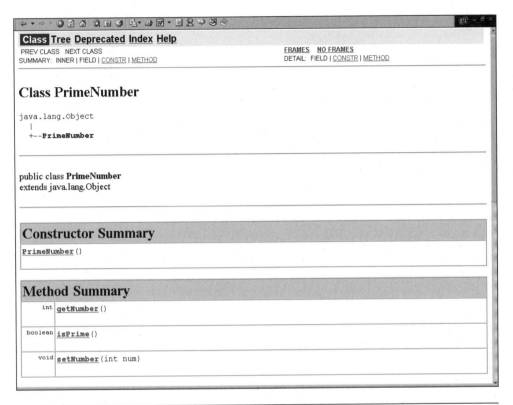

Figure 25-1   The javadoc-generated index

```java
/**
 * Identify a number as prime or not prime.
 */
public class PrimeNumber {
  private int number;
  private boolean primeVal;
  /** Retrieve the number. */
  public int getNumber() {
    return number;
  }
  /** Set the number. */
  public void setNumber(int num) {
    number = num;
  }
  /** Test whether the number is a prime. */
  public boolean isPrime() {
```

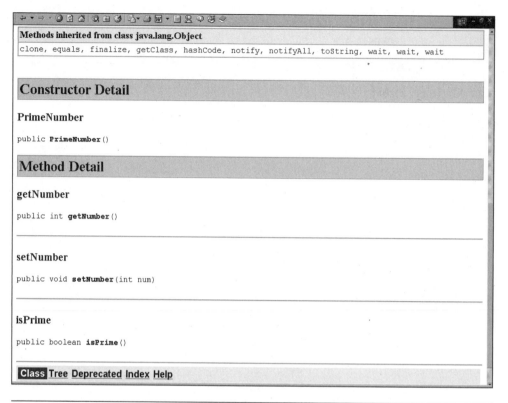

Figure 25-2   The javadoc-generated method documentation

```
/* code to test number */

return primeVal;

    }
}
```

you can generate the documentation shown in Figure 25-3 and Figure 25-4.

javadoc Tags

You can also use special tags within your javadoc comments. javadoc seeks out these tags and creates special documentation based on them. First, let's look at the tags. Then I'll show some examples of how to use them and what their resulting documentation looks like.

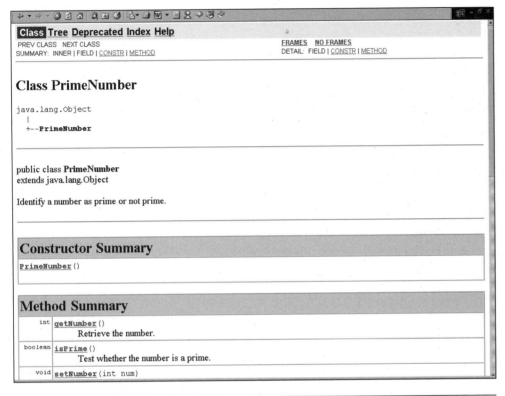

Figure 25-3 The javadoc index, with comments

Variables

When you define a variable, you can use an @see tag to reference a different object or method. There are a few different versions of this tag. First, here's the format for @see to refer to a class:

```
@see classname
```

The classname can simply be the class's name if the class is in the same package as the class defining the comment. The classname can also be fully qualified if it's in a different package. For example, if Lightning is the name of a class, you can write:

```
@see Lightning
```

or

```
@see phenomenon.natural.Lightning
```

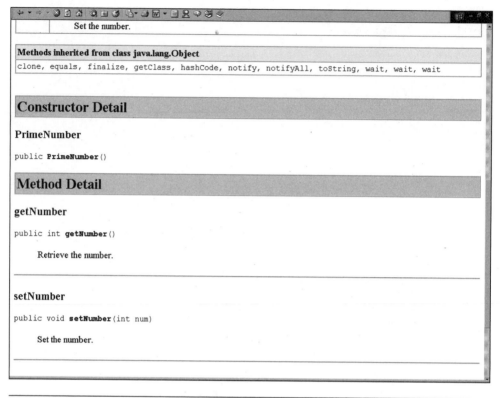

Figure 25-4 The javadoc methods, with comments

You can also reference a method name using the @see tag by writing:

```
@see classname#methodname
```

For example, you might write:

```
@see Lightning#flash
```

As before, you can also fully qualify the class name. The @see tag can refer to a package just like it can refer to a class, method or other API. Other forms of the @see tag use labels and hypertext links:

```
@see name label
@see <a href="linkURL">Link title</a>
```

You can also use @link to create inline text links:

```
{@link APIName label}
```

Now, instead of the link appearing under the See Also heading, the link will be in the text. Note that opening and closing braces are required for the @link tag.

Classes

You can use any of these @see tags with classes. There are also two other tags you can use with the class that are useful only with special keywords passed to javadoc. These tags are @version and @author. In all cases, the text following a particular tag can go over multiple lines.

```
@version anytext
```

With @version you would typically put a version number following this tag, such as 1.0 or 2.1:

```
@version 1.0
@author anytext
```

With @author, you would normally place your name after this tag, as in:

```
@author Albert Einstein
```

To see these @version and @author values in the documentation, you must use the options:

```
-author -version
```

when you invoke javadoc, as in:

```
javadoc -author -version MyClass.java
```

Methods

Methods can use any of the @see tags. In addition, there are four other tags that document the method's signature: @return, @param, @exception, and @throws. In all cases, the text following a particular tag can go over multiple lines.

```
@return anytext
```

For example, you might write:

```
@return a true or false value indicating whether number is prime
@param paramname anytext
```

For example, you might write:

```
@param number a number to test to see if it is a prime or not
@exception exceptionname anytext
```

For example, you might write:

```
@exception ProtocolException Throws this exception when the client
has not supplied data following the agreed-upon protocol
@throws exceptionname anytext
```

The @throws tag serves the same purpose as @exception. The tag is added for convenience since throws is a Java keyword.

Rules for Using javadoc Comments and Tags

A typical javadoc comment and set of javadoc tags follows this format:

```
/**
 * Summary comment line
 * Any number of additional comment lines
 * this could even include HTML
 * @tag any number of lines provided text for this tag
 */
```

There's no need to have a row of asterisks along the left side of the comments like this, but you'll see this done in most Java programs. However, it's perfectly acceptable to also write:

```
/**
    Summary comment line
    Any number of additional comment lines
    this could even include HTML
    @tag any number of lines provided text for this tag
 */
```

Notice that the first line in a javadoc comment is special. It is a summary line, and javadoc uses this in its indices. For example, the method index at the top of the class's HTML file displays this one sentence description, as does the index file AllNames.html for each method and variable. Following this summary line, you can include any number of lines you'd like to. javadoc will strip away any leading spaces (even any leading asterisk as in the first comment sample above), and will wrap the text as appropriate.

Any HTML tags it finds it will use as is, so that you can format your documentation with references, links, bold or italic styles, or code snippets.

Always place all of your tags at the end of your javadoc comments. Since tags can be spread over multiple lines, the only way for javadoc to identify the end of a tag is when it hits the start of a new one.

Examples of javadoc Comments and Tags

Here is an example of class documentation for a class called Tester:

```
/**
 * Test machine for objects.
 * This class tests objects for performance and accuracy
 * by executing standard tests.
 * @see CanBeTested
 * @version 1.0
 * @author William Stanek
 */
public class Tester { . . . }
```

Javadoc will generate the display in Figure 25-5 based on this.

Similarly, based on the following method documentation:

```
/**
 * Performs the standard text.
 * Invokes test() for the object to be tested and informs
 * this method how much testing should be performed.
 * @return A String that explains the results of the test
 * @param target The debug level
 * @see CanBeTested
 */
public String runTest(int debugLevel) { . . . }
```

Javadoc will generate the html file shown in Figure 25-6.

And for this variable documentation:

```
/** Debug output level.
 * @see CanBeTested
 */
public int debugLevel;
```

Javadoc will generate the html file shown in Figure 25-7.

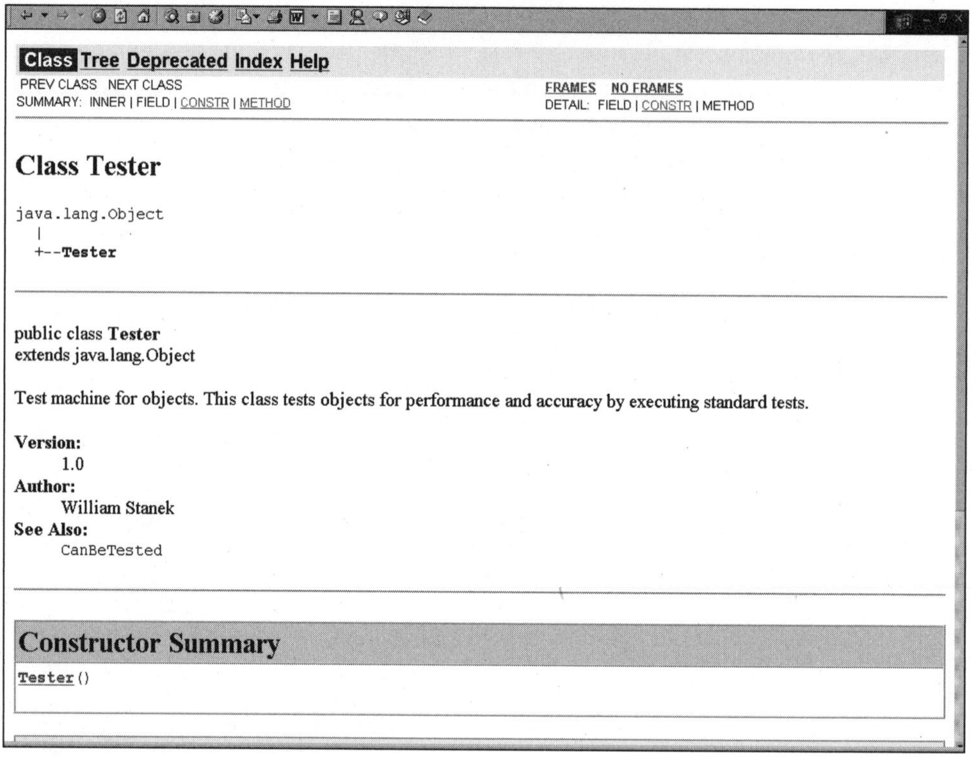
Class Tree Deprecated Index Help
PREV CLASS NEXT CLASS
SUMMARY: INNER | FIELD | CONSTR | METHOD
FRAMES NO FRAMES
DETAIL: FIELD | CONSTR | METHOD
Class Tester
java.lang.Object
|
+--Tester
public class Tester
extends java.lang.Object
Test machine for objects. This class tests objects for performance and accuracy by executing standard tests.
Version:
1.0
Author:
William Stanek
See Also:
CanBeTested
Constructor Summary
Tester()

Figure 25-5 Class documentation

Abstract Classes

Defining an abstract class forces you and other developers to make clear choices. We've already covered abstract classes briefly at the end of Chapter 11, but we wanted to say a word about their role in building an API.

The big difference between an abstract class and a superclass that defines no-op stubs for its methods is that the abstract class forces you and other programmers to use your set of APIs in a particular way. Whereas a programmer can directly instantiate a concrete superclass, a programmer has no such option with an abstract class; he or she must either instantiate a predefined subclass or create her own subclass to instantiate.

This can help clarify your design. For example, imagine a class called Transaction that is to be used in a home banking application. This class has two subclasses: Deposit and Withdrawal. It might make no sense to create an instance of Transaction—a customer

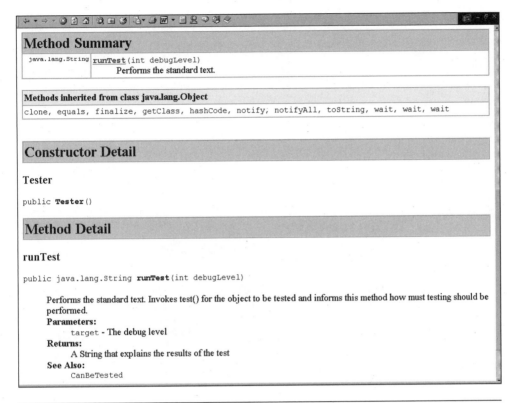

Figure 25-6   Method documentation

doesn't generically announce to a bank teller, "I want to make a transaction," but rather, "I want to make a withdrawal," or "I want to make a deposit." (If a customer does say "I want to make a transaction," the teller will ask him to clarify his intentions.)

You can make your desire for programmers to use only a Deposit or Withdrawal class clear in your design by making Transaction abstract. Now, programmers using your APIs know your intention—you would like them to be specific about the type of transaction they want to perform.

TIP: You know that if you define any abstract methods, you need to make the class abstract. What if you don't have any abstract methods but you still want to make the class abstract? You can do this — just use the abstract keyword for the class. Then, any subclasses are automatically concrete classes (unless, of course, they in turn are declared as abstract).

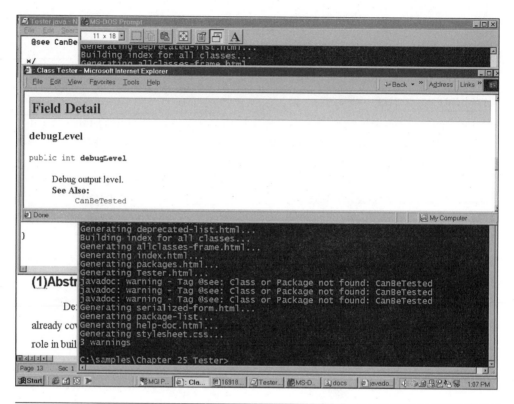

Figure 25-7 Variable documentation

Interfaces

Interfaces define constants and method signatures. Interfaces are not like abstract classes where all of the methods are declared as abstract—interfaces are not classes. Instead, they define, as their name implies, an interface for you to implement.

So what good are they? Why not just define methods in a class rather than fooling around with interfaces? The answer is that interfaces clean up your APIs. Interfaces allow you, as the developer, to make clear to other developers which sets of behavior belong together. Interfaces also help you enforce the proper use of your API.

Grouping Behavior

Identifying related behavior in one place is ideal for an interface. You can find a great example of this in Java 1.1, where interfaces identify related event methods. As one example, an interface called FocusListener defines focusGained() and focusLost(). It's clear that the API expects developers to supply behavior for these two methods to be able to handle focus events.

Enforcing Your API

Because Java can identify classes that implement interfaces by using instanceof, interfaces can also enforce an API. Continuing with the FocusListener example, you must use an object whose class provides the methods focusGained() and focusLost() when you want to handle focus events. To handle focus events, you must register your object as a focus listener by using addFocusListener(). By declaring the parameter in this method to be an instance of type FocusListener, the Java Virtual Machine, compiler, and language, working in conjunction, will not let you pass an object whose class does not properly implement FocusListener.

Identifying Intent

Interfaces can also be used to tag a class. For example, the Cloneable interface does not declare any method; there's nothing for implementers to implement. Instead, any class identified as an instanceof Cloneable lets the Object class's clone() method know that this class can be cloned. The Cloneable interface merely identifies the developer's intent; it does not make the developer implement any behavior.

Exercise 25.1

Image that you have developed a class named Tester that tests other objects. Perhaps it has a testObject() method that, given the name of the object to test, invokes that object's test() method and displays the String results in the standard output.

Naturally, you would like to use any kind of object with your Tester class. How can you define the API so that this will all work well?

Packages

Creating packages can help you clean up your APIs in two important ways:

- You can better restrict access to methods and variables.
- You can define subsystems.

Creating Packages

Chapter 12 already covered how to create packages and place classes inside them. Here's a quick review. To tell the compiler the classes in a particular source file belong in a package, write the keyword package as the first line in your source file, followed by the package name, as in:

```
package MyUtils.MyPackage;
```

To import public classes defined in other packages, specify which packages or specific classes you want to import by writing the keyword import followed by the package or class names, as in:

```
import MyUtils.MyPackage.Average;
import MyUtils.OtherPackage.*;
```

Java will expect your packages to be in a directory structure in which each dot (.) defines a new subdirectory.

Restricting Access

Here's a quick review of restricting access to members. First of all, as we reviewed in Chapter 11, only a public class can be accessed outside of the packages it is defined in. As you also know, there are four ways to specify access control for a class member: you can use the keyword public, protected, or private, or you can leave off an access control keyword and accept the default—public and private have the same effect regardless of whether or not the classes you've defined are in the same package. However, protected and the default are greatly affected by multiple packages.

If all of your classes are in the same package (including the default package), they can access each others' members as long as those members are declared as protected or have no access control specifier (or are declared as public). Sometimes this is what you want. For example, a small class that contains some simple utility methods only meant for use by other classes in its package could restrict outside classes from invoking these methods by leaving off any access control keywords. But keep in mind that a lack of access control keywords should never stem from laziness; it should be your design intent. If it is appropriate only for the class defining a member to access that member, make that member private.

If it is possible that some other package will define a subclass for a class you have defined, and in general you would like subclasses of your class to be able to access specific members in your class, you can give those specific members the protected keyword.

Defining Subsystems

Packages clean up your design by allowing you to think of your application as a collection of cooperating subsystems. You can think of a subsystem as a collection of related classes that accomplish a specific design goal—that fill in one box in a drawing of your application's architecture.

For example, imagine you are creating a database client/server application. You might have a database, a database server, a TCP/IP component that runs on the client side, and a user interface for the client. Perhaps the actual data in the database contains information on birds: their songs, migration paths, and egg colors. If you can generalize the pieces of your application, you could conceivably define four different subsystems which fit the boxes shown in Figure 25-8.

In Java, you can define each of these subsystems by creating classes and placing them into packages. Each package would represent one subsystem. Packages allow you to conceive of your application as a machine constructed out of "tinker-toys." On your next project, if you need a database server and a TCP/IP client that, this time, accesses a database of baseball cards, you can just use these packages as-is and plug them into your new application, which might look like Figure 25-9.

You can place your applet or the class with the main() method in a package, as well as any other classes (rather than letting it be placed in the "default" package). Many programmers don't do this, but this can help keep your class files organized. If you

Figure 25-8   The four pieces of a hypothetical database client/server application

Figure 25-9   A new application using old packages

place a class defining main() called MyClass into a package named MyPackage, for example, you can invoke it by writing:

```
java MyPackage.MyClass
```

Exercise 25.2

Consider these two classes, currently defined in the same source file:

```
class Transaction {
  Amount amount;

  void process() {
  }
}

class Amount {
  int dollars;
  int cents;
}
```

Place each of these classes into a different package so that they can still access all of the same fields and methods they can access now. Call the first package banking and the second package currency.

Defining Access Methods

Rather than allowing other classes to access a class's member variables directly, you should make those members private and supply access methods. For example, this class allows anyone to get and set its instance variables:

```
import java.awt.Point;

public class Circle {
    public Point position;
    public int radius;
    public boolean canDelete;
    public boolean canMove;
}
```

This might seem okay, but perhaps you want to make sure the radius is never set to a negative number. What then? What if you want to make canMove and canDelete read-only? With the above definition, you're stuck.

The better way is to provide getter and setter methods for these values. Here's a new class definition that implements the new requirements listed in the previous para-

graph. It's a little longer, but it's much more flexible. It also uses a new Exception subclass called IllegalGeometryException:

```java
import java.awt.Point;

public class Circle {
    private Point position;
    private int radius;
    private boolean canDelete;
    private boolean canMove;

    public Point getPosition() {
        return position;
    }

    public void setPosition(Point p) {
        position = p;
    }

    public int getRadius() {
        return radius;
    }

    public void setRadius(int r) throws IllegalGeometryException {
        if (r < 0)
            throw new IllegalGeometryException();
        radius = r;
    }

    public boolean getMove() {
        return canMove;
    }

    public boolean getDelete() {
        return canDelete;
    }
}

class IllegalGeometryException extends Exception {}
```

Defining access methods for getting and setting values for your classes is good programming practice. First, only allowing other classes to use access methods hides your
class's implementation and makes these other classes much less dependent on your
class's data layout.

For example, let's go back to the Circle class we defined above. If you decided to
change canMove and canDelete into bit flags, your interface would not have to change
at all. getMove() and getDelete() would still return boolean values. However, rather
than returning the value of a boolean field, your method would perform the appropriate & operation to mask the irrelevant bits.

PART II

Second, you can ensure an object's data integrity. Instead of allowing a class to assign arbitrary values to a field, a setter method can verify that the new value makes sense. If it doesn't, it can fix the problem and possibly throw an exception to inform the caller that the operation did not take place—and possibly present an indication why. That's what we did with the radius for the Circle class. Similarly, a getter can make certain that data is in a valid and consistent state before returning this data to the caller.

Third, you have more control over the data in a multithreading environment. For example, you can make your access methods synchronized, so that one thread is not getting or setting the data while another thread manipulates it elsewhere.

 TIP: What if you have a field that contains a Vector object, but some methods might change the values in the Vector? If you want to ensure that no thread in a multithreaded environment accesses the Vector while it's being used, you should use synchronized methods. Here, you make the methods that manipulate the Vector as well as the access method synchronized.

Fourth, you can make a value read-only or write-only if you desire by only defining a getter or setter. We did this above with the canMove and canDelete fields—perhaps they are dependent on the mode the application is in and cannot be set directly.

You can also define a method called isProperty if the property is read-only and this approach makes sense for your code. For example, I could have defined the methods isMovable() and isDeletable() instead of getMove() and getDelete(), but I chose not to because I'm not convinced that "movable" and "deletable" are real words (I know, details, details . . .).

Java 1.1 introduced many getter and setter methods that used to have other inconsistent names or that used to be variables programmers could access directly. You should make sure your own APIs are as clean as Java's.

Exercise 25.3

Consider two class definitions:

```
public class Employee {
    int employeeNumber;
    Amount salary;
}
class Amount {
    int dollars;
    int cents;
}
```

Our intent is to assign an employee number for each employee when the Employee object is created, and we want to number our employees sequentially. Also, we've created an Amount class to eliminate possible problems with rounding for dollars and cents.

There are three possible problems with these classes. First, anyone can set the employee number. This could lead to errors if the numbers are repeated. Second, anyone can access the Employee salary and set the cents amount to something greater than 99. Third, anyone can set either the dollars or cents amount to less than 0.

Modify these classes to clean up their APIs and eliminate these problems.

Answers to the Exercises

Exercise 25.1

You can define an interface, perhaps named CanBeTested, that declares a test() method, as in:

```
public interface CanBeTested {
  public String test();
}
```

Your Tester class can then require an object in its parameter list for testObject() that requires an instance of CanBeTested:

```
public class Tester {
  public void testObject(CanBeTested obj) {
    System.out.println(obj.test());
  }
}
```

Now, looking at testObject(), it's clear you can only use the Tester class if you have an instance of CanBeTested, which means implementing the CanBeTested interface for the classes you wish to test, which means defining a test() method which testObject() will invoke.

Exercise 25.2

Here is the first source file, which we would call Transaction.java:

```
package banking;

import currency.Amount;
```

```
public class Transaction {
   public Amount amount;

   public void process() {
   }
}
```

Here is the second source file, which we would call Amount.java:

```
package currency;

public class Amount {
   public int dollars;
   public int cents;
}
```

There's a cleaner way to write these interfaces that involves using getters and setters, which the next exercise explores.

Exercise 25.3

Another possible solution would be to throw exceptions if the new Amount values were illegal, and to carry over any cents value in excess of 99 into the dollars field:

```
public class Employee {
   private static int nextNumber;

   private int employeeNumber;
   private Amount salary;

   public Employee() {
      employeeNumber = nextNumber++;
   }

   public int getEmployeeNumber() {
      return employeeNumber;
   }

   public Amount getSalary() {
      return salary;
   }
}

class Amount {
   private int dollars;
   private int cents;

   public int getDollars() {
      return dollars;
   }
```

```
    public void setDollars(int d) {
        if (d >= 0)
            dollars = d;
    }

    public int getCents() {
        return cents;
    }

    public void setCents(int c) {
        if (c >= 0 && c <= 99)
            cents = c;
    }
}
```

Review Questions

1. To make salary in the following class definition read-only:

```
class Employee {
    double salary;
}
```

a good approach would be to

  a. Make the Employee class private.

  b. Make salary protected.

  c. Make salary private and define a method called getSalary().

  d. Make salary private and define methods named getSalary() and setSalary().

2. Which javadoc tags are useful for documenting a class? (For this question, pick all that apply.)

  a. @see

  b. @param

  c. @version

  d. @return

  e. @author

3. If you define an interface without any method declarations,

  a. by default, all classes that implement that interface are abstract.

  b. all classes that implement that interface are concrete (that is, they can be instantiated).

  c. it is illegal to define an interface without any method declarations.

  d. any class that implements this interface is concrete only if the class (or any of its methods) is not declared abstract.

4. If you use the @author tag,

   a. you will see the author when you use javadoc, no options required.

   b. you will only see the author if you use the -author option when you invoke javadoc.

   c. the @author tag never displays the author; it is only used for reference within the source code.

5. The proper use of the @exception tag is

   a. @exception exceptionclassname anytext

   b. @exception anytext

   c. @exception exceptionclassname

   d. There is no @exception tag.

6. What kind of methods can be accessed by classes in the same package? (For this question, pick all the answers that apply.)

   a. public

   b. protected

   c. private

   d. those using the default access control

7. Which statements about the package keyword are true? (For this question, pick all the answers that apply.)

   a. It must be placed at the top of the source file.

   b. It must follow immediately after the import statements.

   c. Only public classes can be placed into a package.

   d. You can have more than one source file whose classes are put into the same package.

Answers to Review Questions

1. **c.** First of all, there is no such thing as a private class. Also, making salary protected doesn't make it read-only. Making it private and providing a getter method (not a setter method too) does the trick.

2. **a, c,** and **e.** The @param tag and @return tag are only useful when documenting a method.

3. **d.** The class is only concrete if it is not declared abstract.

4. **b.** You must invoke javadoc using the -author keyword to see the author information.

5. **a.** Specify the name of the exception class, followed by your own descriptive text.

6. **a, b,** and **d.** Private methods can only be accessed by the same class that defines them. Other than that, any class in the same package can access the other methods.

7. **a** and **d.** The package statement must appear before the import statements. Any type of class (or interface) can be placed into a package.

Accessing and Managing Databases

Objectives for This Chapter

- Implement a simple database using a RandomAccessFile and a class to read from and write to this file.
- Describe how to make a database server thread-safe, so that multiple clients can access it at the same time.
- Describe an n-tiered client/server architecture.
- Define a remote object and access it from another JVM using Remote Method Invocation.
- Use JDBC to access a database via ODBC.

The programming assignment will ask you to access a database. This database could be as simple as a RandomAccessFile, and the class that accesses the database could simply read lines from the file; each line would represent a record. Even though you might develop your own mini-database application for the exam, in real life there's a better way: you can use Remote Method Invocation and Java Database Connectivity. Both of these features are built into Java. We'll review them here.

No matter what method you need to implement on the exam concerning the database, there are some concepts you should know that will help you think through your design. These include how to query a database, how to enable your database to maintain its integrity as different clients attempt to read from and write to it at the same time, what database designers mean when they talk about 2-tier and 3-tier designs, and how to address concerns regarding efficiency.

The original version of the programming assignment involves accessing a database, possibly on a remote machine, using TCP/IP to communicate over the network. It also requires you to implement an application-level protocol for the client and server to communicate with each other. The client and server send Java primitives, such as opcodes, strings, and integers to each other over the network. A class on the back end accesses a RandomAccessFile containing database records.

The first part of this chapter reviews some concepts that can help you understand this architecture. Future versions of the programming assignment may involve JDBC and RMI. Regardless of exactly what is part of the programming assignment and exams, when you become certified in Java others will expect you to know this advanced information. So, this chapter reviews these concepts and APIs.

Roll-Your-Own Databases

Performing database programming in Java can be quite easy for simple programs. At its most basic, all you need is a random access file, a method to read from the file, and a method to write to the file. Each line that you read and write can be one record.

As with any database, you first need to determine the record format. You should have a unique key for each record to search for specific records in the database. For example, let's say you want to keep a database of employees. You can track these employees by social security number. If you hire poets, you might have the following list:

432-82-3212	e e cummings
092-55-3923	John Haines
932-11-5930	Alfred Tennyson

Such a list would represent a table. Each row in the table is a record. A record is made up of fields that keep track of different data types. By reading and writing rows to a file, you can read and write records for your database.

Which field should you use as your key? It might seem you could use either field, but really, only the social security field will be unique. Although you could easily have two employees named John Smith at your company, their social security numbers would still be unique.

To assist with our home-grown database, we might write a class called EmployeeRecord that looks like this:

```
package server;

import java.io.Serializable;
```

```
public class EmployeeRecord implements Serializable {
    private String ssn;
    private String name;

    public EmployeeRecord(String ssn, String name) {
        this.ssn = ssn;
        this.name = name;
    }

    public String getSsn() {
        return ssn;
    }

    public String getName() {
        return name;
    }
}
```

Now that you know what each record will look like, you can define a RandomAccessFile object to act as your database. For example, you could write the following code:

```
package server;

import java.io.*;

public class DB {
    private static final String FILE_NAME = "test.db";
    private RandomAccessFile file;
    private File test;
    private boolean open;

    public DB() throws IOException {
        try {
            test = new File(FILE_NAME);
            file = new RandomAccessFile(FILE_NAME, "rw");
            open = true;
        } catch (IOException x) {
            close();
            throw x;
        }
    }

    public voice void close() {
        if (open) {
            try {
                file.close();
            } catch (IOException x) {
                System.out.println(x.getMessage());
            } finally {
                open = false;
            }
        }
    }
}
```

```
public void finalize() throws Throwable {
    close();
    super.finalize();
}

public void rewind() throws IOException {
    file.seek(0);
}

public boolean moreRecords() throws IOException {
    return (file.getFilePointer() < file.length());
}

public EmployeeRecord readRecord()
    throws IOException, EOFException
{
    String ssn = file.readUTF();
    String name = file.readUTF();
    EmployeeRecord record = new EmployeeRecord(ssn, name);

    return record;
}

public void writeRecord(EmployeeRecord record)
    throws IOException
{
    file.seek(file.length());
    file.writeUTF(record.getSsn());
    file.writeUTF(record.getName());
}

}
```

This class lets us create an object that can access a file called test.db. This file will hold records of type EmployeeRecord. You can see that it knows how to open the file when it's created, and it closes the file if someone invokes its close() method. It also closes the file, if necessary, when the object is garbage collected, because it overrides finalize().

This class provides a way for other objects to use it to read all of the records. Other objects can rewind the file and then keep on checking if there are more records before reading the next one. New records are appended to the end of the file.

If you want to be able to delete records in this database file, one way to proceed would be to prefix each record with a flag that indicated whether that record was active or deleted. To delete a record, then, you would simply change its flag. Periodically, you could copy the database to a new file to get rid of deleted records thereby keeping them from clogging up the database.

> **CAUTION:** The DB class is not appropriate to use with multiple clients. We'll discuss how to update this class so that it is safe for multiple clients in a moment.

Accessing Databases from Multiple Clients

We can create a server class that would allow any number of clients to access this database over a network using TCP/IP. Our architecture would look like Figure 26-1.

We'll look at how to implement a TCP/IP server capable of handling multiple clients in Chapter 27. For now, the issue we're concerned with is what happens if multiple clients are manipulating the database at the same time. What if one client is deleting a record while another client is attempting to read from the database? How can we prevent the clients from interfering with each other?

To keep clients from working on the same record and to keep the database from becoming corrupted, it's important to make the methods that access and change records synchronized. Every method—except, perhaps, for the constructor and finalize()—would be a candidate for becoming synchronized. All you need to do is place the synchronized keyword in front of the method's return type, and voila! The class is thread-safe.

Two-Tiered and Three-Tiered Architectures

We have looked at Figure 26-1 but we have not indicated which machines any of these objects are running on. We could assume that clients connect directly to the machine

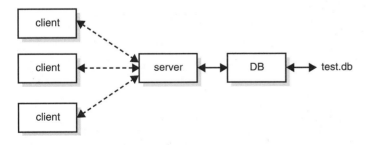

Figure 26-1 A server providing multiple clients access to a database

where the database resides. This is fine, but this is not always the case in the real world. Often, client/server architectures are really client/client/server, or 3-tiered.

This kind of arrangement, where one machine talks to another that talks to another, can go on indefinitely. You can have an n-tiered architecture, where n is essentially any number.

For example, perhaps our physical architecture actually looks like Figure 26-2. Here, there are three different groups of machines. There is a client group, which represents the first tier. There is a server, which represents a middle tier, and there are database engines, which represent the third tier, or the back end. Each box in this diagram could represent a different machine, but because we think of the roles that each machine plays, we think of this as 3-tiered: client, to server, which in turn is a client to the database engines.

This kind of design has a number of interesting aspects. First, it is easily extendible. Our server can act as a gateway to any number of other servers or database engines. The client never has to know that data is coming from 2, 3, or 101 different databases. This means that our server is acting as a kind of gatekeeper. It can establish security precautions, business rules, and can force clients to access data a particular way. What's more, the middle tier, where the server lives, and the back end, where the databases reside, can maintain a very high-speed connection. This helps with performance. By contrast, a different architecture might involve the clients talking over a slower network, such as a dial-up network, with each individual database.

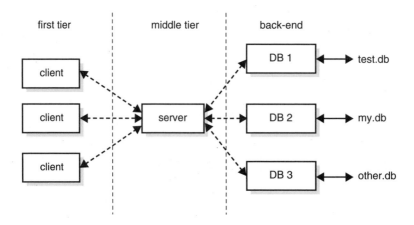

Figure 26-2   A 3-tiered design

Using Java APIs

To help implement this kind of architecture, Java comes with a set of APIs that helps remove you from the low-level chore of creating your own special database and implementing your own application-level protocol used to communicate over TCP/IP networks. These new APIs provide two new features: Remote Method Invocation (RMI) and Java Database Connectivity (JDBC). We'll review each of these over the remainder of this chapter.

Remote Method Invocation

When communicating via TCP/IP, the applications themselves must define the protocol of bytes to pass back and forth. This can be difficult to work with and is definitely error prone. Passing bytes over a network also runs counter to Java's philosophy of helping the programmer concentrate on the application code rather than the protocol details. By providing an API to invoke methods in objects in other JVMs, Java frees you from this chore. Using RMI, you can invoke remote methods and work with remote objects as if they were defined locally in the same application.

You can use RMI to call methods in other Java applications running in different JVMs, where the JVMs are possibly running on different hosts. You can call a method on a remote object once you have a reference to the object. Often, you can get a reference to a remote object as a return value from some other RMI call, but to get your first remote object to begin using RMI, you use a bootstrap naming service provided by RMI.

Figure 26-3 shows the basic concept behind RMI. An object in one application, perhaps on a client machine, invokes a method in another application running on a

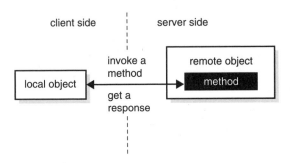

Figure 26-3   Invoking remote objects using RMI

completely different machine, perhaps on a server. The client can pass parameters and even get a return value. RMI uses object serialization to pass parameters and return values between applications.

Once you establish a connection to an object in another program, you can invoke methods on that object as if that object were running in the same program as your own. However, for this to work, everything must be defined and set up just right.

Defining a Remote Interface

You need to define an interface for the remote object. Here are the first steps you need to take to define a remote class:

1. Define an interface that declares the methods that objects will be able to invoke using RMI.

2. Throw RemoteException from the methods that objects will be able to invoke using RMI.

The local object will use this interface to determine what it can do with the remote object. This interface must inherit from another interface called Remote. In the example that we'll pursue here, we'll create a class called DBServer that works with our original DB class but also implements DBInterface. We will define DBServer so that we can invoke methods on its objects remotely:

```
package server;

import java.rmi.RemoteException;
import java.rmi.Remote;
import java.io.IOException;
import java.io.EOFException;

public interface DBInterface extends Remote {
    void close()
        throws RemoteException;
    void rewind()
        throws RemoteException, IOException;
    boolean moreRecords()
        throws RemoteException, IOException;
    EmployeeRecord readRecord()
        throws RemoteException, IOException, EOFException;
    void writeRecord(EmployeeRecord er)
        throws RemoteException, IOException;
}
```

Each method must declare that it throws a RemoteException, in addition to any other application-specific exceptions you would like it to throw. RemoteException indicates that something went wrong in the communication between the local and the remote object.

Defining a Remote Class

Your remote class must extend RemoteObject and implement your remote interface. To define a remote class, you should complete the following steps:

1. Extend the RemoteObject class or one of its subclasses, such as UnicastRemote Object.

2. Implement the remote interface you defined for your remote class' methods.

3. Define a constructor that throws RemoteException.

4. Create and install a security manager.

5. Register the first object others will access via RMI by defining it in RMI's bootstrap naming service.

These steps are examined in the sections that follow.

Defining the Class, Interface, and Constructor

You start defining your remote class by extending RemoteObject or a subclass of RemoteObject such as UnicastRemoteObject. Extending UnicastRemoteObject is a common approach when you are implementing a class whose objects will not be replicated across multiple servers.

You also need to implement the interface that defines your remote methods. You might start by writing:

```
public class DBServer extends UnicastRemoteObject
  implements DBInterface
{
 //source for DBServer class
}
```

Your class would go on to implement all of the methods declared in the interface. In our example, this would involve forwarding the method calls to DB, which we looked at earlier in this chapter. I did rewrite DB so it now looks like this:

```java
package server;

import java.io.*;

public class DB {
    private RandomAccessFile file;
    private boolean open;

    public DB(String fileName) throws IOException {
      file = new RandomAccessFile(fileName, "rw");
      open = true;
    }

    public void close() {
        if (open) {
            try {
                file.close();
            } catch (IOException x) {
                System.out.println(x.getMessage());
            } finally {
                open = false;
            }
        }
    }

    public void finalize() throws Throwable {
        close();
        super.finalize();
    }

    public void rewind() throws IOException {
        file.seek(0);
    }

    public boolean moreRecords() throws IOException {
        return (file.getFilePointer() < file.length());
    }

    public EmployeeRecord readRecord()
        throws IOException, EOFException
    {
        String ssn = file.readUTF();
        String name = file.readUTF();
        EmployeeRecord record = new EmployeeRecord(ssn, name);

        return record;
    }
}
```

```java
    public void writeRecord(EmployeeRecord record)
      throws IOException
    {
        file.seek(file.length());
        file.writeUTF(record.getSsn());
        file.writeUTF(record.getName());
    }

}
```

Here's what DBServer looks like:

```java
package server;

import java.io.*;
import java.rmi.*;
import java.rmi.server.*;

public class DBServer extends UnicastRemoteObject
    implements DBInterface
{
    private static final String FILE_NAME = "test.db";
    private DB db;

    public DBServer() throws RemoteException, IOException {
        db = new DB(FILE_NAME);
    }

    public synchronized void close() throws RemoteException {
        db.close();
    }

public synchronized void rewind()
      throws IOException, RemoteException
    {
        db.rewind();
    }

    public synchronized boolean moreRecords()
        throws IOException, RemoteException
    {
        return db.moreRecords();
    }

    public synchronized EmployeeRecord readRecord()
        throws IOException, EOFException, RemoteException
    {
        return db.readRecord();
    }

    public synchronized void writeRecord(EmployeeRecord record)
        throws IOException, RemoteException
    {
        db.writeRecord(record);
    }
```

```
public static void main(String[] args) {

    // Create and install a security manager
    System.setSecurityManager(new RMISecurityManager());

    try {
        DBServer dbServer = new DBServer();

        Naming.rebind("DBServer", dbServer);
            // located on the same machine as the client

        System.out.println("DBServer bound in registry");
    } catch (Exception e) {
        System.out.println("DBServer err: " + e.getMessage());
        e.printStackTrace();
    }
}

}
```

Your class can define methods not declared in your remote interface, but these other methods cannot be invoked from client-side objects—the client can only invoke those methods that are defined in the interface. Also, one reason why it's necessary to create a special server class that interfaces with the DB class, rather than just interfacing directly with DB, is that interface methods cannot be synchronized.

The class you define that implements the remote interface must define its own constructor. The default no-args constructor won't do, because the object's constructor must declare that it throws a RemoteException.

Installing the Security Manager and Registering the Bootstrap Naming Service

Your remote class must also create and install a security manager and, as with this DBServer object, register itself with the bootstrap naming service. You can create and install a new security manager quite easily by writing:

```
System.setSecurityManager(new RMISecurityManager());
```

A security manager must be running because RMI will be loading classes over the network. Just as with Java applets, Java takes a conservative approach and does not trust the classes that come from anywhere other than the local machine. Java insists that a security manager is up and running to make sure that the classes coming in over the network don't do anything malicious.

The security manager also requires you to have a security policy file with the appropriate permissions. For simplicity, the following security policy file grants all permissions on a system:

```
grant {
  permission java.security.AllPermission;
};
```

This security policy grants all permissions on the system to the application. You shouldn't use this in a live environment but for testing and development, this works well. On Windows NT, the security manager looks for this file in %USERPROFILE%/.java.policy by default.

Registering an object with the bootstrap naming service is also fairly simple. We can create the new object and register it with these two lines of code:

```
DBImplementation db = new DBImplementation();
Naming.rebind("//myhost/DB", db);
```

This says we're going to identify our DBServer object via the String that looks like a URL: "//myhost/DB." This URL enables the client to identify this object later.

You also need to make sure your remote object gets exported. If you do not extend UnicastRemoteObject, you must export your object yourself. You can do this by invoking UnicastRemoteObject.exportObject(). If you extend a class such as UnicastRemoteObject, this will be done for you. This is because UnicastRemoteObject exports the object in its constructor, which is invoked with an implied call to super(). By exporting your object, you start it listening for incoming calls on an anonymous port.

To pass parameters or return values that are objects, they must be serializable. This means that we have to make EmployeeRecord serializable, because it is a return value for one of the methods we've defined. (We don't have to register EmployeeRecord in the bootstrap naming service, because it will be returned. However, we have to make it a remote object just like DBImplementation by defining a Remote interface, and so on. The client also will need to import EmployeeRecord so that it can use it.)

You can also create a *stub* and a *skeleton* for your remote object. A stub represents the remote object on the client side. The skeleton represents the remote object on the server side. Keep in mind that in a pure Java 2 environment the RMI server-side skeletons are not required.

I'll review how Java uses these in just a moment. You can use the RMI compiler named rmic that comes with the JDK to accomplish this. Figure 26-4 shows where we are so far.

Invoking Remote Objects

Figure 26-5 shows what we've accomplished so far on the server side (we'll get to the client side next).

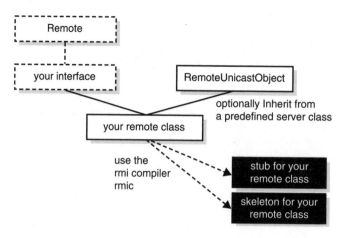

Figure 26-4 Creating the remote class and skeleton

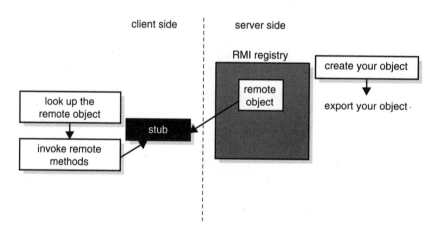

Figure 26-5 The server-client connection via stubs

We've reviewed how to create an object and export it to the registry. Now we'll look at the client side. Calling a method in a remote object from the client side is simple and can be performed in two steps:

1. Obtain a reference to the remote object.

2. Invoke a method in the remote object.

You can obtain a reference by using the static method lookup() in the Naming class and passing it the same URL you used to register your remote object. This method returns a reference to the remote object—actually, the stub representing the remote object—which you can cast to the interface type you want to use.

 CAUTION: Do not cast the remote object to the object type! Remember, you can only invoke methods that are declared in the remote interface. The stub returned declares those methods in the interface. Also, don't forget to import the interface to refer to it.

Once you acquire the stub representing the remote object, you can invoke methods for this object just as if it were a full-blown object residing locally on your machine as part of your local application.

Here's an example of a client that accesses a remote object:

```
package client;

import java.rmi.*;
import java.io.*;
import java.net.MalformedURLException;
import server.DBInterface;
import server.EmployeeRecord;

public class DBClient {
    public static void main(String[] args) {
        EmployeeRecord record;

        try {
            DBInterface db =
              (DBInterface)Naming.lookup("DBServer");

            record = new EmployeeRecord("123-45-6789",
                       "William Blake");
            db.writeRecord(record);

            record = new EmployeeRecord("000-11-2222", "John Dunne");
            db.writeRecord(record);

            db.rewind();
            while (db.moreRecords()) {
                record = db.readRecord();
                System.out.println("Ssn: " + record.getSsn());
                System.out.println("Name: " + record.getName());
            }
        } catch (MalformedURLException e) {
            error(e);
```

```
      } catch (NotBoundException e) {
        error(e);
      } catch (RemoteException e) {
        error(e);
      } catch (EOFException e) {
        error(e);
      } catch (IOException e) {
        error(e);
      }
    }

    private static void error(Exception e) {
      System.out.println("DBClient exception: " + e.getMessage());
      e.printStackTrace();
    }

  }
```

Stubs and Skeletons

Java communicates between the local object and remote object via a stub and a skeleton. For all appearances, the client program might think it has actually acquired a direct reference to the remote object residing on the remote server. But Figure 26-6 shows what is going on under the covers. In reality, the client is communicating with a stub that represents the remote object on the local machine. The stub performs the network operations to communicate with the skeleton on the remote machine; the skeleton then talks to the remote object.

The stub is the client-side representation of the remote object. It defines an interface declaring the methods that the local object can invoke.

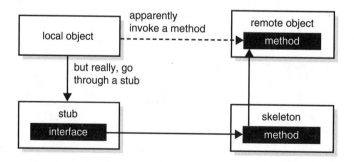

Figure 26-6   Invoking a remote method via stubs and skeletons

When the server-side object responds, the flow of control goes back through the skeleton, which handles the network communication to get back to the stub, where the return values or exceptions are passed back to the local, client-side object.

Getting Things Going

To use RMI, you must start the bootstrap registry before you do anything. You must do this even before starting the server class. You start the RMI registry by executing a command from your operating system's command line named rmiregistry.

You can then start the server, specifying java.rmi.registry.codebase=URL (the URL should include a trailing /), of course replacing URL with your own URL, so that clients can use the URL to find the stubs in the registry.

Finally, you can start your clients. You must have an HTTP server running on the remote machine.

Exercise 26.1

Develop a class that can be accessed remotely. This class should be named NYSE and should respond to a method called dowJonesAvg() to return a double value. This object will not be replicated across multiple servers.

JDBC

JDBC provides an interface to databases. JDBC enables Java programs to access data residing in databases on servers and use that data in the client applet. Programs that use JDBC in Java can access any database that can be queried using Structured Query Language (SQL).

Does this mean you have to know SQL? Unfortunately, the answer is "yes." JDBC does not put any restrictions on the SQL statements you can send to the database. To send SQL statements from a Java client, you need to know the APIs in the JDBC classes. These JDBC classes issue the SQL queries, passing your applet the data they retrieve.

JDBC is good at performing three important tasks as part of accessing data on a server: It can:

- Establish a connection with a database
- Send SQL statements
- Process the results

JDBC is a low-level API because you must issue SQL statements directly. If you want to work at a higher level, you can write an API with method names like getEmployees(), setSalary(), and so on, and have these methods make the translation into the SQL statements that you need.

The Need for Drivers

JDBC interacts with a driver that performs the database-specific connections from the general SQL and JDBC methods. Figure 26-7 shows the connections between a client applet and a back-end database using JDBC.

All drivers contain a static initializer that creates a new instance of itself and registers itself with the DriverManager when it's loaded. You can force a class to be loaded by using the static method forName defined in the class Class. For example, your client might include this line of code:

```
Class.forName("bluehorse.db.Driver");
```

To define a static initializer in the driver itself that registers the new driver object, you can write:

```
static {
  Driver d = new Driver();
  DriverManager.registerDriver(d);
}
```

Using ODBC

There are already a great number of drivers for databases. However, because Java and JDBC are relatively new, most of these drivers conform to a protocol called Open

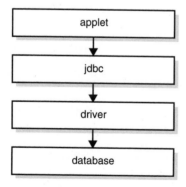

Figure 26-7   Accessing a database from an applet using JDBC

Database Connectivity (ODBC). Does JDBC start from scratch, then, and require a programmer to toss all of this existing work into the recycling bin of history?

No! Although JDBC can interact directly with SQL databases if there's a driver written for it in Java, JDBC can also be used in conjunction with ODBC, which then goes off and interacts with SQL databases. JDBC can interact with ODBC by using what's known as a JDBC-ODBC bridge.

This allows you to take two approaches to interacting with a database: you can write a driver that takes JDBC calls and performs the SQL calls to the database, or you can use an ODBC driver that already does this and connect JDBC to ODBC using a JDBC-ODBC bridge. Figure 26-8 shows what this looks like.

The ODBC driver will be native to the platform it's running on. However, using JDBC to access ODBC enables your applet to remain platform-independent while still taking advantage of ODBC.

The JDBC-ODBC bridge enables a connection to be made to an ODBC Data Source Name (DSN). The DSN specifies either a database or a database server with multiple databases. For example, with MS Access, the DSN would specify the Access database file but with SQL Server, the DSN would specify the SQL Server installation where there are multiple databases.

If the database is on a remote machine, the location of the database is specified in the DSN configuration. The Java program establishing a connection to the database is only aware of the DSN name and perhaps the username and password to access the DSN. The DSN configuration will resolve the DSN to the database. It is possible to explicitly specify remote databases in JDBC, but this requires driver types other than the

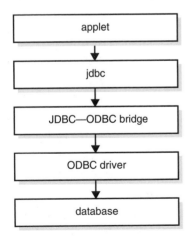

Figure 26-8   Accessing a database using the JDBC-ODBC bridge

type-I bridge drivers. These other driver types are specific to a particular DBMS system and in some cases must be purchased from a third party vendor.

Opening a Connection to a Database

To open a connection to a database, follow these steps:

1. Load the database driver class (which causes it to create an instance of itself and register itself with the DriverManager).

2. Invoke the DriverManager method getConnection() and identify the database driver you will use to connect to the database, the database file name, and optionally as a user ID and password.

With the JDBC-ODBC Bridge, the database driver class and URL (without DSN name) are consistent across database systems. The JDBC URL provides a way of identifying a database so that the appropriate driver will recognize it and establish a connection with it. Driver writers are the ones who actually determine what the JDBC URL looks like. You do not need to worry about how to form a JDBC URL and instead, simply use the URL supplied with the drivers you are using. That said, here's how you can load the JDBC-ODBC bridge that comes with Sun's version of Java:

```
Class.forName("sun.jdbc.odbc.JdbcOdbcDriver");
```

And here is a URL you might use to access a DSN called BaseballCards using the JDBC-ODBC bridge:

```
String url = "jdbc:odbc:BaseballCards";
DriverManager.getConnection(url, "userID", "passwd");
```

Interacting with a Database

Once you've established a connection with the database, you can send it SQL statements and get results. There are three different types of Statement classes. You can use instances of these classes to send SQL statements to a database. These classes are:

- **Statement**   Sends simple SQL statements with no parameters.

- **PreparedStatement (extends Statement)**   Sends precompiled SQL statements.

- **CallableStatement (extends PreparedStatement)**   Executes a database procedure.

There are also two different types of methods you can use to send these SQL statements: executeQuery() and executeUpdate(). Which method you use depends on what

Table 26-1 Methods used with SQL Statements

SQL Statement	Method	What This SQL Statement Does
SELECT	executeQuery( )	Finds records in a datebase with the given criteria
INSERT	executeUpdate( )	Inserts a single record into a table
UPDATE	executeUpdate( )	Updates fields in a table
DELETE	executeUpdate( )	Deletes records matching the criteria
CREATE TABLE	executeUpdate( )	Creates a new table
DROP TABLE	executeUpdate( )	Removes a table

type of SQL statement you create. Table 26-1 shows you which statement you would use with which method, and what that statement does.

The Select statement returns a ResultSet object containing the results of the search. You can use ResultSet methods to iterate over the results. The other SQL statements generally return a result indicating success or failure. Although statement objects are closed automatically by the garbage collector, you should close them yourself as soon as you're done using them to help Java to optimize its memory management chores.

An Example of Using ODBC with Microsoft Access

The following code is one specific example of using JDBC and the JDBC-ODBC bridge. The trouble with any example is that it will be specific for the database and platform you're running on. However, it still might be useful to see a working example, even if your environment is not the same as this one.

I started by creating a very simple database in Microsoft Access. This consisted of a single table and three entries. You'll see when you get to the sample programming assignment in Chapter 29 what this database is supposed to represent (passengers assigned to airplane seats). Figure 26-9 shows what this single table looks like.

I then acquired and installed the ODBC System Administrator from Microsoft. This is free from Microsoft's Web site. I specified my database in this system administrator software as a system data source that used the Microsoft Access ODBC driver.

Then I wrote the code to access this database via JDBC:

```
import java.net.URL;
import java.sql.*;
```

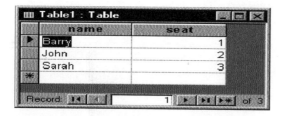

Figure 26-9   A simple table in a database

```java
import sun.jdbc.odbc.*;

class JdbcExample {

    public static void main(String[] args) {

        if (args.length == 0) {
            System.out.println("java JdbcExample <url>");
            System.exit(1);
        }

        try {
            Class.forName("sun.jdbc.odbc.JdbcOdbcDriver");
            Connection con = DriverManager.getConnection(args[0]);

            Statement stmt = con.createStatement();
            ResultSet rs =
                stmt.executeQuery("SELECT name, seat FROM Table1");

            while (rs.next()) {
                String name = rs.getString("name");
                int    seat = rs.getInt("seat");

                System.out.println(name + " " + seat);
            }

            stmt.close();
            con.close();

        } catch (Exception x) {
            System.out.println(x.getMessage());
            x.printStackTrace();
        }
    }
}
```

The JDBC-ODBC bridge translates JDBC method calls into ODBC function calls. It enables JDBC to leverage the database connectivity provided by the ODBC driver that already knows how to work with Microsoft Access.

I ran this program by using this command:

```
java JdbcExample jdbc:odbc:mydb.mdb
```

(mydb.mdb is the name of my Access file.) This program ran, established the connection with the database, read the records in Table 1, and displayed the names and seat assignments in that database:

Barry	1
John	2
Sarah	3

Exercise 26.2

- Establish a connection via the JDBC-ODBC bridge to an ODBC Data Source named "thisdb." "thisdb" can reference any DBMS of your choice, provided you have ODBC drivers for it.

- Execute the SQL statement "INSERT INTO Table1 (name, seat) VALUES('Greg,' 5)."

- Perform any cleanup to complete this connection.

- In the final class definition, be sure to catch any errors using try catch statements.

Answers to the Exercises

Exercise 26.1

First, here is the interface. Remember that it has to extend Remote.

```
import java.rmi.RemoteException;
import java.rmi.Remote;

public interface NYSEInterface extends Remote {
    double dowJonesAvg() throws RemoteException;
}
```

Now, here is the NYSE class. Notice that it has to define a constructor that throws RemoteException. This is true even if you only need a no-args, default constructor.

```java
import java.rmi.*;
import java.rmi.server.*;

public class NYSE extends UnicastRemoteObject
    implements NYSEInterface
{

    public NYSE() throws RemoteException {
    }

    public double dowJonesAvg() throws RemoteException {
        double avg = 0.0;

        // FIND THE AVERAGE

        return avg;
    }

}
```

Exercise 26.2

1. Establish a connection via the JDBC-ODBC bridge to an ODBC Data Source named "thisdb." "thisdb" can reference any DBMS of your choice, provided you have ODBC drivers for it:

```java
Class.forName("sun.jdbc.odbc.JdbcOdbcDriver");
Connection con = DriverManager.getConnection("jdbc:odbc:thisdb");
```

2. Execute the SQL statement "INERT INTO Table1 (name, seat) VALUES('Greg,' 5)":

```java
Statement stmt = con.createStatement();
int result = stmt.executeUpdate("INSERT INTO Table1 (name,
seat) VALUES ('Greg', '5')");
```

3. Perform any cleanup to complete this connection:

```java
stmt.close();
con.close();
```

4. In the final class definition, be sure to catch any errors using try catch statements:

```java
import java.sql.*;

public class DBInsert {

  public static void main(String[] args)
  {
```

```
    try {
      Class.forName("sun.jdbc.odbc.JdbcOdbcDriver");
      Connection con = DriverManager.
      getConnection("jdbc:odbc:thisdb");

        Statement stmt = con.createStatement();
        int result = stmt.executeUpdate("INSERT INTO Table1
              (name, seat) VALUES ('Greg', '5')");
      stmt.close();
      con.close();
    } catch (Exception e) {
      e.printStackTrace(System.out);
    }
  }
}
```

Review Questions

1. You can load Sun's JDBC-ODBC bridge by invoking:
    a. Class.forName("sun.jdbc.odbc.JdbcOdbcDriver");
    b. DriverManager.getConnection()
    c. executeQuery() given a Statement object
    d. You don't have to do anything to load the JDBC-ODBC bridge

2. You can make an object that reads and writes records from a database safe for multiple clients by:
    a. declaring its methods to be synchronized
    b. declaring the method as throwing a RemoteException
    c. implementing the Remote interface
    d. closing the file on finalize()

3. All methods in a remote interface must:
    a. not return a value
    b. throw a RuntimeException
    c. throw a RemoteException
    d. be static methods

4. When an applet obtains a reference to a remote object, that reference is a(n):
    a. stub representing the object
    b. copy of the object
    c. direct reference to the object
    d. instance of RemoteObject

5. To create an object that others can access remotely, you must implement which interface?
   a. Clonable
   b. Throwable
   c. RemoteObject
   d. Remote

Answers to Review Questions

1. **a.** Class.forName() loads a class. (Database drivers should register themselves with the DriverManager when they load.)

2. **a.** By synchronizing the methods that access and update a database file, multiple clients can work with the object responsible for this file at the same time.

3. **c.** All methods that you want to invoke remotely must declare that they throw a RemoteException.

4. **a.** When you find an object on a remote JVM, RMI passes back a stub representing the object.

5. **d.** You must implement the Remote interface. Typically, you extend the Remote interface by defining an interface specific to your application. Then, you implement this new interface. Ultimately, however, your new remote class is an instanceof Remote.

CHAPTER 27

Network Programming and Communication

Objectives for This Chapter

- Describe what IP addresses are and how they work.
- State why TCP makes it possible to send streams of data over the Internet.
- Identify what a socket is and what it represents.
- Identify the classes in java.net used to communicate via TCP/IP.
- Use Java to establish network connections.
- Write a client/server application.
- Write a server that can handle more than one client.

With Java, network programming is—dare I say it—fun. The package java.net contains a few classes that hide what's happening at the Transport Control Protocol/Internet Protocol (TCP/IP) layer and make programs that communicate over the Internet relatively easy to write. However, to use these classes effectively, you've got to know how TCP/IP works, what sockets are, and the strategies for writing a client/server application. We'll review all of these topics in this chapter.

The programming assignment requires you to write a client/server application. The client and server talk to each other using TCP/IP. You will pass data between the client and server using sockets.

A TCP/IP Primer

The programming assignment for the Developer exam requires you to understand TCP/IP. If you're a little fuzzy on these protocols, or are not quite sure what this acronym even stands for, have no fear. I'll cover them in this section, and you'll even write your own simple client/server programs using TCP/IP in the exercises.

TCP/IP stands for *Transport Control Protocol/Internet Protocol*. TCP and IP are really two different protocols, but together they define the way things work on the Internet. The Internet Protocol (IP) identifies computers on the Internet. Computers are identified by a four-byte value. The four-byte value is usually written in a form called a *dotted octet* where the values of each of the bytes are separated by a period, such as:

206.26.48.100

Given this number, one computer on the Internet can find and identify another computer. That's the IP.

Since it's not always easy to remember numbers like this, these numbers are often mapped to human names, called *domain names*, such as java.sun.com. There are special servers on the Internet that perform this mapping, called *Domain Name Servers*. If you ask your Web browser to connect to **www.javasoft.com,** for example, it finds a Domain Name Server, looks up its dotted octet, and connects to that machine.

Before we look at how that connection occurs, let's look at the other protocol—Transport Control Protocol, or TCP. TCP enables you to treat any Internet resource as a stream. It does this by guaranteeing two things:

- Data sent to a particular machine arrives at that machine.

- If the data sent to a particular machine had to be divided into smaller pieces and sent separately, all of these pieces are reassembled on the receiving end in the correct order.

Here's an example of why this is important and how it's used. Let's say you are about to send a memo to your boss asking for a raise. You've stated all the important reasons why you deserve a raise. Since you're thorough, the message is quite long. You want to make certain your boss knows each and every reason why you're worth more than his penny-pinching mind currently comprehends.

You hit "send" on your e-mail program. The e-mail program wants to send this out over the Internet to the IP address you've specified. But it can't. Why? Because the message is too big! You were too thorough. Does the e-mail program ask you to rewrite your message and state your reasons in 50 words or less? No! It takes matters into its own hands. It divides the message you wrote into lots of smaller messages, each one small enough to travel over the Internet. This first step is shown in Figure 27-1.

Figure 27-1 Preparing to send a message over the internet

Because of TCP, each piece contains a header that indicates where it's going and identifies its place in the sequence to be received. Each piece of the message—each packet—goes out into the Internet. (For the sake of completeness, here's a simple definition of the Internet: a network of networks that relies on TCP/IP.)

As each packet travels from computer to computer—from node to node—on its way to its IP destination, perhaps not all pieces of this monster message go the same way. Perhaps some pieces get rerouted. Perhaps a machine in the stepping stones across the net goes down after sending packet 16 but before sending packet 17. TCP/IP still works its magic—the pieces of your message still arrive at their correct destination—but now they start arriving in a different order from the order you sent them. This is shown in Figure 27-2.

Naturally, you don't want an argument left out because it didn't arrive. And you don't want your e-mail in a jumbled order when your boss looks at it. You want to keep your argument cogent and focused, building to a crescendo by the time you ask for a raise at the end.

This is where TCP kicks into high gear. Not only have all your message pieces arrived (guaranteed delivery), but now they are reassembled into the correct order. After the pieces are reassembled, they're accepted by your boss' e-mail program. Your boss now has an impressive piece of e-mail to read. This is illustrated in Figure 27-3.

Ports and Sockets

This is fine as far as it goes, but I left out one crucial step: how does the computer receiving the e-mail message know that this message is an e-mail message? What if there is also a Web server on your boss' machine, serving up pages to the people in your group?

Figure 27-2 Packets don't have to take the same route to their destination.

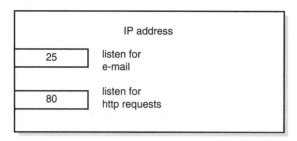

Figure 27-3   Packets are reassembled into their proper order.

How can the Web server and the e-mail program both be running at the same time and be paying attention only to the data meant for them when they're both talking TCP/IP? After all, both programs are running on the same machine, and that machine has only one IP address.

The solution to this riddle is that there is one more piece of information that distinguishes where the data should go. That piece of information is a port number.

Each server program listens to a different *port*. There are 2 to the 16th different ports, and each is assigned a number.

By convention, these numbers are divided into two groups:

• Port numbers below 1024 are reserved for well-known system uses, such as Web protocols, e-mail, ftp, and so on.

• Port numbers above 1024, up to 2 to the 16th minus 1 (because port numbers start at 0), are all yours, and you can assign your own programs and services to these port numbers.

So, the e-mail program is listening to one port, and the Web server is listening to another port. E-mail might arrive looking for port 25 (which is the port usually associated with SMTP, or Simple Mail Transfer Protocol), while requests for Web pages might arrive looking for port 80 (which is the port usually associated with HTTP, or HyperText Transport Protocol). Each server only listens for data arriving on its particular port. Figure 27-4 gives a sense of this.

The combination of *IP address* and *port number* uniquely identifies a service on a machine. This service could be a server program, such as a Web server. Client programs also listen to a particular port for data from the server. Just as the client uses this combination of IP address and port to send data to the server, the server also uses this combination of IP address and port to send data back to the client. Such a combination of IP address and port is known as a *socket*.

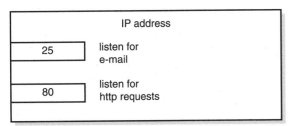

IP address	
25	listen for e-mail
80	listen for http requests

Figure 27-4 Server software listening to specific ports

A socket identifies one end of a two-way communication. When a client requests a connection with a server on a particular port, the server identifies and keeps track of the socket it will use to talk to the client.

This might help explain how a server can keep track of and talk to multiple clients at once. Even though the server is communicating over the same *port* with many clients, it uses *sockets* (remember, *port* + *IP address*) to determine the destination and source of that communication. The server keeps track of each client's socket. The server knows data arriving on one socket comes from a different client than data arriving on another socket. The server knows that it can respond to a client by passing data back to that client's socket.

Figure 27-5 gives a sense of the role that sockets play in this client/server communication. (We'll look at exactly what's happening on the server side regarding port numbers shortly.)

Streams

With IP addressing, TCP's guaranteed delivery and sequencing of data, and with sockets to identify the end points of two-way communications, data passing over the Internet can be treated by an application as a stream. In other words, you can read from a socket just as if you were reading from a file, because TCP ensures that all the data sent from the machine on the other end of the Internet connection is received in order. TCP hides the fact that the data is arriving via the Internet and, at the level of the public interfaces declared by Java's Stream classes, makes the data indistinguishable from data read from a local file.

You can attach a Stream class to a socket and read from it or write to it just as you learned about in Chapter 19. We'll look at some examples in a moment.

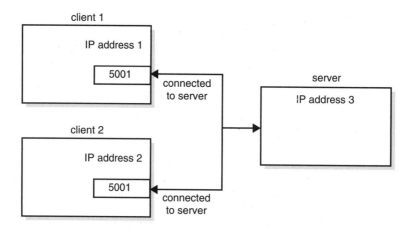

Figure 27-5   Sockets uniquely identify the end point of a two-way communication.

Designing Servers and Clients

To develop an application that communicates over the Internet, you'll develop a server and a client. The server listens for connections on a particular port; when it receives a connection, it obtains a socket to use for the communication and begins a dialog with the client at the other end of that socket. The client initiates the connection and communicates with the server via a socket representing that server.

A classic design for a server is one that runs forever, listening for connections with clients, and then taking part in a dialog with the client (by reading data from the client and writing data to the client, as appropriate). Figure 27-6 shows the basic steps that a client and server take in communicating with each other.

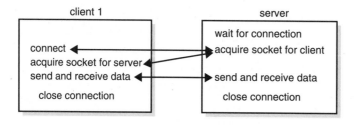

Figure 27-6   The basic interaction between a server and a client

Handling Multiple Clients

As long as the server only uses a single thread, other clients attempting to communicate with the server wait in a queue until the server is through with its current client and closes its connection with that client. If you only anticipate having one client communicate with the server, then the possibilities of other clients waiting in a queue is not a concern. If you might have multiple clients talking to the server, you need a design that can handle this situation.

Regardless of whether the communication between the server and client is lengthy or relatively short, there's really no need to fear implementing a server that can handle more than one client. In Java, with its ability to easily implement multithreading, synchronize between multiple threads, and work directly with sockets, it's quite straight-forward to create a multithreading server.

You might wish to implement a server that follows the basic flow chart shown in Figure 27-7.

Threads introduce new wrinkles to the server. The first wrinkle you might want to iron out is making the server thread-safe. For example, let's say the server is accessing a database. If one thread is reading from the database at the same time that another thread is writing to it, clearly this is trouble. Fortunately, it's simple to lock the dependent methods in Java by declaring them to be synchronized. You'll see an example of a working server in a few more pages.

That's great as far as interacting with the database. But how does the server keep track of multiple clients? How does the server know which data read from a port goes with a particular thread? The answer is that TCP/IP takes care of this data routing for you, and TCP is the protocol layer below sockets—which you probably won't ever have to deal with directly if you program in Java.

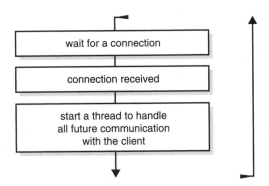

Figure 27-7   A basic flow chart for a multithreading server

Remember, sockets encode both the port number and the IP address. This means each client is uniquely identified. When a server accepts a connection, it acquires the client's socket. From then on, all data received from or sent to the client is read from or written to this socket. The TCP protocol below the socket layer ensures the data sent from a particular client goes to the correct socket in the correct server thread.

Because the server uses a socket to interact with the client, the server is born ready for multithreading.

NOTE: Assigning each socket communication with a client to its own thread also has the great benefit that if something goes terribly wrong with the communication between the server and a particular client, only the thread that's dealing with that client will be in trouble (and possibly end with an exception); the rest of the server will continue chugging along.

Client Issues

Let's look briefly at some design issues involving the client. Here are some questions you might want to think about for your client. The answers will depend on the needs of your particular client application.

If the client sends a request to the server and the server takes some time to answer it, will the user interface freeze because it is waiting for a response from the client, or will it continue working? If the user interface continues working, what will happen if the user then issues another request? Should this second request supersede the first one?

You have a number of strategies in implementing your client, and the right approach will take into account numerous factors that depend on your particular situation. You've got to decide how sophisticated to make your user interface, and whether that sophistication is worth the price of increased development and maintenance. Here are some possible strategies for you to contemplate:

- Block all user input until (and hopefully when) the server responds. You might want to change the cursor to a busy cursor during this communication time.

- Spawn a separate thread to communicate with the server. When the server responds, have that thread invoke a method that updates the user interface appropriately. Work at recovering gracefully if the user interface changes before the server responds.

- Spawn a separate thread that displays a modal dialog that allows the user the option of canceling the communication with the server. The modal dialog should disappear when the server does respond. Because it is modal, it will keep the user from altering the user interface if communication with the server is still taking place.

Two other important considerations in writing a client/server application are:

- Does the server need to save state for each individual client, or will all clients manipulate the same data source on the server? If the server needs to save state for each client, it will either need objects that store the relevant information, or better (in case the connection is dropped prematurely), a file where it can keep the information for the various clients (or perhaps the server can keep one file per client).

- Does the server communicate with each client independently of the others, or will the server broadcast information to all the clients connected to it? If the clients are operating independently of each other, the server does not need to keep track of each thread in the server. However, if the server will broadcast information to all connected clients (as in a multiclient chat program), the server will need to keep some kind of list of the threads handling communication with the various clients.

The Networking Package

Java makes working with TCP/IP easy, because it has built-in support for these protocols. Java provides this support in the form of classes. In particular, you'll find that three classes are particularly useful for this kind of low-level communication. They are

- InetAddress
- Socket
- ServerSocket

InetAddress

The InetAddress class encodes an IP address. You obtain InetAddress objects not by creating them with a constructor, but by calling one of three static methods defined by InetAddress.

One of these is called getByName(). This method takes a String object that contains the IP address either as a dotted octet or as its Domain Name Server equivalent. You can create a new InetAddress object either with this line of code:

```
InetAddress ipAddress = InetAddress.getByName("206.26.48.100");
```

or with this one:

```
InetAddress ipAddress = InetAddress.getByName("java.sun.com");
```

You can obtain the IP address of the machine which your code is running on by writing:

```
InetAddress ipAddress = InetAddress.getByLocalHost();
```

This creates an InetAddress object that represents the local machine.

The InetAddress class defines two instance methods: getAddress(), which returns an array of four bytes, and getHostName(), which returns a String. Each returns the IP address. getAddress() returns the dotted octet, whereas getHostName() returns the name found in the Domain Name Server.

You'll see next how you can use an InetAddress object to create a socket used to communicate with another computer over the Internet.

Socket and ServerSocket

The Socket class defines a socket—one end of a two-way communication. You need an IP address and a port to create a Socket object. Here's an example:

```
InetAddress ipAddress = InetAddress.getByName("java.sun.com");
Socket s = new Socket(ipAddress, 5001);
```

The first line obtains the IP address of the server. The second line creates a socket connected to that server if it's listening to port 5001 for client connections. This constructor establishes a dedicated connection between the local machine and the server. Figure 27-8 shows the first step in this process.

For this constructor to work, the server must already be waiting for clients to connect to it. The server first creates a ServerSocket object listening on a specified port:

```
ServerSocket serverSock = new ServerSocket(5001);
```

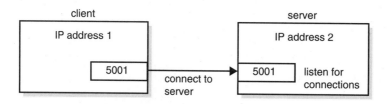

Figure 27-8   The client requests a connection with a server.

Then, the server waits for clients to connect to it by executing

```
Socket sock = serverSock.accept();
```

The accept() method waits until a client connects with the server. At this point, the accept() method does something very interesting: it tells the client that it should use a different port to continue the communication. This is shown in Figure 27-9.

For example, the server might obtain a new, free port to use to communicate with the client whose number is 1070. The client now communicates using local port 5001 and remote port 1070 (the remote port is the server's port from the client's point-of-view). Similarly, the server communicates using local port 1070 and remote port 5001 (the remote port is the client's port from the server's point-of-view). The server needs to obtain a new port so that it can continue to listen for other clients trying to connect to it on port 5001. This is shown in Figure 27-10.

All you need to know as an application programmer is the original port that the server is listening to: the port that the server and client agree to use for their dedicated connection is not something you need to decide on. Java's classes will handle this detail for you. In fact, if you do not invoke getLocalPort() and getPort() on the sockets you

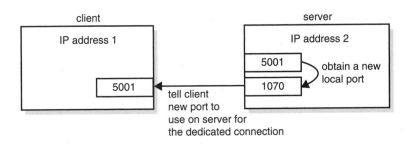

Figure 27-9   The server obtains a new local port and tells the client what it is.

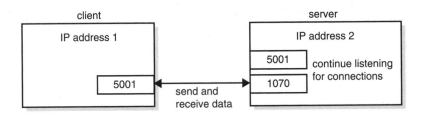

Figure 27-10   The server and client can now have a dedicated connection.

create to identify the local and remote ports, respectively, you'll never realize that ServerSocket's accept() method has reassigned the server's port for you.

 NOTE: This is really just background information — you won't have to deal with these ports directly, other than knowing which port the server is listening to initially. However, it's useful to know what's going on under the hood.

There are other constructors, as well, for both ServerSocket and Socket. For example, you can specify the local port as a different number from the remote port. For example, perhaps you want your socket's local port to be 3333, but you still want to connect to the server listening to port 5001. You can create your socket and connect to the server by writing:

```
Socket sock = new Socket(ipServer, 5001, ipLocal, 3333);
```

By default, the ServerSocket object you create will accept connections with up to 50 clients. You can also create a ServerSocket where you indicate this limit directly. For example, you can write:

```
ServerSocket serverSock = new ServerSocket(5001, 25);
```

This server socket can only accept up to 25 simultaneous connections. If a 26th client tries to connect to it, the server socket refuses the connection.

Internet Streams

At this point, once you've established a dedicated connection between client and server, you can use everything you're familiar with from the review of streams in Chapter 19. For example, you can acquire an InputStream object that has a socket as its source. Then, you can create a new Filter stream object and attach it to this InputStream. You might create a new DataInputStream object and use it to read bytes from the socket. Here's a code snippet that does this.

Let's say you have a Socket object in the variable sock. You can get an InputStream object by writing:

```
sock.getInputStream();
```

From this, you can create a DataInputStream by passing this value to its constructor. You might write this all-in-one line of code:

```
DataInputStream remoteIn = new
  DataInputStream(sock.getInputStream());
```

You can then use remoteIn to read from the socket and receive data from the machine you're connected to. For example, to read an integer, you can write:

```
int myInt = remoteIn.readInt();
```

To send data, you need to acquire an output stream for the client by using the method getOutputStream():

```
DataOutputStream remoteOut = new
  DataOutputStream(sock.getOutputStream());
```

You can then use remoteOut to write to the socket and send data to the machine you're connected to. For example, to write the number 5, you might write:

```
remoteOut.writeInt(5);
```

You've got to be sure to handle all of the exceptions appropriately. In particular when reading and writing using streams, you need to wrap your read() and write() calls in try-catch blocks and be prepared to catch IOException.

Of course, you need to read and write according to a protocol that both the server and client know how to speak. When your client reads, the server better send you something. Similarly, when your client writes, the server better try to read it. There are some read() methods that will time out if nothing appears. However, if you don't use these, read() will block forever until data finally arrives.

When your protocol is clearly established and you're reading and writing in the right sequence, you'll find that you're communicating over the Internet with just a few lines of code. Once you have completed your connection, you should close any streams you've created. After this, you should close the socket connection. You can invoke close() for both a stream and a socket to accomplish this.

Client-Server Examples

You've learned the basics of TCP/IP, seen the design issues and approaches for servers and clients, and learned about the networking classes available in Java to help you work with TCP/IP. Now, let's look at how to write a client/server application in Java by writing two types of chat programs.

In the first program, we'll write a simple chat program that connects one computer with another and passes messages back and forth. In the next program, we'll write a server that allows any number of clients to connect to it. In this second version, the server will broadcast each message it receives from a client to all other connected clients.

These servers do not require synchronization. To see how to synchronize between multiple clients, work through the practice programming assignment for the Developer exam, located in Chapter 30.

You'll find that you've seen some of this code in the snippets presented in the chapter so far. Now, you'll see these snippets as part of a working program.

Writing a Single-Client Server in Java

Let's take a look at how the single-client chat program works. You can launch this program from the command line; it runs as a standalone graphical application, not as an applet. If you specify no command-line arguments, it's launched as a server, waiting for a connection from a client.

You can also launch it as a client by specifying the name of the host to connect to. If you are running both the client and the server on the same machine, you can pass it the name "local." In other words, this program can act as either the client or the server, depending on whether or not you have supplied a command line parameter.

When you first launch the program as a server (without a command line parameter), by typing:

java SingleChat

It will appear as in Figure 27-11.

Then, when you launch the program as a client (by specifying the host where the server is already running), by typing

java SingleChat local

the new program runs and displays the user interface shown in Figure 27-12.

These two graphical user interfaces look mighty similar; the difference is in the title of the frame (and what went on behind the scenes, which we'll look at in a moment). Notice the title of the client states that it has connected to the server named localhost. In the meantime, the title of the server application changed to indicate it has "Accepted connection from localhost."

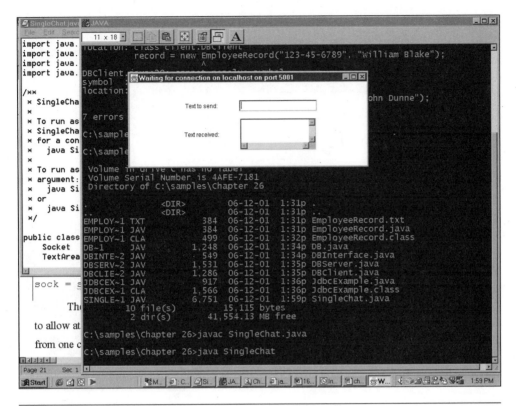

Figure 27-11 The SingleChat application launched as a server

Now whenever one person types text into the field labeled "Text to send" and hits enter, the text is sent over the network connection using TCP/IP to the other version of SingleChat it is connected with. This is shown in Figure 27-13 and Figure 27-14. The first figure shows text being typed into the Text to send text field. Then, after the user hits enter, the text is sent to the other SingleChat application. The text is received and displayed in the Text received text area shown in the second figure.

So how does this work? Let's look at the basic architecture first. Then I'll present the entire source code, and then we'll examine the lines of code specific to TCP/IP.

The SingleChat class is a Panel. It creates a Frame in main() so that it can appear on the screen. It lays out its user interface using a GridBagLayout.

SingleChat invokes one of two methods, client() or server(), depending on whether or not the user has supplied a command line parameter. Without a parameter, it runs

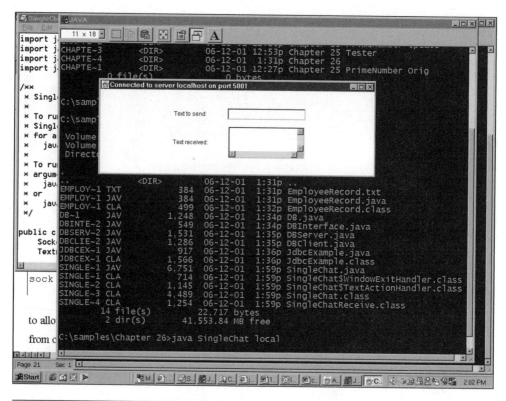

Figure 27-12 The SingleChat application launched as a client with a server already running

as a server. With a parameter, it runs as a client, and the server's name is passed to client().

The server() method waits for a connection. When a client connects to it, it obtains a socket for the client and spawns a thread that loops forever. This thread listens to this socket for data sent by the client.

The client() method tries to establish a connection with the server given the name of the machine the server is running on. Once it establishes this connection, it obtains a socket for the server and spawns a thread that loops forever. This thread listens to this socket for data sent by the server.

When the user hits the enter key in the text field labeled Text to send, the application gets the text in this text field and writes it to the socket it obtained when the two applications connected. When data arrives on the socket, as monitored in the thread that's continually looping, the application takes this text and displays it in the text area labeled Received text.

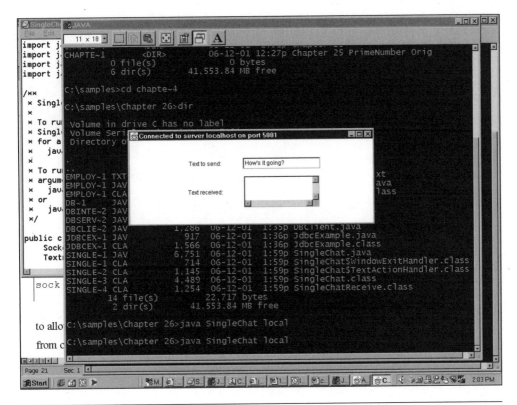

Figure 27-13 Text typed into the Text to send text field

Here is the complete code listing. It is under 200 lines of code, including comments:

```java
import java.io.*;
import java.net.*;
import java.awt.*;
import java.awt.event.*;

/**
 * SingleChat -- A chat program between a server and one client.
 *
 * To run as a server, do not supply any command line arguments.
 * SingleChat will start listening on the default port, waiting
 * for a connection:
 *    java SingleChat
 *
 * To run as a client, name the server as the first command line
 * argument:
 *    java SingleChat bluehorse.com
 * or
 *    java SingleChat local          // to run locally
 */
```

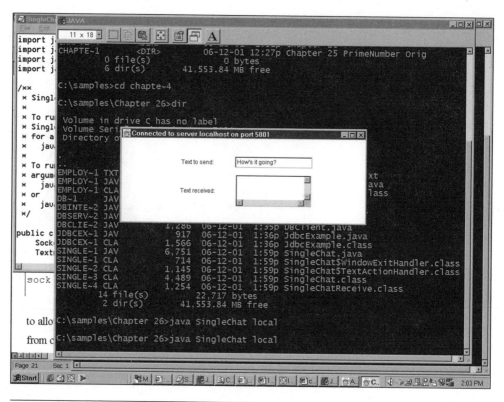

Figure 27-14 Text received and displayed in the Text received text area

```java
public class SingleChat extends Panel {
    Socket      sock;
    TextArea    receivedText;

    private GridBagConstraints c;
    private GridBagLayout       gridBag;
    private Frame               frame;
    private Label               label;
    private int                 port = 5001;    // The default port.
    private TextField           sendText;
    private DataOutputStream    remoteOut;


    public static void main(String args[]) {
        Frame f = new Frame("Waiting for connection...");

        String s = null;
        if (args.length > 0)
            s = args[0];
```

```
    SingleChat chat = new SingleChat(f);
    f.add("Center", chat);
    f.setSize(350, 200);
    f.show();

     // Make the connection happen.
     if (s == null)
        chat.server();
     else
        chat.client(s);
}

public SingleChat(Frame f) {
    frame = f;
    frame.addWindowListener(new WindowExitHandler());

    // Build the user interface.
    // Insets(bot, lf, rt, top)
    Insets insets = new Insets(10, 20, 5, 10);
    gridBag = new GridBagLayout();
    setLayout(gridBag);

    c = new GridBagConstraints();

    c.insets = insets;
    c.gridy = 0;
    c.gridx = 0;

    label = new Label("Text to send:");
    gridBag.setConstraints(label, c);
    add(label);

    c.gridx = 1;

    sendText = new TextField(20);

    sendText.addActionListener(new TextActionHandler());
    gridBag.setConstraints(sendText, c);
    add(sendText);

    c.gridy = 1;
    c.gridx = 0;

    label = new Label("Text received:");
    gridBag.setConstraints(label, c);
    add(label);

    c.gridx = 1;

    receivedText = new TextArea(3, 20);
    gridBag.setConstraints(receivedText, c);
    add(receivedText);

}
```

```java
// As a server, we create a server socket bound to the specified
// port, wait for a connection, and then spawn a thread to
// read data coming in over the network via the socket.

private void server() {
    ServerSocket serverSock = null;
    try {
        InetAddress serverAddr = InetAddress.getByName(null);

        displayMsg("Waiting for connection on " +
                serverAddr.getHostName() +
                " on port " + port);

        // We'll only accept one connection for this server.
        serverSock = new ServerSocket(port, 1);
        sock = serverSock.accept();

        displayMsg("Accepted connection from " +
                sock.getInetAddress().getHostName());

        remoteOut = new DataOutputStream(sock.
        getOutputStream());
        new SingleChatReceive(this).start();

    } catch (IOException e) {
        displayMsg(e.getMessage() +
            ": Failed to connect to client.");

    } finally {
        // At this point, since we only establish one connection
        // per run, we don't need the ServerSocket anymore.
        if (serverSock != null) {
            try {
                serverSock.close();
            } catch (IOException x) {
            }
        }
    }
}


// As a client, we create a socket bound to the specified port,
// connect to the specified host, and then spawn a thread to
// read data coming in over the network via the socket.

private void client(String serverName) {
    try {
        if (serverName.equals("local"))
            serverName = null;

        InetAddress serverAddr = InetAddress.
        getByName(serverName);
        sock = new Socket(serverAddr.getHostName(), port);
        remoteOut = new DataOutputStream(
        sock.getOutputStream());
```

```
            displayMsg("Connected to server " +
                    serverAddr.getHostName() +
                    " on port " + sock.getPort());

            new SingleChatReceive(this).start();

        } catch (IOException e) {
            displayMsg(e.getMessage() +
                ": Failed to connect to server.");
        }
    }

    void displayMsg(String s) {
        frame.setTitle(s);
    }

    protected void finalize() throws Throwable {
        try {
            if (remoteOut != null)
                remoteOut.close();
            if (sock != null)
                sock.close();
        } catch (IOException x) {
        }
        super.finalize();
    }

    class WindowExitHandler extends WindowAdapter {
        public void windowClosing(WindowEvent e) {
            Window w = e.getWindow();
            w.setVisible(false);
            w.dispose();
            System.exit(0);
        }
    }

    class TextActionHandler implements ActionListener {
        public void actionPerformed(ActionEvent e) {
            try {
                // Send it.
                remoteOut.writeUTF(sendText.getText());
                // Clear it.
                sendText.setText("");
            } catch (IOException x) {
                displayMsg(x.getMessage() +
                ": Connection to peer lost.");
            }
        }
    }

}

/**
 * SingleChatReceive takes data sent on a socket and displays it in
```

```
 * a text area. This receives it from the network.
 */
class SingleChatReceive extends Thread {
    private SingleChat chat;
    private DataInputStream remoteIn;
    private boolean listening = true;

    public SingleChatReceive(SingleChat chat) {
        this.chat = chat;
    }

    public synchronized void run() {
        String s;
        try {
            remoteIn = new DataInputStream(
            chat.sock.getInputStream());

            while (listening) {
                s = remoteIn.readUTF();
                chat.receivedText.setText(s);
            }

        } catch (IOException e) {
            chat.displayMsg(e.getMessage() +
                ": Connection to peer lost.");

        } finally {
            try {
              if (remoteIn != null)
                  remoteIn.close();
            } catch (IOException x) {
            }
        }
    }
}
```

Here are the key lines of code as far as TCP/IP is concerned.

server( )

First, here is how the server() method works. The two lines that actually wait for a client to connect to it and then accept this connection are:

```
serverSock = new ServerSocket(port, 1);
sock = serverSock.accept();
```

The constructor for ServerSocket takes a port number and, optionally, the number of connections to allow at one time. The default is 50; in this version of the chat program, we only allow one connection from one client. In the next version, we'll allow multiple clients to be connected to the server simultaneously.

PART II

The ServerSocket's accept() method waits for a connection from a client. When it accepts a connection and returns, it passes back a Socket object that represents the client.

Before these two lines, this method simply acquires the machine name that this server is running on so that it can display this to the user. After these two lines, it formats and displays a message containing the client's name. It then acquires a stream to use to write to the socket and starts a thread going that waits for data coming in on this socket.

client( )

The two lines that connect with the server are:

```
InetAddress serverAddr = InetAddress.getByName(serverName);
sock = new Socket(serverAddr.getHostName(), port);
```

serverName is a String that represents the IP address (either the dotted octet or the Domain Name Server name) where the server is running. If this name is null, then get-ByName() returns the name of the local machine. When the constructor for the socket returns, you will have obtained a socket you can use to communicate with the server.

Before these two lines, this method sets the serverName String to null if the name is "local," so that the Java methods will work with the local host. After these two lines, it formats and displays a message containing the server's name. It then acquires a stream to use to write to the socket and starts a thread that waits to process data arriving on this socket.

NOTE: As we covered already, the actual remote port number that this socket contains will be a port the server has decided it will use to establish the dedicated connection with the client. As I indicated earlier, this is a detail that is handled by Java classes, though it is useful to keep this in mind while trying to understand what is going on.

---

action( )

When the user types some text into the text field labeled Text to send and hits enter, the application finds out about it in action(). Since we have already acquired a DataOutputStream object, we can use any DataOutputStream method and write the data to the socket. From there, Java handles the TCP/IP and makes sure the data goes out over the network and finds its destination.

run() for SingleChatReceive

The first thing this method does is acquire a DataInputStream object with the line:

```
remoteIn = new DataInputStream(chat.sock.getInputStream());
```

We reference this socket via the SingleChat object, since SingleChatReceive is a different class from SingleChat.

Then, this thread loops forever, reading text from the socket and displaying it in the text area.

Cleaning Up

You'll notice that this application is very careful to clean up after itself. If we fall out of the listening loops, or if this object is finalized, it first closes the streams and then closes the sockets.

Writing a Multi-Client Server in Java

The SingleChat server is a little bit unusual in that it only communicates with one client during its life. Let's write a server that accepts connections from multiple clients.

When one client sends the server a message, the server will broadcast this message to all clients attached to it. As with the single-chat application, we'll look first at how it works. Then, we'll look at the basic architecture, view the source code, and examine the lines of code that make this a good multi-client, multithreaded server.

For this application, it was easier to write two different programs. One program is the server, which runs as a standalone character-mode program. (It doesn't really have much of an interface at all.) The other program is a client program that looks and acts very similar to the client program we looked at already.

When you launch the server (called MultiChatServer) by typing:

java MultiChatServer

at the command line, the program writes the following messages to the screen:

Hit CONTROL-C to exit the server.

Waiting for first connection on localhost on port 5001

At this point, it's ready for clients to connect to it. There is a hard limit in the code of 50 clients, set somewhat arbitrarily, with the intent of ensuring the server doesn't get swamped with requests. Otherwise, the server might get bogged down keeping track of network connections causing performance to become slow. The server will run forever, until the user hits CONTROL-C to actually break out of the program with this interrupt.

Once the server is running, the user can launch clients—any number theoretically, but up to 50 in this case—that connect to the server. To launch a client for this multi-chat application, specify two command line parameters: the name of the person taking part in the chat session, and the name of the host where the server is running. As before, you can type local to run locally, with the server and the client on the same machines. The name of this program is MultiChat. For example, you might type:

java MultiChat Shakespeare local

This will launch the client, this time putting the user's name in the title of the frame. Other clients can also connect to the same server. Now, when the user types into the text field labeled Text to send and hits enter, all other clients connected to the server will receive that message, with the client's name also displayed as a prefix, as in:

Shakespeare: If music be the food of love play on.

This identifies whom this message came from.

Now, here's the architecture. The server loops forever, waiting to accept connections from clients. When a client does connect with the server, the server acquires a stream to use to write to the socket and saves this stream in a list. It then creates a new thread that will handle all future communication with the client. It passes the client's socket to the thread and this output stream, since the thread will use this socket to communicate with the client. The server also passes the server instance to the thread, because the thread will later need to invoke some server methods.

> **NOTE:** Even if multiple clients can connect with the server, there might not be a need to keep track of all of the currently connected clients in a list in the server. If the clients do not need to interact with each other, the server can just spawn a new thread that handles the connection with the client, independently of the other client-handling threads. It is only because each client's message is broadcast to all the other clients that the server must keep track of all of the clients in this application.

The thread that interacts with the client also loops forever, waiting to receive data from the client. When it receives a message from the client, it invokes a method called broadcast(). This method loops through the different client output streams and sends the message to each of them.

After setting up the user interface, the client establishes a connection with the server and starts a thread that will listen for messages from the server. This thread listening for server messages loops forever. When it receives a message, it displays it in the text area labeled Received text. Whenever the user types into the text field labeled Text to send and hits Enter, the action() method sends this text to the server (where it is broadcast to all other clients connected to the server).

Now that you've gotten an overview of the architecture for both the client and the server, let's look at the source code. There are two separate source files for this application—one representing the server, and one representing the client. After each listing, I'll go over the lines of code you need to pay particular attention to.

First, here's the server:

```
import java.io.*;
import java.net.*;
import java.util.Vector;
import java.util.Enumeration;

/**
 * MultiChatServer -- A chat program between any number of clients.
 *
 * The server acts as the central clearing house of all messages.
 * To run as a server, do not supply any command line arguments.
 * MultiChat will start listening on the default port, waiting
 * for a connection:
 *
 *    java MultiChatServer
 */

public class MultiChatServer {
    private int        port = 5001;     // The default port.
    private boolean    listening = true;
    private Vector     clients = new Vector();

    public static void main(String args[]) {
        System.out.println("Hit control-c to exit the server.");
        new MultiChatServer().server();
    }

    // As a server, we create a server socket bound to the specified
    // port, wait for a connection, and then spawn a thread to
    // read data coming in over the network via the socket.

    private void server() {
        ServerSocket serverSock = null;

        try {
            InetAddress serverAddr = InetAddress.getByName(null);

            System.out.println("Waiting for first connection on " +
                    serverAddr.getHostName() +
                    " on port " + port);
```

```
        // Accept up to 50 connection at a time.
        // (This limit is just for the sake of performance.)
        serverSock = new ServerSocket(port, 50);

    } catch (IOException e) {
        System.out.println(e.getMessage() +
            ": Failed to create server socket.");
        return;
    }

    while (listening) {

        try {
            Socket socket = serverSock.accept();
            System.out.println("Accepted connection from " +
                socket.getInetAddress().getHostName());
            DataOutputStream remoteOut =
                new DataOutputStream(socket.getOutputStream());
            clients.addElement(remoteOut);
            new ServerHelper(socket, remoteOut, this).start();

        } catch (IOException e) {
            System.out.println(e.getMessage() +
                ": Failed to connect to client.");
        }
    }

    if (serverSock != null) {
        try {
            serverSock.close();
        } catch (IOException x) {
        }
    }
}

synchronized Vector getClients() {
    return clients;
}

synchronized void removeFromClients(DataOutputStream
remoteOut) {
    clients.removeElement(remoteOut);
}

}

/**
 * ServerHelper handles one client. The server creates one new
 * ServerHelper thread for each client that connects to it.
 */
class ServerHelper extends Thread {
    private Socket sock;
    private DataOutputStream remoteOut;
```

```
private MultiChatServer server;
private boolean listening = true;
private DataInputStream remoteIn;

ServerHelper(Socket sock, DataOutputStream remoteOut,
    MultiChatServer server) throws IOException
{
    this.sock = sock;
    this.remoteOut = remoteOut;
    this.server = server;
    remoteIn = new DataInputStream(sock.getInputStream());
}

public synchronized void run() {
    String s;

    try {
        while (listening) {
            s = remoteIn.readUTF();
            broadcast(s);
        }

    } catch (IOException e) {
        System.out.println(e.getMessage() +
            ": Connection to peer lost.");

    } finally {
        try {
            cleanUp();
        } catch (IOException x) {
        }
    }
}

// Send the message to all the sockets connected to the server.
private void broadcast(String s) {
    Vector clients = server.getClients();
    DataOutputStream dataOut = null;

    for (Enumeration e = clients.elements();
    e.hasMoreElements(); ) {
        dataOut = (DataOutputStream)(e.nextElement());

        if (!dataOut.equals(remoteOut)) {

            try {

                dataOut.writeUTF(s);

            } catch (IOException x) {
                System.out.println(x.getMessage() +
                    ": Failed to broadcast to client.");
                server.removeFromClients(dataOut);
            }
```

```
            }
        }
    }

    private void cleanUp() throws IOException {
        if (remoteOut != null) {
            server.removeFromClients(remoteOut);
            remoteOut.close();
            remoteOut = null;
        }

        if (remoteIn != null) {
            remoteIn.close();
            remoteIn = null;
        }

        if (sock != null) {
            sock.close();
            sock = null;
        }
    }

    protected void finalize() throws Throwable {
        try {
            cleanUp();
        } catch (IOException x) {
        }

        super.finalize();
    }

}
```

server( )

This time, we allow up to 50 clients to connect to the server. We accomplish this with the following line of code:

```
serverSock = new ServerSocket(port, 50);
```

Then, the server loops forever (until the user hits CONTROL-C). At each iteration in the loop, the server waits to accept a connection with a client:

```
Socket socket = serverSock.accept();
```

If the clients were operating independently of each other (for example, in a database server), the server could simply spawn a new thread to handle all future communication with that client, handing that thread the socket it just acquired. However, in this program, we need to keep track of all of the clients connected to the server—that's how we'll know who to broadcast the message to.

So, we create a DataOutputStream object, save this object in a list of all the other client DataOutputStreams, and then start our new thread, which we've called ServerHelper. Now, ServerHelper will handle all future communication with the client —but it will turn to this list of output streams to broadcast any messages it receives from the client it's handling:

```
DataOutputStream remoteOut =  new
  DataOutputStream(socket.getOutputStream());
clients.addElement(remoteOut);
new ServerHelper(socket, remoteOut, this).start();
```

run( )

The run() method in ServerHandler loops forever, simply reading data from the socket and broadcasting it to other clients also connected to the server.

```
while (listening) {
  s = remoteIn.readUTF();
  broadcast(s);
}
```

broadcast( )

This method simply enumerates over the list of clients connected to the server, and as long as the DataOutputStream object in this list is not from the client that sent the message, it writes the message to that client.

cleanUp( )

As always, we're very careful to close all the streams and sockets when we're through with them.

The Client

Now, here's the client (it's very similar to the SingleChat program in many ways):

```
import java.io.*;
import java.net.*;
import java.awt.*;
import java.awt.event.*;

/**
 * MultiChat -- A chat program between any number of clients.
 *
 * To run as a client, supply two parameters:
 *   1. The name of the person to identify this user
 *   2. the name the server:
```

```
 *      java MultiChat Spielberg bluehorse.com
 * or
 *      java MultiChat Spielberg local          // to run locally
 */

public class MultiChat extends Panel {
    TextArea   receivedText;
    Socket     sock;                 // The communication socket.

    private GridBagConstraints c;
    private GridBagLayout       gridBag;
    private Frame               frame;
    private Label               label;
    private int                 port = 5001;   // The default port.
    private TextField           sendText;
    private String              hostname;
    private String              username;
    private DataOutputStream    remoteOut;

    public static void main(String args[]) {
        if (args.length != 2) {
            System.out.println(
            "format is: java MultiChat <username> <hostname>");
            return;
        }

        Frame f = new Frame(args[0]);

        MultiChat chat = new MultiChat(f, args[0], args[1]);
        f.add("Center", chat);
        f.setSize(350, 200);
        f.show();

        // Make the connection happen.
        chat.client();

    }

    public MultiChat(Frame f, String user, String host) {
        frame = f;
        frame.addWindowListener(new WindowExitHandler());
        username = user;
        hostname = host;

        // Build the user interface.
        //Insets(bot, lf, rt, top)
        Insets insets = new Insets(10, 20, 5, 10);
        gridBag = new GridBagLayout();
        setLayout(gridBag);

        c = new GridBagConstraints();

        c.insets = insets;
        c.gridy = 0;
        c.gridx = 0;
```

```
                   label = new Label("Text to send:");
                   gridBag.setConstraints(label, c);
                   add(label);

                   c.gridx = 1;

                   sendText = new TextField(20);
                   sendText.addActionListener(new TextActionHandler());
                   gridBag.setConstraints(sendText, c);
                   add(sendText);

                   c.gridy = 1;
                   c.gridx = 0;

                   label = new Label("Text received:");
                   gridBag.setConstraints(label, c);
                   add(label);

                   c.gridx = 1;

                   receivedText = new TextArea(3, 20);
                   gridBag.setConstraints(receivedText, c);
                   add(receivedText);

              }

        // As a client, we create a socket bound to the specified port,
        // connect to the specified host, and then spawn a thread to
        // read data coming coming in over the network via the socket.

        private void client() {
              try {
                   if (hostname.equals("local"))
                        hostname = null;

                   InetAddress serverAddr =
                     InetAddress.getByName(hostname);
                   sock = new Socket(serverAddr.getHostName(), port);
                   remoteOut = new
                     DataOutputStream(sock.getOutputStream());

                   System.out.println("Connected to server " +
                           serverAddr.getHostName() +
                           " on port " + sock.getPort());

                   new MultiChatReceive(this).start();

              } catch (IOException e) {
                   System.out.println(e.getMessage() +
                        ": Failed to connect to server.");
              }
        }
```

```
      protected void finalize() throws Throwable {
          try {
              if (remoteOut != null)
                  remoteOut.close();
              if (sock != null)
                  sock.close();
          } catch (IOException x) {
          }
          super.finalize();
      }

      class WindowExitHandler extends WindowAdapter {
        public void windowClosing(WindowEvent e) {
          Window w = e.getWindow();
          w.setVisible(false);
          w.dispose();
          System.exit(0);
        }
      }

      // Send data out to the socket we're communicating with when
      // the user hits enter in the text field.
      class TextActionHandler implements ActionListener {
        public void actionPerformed(ActionEvent e) {
          try {
            // Send it.
            remoteOut.writeUTF(sendText.getText());
            // Clear it.
            sendText.setText("");
          } catch (IOException x) {
            System.out.println(x.getMessage() +
              ": Connection to peer lost.");
          }
        }
      }
}


/**
 * MultiChatReceive takes data sent on a socket and displays it in
 * a text area. This receives it from the network.
 */
class MultiChatReceive extends Thread {
    private MultiChat chat;

    MultiChatReceive(MultiChat chat) {
        this.chat = chat;
    }

    public synchronized void run() {
        String s;
        DataInputStream remoteIn = null;
```

```
        try {
            remoteIn = new DataInputStream(
            chat.sock.getInputStream());

            while (true) {
                s = remoteIn.readUTF();
                chat.receivedText.setText(s);
            }

        } catch (IOException e) {
            System.out.println(e.getMessage() +
                ": Connection to peer lost.");

        } finally {
            try {
                if (remoteIn != null)
                    remoteIn.close();
            } catch (IOException x) {
            }
        }
    }
}
```

The only real difference between the client version of MultiChat and the client portion of SingleChat is that one of the command-line parameters is the user's name. This name is placed in front of the user's message to identify the speaker when the message is broadcast.

Cleaning Up

You'll also notice that, once again, we're very careful about closing the streams and sockets after we're through with them.

Exercise 27.1

Write a standalone character-mode client/server chat application using sockets. The server should accept only one connection from the client. Each peer should write what the user types via the keyboard to its communication socket. the peer should also read what comes in over this communication socket and display it in the standard output.

Exercise 27.2

Write a standalone character-mode client/server application where the client guesses a number between 0 and 9 chosen by the server. The client should send messages that follow this protocol:

If the client wants to know whether the number chosen by the server is greater than some number, it should send a String in the format:

```
>#
```

For example, to guess if the number is greater than 5, the client can send:

```
>5
```

To ask whether the number is less than a value, the client can send:

```
<#
```

To guess if the number is equal to a particular value, the client can send:

```
=#
```

The server should send true or false, depending on the number it has chosen and on the client's guess. When the client has guessed the number correctly, the server should send a congratulatory message and then end the connection to the client.

Uniform Resource Locator

Here's a quick word about URLs (you won't really have to program using URLs on the programming assignment).

Java defines a class called URL. When you use this class, you don't have to concern yourself with what's really going on with TCP/IP. All you have to do is point to the Internet address you are interested in and use the java.io classes to read from (and write to) that location.

The basic format of a URL address is:

```
access-method://server-name[&port]/dir/file&]
```

As you can see from this, a URL indicates the access method, server name, and file name of an Internet resource. Typically, the access method is something like http or ftp. The server name for a Web address might be **www.tvpress.com**. The server name for an ftp address might be ftp.tvpress.com. The directory and file name refer to the directory structure of the server.

You can create a URL object using a variety of constructors. The easiest way is to create a new URL like this:

```
URL myHome = new URL("www.tvpress.com");
```

You can then use a method called openConnection() to begin reading from this URL, using the same I/O classes and methods you've already learned about. The open-Connect() method returns a URLConnection object. With this, you can obtain an input stream or an output stream by calling getInputStream() or getOutputStream(). As you might suspect, you can then use this stream to access the resource.

Answers to the Exercises

Exercise 27.1

The only important change in this particular solution, compared to the example programs in the text, is that I used two threads: one to continually monitor what the user types and one to read from the socket.

```java
import java.io.*;
import java.net.*;
import java.awt.*;

/**
 * CharChat -- A chat program between a server and one client.
 *
 * To run as a client, name the server as the first command line
 * argument:
 *    java CharChat bluehorse.com
 * or
 *    java CharChat local          // to run locally
 */

public class CharChat {
    private int                  port = 5001;     // The default port.

    public static void main(String args[]) {

        String s = null;
        if (args.length > 0)
            s = args[0];

        CharChat chat = new CharChat();
        if (s == null)
            chat.server();
        else
            chat.client(s);
    }

    // As a server, we create a server socket bound to the specified
    // port, wait for a connection, and then spawn a thread to
    // read data coming in over the network via the socket.
```

```java
private void server() {
    Socket sock = null;
    ServerSocket serverSock = null;

    try {
        serverSock = new ServerSocket(port, 1);

        //We'll only accept one connection for this server.
        sock = serverSock.accept();

        new CharChatSend(sock).start();
        new CharChatReceive(sock).start();

    } catch (IOException x) {
        System.out.println(x.getMessage() +
            ": Failed to connect to client.");
        System.exit(1);

    } finally {

        // At this point, we don't need the ServerSocket
        // anymore.
        if (serverSock != null) {
            try {
                serverSock.close();
            } catch (IOException x) {
            }
        }
    }

}

// As a client, we create a socket bound to the specified port,
// connect to the specified host, and then spawn a thread to
// read data coming coming in over the network via the socket.

private void client(String serverName) {
    try {
        if (serverName.equals("local"))
            serverName = null;

        InetAddress serverAddr =
            InetAddress.getByName(serverName);
        Socket sock = new
            Socket(serverAddr.getHostName(), port);

        new CharChatSend(sock).start();
        new CharChatReceive(sock).start();

    } catch (IOException e) {
        System.out.println(e.getMessage() +
            ": Failed to connect to server.");
    }
}

}
```

```
/**
 * CharChatReceive takes data sent on a socket and displays it in
 * the standard output.
 */
class CharChatReceive extends Thread {
    private Socket sock;
    private DataInputStream remoteIn;
    private boolean listening = true;

    public CharChatReceive(Socket sock) throws IOException {
        this.sock = sock;
        remoteIn = new DataInputStream(sock.getInputStream());
    }

    public synchronized void run() {
        String s;
        try {

            while (listening) {
                s = remoteIn.readUTF();
                System.out.println(s);
            }

        } catch (IOException e) {
            System.out.println(e.getMessage() +
                ": Connection to peer lost.");
        } finally {
            try {
                if (remoteIn != null) {
                    remoteIn.close();
                    remoteIn = null;
                }

                if (sock != null) {
                    sock.close();
                    sock = null;
                }

            } catch (IOException x) {
            }
        }
    }

    protected void finalize() throws Throwable {
        try {
            if (remoteIn != null)
                remoteIn.close();
            if (sock != null)
                sock.close();
        } catch (IOException x) {
        }
        super.finalize();
```

```
    }

}

/**
 * CharChatSend takes data entered on the standard input and
 * sends it out over a socket.
 */
class CharChatSend extends Thread {
    private Socket sock;
    private DataOutputStream remoteOut;
    private boolean listening = true;

    public CharChatSend(Socket sock) throws IOException {
        this.sock = sock;
        remoteOut = new DataOutputStream(sock.getOutputStream());
    }

    public synchronized void run() {
        BufferedReader in = null;
        String s;
        try {

            in = new BufferedReader(new
              InputStreamReader(System.in));

            while (listening) {
                s = in.readLine();
                if (s.equals(""))
                    break;
                remoteOut.writeUTF(s);
            }

        } catch (IOException e) {
            System.out.println(e.getMessage() +
                ": Connection to peer lost.");

        } finally {
            try {
                if (in != null)
                    in.close();

                if (remoteOut != null) {
                    remoteOut.close();
                    remoteOut = null;
                }

                // Socket closed in receive thread

            } catch (IOException x) {
            }
        }
    }
```

```
protected void finalize() throws Throwable {
    try {
        if (remoteOut != null)
            remoteOut.close();

        // Socket closed in receive thread

    } catch (IOException x) {
    }
    super.finalize();
}

}
```

Exercise 27.2

Here is the client:

```
import java.io.*;
import java.net.*;
import java.awt.*;

/**
 * NumberClient -- The client program for the guessing game.
 *
 * To run as a client, name the server as the first command line
 * argument:
 *    java NumberClient bluehorse.com
 * or
 *    java NumberClient local          // to run locally
 */

public class NumberClient {
    private int              port = 5001;    // The default port.
    private Socket           sock;
    private DataInputStream  remoteIn;
    private DataOutputStream remoteOut;
    private boolean          listening = true;

    public static void main(String args[]) {

        if (args.length != 1) {
            System.out.println (
            "format is: java NumberClient <hostname>");
            return;
        }

        new NumberClient().client(args[0]);
    }

    // As a client, we create a socket bound to the specified port,
    // connect to the specified host, and then start communicating
    // over the network via the socket.
```

```java
private void client(String serverName) {
    BufferedReader in = new BufferedReader(new
    InputStreamReader(System.in));

    try {
        if (serverName.equals("local"))
            serverName = null;

        InetAddress serverAddr =
          InetAddress.getByName(serverName);
        sock = new Socket(serverAddr.getHostName(), port);
        remoteIn = new
          DataInputStream(sock.getInputStream());
        remoteOut = new
          DataOutputStream(sock.getOutputStream());

        while (listening) {
            String s = in.readLine();
            if (s.equals(""))
                listening = false;
            else
                remoteOut.writeUTF(s);

            String response = remoteIn.readUTF();
            System.out.println(response);
        }

    } catch (IOException e) {
        System.out.println(e.getMessage() +
            ": Connection with server closed.");

    } finally {
        try {
            if (remoteIn != null) {
                remoteIn.close();
                remoteIn = null;
            }

            if (remoteOut != null) {
                remoteOut.close();
                remoteOut = null;
            }

            if (sock != null) {
                sock.close();
                sock = null;
            }

        } catch (IOException x) {
        }
    }
}
```

```
        protected void finalize() throws Throwable {
            try {
                if (remoteIn != null)
                    remoteIn.close();
                if (remoteOut != null)
                    remoteOut.close();
                if (sock != null)
                    sock.close();
            } catch (IOException x) {
            }
            super.finalize();
        }

}
```

Here is the server:

```
import java.io.*;
import java.net.*;
import java.awt.*;

/**
 * NumberServer -- The server for a number guessing application.
 *
 * To run as a server, name the server as the first command line
 * argument:
 *    java NumberServer bluehorse.com
 * or
 *    java NumberServer local          // to run locally
 */

public class NumberServer {
    private int              port = 5001;    // The default port.
    private boolean          listening = true;

    public static void main(String args[]) {
        new NumberServer().server();
    }

    // As a server, we create a server socket bound to the specified
    // port, wait for a connection, and then spawn a thread to
    // read data coming in over the network via the socket.

    private void server() {
        ServerSocket serverSock = null;

        try {
            serverSock = new ServerSocket(port, 50);
        } catch (IOException x) {
            System.out.println(x.getMessage() +
                ": Failed to create server socket.");
            System.exit(1);
        }
```

```
        while (listening) {
            try {

                Socket sock = serverSock.accept();
                new HandleGuesses(sock).start();

            } catch (IOException x) {
                System.out.println(x.getMessage() +
                    ": Failed to connect to client.");
                System.exit(1);
            }
        }

        // At this point, we don't need the ServerSocket anymore.
        if (serverSock != null) {
            try {
                serverSock.close();
            } catch (IOException x) {
            }
        }

    }

}


/**
 * HandleGuesses communicates with the client.
 */
class HandleGuesses extends Thread {
    private Socket sock;
    private DataInputStream remoteIn;
    private DataOutputStream remoteOut;
    private boolean listening = true;
    private int num = (int)(Math.random() * 10);

    public HandleGuesses(Socket sock) throws IOException {
        this.sock = sock;
        remoteIn = new DataInputStream(sock.getInputStream());
        remoteOut = new DataOutputStream(sock.getOutputStream());
    }

    public synchronized void run() {
        String s;
        String op;
        String guessString;
        int guessInt;
        try {

            while (listening) {
                s = remoteIn.readUTF();
                op = s.substring(0, 1);
                guessString = s.substring(1, 2);
                guessInt = new Integer(guessString).intValue();
```

```
                    if (op.equals(">"))
                        handleGreaterThan(guessInt);
                    else if (op.equals("<"))
                        handleLessThan(guessInt);
                    else
                        handleEquals(guessInt);
                }

        } catch (NumberFormatException x) {
            System.out.println(x.getMessage() +
                ": Protocol problem: expected a number.");

        } catch (IOException x) {
            System.out.println(x.getMessage() +
                ": Connection to peer lost.");

        } finally {
            try {
                if (remoteIn != null) {
                    remoteIn.close();
                    remoteIn = null;
                }

                if (remoteOut != null) {
                    remoteOut.close();
                    remoteOut = null;
                }

                if (sock != null) {
                    sock.close();
                    sock = null;
                }

            } catch (IOException x) {
            }
        }
    }

    private void handleGreaterThan(int i) throws IOException {
        if (num > i)
            remoteOut.writeUTF("true");
        else
            remoteOut.writeUTF("false");
    }

    private void handleLessThan(int i) throws IOException{
        if (num < i)
            remoteOut.writeUTF("true");
        else
            remoteOut.writeUTF("false");
    }
```

```
    private void handleEquals(int i) throws IOException {
        if (i == num) {
            remoteOut.writeUTF("You guessed it!");
            listening = false;
        }

        else
            remoteOut.writeUTF("false");
    }

    protected void finalize() throws Throwable {
        try {
            if (remoteIn != null)
                remoteIn.close();
            if (remoteOut != null)
                remoteOut.close();
            if (sock != null)
                sock.close();
        } catch (IOException x) {
        }
        super.finalize();
    }

}
```

Review Questions

1. A socket encodes:
   a. a port number
   b. an IP address
   c. both a port number and an IP address
   d. none of these

2. To wait for a client to request a connection, your server can use the class:
   a. Socket
   b. ServerSocket
   c. Server
   d. URL

3. When you create a new Socket instance using a constructor that takes a host address:
   a. java attempts to establish a connection over the Internet with the host.
   b. java starts a server running on the host.
   c. nothing special happens until you invoke the Socket's accept() method.

4. To acquire an output stream to use to communicate via a socket given a Socket instance named sock, you can write:
   a. sock.accept();
   b. sock.getDataOutputStream();
   c. sock.getOutputStream();
   d. new DataOutputStream(sock);

5. The ServerSocket's accept() method returns an object of type:
   a. Socket
   b. ServerSocket
   c. Server
   d. URL

6. TCP is used to:
   a. Identify a machine on the Internet based on a dotted octet or domain name.
   b. Ensure packets arrive in the same order they are sent.
   c. Both a and b.
   d. Neither of these.

Answers to Review Questions

1. c. A socket encodes both a port number and an IP address.

2. b. Invoke the ServerSocket's accept() method to wait for an incoming request.

3. a. Creating a Socket using a constructor that specifies a host causes Java to attempt to establish a connection with that host.

4. c. Use getOutputStream() to acquire a stream. You can then create a DataOutput-Stream by passing this stream to its constructor.

5. a. The ServerSocket's accept() method returns an instance of class Socket, which the server can use to communicate with the client.

6. b. Transport Control Protocol (TCP) guarantees packets arrive in the same order they are sent. Internet Protocol (IP) identifies machines on the Internet.

Designing Application Interfaces

Objectives for This Chapter

- Use layout managers to size and space components as you intend.
- Embed layout managers within other layout managers to achieve sophisticated effects.
- Set fonts and colors for your components.
- Change a component after it has been displayed.
- Place user interface elements within top-level frames.

If you've been reading this book straight through, you've already read Chapters 18 and 19 where we discussed the basics of creating a graphical user interface. With that knowledge, you can probably fish around in the APIs for the methods you need, piece together more complicated user interfaces, and add the little flourishes that will make your interface behave exactly as you would like. However, there's no need to waste your time through trial and error. This chapter helps point you in the right direction when building advanced graphical user interfaces.

Imitating a typical real-world situation, the programming assignment requires you to create a graphical user interface that exactly matches a set of specifications. The assignment provides diagrams that show you how the user interface should look when it first appears, and how it should look if the user enlarges the enclosing frame.

To meet the specifications, you've got to create a hierarchy of containers within other containers, using a combination of different layout managers. You've also got to know how to change components after they've been displayed on the screen.

The programming assignment is a standalone graphical application. This means that there is no appletviewer or Web browser to create an enclosing frame for you. You need to know how to write your own.

Mix and Match!

We briefly looked at how components are sized back in Chapter 18. However, our objective then was to understand enough to pass the programmer's test. Now, our objective is a little broader: to use the proper layout manager in the proper way to achieve a specific look.

You can create arbitrarily complex arrangements in your user interface by nesting layout managers. Here are some scenarios.

Let's say you want to arrange five buttons along the top of an applet. You might want these five buttons in any number of appearances:

- All with a width equal to the widest button
- Each only as large as necessary to contain its label
- Centered, left-aligned, or right-aligned
- Centered but equal in width

and so on. Achieving the look you want involves two things:

- Using the right layout manager to stretch or not stretch the buttons as appropriate
- Using the right combination of layout managers so that the buttons are aligned and arranged correctly in relation to each other

Using One Layout Manager

Let's look at the simplest situations first: using one layout manager to achieve the button layouts. A BorderLayout is not the best choice to use directly for laying out five buttons—each region (North, South, and so on) can only contain one component, so the look of all five regions being used by five buttons is unusual. This arrangement is shown in Figure 28-1.

Each button expands to fill up its region. In particular, the North and South buttons expand horizontally, whereas the East and West buttons expand vertically. The Center button takes up the remaining space.

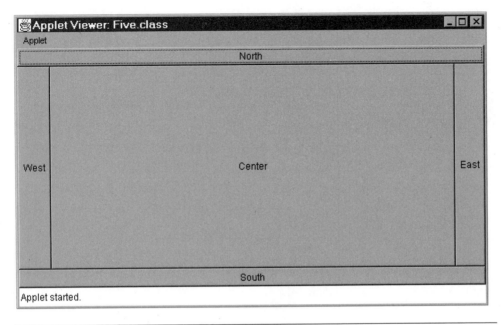

Figure 28-1   Five buttons arranged in a BorderLayout

The code for this (which you saw back in Chapter 21) is:

```
import java.awt.*;
import java.applet.*;

public class Five extends Applet {
   public void init() {
       setLayout(new BorderLayout());
       add(new Button("North"), BorderLayout.NORTH);
       add(new Button("South"), BorderLayout.SOUTH);
       add(new Button("East"), BorderLayout.EAST);
       add(new Button("West"), BorderLayout.WEST);
       add(new Button("Center"), BorderLayout.CENTER);
   }
}
```

A GridLayout is probably not what you want either, if a GridLayout is the only layout manager you're using. For example, arranging five buttons in a grid that is 1 row by 5 columns looks like Figure 28-2.

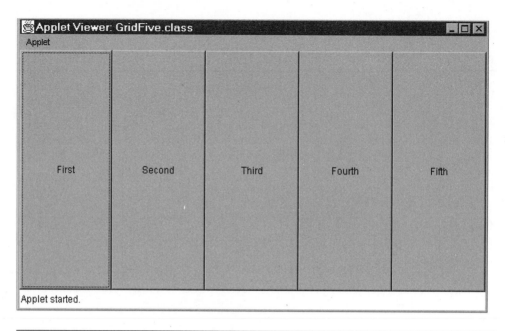

Figure 28-2 Five buttons in a GridLayout

As you can see, the buttons are all equally sized and take up the full region of the grid cell. The code is

```
import java.awt.*;
import java.applet.*;

public class GridFive extends Applet {
    public void init() {
        setLayout(new GridLayout(1, 5));
        add(new Button("First"));
        add(new Button("Second"));
        add(new Button("Third"));
        add(new Button("Fourth"));
        add(new Button("Fifth"));
    }
}
```

You can also create the GridLayout using a constructor where you define space around the cells. For example, creating the GridLayout with this line of code:

```
setLayout(new GridLayout(1, 5, 10, 0));
```

creates the display in Figure 28-3.

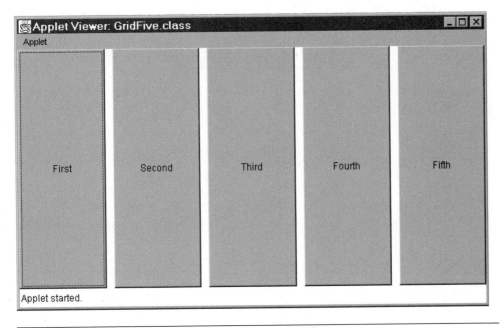

Figure 28-3   A GridLayout with space around each cell

If there were multiple rows, we could also specify a vertical gap. In the snippet above, we pass 0 to the constructor for GridLayout for the vertical gap, since we have only one row.

A FlowLayout will arrange the buttons first left to right, and then, as it runs out of room on each row, top to bottom. The buttons take on their natural size. By default, each row is centered, as in Figure 28-4.

Here's the code that produced Figure 28-4:

```
import java.awt.*;
import java.applet.*;

public class FlowFiveA extends Applet {
    public void init() {
        setLayout(new FlowLayout());
        add(new Button("First"));
        add(new Button("Second"));
        add(new Button("Third"));
        add(new Button("Fourth"));
        add(new Button("Fifth"));
    }
}
```

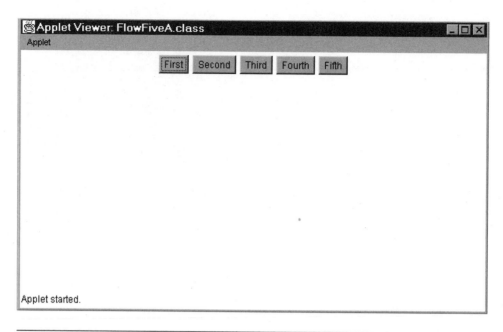

Figure 28-4 A FlowLayout arranging five buttons

However, you don't have to accept that each row is centered. You can use the constants FlowLayout.LEFT, FlowLayout.CENTER, and FlowLayout.RIGHT to set the alignment. One of the constructors allows you to pass in this alignment value.

You can also specify horizontal and vertical gaps between components and rows by invoking the constructor that takes three parameters: the alignment, the horizontal gaps, and the vertical gaps. For example, creating the FlowLayout with this line of code:

```
setLayout(new FlowLayout(FlowLayout.LEFT));
```

creates the display shown in Figure 28-5.

As you can see, there's only so much you can achieve when you use layout managers one at a time. The power comes from using them in combination.

For example, to arrange the five buttons along the bottom of an applet and make them left-aligned, you can write the following code:

```
import java.awt.*;
import java.applet.*;
public class FlowFiveB extends Applet {
    public void init() {
```

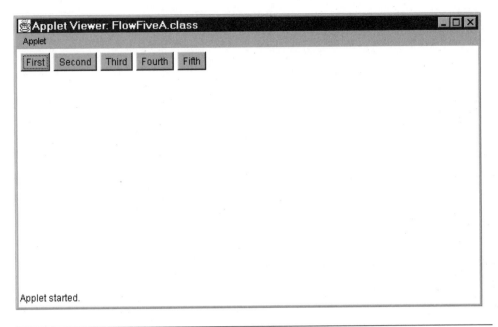

Figure 28-5   A FlowLayout arrangement where the components are left-aligned

```
Panel p = new Panel();
p.setLayout(new FlowLayout(FlowLayout.LEFT));
p.add(new Button("First"));
p.add(new Button("Second"));
p.add(new Button("Third"));
p.add(new Button("Fourth"));
p.add(new Button("Fifth"));

setLayout(new BorderLayout());
add(p, BorderLayout.SOUTH);
    }
}
```

In this code, we first place the buttons into a Panel object that uses a FlowLayout to left-align them. Then, we add the Panel object to the applet, which uses a BorderLayout. This program produces the display shown in Figure 28-6.

What if you want to make each button the same size, but still align them on the left at the bottom of the applet? Then you have to use three layout managers in combination. That's no problem at all; just think through your design carefully so that it all comes together in the end.

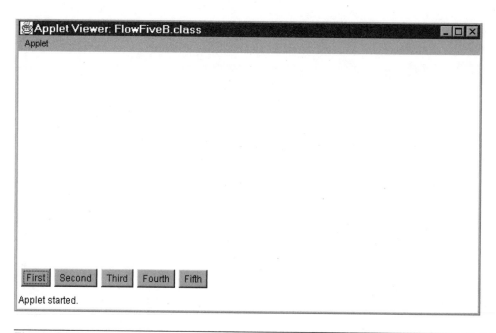

Figure 28-6 Using BorderLayout and FlowLayout together

First, you want to make all the buttons the size of the largest one (you can use a GridLayout to achieve this effect). Then, you want to align this group of buttons on the left (you can use a FlowLayout to accomplish this). Finally, you want the left-aligned buttons on the bottom of the applet (naturally, you use a BorderLayout to make this happen).

Figure 28-7 shows the layout you want.

And here's the code:

```
import java.awt.*;
import java.applet.*;

public class FlowFiveC extends Applet {
    public void init() {
        Panel p1 = new Panel();
        p1.setLayout(new GridLayout(1, 5));
        p1.add(new Button("First"));
        p1.add(new Button("Second"));
        p1.add(new Button("Third"));
        p1.add(new Button("Fourth"));
        p1.add(new Button("Fifth"));
        Panel p2 = new Panel();
        p2.setLayout(new FlowLayout(FlowLayout.LEFT));
```

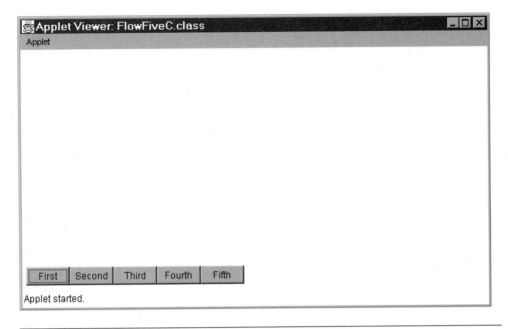

Figure 28-7   A layout involving three layout managers

```
        p2.add(p1);

        setLayout(new BorderLayout());
        add(p2, BorderLayout.SOUTH);
    }
}
```

The examples so far have involved buttons, because it's clear where the layout managers are placing each one. You can achieve the same effects with the other components. Button, Label, TextField, TextArea, Choice, and List will all stretch in GridLayout and BorderLayout regions. Checkbox will not.

Exercise 28.1

Create a user interface that looks like the display shown in Figure 28-8.

This is the interface for a word processing application. There are two rows of options on the bottom of the applet. The first row contains checkboxes indicating possible text colors: black, blue, and red. Notice that these are evenly spaced in their row. Naturally, they should be mutually exclusive. The second row offers a list of font types (Courier, Helvetica, and Times Roman) and point sizes (8, 10, and 12). Notice that these are centered.

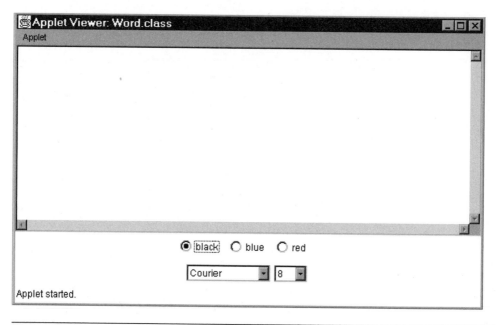

Figure 28-8   An interface with a text area and two rows of options

The text area should take up the rest of the applet. It should be 60 columns wide and 10 rows high. (It's not necessary to make this applet functional now.)

Changing Your Look

Just because you've displayed a component doesn't mean it's out of your hands entirely. As long as you can find it through an object reference, you can continue to change its appearance.

Text

One common task is to change the text in a label. For example, you might have a label that displays a status message. You can use the method setText() to change what a Label object displays and pass this method a new String to use.

Updating a label or a button can be tricky in certain situations. If the label is in a BorderLayout in the North or South region, it will already be stretched to its widest and you won't have to concern yourself with the label's size. However, if the label is in a flow layout, the label will not change its size if the new text is longer than the old text. This can cause your new text to be clipped.

If your label won't stretch because it is in a flow layout, and it won't display any text initially, you may want to create the label with some blank spaces. That way, when you do place text into it, the label is already sized large enough to contain the text.

Font and Color

Here are some important classes and methods to keep in mind regarding changing the appearance of a component:

- The Font class defines a font. To define a new Font object, you supply the font name, font style (from a set of constants defined by the Font class), and the size of the font. You can then set the font used by a component by invoking setFont() and passing your new Font object.

- Courier is a proportional font, which means that each letter's width is the same. It's convenient to use a proportional font when you want your text to line up with text in other lines (such as in a text area or list).

- You can use setForeground() to set the text color for components. You can also use setBackground() to set the component's background color. Pass both of these methods a Color object. Almost always, you will use a predefined Color object referenced from the Color class, such as Color.blue, Color.red, or Color.gray, to name three colors. Many common colors are represented as static variables like this in the Color class.

Replacing a Component

To remove a component from a container, invoke the remove() method, passing this method the object reference of the component that you want to remove.

You can even add a component by invoking add() at any time—not just when you initially build your user interface. Invoking remove() and add() back-to-back can replace a component. However, there are a number of gotchas.

First of all, you may have to force the user interface to lay itself out again after you've tinkered with it. You can do this by invoking validate().

Second of all, and perhaps most importantly, you have to be aware of the order in which you added components to your container. If you are attempting to replace the third button in a grid that is 2 rows by 3 columns, you can't just remove the third button and replace it by invoking add(). That would cause the new button to be added to the end of the grid.

Instead of using add() and only passing the component to add, you can use an over-loaded version of add() that also takes a position index indicating where it should be added to the container. So, to replace the third button in this scenario, you can write:

```
remove(oldButton);
add(newbutton, 2); // 0 based
```

Sometimes, if you want to replace components in a panel or replace the text in a choice or list, the best way to achieve a smooth look is to create a new component or set of components, and then replace the ones onscreen—rather than changing the on-screen components as you go, which can cause the display to look messy while the change is taking place.

Exercise 28.2

Extend the applet you wrote in Exercise 28.1 so that the text in the text area matches the selections in the options on the bottom two rows.

Working with Frames

If you climb the container hierarchy to the top, you'll always find a Frame. All compo-nents must ultimately be contained inside a Frame. You can either create this enclosing Frame yourself, or, in the case of an applet, you might use the Frame the appletviewer or Web browser provided.

It's important to know that you need a top level Frame for a number of reasons:

- If you want to display a window separately from your applet, perhaps outside of the Web browser, you'll need to create a Frame to contain this separate window.

- If you don't create an applet, you must create a Frame for any standalone graphi-cal user interfaces you create.

- You need a Frame to show dialogs.

Let's start our work with Frames by looking at a snippet (which we'll improve upon) to display a standalone, graphical user interface contained in an object reference named panel:

```
Frame f = new Frame();
f.add(panel, BorderLayout.CENTER); // BorderLayout is the default
for frame
f.pack();
f.show();
```

Let's examine this snippet for a moment. First, the Frame's title will say Unknown, because we haven't explicitly supplied our own title. Second, the application won't close or exit when the user clicks the Close button in this Frame. In fact, in Windows and Solaris, the user has to use CONTROL-C in the window the user launched this program from to end it. That's not exactly a graceful user interface.

Closing the Frame

We can fix the lack of a title in the Frame by passing one to the Frame's overloaded constructor. But the inability to exit when the user clicks the Close button can best be fixed by providing a WindowListener for the Frame and handle the windowClosing() event, like this:

```
import java.awt.Window;
import java.awt.event.WindowAdapter;
import java.awt.event.WindowEvent;

/**
 * This handler helps a window (such as a top-level Frame)
 * exit gracefully.
 */
public class WindowCloser extends WindowAdapter {
    public void windowClosing(WindowEvent e) {
        Window w = e.getWindow();
        w.setVisible(false);
        w.dispose();
        System.exit(0);
    }
}
```

Then, add an instance of this class to the window listeners for the window or frame you want to be able to close. For example, if your Frame is in a reference named topFrame, and your instance of WindowCloser is in a reference named closer, you can write:

```
topFrame.addWindowListener(closer);
```

Making an Applet
a Standalone Application

If you would like to turn an applet into a standalone application so you can run it outside of a Web browser (free of many security requirements related to accessing servers and the file system), you can write a main() method for your applet. That way, you can invoke it from the command line.

To make this work, you've got to handle the chores that the Web browser used to handle.

As far as Java is concerned, a Web browser's chores include

- Creating an instance of your applet.

- Making sure your applet progresses through its life-cycle—especially so that it creates and arranges its user interface components. (If your applet creates a user interface in init(), make sure any frame you write that replaces the applet also invokes init().)

- Creating a top-level frame for your applet and placing your applet in this frame.

- Setting this frame to its appropriate size. (You can either set the frame's size directly using setSize()or you can invoke pack() to shrink-wrap the frame around your user interface.)

- Making this frame appear on the screen. (You can accomplish this by invoking your frame's setVisible(true) method.)

Exercise 28.3

Take the word processing applet you wrote in Exercises 28.1 and 28.2 and add a main() method to this applet so that it can run as a standalone application.

Answers to the Exercises

Exercise 28.1

This code contains a few instance variables in preparation for making this interface operative:

```
import java.awt.*;
import java.applet.Applet;

public class Word extends Applet {
    private TextArea area;
    private Choice fonts;
    private Choice sizes;

    private String currentFont = "Courier";
    private int currentSize = 8;
    private int style = Font.PLAIN;
    private Color currentColor = Color.black;

    public void init() {
        setLayout(new BorderLayout());
```

```
        area = new TextArea(10, 60);
        area.setFont(new Font(currentFont, style, currentSize));
        area.setForeground(currentColor);
        add(area, BorderLayout.CENTER);

        Panel p = new Panel();
        p.setLayout(new GridLayout(2,1));

        Panel firstRow = new Panel();
        CheckboxGroup group = new CheckboxGroup();
        firstRow.add(new Checkbox("black", group, true));
        firstRow.add(new Checkbox("blue", group, false));
        firstRow.add(new Checkbox("red", group, false));
        p.add(firstRow);

        Panel secondRow = new Panel();
        fonts = new Choice();
        fonts.addItem("Courier");
        fonts.addItem("Helvetica");
        fonts.addItem("Times Roman");
        secondRow.add(fonts);

        sizes = new Choice();
        sizes.addItem("8");
        sizes.addItem("12");
        sizes.addItem("16");
        secondRow.add(sizes);

        p.add(secondRow);

        add(p, BorderLayout.SOUTH);
    }

}
```

Exercise 28.2

```
import java.awt.*;
import java.awt.event.*;
import java.applet.Applet;

public class Word extends Applet {
    private TextArea area;
    private Choice fonts;
    private Choice sizes;

    private String currentFont = "Courier";
    private int currentSize = 8;
    private int style = Font.PLAIN;
    private Color currentColor = Color.black;
```

```java
public void init() {
    setLayout(new BorderLayout());

    area = new TextArea(10, 60);
    area.setFont(new Font(currentFont, style, currentSize));
    area.setForeground(currentColor);
    add(area, BorderLayout.CENTER);

    Panel p = new Panel();
    p.setLayout(new GridLayout(2,1));

    Panel firstRow = new Panel();
    CheckboxGroup group = new CheckboxGroup();
    Checkbox[] checkBoxes = {new Checkbox("black", group, true),
                             new Checkbox("blue", group, false),
                             new Checkbox("red", group, false)};
    for (int i = 0; i<checkBoxes.length; i++) {
      checkBoxes[i].addItemListener(new ChooseColorHandler());
      firstRow.add(checkBoxes[i]);
    }
    p.add(firstRow);

    Panel secondRow = new Panel();
    fonts = new Choice();
    fonts.addItem("Courier");
    fonts.addItem("Helvetica");
    fonts.addItem("Times Roman");
    fonts.addItemListener(new ChooseFontStyleHandler());
    secondRow.add(fonts);

    sizes = new Choice();
    sizes.addItem("8");
    sizes.addItem("12");
    sizes.addItem("16");
    sizes.addItemListener(new ChooseFontSizeHandler());
    secondRow.add(sizes);

    p.add(secondRow);

    add(p, BorderLayout.SOUTH);
}


class ChooseFontSizeHandler implements ItemListener {

  public void itemStateChanged(ItemEvent ie) {
    Choice c = (Choice)ie.getSource();
    currentSize =
      Integer.valueOf(c.getSelectedItem()).intValue();
    area.setFont(new Font(currentFont, style, currentSize));
  }
}
```

```
class ChooseFontStyleHandler implements ItemListener {

  public void itemStateChanged(ItemEvent ie) {
    Choice c = (Choice)ie.getSource();
    currentFont = c.getSelectedItem();
    area.setFont(new Font(currentFont, style, currentSize));
  }
}

class ChooseColorHandler implements ItemListener {

  public void itemStateChanged(ItemEvent ie) {
    Checkbox c = (Checkbox)ie.getSource();
    String s = c.getLabel();
    if (s.equals("black"))
      currentColor = Color.black;
    else if (s.equals("blue"))
      currentColor = Color.blue;
    else
      currentColor = Color.red;

    area.setForeground(currentColor);
  }
}
}
```

Exercise 28.3

You can use the WindowCloser class provided in the text. Here's how you can write a main() method for the Word applet:

```
public static void main(String[] args) {
    Word w = new Word();
    w.init();
    Frame frame = new Frame("Word processor");
    frame.add(w, BorderLayout.CENTER);
    frame.addWindowListener(new WindowCloser());
    frame.pack();
    frame.show();
}
```

Review Questions

1. How can you display three labels that line up top-to-bottom along the right-hand side of an interface and are sized equally?

   a. Place the labels into a GridLayout.

   b. Place the labels into a BorderLayout.

c. Place the labels in a container that uses a BorderLayout, and then place this container into another container that uses a GridLayout.

d. Place the labels in a container that uses a GridLayout, and then place this container into another container that uses a BorderLayout.

2. What is the cleanest way to make a window vanish permanently?
a. Invoke dispose().
b. Invoke setVisible(false).
c. Invoke dispose() and then setVisible(false).
d. Invoke setVisible(false) and then dispose().

3. To force a layout manager to relayout the components in a container, you can invoke the container method named:
a. validate()
b. repaint()
c. layout()
d. update()

4. To set the text color for a component, you can use the component method:
a. setColor()
b. setFont()
c. setForeground()
d. setBackground()

5. What method can you invoke for a Frame enclosing a user interface so that it fits perfectly around that interface?
a. resize()
b. size()
c. pack()
d. show()

Answers to Review Questions

1. **d.** You can place the components first into a container using a GridLayout that is 3 rows by 1 column. Then, you can place this container into another container using a BorderLayout on the East side.

2. **d.** You should always hide the window before disposing of it to make sure the interface looks clean.

3. **a.** The validate() method forces a layout manager to lay out the components again.

4. **c.** setColor() sets the drawing color, setFont() changes the font type, and setBackground() sets the background color. setForeground() changes the text color.

5. **c.** The pack() method makes the Frame shrink or expand as necessary to contain the interface.

Sun Certified Developer Practice Programming Assignment

Developer certification takes place in stages. First, you complete a programming assignment that you download from the Web. Then, you take a test that asks you to justify decisions you made in completing the programming assignment.

The assignment consists of implementing a client/server application, where the client and server talk to each other using TCP/IP. While the actual assignment is, of course, different from this one, the two are similar in scope and the topics they cover.

Read over the scenario and instructions for this assignment, and then go to it.

The Scenario

Aunt Edna's Airlines started as a one-woman operation. Edna rented a small two-seater and flew passengers to the San Juan Islands from Seattle, a short hop of less than an hour. No one thought her business would make it, but her flying was flawless and her service professional. She now owns two planes, capable of carrying five passengers each. She hired her niece as the other pilot. She set up regular flight schedules.

Edna has been taking reservations over the phone, but with business booming, that has became too cumbersome. She has allowed travel agents to mail in reservations, but this is not a very efficient system. What's more, they keep on booking passengers in the same seats (numbered 1 through 5) because there is no coordination between them.

643

(Remember the discussion of this scenario back in Chapter 15 when we talked about threads?)

Edna talked things over with her niece, and they came up with a plan. They have this idea that travel agents would tap directly into their reservation computer over the Internet. They could maintain a simple database that travel agents could use to make reservations and assign passengers to seats.

Her niece worked on a piece of this program for a few days when it was rainy and no one wanted to visit the San Juans. Being a Mac person, she bought *Learn Java on the Macintosh*. She got as far defining what the prototype database would look like and providing a few simple methods to access the database. However, business soon picked up, and she headed back into the skies (where she preferred to be, anyway).

Edna has looked around for a qualified Java programmer, and since you are Sun Certified as a Java Programmer, she thought you would be ideal for the task. She would like you to write a prototype system so that she can begin to get a sense of what this might look like. The prototype is only proof of a concept that she hopes will do the following things:

- Offer a simple user interface that displays the date, flight number, and passenger list.

- Allow the user to make a new reservation, type in the passenger's name, and assign the passenger a seat from a list of those available.

- Let the user delete a reservation.

- Provide access to the database over the Internet, possibly by multiple travel agents at a time.

She wants this done in a very particular way, because she wants to make sure that, if you decide to move on to other projects after implementing the prototype, her niece can understand how the program works and maintain it. This means that you should favor code that is easy to understand over code that might be slightly more efficient. And you should provide all of the javadoc-style comments necessary so that the code is well-documented, without being filled with unnecessary, trivial comments.

The Prototype Specifications

The rest of this document describes the following:

- The design completed so far
- The protocol you will use to communicate between the client and server

- The code completed so far
- What you will add to the code
- What the user interface will look like

The Design Completed So Far

The current design identifies the class names for the prototype. However, the only classes that have been completed are those for the record layout for the database (the classes PassengerRecord and FileHeader) and some support methods to manipulate the database file (in the class DB). The database file is simply an ASCII file that we'll read from and write to using the java.io classes—especially RandomAccessFile. There is also an interface called CanUpdate and two new Exception classes that are complete, but their definitions are very simple. You will implement all of the other classes yourself as you think best, but you should try to follow the designs presented here.

Figure 29-1 shows the user interface classes for the prototype. The only one of these currently written is an interface called CanUpdate. This interface defines a single method that other classes can call to force the user interface to update to reflect the current state of the database.

Figure 29-1 shows the intended flow of control between these classes. A user can launch the client by invoking the Java interpreter and passing it a top-level frame. The

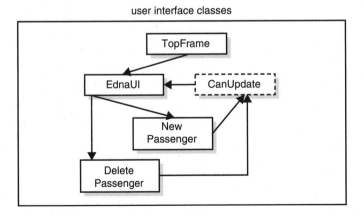

Figure 29-1   The current design

main() method of this new Frame subclass creates an instance of a Panel subclass called EdnaUI. EdnaUI implements the CanUpdate interface.

When the user wants to add a new passenger to the passenger list, the user interface will bring up a new window—a Frame subclass called NewPassenger. (I'll discuss the exact look and feel of the user interface in the section of this chapter entitled, "What the User Interface Should Look Like when You're Done.") When the user wants to delete a passenger from the passenger list, the user interface will bring up a new window—a Frame subclass called DeletePassenger.

Once the user has added or deleted a passenger, these Frame subclasses invoke updateUI() for the EdnaUI object. The method updateUI()is the method defined by the CanUpdate interface and implemented by EdnaUI, so that the user interface reflects the new state of the database.

If this were not to be a client/server application, NewPassenger and DeletePassenger could access the database directly, as shown in Figure 29-2.

The DB class reads from and writes to a file called Reservations.db. It uses the File-Header and PassengerRecord classes to keep track of the data in each record. There are also two exceptions that the DB class can use if it encounters any trouble assigning seats.

All of the classes are currently part of the same default package.

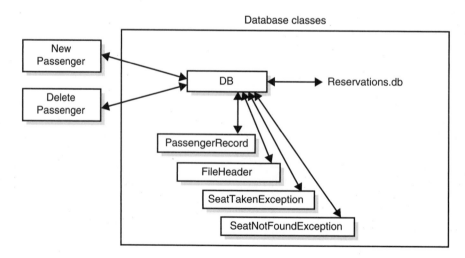

Figure 29-2   Directly accessing the database

The New Design

To complete this assignment, you should place the classes into one of two packages: client or server. Any new classes you create should go into one of these packages. You can import classes from one package to another as you require. However, you may only need to import a class called server.Server (which I'll discuss shortly) in the a class called client.Client. You can probably find ways around this, if you would like to.

Figure 29-3 shows the new design on the client side. This is the final design that you should achieve in your solution.

NewPassenger and DeletePassenger do not communicate directly with the database. Instead, they create a new instance of a class called Client. Client defines methods that establish a TCP/IP connection with a server and communicate with the server to perform database operations.

Two new classes are on the server side. These are shown in Figure 29-4.

The first server class is called Server. This class simply loops forever, waiting for a client to connect to it. When it establishes a connection, Server creates a new instance of a Thread subclass called ClientServerThread and starts this thread. This thread reads data from the network, interacts with the database, and passes the appropriate data back over the network.

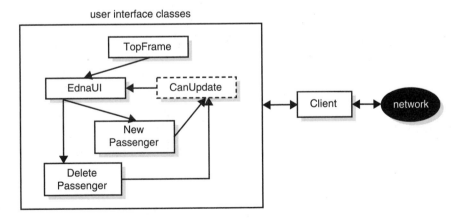

Figure 29-3   The design on the client side

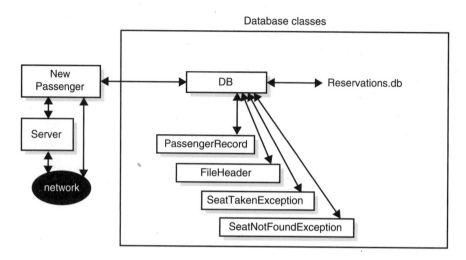

Figure 29-4   The design on the server side

The Code Completed So Far

You must use the following code as part of your solution. This code defines the database entries and specifies how you will access the database. Optimizations such as compressing the database by squeezing out deleted records will be a future consideration, implemented at some point after the prototype is completed, so don't concern yourself with this now.

Here are two classes that define the record layout. Each record consists of a header and passenger information.

The class FileHeader can be placed in the file DB.java (which I'll discuss next):

```
class FileHeader {

    int totalRecords;
    int numPassengers;
}
```

The class PassengerRecord must be placed in its own file, PassengerRecord.java:

```
package server;
public class PassengerRecord {
    private long ptr;
    private String name;
    private int seat;
    public String getName() {
        return name;
    }
```

```
    public void setName(String n) {
        name = n;
    }
    public int getSeat() {
        return seat;
    }
    public void setSeat(int s) {
        seat = s;
    }
    public long getPtr() {
        return ptr;
    }
    public void setPtr(long p) {
        ptr = p;
    }
}
```

The following code provides the start of the class called DB that is used to manipulate a database (there are three methods still to implement). This class is defined in DB.java:

```
package server;
import java.io.*;
/**
 * Record format is:
 * <num records>
 * <name> <seat #>
 * repeat as necessary
 */
public class DB {
    public static final String FILE_NAME = "Reservations.db";
    public static final int MAX_SEATS = 5;
    private static final int ACTIVE_REC = 0;
    private static final int DELETED_REC = 1;
    private boolean open;
    private RandomAccessFile file;
    public DB() throws IOException {
        try {
            File test = new File(FILE_NAME);
            boolean alreadyExisted = test.exists();
            file = new RandomAccessFile(FILE_NAME, "rw");
            open = true;
            if (!alreadyExisted) {
                FileHeader header = new FileHeader();
                writeHeader(header);
            }
        } catch (IOException x) {
            close();
            throw x;
        }
    }
    public synchronized String[] getPassengerList() throws
IOException {
```

```
            String[] reservations = null;
            // PLACE YOUR CODE HERE.
            return reservations;
        }

    public synchronized int getSeat(String passenger)
        throws IOException, SeatNotFoundException
    {
        int seat = 0;
        // PLACE YOUR CODE HERE.
        return seat;
    }
    public synchronized void reservePassenger(String passenger, int
seat)
        throws IOException, SeatTakenException
    {

        // PLACE YOUR CODE HERE.

    }
    public synchronized int[] getOpenSeats() throws IOException {
        PassengerRecord record;
        FileHeader header = readHeader();
        // Do the case where there are no seats:
        if (header.numPassengers == MAX_SEATS)
            return new int[0];
        // Do the case where all seats are still available.
        if (header.numPassengers == 0) {
            int[] open = {1, 2, 3, 4, 5};
            return open;
        }
        // Determine the open seats from the reserved seats.
        boolean[] reserved = new boolean[MAX_SEATS];
        String passenger;
        for (int i = 0; i < header.numPassengers; i++) {
            record = readNextRecord();
            reserved[record.getSeat() - 1] = true;
        }
        // Make the int array only as large as it needs to be.
        int[] open = new int[MAX_SEATS - header.numPassengers];
        int next = 0;
        for (int i = 0; i < MAX_SEATS; i++) {
            if (reserved[i] == false)
                open[next++] = i + 1;
        }
        return open;
    }
    public synchronized void deletePassenger(String name)
        throws IOException
    {
        FileHeader header = readHeader();
        boolean found = false;
        PassengerRecord record = null; // make the compiler happy
        for (int i = 0; i < header.numPassengers && !found; i++) {
```

```
            record = readNextRecord();
            if (name.equals(record.getName()))
                found = true;
        }
        // Delete at the position before we read the record to
        // be deleted.
        if (found) {
            file.seek(record.getPtr());
            file.write(DELETED_REC);
            header.numPassengers--;
            writeHeader(header);
        }
    }
    public synchronized void close() {
        if (open) {
            try {
                file.close();
            } catch (IOException x) {
                System.out.println(x.getMessage());
            } finally {
                open = false;
            }
        }
    }
    public void finalize() throws Throwable {
        close();
        super.finalize();
    }
    private synchronized PassengerRecord readNextRecord()
        throws IOException
    {
        boolean looking = true;
        PassengerRecord record = new PassengerRecord();
        try {
            while (looking) {
                record.setPtr(file.getFilePointer());
                int type = file.readInt();
                record.setName(file.readUTF());
                record.setSeat(file.readInt());
                if (type == ACTIVE_REC)
                    looking = false;
            }
        } catch (EOFException x) {
            System.out.println("read past the end of the file");
        }
        return record;
    }
    private synchronized void writeRecord(PassengerRecord record)
        throws IOException
    {
        FileHeader header = readHeader();
        header.totalRecords++;
        header.numPassengers++;
```

```
            writeHeader(header);
            file.seek(file.length());
            file.writeInt(ACTIVE_REC);
            file.writeUTF(record.getName());
            file.writeInt(record.getSeat());
        }
    private synchronized FileHeader readHeader() throws IOException
{
        FileHeader header = new FileHeader();
        file.seek(0);
        header.totalRecords = file.readInt();
        header.numPassengers = file.readInt();
        return header;
    }
    private synchronized void writeHeader(FileHeader header)
        throws IOException
        {
        file.seek(0);
        file.writeInt(header.totalRecords);
        file.writeInt(header.numPassengers);
        }
    }
}
```

The three methods you need to implement are getPassengerList(), getSeat(), and reservePassenger(). You will invoke these methods from ClientServerThread when appropriate. The two other methods that you will invoke from ClientServerThread are deletePassenger() and getOpenSeats(), which are already implemented for you.

There is a new exception called SeatNotFoundException defined in SeatNot-FoundException.java like this:

```
package server;
public class SeatNotFoundException extends Exception { }
```

There is also a new exception called SeatTakenException defined in SeatTakenException.java like this:

```
package server;
public class SeatTakenException extends Exception { }
```

On the client side, the interface CanUpdate looks like this:

```
package client;
public interface CanUpdate {
    void updateUI();
}
```

(You will find all this code on the CD-ROM included with this book.)

What You Will Add to the Code

You need to complete the DB class, create the user interface for accessing the database, and turn this into a client/server application by defining client and server classes.

The Database

The basic structure of the database has already been implemented for you. However, here's what's going on, if it helps you to write your software.

The database consists of a header followed by any number of records. Only five records will be active at a time; if there are more, it is only because the others have been deleted.

The database's header consists of two numbers: the total number of records in the database, and the total number of passengers. (Nothing is currently done with the integer for the total number of records.)

Each record in the database consists of an integer indicating whether it is active or deleted, a String indicating the passenger's name, and an integer specifying the passenger's seat assignment.

The DB class already implements methods to append a new record to the database, delete a record, and retrieve the open seats.

The Server

The server should be able to handle multiple clients. Each transaction with a client should be one complete connect-process-close cycle. For example, if the client wants to add a new passenger to the database, it should connect with the server and pass the server the new passenger name and seat assignment. The server should add this passenger to the database if it can, and tell the client whether or not it was successful. Then, the connection ends.

The server and the client can both run on the local machine by default for the purposes of this exercise. However, all of the proper TCP/IP should be in place so that they could reside on different machines if necessary. (You can pick a port you think is appropriate for the client and server to use to communicate. The port number 5001 is one candidate.)

The server consists of the Server class and the ClientServerThread class. The server handles connections arriving over the network and interacts with the DB class to work with the database.

The Client

The client consists of the user interface and a class called Client that knows how to establish a connection with the server, communicate with the server, and close the connection. The Client class can define different methods to perform different transactions —add a new passenger to the list, delete a passenger, and so on.

The User Interface

The user interface is discussed in the following section, after the discussion of protocol. Your user interface should match the figures in this chapter as closely as possible. The user interface can create a new Client instance when it needs to talk to the server, and invoke the proper method in the Client instance to make the client communicate with the server.

The Protocol

For the client and the server to talk to each other, they have to speak the same language. In other words, they need to agree on a protocol. Each transaction represents a new connection between the client and the server.

Making a New Reservation

The client sends an integer opcode that means "make a new reservation," followed by a String representing the passenger name, followed by an integer for the seat number. The server returns a 0 if the reservation was made successfully, or a 1 if it was not.

Delete a Passenger's Reservation

The client sends an integer opcode that means "delete this reservation," followed by a String representing the passenger name.

The server a 0 if the reservation was deleted successfully, or a 1 if it was not.

Finding a Passenger's Seat

The client sends an integer opcode that means "get this passenger's seat," followed by a String representing the passenger name.

If the passenger's seat is found, the server an integer representing the passenger's seat number. For the case when a passenger's seat is not found, a SeatNotFoundException occurs.

Finding All Open Seats

The client sends an integer opcode that means "find all open seats."

The server an integer that indicates how many open seats there are, followed by integers that specify the open seat numbers. If there are no open seats, the first integer is 0, followed, of course, by no other numbers.

Retrieving the List of Passengers

The client sends an integer opcode that means "return the passenger list."

The server an integer that indicates how many passengers there are, followed by Strings that contain the passenger names. If there are no passengers, the first integer is 0, followed by no other Strings.

What the User Interface Should Look Like when You're Done

Figure 29-5 shows what will first appear on the screen when the user launches the client.

(The client is a standalone graphical program. It does not run within a Web browser.) There are three regions to this user interface:

- At the top are the date and flight number. These can be labels purely for aesthetic purposes that don't have to reflect any real data.

- In the center is the list of passengers. This list will reflect the current state of the database.

- At the bottom is a button that allows the user to make new reservations.

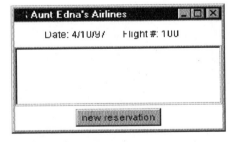

Figure 29-5   The initial client interface

When the user first launches the client, it should connect with the server. Once it establishes a connection, it should update the passenger list if there is already data in the database, so that the user interface displays any passenger data when it first appears.

As the user enters data into the database, the center portion of the user interface will show this data. Figure 29-6 shows the list of passengers after the user has made three new reservations.

The database method getPassengerList() returns an array of Strings that you can use to display in this list, one String per list item.

To make this clearer, Figure 29-7 shows the generic arrangement of the user interface components you need to implement.

There are two other features of this user interface that you should implement:

- The new reservation button becomes disabled when the flight is full (that is, when there are five passengers).

- The client program ends when the user clicks the close button in the frame enclosing this interface.

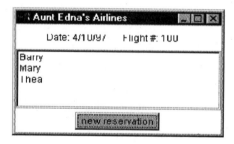

Figure 29-6   The list of passengers

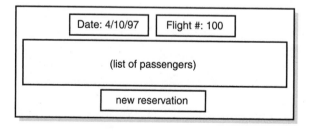

Figure 29-7   The user interface components

In addition to these, clicking the new reservation button and double-clicking a list entry both cause the user interface to bring up other windows. The new reservation button brings up a window that enables you to add passengers to the database. Double-clicking a list entry brings up a window that allows you to delete that passenger.

Updating the Passenger List

When the user clicks the new reservation button, a new window appears that floats separately from the main user interface. This window should look like Figure 29-8.

The only entries in the choice box should be those for the open seats. (The seats are numbered 1 through 5.) You can use the database method getOpenSeats() to determine which entries to place into the choice box. The user will type the passenger name into the text field and click the reserve seat button to make the reservation. To make this work, you'll have to implement the database method reservePassenger(). If the seat the user is trying to reserve is already taken (because another thread has beaten the user to it), then no reservation should be made. (If the text field is all spaces or blank, the reserve seat button should not change the database.)

Then, the window should vanish. If the user clicks the close button for this enclosing frame, the floating window should go away without the user having made a reservation.

When the window vanishes, the main user interface's list of passengers should be updated to reflect the new passenger in the database. To do this, the window can invoke EdnaUI's implementation of updateUI().

When the user double-clicks an entry in the list, a new window appears that floats separately from the main user interface. This window should look like Figure 29-9.

This window shows the passenger's name and seat assignment. To show the seat assignment, you'll have to implement the database method getSeat(). Two buttons on the bottom of this floating window allow the user to either keep or delete this reservation. If the user clicks delete, the passenger should be removed from the database. (To do this, you should implement the database's deletePassenger() method.) Then, the

Figure 29-8   The new passenger window

Figure 29-9   The delete passenger window

window should vanish. If the user clicks keep or clicks the Close button in the enclosing frame, the floating window should simply go away.

Again, when the window vanishes, the main user interface's list of passengers should be updated to reflect the change to the database.

Final Words of Advice

Implement this as you think best. Keep in mind the chapters we've covered in the previous section, especially regarding TCP/IP and building user interfaces by placing layout managers inside other layout managers.

I have provided few lines of working code on purpose. The more you work through the issues yourself, the easier you'll find the actual developer programming assignment. Don't worry if it takes some time.

You can always look at the answer at the end of this chapter if you get stuck. But try to get as far as you can to really think about what's happening.

One Possible Answer for the Client Side

Client.java

```
package client;

import java.io.*;
import java.net.*;
import server.Server;

/**
 * Communicates with the database server.
 * @see server.Server
 * @version 1.1
```

```
 * @author Barry Boone / William Stanek
 */
public class Client {

    /* Data stream to read from server. */
    DataInputStream remoteIn;

    /* Data stream to write to server. */
    DataOutputStream remoteOut;

    private int port = 5001;
    private Socket sock;
    private String server = null;
        // name of the remote server (null if on same machine)

    /**
     * Establish a connection with the database server.
     * @exception IOException  Thrown if there's trouble
     *    connecting to the server
     */
    void establishConnection() throws IOException {
        try {
            InetAddress serverAddr = InetAddress.getByName(server);
            sock = new Socket(serverAddr.getHostName(), port);

            remoteIn = new DataInputStream(sock.getInputStream());
            remoteOut = new DataOutputStream(sock.getOutputStream());

        } catch (IOException e) {
            System.out.println(e.getMessage() +
                ": Failed to connect to server.");
            throw e;
        }

    }

    /*
     * Close the connection with the database server.
     */
    void closeConnection() {
        try {
            if (remoteOut != null) {
                remoteOut.close();
                remoteOut = null;
            }

            if (remoteIn != null) {
                remoteIn.close();
                remoteIn = null;
            }

        } catch (IOException x) {
            System.out.println(x.getMessage());
```

```
      } finally {
        try {
          if (sock != null) {
            sock.close();
            sock = null;
          }
        } catch (IOException x) {
          System.out.println(x.getMessage());
        }
      }
    }

    int[] getOpenSeats() throws IOException {
      establishConnection();
      remoteOut.writeInt(Server.OP_GET_OPEN_SEATS);
      int numSeats = remoteIn.readInt();
      int[] seats = new int[numSeats];
      for (int i = 0; i < numSeats; i++)
        seats[i] = remoteIn.readInt();

      closeConnection();
      return seats;
    }

    String[] getPassengerList() throws IOException {
      establishConnection();
      remoteOut.writeInt(Server.OP_GET_PASSENGER_LIST);
      int numPassengers = remoteIn.readInt();
      String[] passengers = new String[numPassengers];
      for (int i = 0; i < numPassengers; i++)
        passengers[i] = remoteIn.readUTF();

      closeConnection();
      return passengers;
    }

    int reservePassenger(String name, int seat) throws IOException{
      establishConnection();
      remoteOut.writeInt(Server.OP_MAKE_RESERVATION);
      remoteOut.writeUTF(name);
      remoteOut.writeInt(seat);
      int rv = remoteIn.readInt();
      closeConnection();
      return rv;
    }

    int deletePassenger(String name) throws IOException {
      establishConnection();
      remoteOut.writeInt(Server.OP_DELETE);
      remoteOut.writeUTF(name);
      int rv = remoteIn.readInt();
      closeConnection();
```

```
          return rv;
       }

   int getSeat(String name) throws IOException {
       establishConnection();
       remoteOut.writeInt(Server.OP_GET_SEAT);
       remoteOut.writeUTF(name);
       int seat = remoteIn.readInt();
       closeConnection();
       return seat;
   }

   protected void finalize() throws Throwable {
       super.finalize();
       closeConnection();
   }

}
```

TopFrame.java

```
package client;

import java.awt.*;
import java.awt.event.*;

public class TopFrame extends Frame {
    public TopFrame(String s) {
        super(s);

        WindowAdapter closeHandler = new WindowAdapter() {
          public void windowClosing(WindowEvent e) {
            Window w = e.getWindow();
            w.setVisible(false);
            dispose();
            System.exit(0);
          }
        };
        addWindowListener(closeHandler);
    }

    public static void main(String[] args) {
        TopFrame frame = new TopFrame("Aunt Edna's Airlines");
        EdnaUI ui = new EdnaUI();
        frame.add("Center", ui);
        frame.pack();
        frame.show();

        ui.updateUI();
    }
}
```

PART II

EdnaUI.java

```java
package client;

import java.awt.*;
import java.awt.event.*;
import java.util.Date;
import java.util.StringTokenizer;
import java.io.IOException;

public class EdnaUI extends Panel implements CanUpdate {
    private static final int MAX_SEATS = 5;

    private List     passengerList;
    private Button   reserve;

    public EdnaUI() {
        setLayout(new BorderLayout());

        Panel p;
        p = new Panel();

        p.add(new Label("Date: 4/10/97"));
        p.add(new Label("Flight #: 100"));

        add("North", p);

        passengerList = new List(5, false);
        add("Center", passengerList);

        p = new Panel();
        reserve = new Button("new reservation");
        p.add(reserve);

        add("South", p);

        /*
         * Show frame to make a new reservation when the user clicks
         * the "new reservation" button.
         * Show frame to delete a reservation when the user
         * doubleclicks the list.
         */
        ActionListener actionHandler = new ActionListener() {
          public void actionPerformed(ActionEvent e) {
            try {
                if (e.getSource() == reserve)
                    showNewWindow();
                else if (e.getSource() == passengerList)
                    showDeleteWindow();
            } catch (IOException x) {
                System.out.println("could not edit passenger list");
            }
          }
        }
```

```
      };
      reserve.addActionListener(actionHandler);
      passengerList.addActionListener(actionHandler);

   }


   private void showDeleteWindow() throws IOException {
      Frame pass;

      // Get the selected entry in the list, if there is one.
      String name = passengerList.getSelectedItem();
      if (name != null) {
         pass = new DeletePassenger(name, this);
         pass.pack();
         pass.show();
      }
   }

   private void showNewWindow() throws IOException {
      Frame pass;

      pass = new NewPassenger(this);
      pass.pack();
      pass.show();
   }


   public void updateUI() {
      String[] reservations;
      try {
         reservations = new Client().getPassengerList();
      } catch (IOException x) {
         System.out.println("Unable to show list");
         System.out.println(x.getMessage());
         return;
      }
      passengerList.removeAll();

      int total = reservations.length;
      for (int i = 0; i < total; i++)
         passengerList.add(reservations[i]);

      // Update the "make reservation" button as appropriate.
      if (reservations.length == MAX_SEATS)
         reserve.setEnabled(false);
      else
         reserve.setEnabled(true);

      validate();
   }

}
```

NewPassenger.java

```java
package client;

import java.awt.*;
import java.awt.event.*;
import java.io.IOException;

public class NewPassenger extends Frame {
    String     thePassenger;
    TextField  passengerField;
    Choice     seatNumber;
    Button     makeRes;
    CanUpdate  ui;
    int[]      openSeats;

    public NewPassenger(CanUpdate edna) throws IOException {
        super("Make New Reservation");

        ui = edna;

        setLayout(new GridLayout(3, 1));
        Panel p;

        p = new Panel();
        p.add(new Label("passenger: "));

        passengerField = new TextField(30);
        p.add(passengerField);
        add(p);

        p = new Panel();
        openSeats = new Client().getOpenSeats();

        seatNumber = new Choice();
        for (int i = 0; i < openSeats.length; i++) {
            String s = new Integer(openSeats[i]).toString();
            seatNumber.addItem(s);
        }
        p.add(seatNumber);

        add(p);

        p = new Panel();
        makeRes = new Button("make reservation");
        p.add(makeRes);
        add(p);

        WindowAdapter closeHandler = new WindowAdapter() {
            public void windowClosing(WindowEvent e) {
                Window w = e.getWindow();
                w.setVisible(false);
            }
        };
        addWindowListener(closeHandler);
```

```
        ActionListener actionHandler = new ActionListener() {
          public void actionPerformed(ActionEvent e) {

            String passenger = passengerField.getText();
            passenger = passenger.trim();
            if (passenger.length() > 0) {
              int seatIndex = seatNumber.getSelectedIndex();
              int seatNum = openSeats[seatIndex];
              try {
                new Client().reservePassenger(passenger, seatNum);
              } catch (IOException x) {
                System.out.println("Unable to reserve " + passenger
+
                    "for seat number " + seatNum);
              }
            }

            hide();
            ui.updateUI();
          }
        };
        makeRes.addActionListener(actionHandler);
    }
}
```

DeletePassenger.java

```
package client;

import java.awt.*;
import java.awt.event.*;
import java.io.IOException;

public class DeletePassenger extends Frame {
    String    thePassenger;
    Button    keepRes;
    Button    deleteRes;
    CanUpdate ui;

    public DeletePassenger(String s, CanUpdate edna) throws
IOException {
        super("Delete Reservation");

        thePassenger = s;
        ui = edna;

        setLayout(new GridLayout(2, 1));
        Panel p;

        p = new Panel();
        p.add(new Label("passenger: " + thePassenger));

        int seat = new Client().getSeat(thePassenger);
```

```
                p.add(new Label("seat #: " + seat));

                add(p);

                p = new Panel();
                keepRes = new Button("keep");
                p.add(keepRes);
                deleteRes = new Button("delete");
                p.add(deleteRes);

                add(p);

                WindowAdapter closeHandler = new WindowAdapter() {
                  public void windowClosing(WindowEvent e) {
                    Window w = e.getWindow();
                    w.setVisible(false);
                  }
                };
                addWindowListener(closeHandler);

                ActionListener actionHandler = new ActionListener() {
                  public void actionPerformed(ActionEvent e) {

                    if (e.getSource() == keepRes)
                      setVisible(false);
                    else if (e.getSource() == deleteRes) {
                      try {
                        new Client().deletePassenger(thePassenger);
                      } catch (IOException x) {
                        System.out.println(x.getMessage());
                      }
                      setVisible(false);
                      ui.updateUI();
                    }
                  }
                };
                keepRes.addActionListener(actionHandler);
                deleteRes.addActionListener(actionHandler);
            }
        }
```

One Possible Answer for the Server Side

Server.java (Including ClientServerThread)

```
package server;

import java.io.*;
import java.net.*;
```

```
/**
 * The DataServer processes requests from clients to
 * access the database. The DataServer runs until
 * you hit control-c. It is a multithreaded server
 * and spins off threads to process each connection
 * from a client.
 * @see server.DB
 * @version 1.1
 * @author Barry Boone / William Stanek
 */
public class Server {

    /** opcode for making a reservation. */
    public static final int OP_MAKE_RESERVATION = 1;

    /** opcode for deleting a reservation. */
    public static final int OP_DELETE = 2;

    /** opcode for getting a passenger's seat. */
    public static final int OP_GET_SEAT = 3;

    /** opcode for getting all open seats. */
    public static final int OP_GET_OPEN_SEATS = 4;

    /** opcode for getting all passengers. */
    public static final int OP_GET_PASSENGER_LIST = 5;

    private int port = 5001;
    private boolean listening = true;
    private DB db;
    private ServerSocket serverSock;

    /** Start the database server spinning. */
    public static void main(String args[]) {
        int portnum = 5001;

        System.out.println("The Server runs until you hit control-
c");

        try {
            Server server = new Server();
            server.start();
        } catch (IOException x) {
            System.out.println("Could not create server socket: " +
                x.getMessage());
            System.exit(1);
        }
    }

    /**
     * Put the Server object into action.
     * @exception IOException thrown if we cannot create a
ServerSocket
```

```
*       bound to the specified port
 */
public void start() throws IOException {

    serverSock = null;
    Socket sock;

    db = new DB();

    try {
       serverSock = new ServerSocket(port, 50);

       while (listening) {

           // Wait for a client to connect with server socket.
           // Then spin off a thread to handle the connection
           // with the client, repeat.
           try {
               // Wait here until contacted by a client.
               sock = serverSock.accept();

               new ClientServerThread(sock, db).start();
           } catch (IOException e) {
               System.out.println("Connection dropped?: " +
                   e.getMessage());
           }
       }

    } finally {
       serverSock.close();
       serverSock = null;
    }
}

protected void finalize() throws Throwable {
    super.finalize();
    if (serverSock != null) {
       serverSock.close();
       serverSock = null;
    }
}
}

// Handles one transaction with a client.
class ClientServerThread extends Thread {

    private static final int SUCCESS = 0;
    private static final int FAILURE = 1;

    private static final int PAUSE_FOR = 50;

    private DB db;
    private Socket sock;
```

```
private DataInputStream remoteIn;
private DataOutputStream remoteOut;

ClientServerThread(Socket sock, DB db) {
    this.sock = sock;
    this.db = db;
}

// This run() method processes just one request from a client
// and then ends.

public void run() {
    try {
        remoteIn = new DataInputStream(sock.getInputStream());
        remoteOut = new DataOutputStream(sock.getOutputStream());

        // Get the opcode so we know how to handle this
        // transaction.
        int opcode = remoteIn.readInt();

        switch (opcode) {
            case (Server.OP_MAKE_RESERVATION):
                makeReservation();
                break;
            case (Server.OP_DELETE):
                delete();
                break;
            case (Server.OP_GET_SEAT):
                getSeat();
                break;
            case (Server.OP_GET_OPEN_SEATS):
                getOpenSeats();
                break;
            case (Server.OP_GET_PASSENGER_LIST):
                getPassengerList();
                break;
            default:
                done();
                return;
        }

    } catch (IOException e) {
        error(e);
    }
}

// Make a reservation.
// in:  <opcode> <passenger name> <seat number>
// out: <0 OR 1 (success or failure)>
private void makeReservation() {
    try {
        String name = remoteIn.readUTF();
        int seat = remoteIn.readInt();
```

```
            db.reservePassenger(name, seat);
            sendToClient(SUCCESS);
        } catch (SeatTakenException x) {
            sendToClient(FAILURE);
        } catch (IOException x) {
            System.out.println(x.getMessage());
            sendToClient(FAILURE);
        } finally {
            done();
        }
    }

    // Delete a reservation.
    // in:  <opcode> <passenger name>
    // out: <0 OR 1 (success or failure)>
    private void delete() {
        try {
            String name = remoteIn.readUTF();
            db.deletePassenger(name);
            sendToClient(SUCCESS);
        } catch (IOException e) {
            error(e);
            sendToClient(FAILURE);
        } finally {
            done();
        }
    }

    // Get a seat given a passenger.
    // in:  <opcode> <passenger name>
    // out: <seat number> (-1 if no seat found)
    private void getSeat()
    {
        try {
            String name = remoteIn.readUTF();
            int seat = db.getSeat(name);
            sendToClient(seat);
        } catch (Exception x) {
            sendToClient(FAILURE);
        } finally {
            done();
        }
    }

    // Get all open seats.
    // in:  <opcode>
    // out: <number of open seats> { <seat number> }
    private void getOpenSeats()
    {
        try {
            int[] seats = db.getOpenSeats();
            sendToClient(seats.length);
            for (int i = 0; i < seats.length; i++)
```

```
            sendToClient(seats[i]);
        } catch (Exception x) {
        } finally {
            done();
        }
    }

// Get passenger list.
// in:  <opcode>
// out: <number of passengers> { <passenger name> }
private void getPassengerList()
{
    try {
        String[] passengers = db.getPassengerList();
        sendToClient(passengers.length);
        for (int i = 0; i < passengers.length; i++)
            sendToClient(passengers[i]);
    } catch (Exception x) {
    } finally {
        done();
    }
}

// Close the connection with the client.
private void done() {
    try {
        if (remoteOut != null) {
            remoteOut.close();
            remoteOut = null;
        }

        if (remoteIn != null) {
            remoteIn.close();
            remoteIn = null;
        }
    } catch (IOException x) {
        error(x);
    } finally {
        try {
            if (sock != null) {
                sock.close();
                sock = null;
            }
        } catch (IOException x) {
            error(x);
        }
    }
}

private void sendToClient(int i) {
    try {
        remoteOut.writeInt(i);
    } catch (IOException x) {
```

```
        error(x);
      }

      pause();
    }

    private void sendToClient(String s) {
      try {
        remoteOut.writeUTF(s);
      } catch (IOException x) {
        error(x);
      }

      pause();
    }

    // On Windows95/98, at least, when the client and server are
    // running on the same machine, we have to pause for the
    // client to read the data when the server writes it to the
    // socket. Otherwise, the client hangs.
    private void pause() {
      try {
        sleep(PAUSE_FOR);
      } catch (InterruptedException x) {
        error(x);
      }
    }

    private void error(Exception x) {
      System.out.println("Connection dropped?: " +
x.getMessage());
    }

    protected void finalize() throws Throwable {
      super.finalize();
      done();
    }

  }
```

The Three Missing Methods from DB.java

```
public synchronized String[] getPassengerList() throws IOException
{
    String[] reservations = null;
    PassengerRecord record;

    FileHeader header = readHeader();

    reservations = new String[header.numPassengers];
```

```
        for (int i = 0; i < header.numPassengers; i++) {
            reservations[i] = readNextRecord().getName();
        }
        return reservations;
    }

    public synchronized int getSeat(String passenger)
        throws IOException, SeatNotFoundException
    {
        boolean found = false;
        PassengerRecord record;

        int seat = 0; // satisfy the compiler
        FileHeader header = readHeader();

        for (int i = 0; i < header.numPassengers && !found; i++) {
            record = readNextRecord();
            if (passenger.equals(record.getName())) {
                found = true;
                seat = record.getSeat();
            }
        }

        if (!found)
            throw new SeatNotFoundException();

        return seat;
    }

    public synchronized void reservePassenger(String passenger, int
seat)
        throws IOException, SeatTakenException
    {
        // Make sure the seat is still available
        boolean taken = true; // prove it false
        int[] open = getOpenSeats();
        for (int i = 0; i < open.length && taken; i++) {
            if (seat == open[i])
                taken = false;
        }

        if (taken)
            throw new SeatTakenException();

        PassengerRecord record = new PassengerRecord();
        record.setName(passenger);
        record.setSeat(seat);
        writeRecord(record);
    }
```

30

Sun Certified Developer Practice Essay Exam

For the essay exam, there are no absolute right or wrong answers. Instead, there are five to ten essay questions. Each of these questions asks you to justify your design decisions, comment on your approach to designing applications in Java, and, to some extent, explain how an aspect of Java works in the first place.

You have 90 minutes to answer these questions. On the test, you read over the question (which often has multiple parts), and then, by clicking a button marked comment, you open a window to type in your response. You can open the comment window as many times as you would like to so that you can keep on adding to or tweaking your answer. At the end, you can easily go back over your answers and change them yet again before submitting them.

Once you do submit them, you'll have to wait until Sun Microsystems has looked over your answers, which can take up to four weeks. So relax until then; you have no choice, anyway. You'll generally know if you did okay. Remember, there are no right or wrong answers. If you justified your design decisions in a way that makes sense, you'll do fine.

So that you don't have to worry about whether you've written too much or not enough, the question instructions state very clearly the maximum number of sentences, words, or some other appropriate measure you should stay within as you're typing.

These practice questions relate to the sample programming assignment from Chapter 29. Of course, the questions on the real exam relate to the programming assignment you're asked to complete after you pass the Programmer Certification exam.

Questions

1. In order for the client and server to talk to each other, they need to agree on a protocol involving opcodes.

   a. Where did you define the opcodes? Did you define these in one place, or in more than one? If you only defined the opcodes in one place, how did you use the opcode numbers in other classes? (If you did not need to use opcodes in more than one class, explain why.)

   b. How did you define the opcodes? For example, what did the opcode for making a reservation look like (its value is equal to 1)? Did you create a constant, or did you use these numbers inline, written directly in the code? In either case, describe your design decisions that led to your choice.

2. Many of the methods of the DB class are synchronized.

   a. In a paragraph, explain why you think this is. What might happen if they were not synchronized?

   b. The reservePassenger() method in DB is one of the three methods in that class that you were asked to implement. Did you throw a SeatTakenException (the method declares this method might throw such an exception)? Why or why not? In no more than two paragraphs, describe how it might be possible for this situation to arise (that is, for a seat to be already taken when you call this method) even though most of the DB methods are synchronized.

3. What types of layout managers did you use in EdnaUI?

   a. What did you use for the overall layout manager for EdnaUI? In no more than two sentences, describe what led to your choice.

   b. How did you center the new reservation button in the bottom of EdnaUI without stretching from side to side? If your button did stretch from side to side, how might you use a combination of layout managers so that this does not occur?

4. Describe how TCP/IP works in relation to this program by answering the following questions.

   a. In not more than three paragraphs, describe how the client and server establish a dedicated connection with each other.

   b. In an additional one or two paragraphs, explain how it is possible for there to be two clients and one server all with dedicated connections on the same machine. (In your answer, mention how sockets are used in Java.)

5. The following questions relate to how you might extend the client's design.

    a. When your client communicates with the server, does your client wait for the server to respond before it continues? If so, provide an overview in no more than 100 words on how you might redesign your client so that the user has the ability to cancel the client's wait for a response, so that the client does not hang indefinitely if the server is no longer running. If your client already does this, describe your design.

    b. Does your client provide some kind of feedback when it is attempting to communicate with the server? Describe at least two ways to provide feedback and name one advantage for each of them.

Answers

1. **a.** The opcodes were defined in the Server class. This is the only place they were defined. So, when the Client class in the client package needed them, it had to import the Server class, like this:

```
import server.Server;
```

    b. The Server class created constants to define each of the opcodes. The opcode for making a reservation, looked like the following:

```
public static final int OP_MAKE_RESERVATION = 1;
```

2. **a.** The methods in DB that are synchronized are those that access and change the database. If they were not synchronized, then multiple threads could act on different parts of the database at once. This could easily result in the database becoming corrupted. For example, imagine one thread that deleted records as another added records. This could throw off the record count, or cause records to be overwritten.

    b. Even though the methods in DB are synchronized, that does not mean you don't have to guard against data becoming corrupted by some other mechanism. Synchronized methods cannot be executed at the same time by multiple threads. However, in a client/server application such as this one, a client can acquire data, then disconnect, and then connect again to act on that data.

    That's exactly what happens when a client gets the open seats, then allows a user to pick an open seat. If more than one client is active at a time, both clients will obtain the open seats (one at a time), and then (again, one at a time), they will try to reserve a seat. This means that there's nothing stopping one client from booking a passenger in the same seat as another client—that's why you must check for the seat still being available and inform the client if it is not.

3. **a.** The EdnaUI object uses a BorderLayout overall. The specifications indicate it should arrange objects within it in three sections, which happen to fall naturally into a North, Center, and South arrangement.

   b. Since EdnaUI uses a BorderLayout, if the new reservation button were added directly in the South region, it would stretch from the left edge of EdnaUI to the right. To stop this from happening, we can place the button in a panel. This keeps the button centered and at its natural size. We can then place the panel South in EdnaUI's BorderLayout.

4. **a.** An instance of class ServerSocket waits for a connection by invoking accept(). At this point, the ServerSocket is listening on a particular port for a client to try to connect with it. A client tries to establish a connection by creating a Socket instance, specifying the server and the port the server is listening to.

   The ServerSocket passes back a new port number to the client that the client should use for all further communication with the server. This port number gets encoded into the Socket object the client creates; it also is encoded into the Socket object returned by accept().

   b. Once the client has a port to use for the dedicated connection, the server continues to listen for more connections on the original port. Each new client, even if it's on the same machine, uses a different port to communicate with the server (even though each client originally connects to the server on the server's one known port).

   Java uses Socket objects to communicate via TCP/IP. A Java socket object encodes an IP address and a port to use for communication. ServerSocket ensures each port is different, so each socket is different, and multiple clients can communicate with the same server—each is using a different port.

5. **a.** The client could spawn a separate thread to perform the communication with the server. In addition, the client could display a window that contained a stop button. If the user clicked stop, this button would halt the communication thread. Otherwise, this window would go away by itself when the server responded. (Note

that we could make this even better, and make the cursor a busy cursor over all parts of the application except for the stop button.)

b. Two ways to provide feedback to the user are to change the cursor and provide a window containing an informative message. With a cursor, the user knows that any click he makes will be ineffective until the cursor changes back to a normal cursor. With a message, the user can read exactly what the application is doing because the message can explain it to him in detail. (A combination of these two approaches might also work well.)

PART III

Appendices

What's on the CD-ROM

The CD that comes with this book contains resources to help you use this book more effectively. We've included all the source code in the chapter and exercises, as well as Sun's latest JDK and the javadoc-style API files for the Java packages in HTML format. You'll also find a Java Certification testing engine that simulates the Sylvan Prometric testing environment.

How the CD is Organized

On the CD, you'll find that the source files and HTML pages are organized like a Web site. At the top level of the CD, you'll find a directory named "Source Code." Within this there's a file called index.html. You can view this HTML file with any standard Web browser.

We have included links to these categories:

- Code Listings for the Chapter Text
- Code Listings for the Exercises
- Answers to the Exercises
- Code Listings for the Review Questions
- Code for the Programming Assignment
- Where to Find More About Java and Java Certification

Source Code

The code listings are organized by chapter. Just follow the links until you're looking at Java code.

Sun's JDK

The reason this book includes the JDK is that the exam assumes you are using the JDK to develop your code. You can always grab newer versions of the JDK off the JavaSoft Web site, but for convenience it's included on the CD, as well. To find installation notes and troubleshooting ideas for the JDK, you can visit **http://java.sun.com/j2se/**.

Where to Find More

For all the latest and greatest information concerning this book and Java certification, we've included links to places on the Web. You'll find this on the CD in the HTML files by following the link titled "Where to Find More About Java and Java Certification."

What Is the Test Engine?

The Test Engine is a training tool to prepare for the Sun Certified Programmer for the Java 2 Platform Platform exam (Exam number 310-025). The program provides an interactive training environment and an exam simulator. The test engine does an excellent job of simulating the test environment used by Sylvan Prometric.

The JDK

The Programmer test assumes you are using Sun's Java Development Kit. The JDK often insists on things being a certain way, and it has its own commands and characteristics not shared by all development environments. Let's take a quick look at how to use the JDK. I'll also touch some aspects of the JDK that might appear on the test.

The Pieces of the JDK

First, in case you're using a different development environment, you might find it useful to get an overall picture of the JDK. This environment is not graphical; instead, you issue commands from the command line. For example, to compile a program, you type **javac,** list any options, and then type the name of the file or files you want to compile.

The JDK comes with:

- A compiler
- A Java Virtual Machine runtime environment for stand-alone programs
- An applet viewer to run applets without the need for starting a full-blown Web browser
- A debugger
- A program that extracts javadoc comments and generates HTML documentation

The debugger is not mentioned on the exam. That leaves the compiler, the runtime environment for stand-alone programs, the documentation tool, and the applet viewer.

The Compiler

Execute the compiler using the command javac. Invoking javac can be as simple as naming the Java source file you want to compile:

```
javac Bagel.java
```

Here are three compiler options you might find useful:

- You can specify the -classpath path option to tell the compiler where your class files exist. Without this option, the compiler relies on the CLASSPATH environment variable to find where your class files are that you want to include.

- The -d directory option tells the compiler to place the classes it generates into a particular directory. You can use this option when creating classes that belong in packages. For example, if you have defined a source file named CertClass.java that contains code like this:

```
package cert.util;
class CertClass { }
```

You can compile this class and generate the directory structure Java expects to be in place with packages by issuing the command:

```
javac -d . Certclass.java
```

javac will create a new directory at the same node as your source file, called cert. Below that, it will create a directory called util. And it will place CertClass.class within util.

There's also a compiler option -O that allows the compiler to generate inline code for static, final, and private methods. This option stands for "optimize."

The JDK enforces the rule that public classes must be placed in a file named after the class. So, if CertClass were declared as public, it would have to be placed in a file named CertClass.java. While you can place as many classes in the same source file as you would like, you can only have one public class per file.

The Runtime Environment for Stand-Alone Programs

You can invoke the Java interpreter using the command java. You pass the interpreter the name of the class you want to run (not the filename). For example, you can run the Bagel class by typing:

```
java Bagel
```

The interpreter will seek out this class's public, static main() method. This method must not return a value, and it must take an array of String objects. If the main() method is declared in any other way, the interpreter will complain that it could not find the main() method it was looking for, and it will not run your class.

You might be interested in the -classpath, -noasyncgc, and -verbosegc options.

- As with the compiler, you can specify the -classpath path option to tell the compiler where your class files are. Without this option, the compiler relies on the CLASSPATH environment variable to find where your class files are that you want to include.

- The -noasyncgc option turns off garbage collection.

- The -verbosegc option asks the interpreter to tell you when it has performed garbage collection.

The Documentation Tool

You use Java's documentation tool (javadoc) to generate documentation in HTML format for all your public classes, and your public and protected variables and methods. The documentation tool creates an HTML file for each class that lists the fields, constructors, or methods for a particular class. It also places a class hierarchy at the top of the HTML file and provides an index to the fields, constructors, and methods after the class hierarchy.

All you have to do to generate documentation is run the command javadoc and place the resulting HTML files into the same directory as the API files for the JDK. Javadoc can use special comment tags and variables to add information to the documentation. For more information on the documentation tool, see Chapter 25.

The Applet Viewer

You can use the appletviewer command to test an applet without ever starting a full-fledged Web browser. You pass the appletviewer command the name of an HTML file that references your applet class. For example, if you have an HTML file named Bagel.html that includes an <applet> tag referencing an Applet subclass, you can type

```
appletviewer Bagel.html
```

You don't have to only provide the name of a local HTML file. You can supply any URL as the parameter to appletviewer.

A useful feature is the -debug option, which writes debugging messages to the standard error.

INDEX

INTERNATIONAL CONTACT INFORMATION

AUSTRALIA
McGraw-Hill Book Company Australia Pty. Ltd.
TEL +61-2-9417-9899
FAX +61-2-9417-5687
http://www.mcgraw-hill.com.au
books-it_sydney@mcgraw-hill.com

CANADA
McGraw-Hill Ryerson Ltd.
TEL +905-430-5000
FAX +905-430-5020
http://www.mcgrawhill.ca

GREECE, MIDDLE EAST,
NORTHERN AFRICA
McGraw-Hill Hellas
TEL +30-1-656-0990-3-4
FAX +30-1-654-5525

MEXICO (Also serving Latin America)
McGraw-Hill Interamericana Editores S.A. de C.V.
TEL +525-117-1583
FAX +525-117-1589
http://www.mcgraw-hill.com.mx
fernando_castellanos@mcgraw-hill.com

SINGAPORE (Serving Asia)
McGraw-Hill Book Company
TEL +65-863-1580
FAX +65-862-3354
http://www.mcgraw-hill.com.sg
mghasia@mcgraw-hill.com

SOUTH AFRICA
McGraw-Hill South Africa
TEL +27-11-622-7512
FAX +27-11-622-9045
robyn_swanepoel@mcgraw-hill.com

UNITED KINGDOM & EUROPE
(Excluding Southern Europe)
McGraw-Hill Publishing Company
TEL +44-1-628-502500
FAX +44-1-628-770224
http://www.mcgraw-hill.co.uk
computing_neurope@mcgraw-hill.com

ALL OTHER INQUIRIES Contact:
Osborne/McGraw-Hill
TEL +1-510-549-6600
FAX +1-510-883-7600
http://www.osborne.com
omg_international@mcgraw-hill.com